Race, Racism, and Science

Forthcoming titles in
ABC-CLIO's

Science and Society

Series

The Environment and Science, Christian C. Young

Exploration and Science, Michael S. Reidy, Gary Kroll, and Erik M. Conway

Imperialism and Science, George N. Vlahakis, Isabel Maria Malaquias,
Nathan M. Brooks, François Regourd, Feza Gunergun, and David Wright

Literature and Science, John H. Cartwright and Brian Baker

Women and Science, Suzanne Le-May Sheffield

Advisory Editors
Paul Lawrence Farber and Sally Gregory Kohlstedt

Race, Racism, and Science

Social Impact and Interaction

John P. Jackson, Jr.,
and Nadine M. Weidman

ABC-CLIO

Santa Barbara, California • Denver, Colorado • Oxford, England

Library of Congress Cataloging-in-Publication Data

Jackson, John P., 1961–
    Race, racism, and science : social impact and interaction /
    John P. Jackson and Nadine M. Weidman.
        p. cm. — (Science and society)
    Includes bibliographical references and index.
    ISBN 1-85109-448-2 (hardcover : alk. paper) ISBN 1-85109-453-9 (e-book)
1. Race. 2. Race awareness—History. 3. Racism—History. 4. Social evolution. 5.
Human evolution. 6. Race discrimination—History. I. Weidman, Nadine M., 1966– II.
Title. III. Series: Science and society (Santa Barbara, Calif.)

    HT1521.J33 2004
    305.8—dc22   2004006531

This book is also available on the World Wide Web as an e-book.
Visit abc-clio.com for details.

ABC-CLIO, Inc.
130 Cremona Drive, P.O. Box 1911
Santa Barbara, California 93116-1911

This book is printed on acid-free paper.
Manufactured in the United States of America

Contents

Series Editor's Preface

The discipline of the history of science emerged from the natural sciences with the founding of the journal *Isis* by George Sarton in 1912. Two and a half decades later in a lecture at Harvard Sarton explained, "We shall not be able to understand our own science of to-day (I do not say to use it, but to understand it) if we do not succeed in penetrating its genesis and evolution." Historians of science, many of the first trained by Sarton and then by his students, study how science developed during the sixteenth and seventeenth centuries and how the evolution of the physical, biological, and social sciences over the past 350 years has been powerfully influenced by various social and intellectual contexts. Throughout the twentieth century the new field of the history of science grew with the establishment of dozens of new journals, graduate programs, and eventually the emergence of undergraduate majors in the history, philosophy, and sociology of science, technology, and medicine. Sarton's call to understand the origins and development of modern science has been answered by the development of not simply one discipline, but several.

Despite their successes in training scholars and professionalizing the field, historians of science have not been particularly successful in getting their work, especially their depictions of the interactions between science and society, into history textbooks. Pick up any U.S. history textbook and examine some of the topics that have been well explored by historians of science, such as scientific racism, the Scopes trial, nuclear weapons, eugenics, industrialization, or the relationship between science and technology. The depictions of these topics offered by the average history textbook have remained unchanged over the last fifty years, while the professional literature related to them that historians of science produce has made considerable revision to basic assumptions about each of these subjects.

The large and growing gap between what historians of science say about certain scientific and technological subjects and the portrayal of these subjects in most survey courses led us to organize the Science and Society series. Obviously, the rich body of literature that historians of science have amassed is not regularly consulted in the production of history texts or lectures. The authors and editors of this series seek to overcome this disparity by offering a synthetic, readable, and chronological history of the physical, social, and biological sciences as they developed within particular social, political, institutional, intellectual, and economic contexts over the past 350 years. Each volume stresses the reciprocal relationship between science and context; that is, while various circumstances and perspectives have influenced the evolution of the sciences, scientific disciplines have conversely influenced the contexts within which they developed. Volumes within this series each begin with a chronological narrative of the evolution of the natural and social sciences that focuses on the particular ways in which contexts influenced and were influenced by the development of scientific explanations and institutions. Spread throughout the narrative, readers will encounter short biographies of significant and iconic individuals whose work demonstrates the ways in which the scientific enterprise has been pursued by men and women throughout the last three centuries. Each chapter includes a bibliographic essay that discusses significant primary documents and secondary literature, describes competing historical narratives, and explains the historiographical development in the field. Following the historical narratives, each book contains a glossary, timeline, and most importantly a bibliography of primary source materials to encourage readers to come into direct contact with the people, the problems, and the claims that demonstrate how science and society influence one another. Our hope is that students and instructors will use the series to introduce themselves to the large and growing field of the history of science and begin the work of integrating the history of science into history classrooms and literature.

—*Mark A. Largent*

Prologue

Asking Questions and Defining Terms

Our common sense seems to tell us that people belong to different groups. We look around in a crowded theater or shop and we can see that some people are female and others are male, for example. Similarly, there are people who would belong to the group children and others who seem to be adults. Then there are the groups we think of as "racial." Our eyes seem to tell us that we can divide humanity into groups of people based on physical characteristics such as skin color, hair type, or the shape of the eye. In common American usage, someone with straight black hair, epicanthic folds around their eyes, and yellow skin is a member of the Asian race. Similarly someone with blonde hair, blue eyes, and white skin is a member of the white race.

Yet, merely because common sense tells us something does that necessarily make it so? In particular, because common sense tells us that there are racial differences between people, does that mean that these differences can be proven to exist scientifically? After all, science sometimes tells us things that contradict what our common sense tells us. Science tells us, for example, that solid objects are made up of atoms and molecules and are mostly empty space rather than solid matter. Yet this scientific truth is small consolation to a person hit in the head by a foul ball at a baseball game.

So, take our examples of common sense racial differences. Clearly, people do differ by skin color. But why do we choose skin color as the important physical trait for racial classification? Why not some other physical trait, perhaps height, foot size, or handedness? Why aren't left-handed people and right-handed people considered different races? Why aren't people over, say, 5'8" considered members of one race and people under that height considered another? Why is skin color or eye shape an important factor for defining racial groups when these other physical characteristics are not?

The answer is that, historically, some physical characteristics, especially skin color, have been imputed to have great social and scientific significance for human differences and others have not. In the United States and much of Europe, skin color has been seen as an indicator of a person's moral and intellectual worth while other physical characteristics have not. Left-handed people may have experienced some inconveniences in a predominately right-handed world, but they were never enslaved because they were left-handed.

So, our common sense about racial groups is the product of social circumstances rather than anything natural or essential about skin color. As we will explore in this book, any number of physical factors have been taken to be scientific "proof" of racial differences. Although it may seem strange to us, physical factors such as head shape or nose shape have been taken to be the key to dividing up people racially.

As we will see, what counts as a racial group in one time and place may not count as a racial group at different times and places. In our time and place, people may speak of someone as Asian American. Yet, does this mean that there really is some natural racial group of Asians? Asia is the largest, most populous continent, and its residents do not by any means think of themselves as one race. A Korean and a Japanese person could be horrified to find out that many Americans think of them simply as Asians.

Is there a British "race"? Many in the United Kingdom would draw some sort of distinction between an English person, a Welsh person, a Scottish person, and an Irish person. Presently these differences would probably not be thought of as "racial" but one hundred years ago they might have been. Are the Jews a race? Sixty years ago, in Nazi Germany, many believed they were. A century ago, in the United States, many thought they were. Today, few would make that claim.

In this book, we will try to make sense out of these puzzles. In particular we will try to answer the following questions:

- What, historically, has the term "race" meant? How has the term been used and how has its meaning changed? How, if at all, has it differed from "ethnicity" or "culture"? How has its appropriation by scientists influenced, and been influenced by, its folk meanings? How is it that a given group of people, most notably Jews, can be considered a "racial" group at one time and not considered a racial group at another?

- What has the relationship been between the scientific study of race and racism? Has "racial science" always meant "scientific racism"? What attempts have been made to pry the two apart?

- How have the debates about and the changing consensus on the physical reality of race affected, and been affected by, the concept's social power? Rather than trying to separate the questionable physical reality of race from its immense social power, we will show how the two are interconnected and mutually constitutive.

In order to answer these questions, this volume will survey scientific ideas about race from 1500 to the present as they developed mainly in Europe and North America but will also set them in a global context, considering their impact on and shaping by imperialism, colonialism, the slave trade, genocide, and world war. We will consider it as important to explain the rise of racist thinking in the sciences—including anthropology, psychology, genetics, and medicine—as to understand why scientists ever began to turn their backs on racism. The popular assumption is that scientific racism results from the political or religious biases of individual scientists, and that these biases prevent scientists from seeing the truth (which is whatever we believe today). When the biases are removed (through the self-correcting nature of science), racism in science naturally disappears. The more our science progresses, the less racist we will become.

This volume will reject such a simplistic assumption and argue instead that the growth of antiracism in the sciences, especially in the latter half of the twentieth century, needs to be explained as much as the flourishing of racist ideas. If the concept of race arose with the establishment of modern science, then we cannot simply conclude that the growth of science naturally banishes the concept. The development of the concept of race in the sciences, its fluctuating fortunes, and its connections both to racism and antiracism, all stand in need of sophisticated historical explanation. Thus, we will argue, the transparent social construction of racial science, its shaping by political, social, and moral beliefs, makes it more—not less—difficult to understand historically.

All of these beliefs and attitudes regarding race can be thought of as an ideology. By ideology we mean a structured set of beliefs and attitudes that people within a society bring with them when they view the world; hence we will use the word interchangeably with "worldview." Often, people are unaware of any ideology that they hold. Ideologies are the background assumptions that are unquestioned by those holding them, and they not only affect what people see in the world but also affect how people behave or prescribe the behavior of others.

There are five basic beliefs that underlie racial ideology:

1. People can be classified into distinct, biological groups on the basis of physical characteristics, either phenotypic or genotypic.
2. These groups can be ranked on a hierarchy with some better than others.
3. Outer characteristics of people are linked to inner characteristics. In other words, some physical characteristics, such as skin color, are a sign of inner, unobservable attributes, such as intelligence, temperament, or moral capacity.
4. These outer signs and inner capacities mentioned above are inherited and innate. You are born into your race and you are always the same race as your parents.

5. These differentiated races are fixed either by nature or God. You cannot
   escape your racial classification.

Certain aspects of this list need comment. For example, the first belief seems more "scientific" than some of the other beliefs. Certainly it is simply a factual matter to decide if people can be divided into separate groups. Science excels at classification, after all: there are three kinds of rocks (sedimentary, igneous, and metamorphic); there are five kinds of vertebrate animals (fish, amphibians, reptiles, birds, and mammals). As we will see, however, dividing people into different racial groups has been a profound problem that defied any sort of scientific consensus from the earliest attempts in the seventeenth century to those scientists currently working on the human genome project. No list of physical characteristics has ever been agreed upon to be the correct one for dividing people into racial groups. When geneticists started dividing people into population groups in the twentieth century, their divisions had little or nothing to do with our "common sense" ways of identifying races.

If the first belief seems scientific on first glance, the second, that some races are better than others, seems to violate what we consider good science. Modern science is built on the notion that there is a sharp division between "facts" and "values." By calling for an explicit value judgment, the second belief seems unscientific. However, as we will show in the chapters that follow, this value judgment about the worth of races was built into the concept of race from its very beginning. Value judgments, especially aesthetic judgments about physical beauty, were explicitly tied to almost every definition of race from the seventeenth century onward.

Philosopher K. Anthony Appiah has called the belief that humankind can be divided into distinct races "racialism." It is possible, at least in principle, to be a racialist without being a racist. It is the addition of the value judgment that the races are ordered on a hierarchy that transforms "racialism" into "racism." Once a society has judged some races to have more moral worth than others, social power is often allocated accordingly. In the United States, racism has meant that members of the "white race" made sure that members of the "black race" were first systematically enslaved, then legally disenfranchised. Similarly, members of the "Chinese race" were judged to be unfit for citizenship for much of the country's history. In Nazi Germany members of "racially valueless" groups—Jews, Roma, and Sinti ("Gypsies")— were confined to concentration camps and eventually exterminated.

Racism can be distinguished from ethnocentrism—the belief that one's culture, beliefs, and value system are superior to those of other groups. Like racism, ethnocentrism is a value judgment that one group of people makes about other groups. The difference between ethnocentrism and racism is in the last three beliefs of the racial ideology outlined above. Unlike a racist society, an ethnocentric society allows those from other societies to escape their inferior position by throwing off their "wrong" beliefs and values and adopting the "correct" beliefs and values of the dominant group.

Anti-Semitism (anti-Jewish prejudice) is a useful example of the difference between ethnocentrism and racism. For much of European history Christian governments and communities persecuted Jews. Christians justified this persecution because Jews have rejected the Savior, Jesus Christ. In most of these cases, Jews could escape this persecution by accepting the Savior and converting to Christianity. This would be an example of ethnocentric behavior by the Christians because they allowed the possibility that Jews could escape their social oppression by casting off their culture and accepting that of the dominant group (though few Jews did, in practice). Contrast the ethnocentrism of much of European history with the racism of the Nazi regime. For the Nazis, "Jewishness" was defined racially: if you had one grandparent who was Jewish, you were Jewish. It did not matter to the Nazis if you had never practiced Judaism in your life, you were born Jewish and could do nothing to escape your Jewishness. This was a racial form of persecution that offered no escape through a cultural conversion to the dominant society.

In the chapters that follow, we will trace how science contributed to the rise of racial ideology outlined above. As we will see, ethnocentric ideas of the seventeenth and eighteenth century hardened into a full-blown racial ideology in the nineteenth century and the first part of the twentieth century. Then science, which had contributed much to the rise of racial thinking, contributed to the demise of racism in the second half of the twentieth century.

The Origins of Racial Science, Antiquity–1800

T he history of the scientific study of race is a series of puzzles. There is no gradual progression from "primitive" ideas to more enlightened ideas regarding race and its scientific investigation; rather there are a number of seemingly intractable problems. Why is it that race, a seemingly inevitable part of our world, did not even exist as a concept in intellectual thought until a few hundred years ago? Why did the period of European history known as the "Enlightenment," which brought forth the fundamental ideas of our modern democracies, also bring with it a brutal form of racialized slavery? How did the growth of a supposedly objective science during the seventeenth century generate a science of race that made explicit value judgments regarding the aesthetic and moral worth of specific races?

These are difficult and disturbing questions. The answers to them lie in the profound scientific, social, economic, political, and ideological changes in Western Europe as it moved from medieval to modern times. Although many of the ideas explored in this chapter are, to modern eyes, "unscientific," what counts as good science changes over time and space. Indeed, the word "science" did not take on its modern meaning until the nineteenth century, after the time period covered in this chapter. The ideas here were often propounded by men (there were almost no women) who called themselves "natural philosophers." Natural philosophy and natural history were the immediate predecessors to modern science. The first natural philosophers were in ancient Greece.

Was There Race in Antiquity?

At the beginning of the twentieth century, scholars, including historians, were so sure that race was real and that racism was justified that they looked for evidence in the works of ancient authors, such as Plato and Aristotle, in order to prove that early-twentieth-century views about race were supported by ancient

Statue of Aristotle in the village of Stayira, Halkidiki, Greece (Corel Corporation)

philosophers. The Greek philosopher Aristotle (384–322 B.C.E.) developed a system of thought that, with modifications and adjustments, was the most prevalent in Western European history until the end of the eighteenth century. The idea often interpreted as racist is found in his *Politics*, in which he wrote that the defining feature of man was that he was a "political animal." Aristotle believed that men could be identified by "essence," which was the immutable, unchanging truths behind material things. Because essence was unchanging, they were more "real" than material bodies, which Aristotle considered mere surfaces that hid the real essence of a human being. So, when Aristotle claimed that man was a political animal, he meant that men were material animals, but that their essence (hence, their reality) was their ability to participate in politics. By politics, Aristotle meant the ability of men to come together in a public space and work together to form rules for a society governed by men themselves, rather than by autocratic rulers. Remember that the ancient Greek city-states were the first democracies. Aristotle also wrote a book called *Rhetoric*, which he meant as a guide for citizens making arguments and speeches in a public space in order to take part in democracy effectively. Through the use of rhetoric, or the art of persuasion, Aristotle believed that men could govern themselves without resorting to violence. So when Aristotle claimed that man was a political animal, he meant that the essence of man was his ability to participate in the public sphere to form a civilized and peaceful democracy. The ability to participate in politics was what separated man from the animals.

There was an obvious limitation in Aristotle's otherwise noble vision of the political animal. Aristotle meant only "men," not "people." Women were not included in Aristotle's democracies because they were thought unfit to participate in public life and govern themselves. Aristotle also drew a sharp distinction between Greek citizens and "barbarians" (meaning those who did not speak Greek), who were, like women, unfit for self-governance. Moreover, Aristotle defended slavery. According to Aristotle, a slave was a mere extension of his or her master's will. A slave was a tool that could be used by someone else, but a slave had no will of his or her own.

For Aristotle, what made a person a natural slave or a barbarian had nothing to do with those physical markers modern people take as "racial." In some of his other writings, Aristotle examined color and physiognomy—the study of the shape of the face— but dismissed them as a lesser form of knowledge than philosophy, which was the study of essences. For Aristotle physical appearance had little or nothing to do with determining servile status; that was determined by the ability to participate in self-governance.

Enslaved barbarians, who were often prisoners taken in war, were not racially different from the Greeks who enslaved them. Slavery is as old as civilization itself and was practiced in those Mesopotamian and Egyptian civilizations that were ancient even in Aristotle's time. For all those millennia, however, slavery was not the racialized system of oppression so familiar to us from the history of the United States and South America. For much of human history people became slaves because they lived in territories conquered by a foreign power or were considered members of an "infidel" religion. Some people were enslaved because they fell into debt and needed to sell themselves (or perhaps their children) into servitude. For five millennia, however, slavery was not "racial" in the modern sense of the world. To conclude that Aristotle's approval of slavery meant that he approved of racism is simply to read into his work a modern understanding of slavery and impose it on a time when that understanding of slavery did not exist.

The Curse of Ham and Medieval Racial Thought

The legacy of the Greek city-states continued under the Roman Republic and Empire until Alaric and the Goths sacked Rome in 410. The medieval world that followed for the next thousand years replaced the ancient political ideas of Aristotle with a Christian worldview. After the rise of Islam in the 630s there was a series of conflicts between Islam and Christianity. The religious conflicts of the medieval world were not themselves racial in nature but did establish some important precedents for racial thought that came to fruition after 1500. But the important division between people at this time was religious, not racial.

One supposedly ancient Christian justification for slavery is the biblical "Curse of Ham." In the biblical account of the Great Flood that destroyed all of humanity, save for Noah and his family, Ham was one of Noah's three sons. After the Flood, Noah fell asleep in a drunken stupor after drinking wine. Ham saw his father naked and mocked him. Ham invited his two brothers, Shem and Japheth to join him, but they refused. When Noah awoke and discovered what happened, he cursed Ham and his descendents: from that day forward they would have black skins. Each son was then assigned a continent of the world: Shem got Asia, Japheth got Europe, and Ham got Africa. The Curse of Ham explained why the inhabitants of Africa have been "cursed" to eternal servitude.

Historians and other scholars have argued that the Curse of Ham was used to justify the enslavement of Africans during the medieval period. Upon close examination we discover that this is another example of people reading into the past what they want to find there. In the medieval world the Bible was available to only a select few in the church, and then only in the form of select passages, always accompanied by extensive commentaries that left serious doubt as to the passage's true meaning. The medieval manuscripts show that Ham was seldom portrayed as having black skin, seldom confined to Africa, and not always seen as a wretched individual. So there was no medieval portrayal of people with black skins as being cursed by God in any special way.

Another problem with looking for medieval belief in some sort of special curse on Africa is that the science of cartography (mapmaking) was much different then. Although modern eyes see in a map a representation of the world's physical being, the idea that Ham was confined to Africa and that Africa was a separate place from Europe or Asia was simply not part of the medieval worldview.

Europeans had been trading and fighting with Africans and Asians since antiquity—the Mediterranean Sea made such interactions relatively easy. But the notion that these areas were part of different continents, rather than merely bits of shoreline along a common sea, was alien to medieval people and was reflected in their representations of the world. Medieval maps represented the world in a spiritual, rather than physical way. Africa, Asia, and Europe were not represented as separate physical continents but as parts of one unified world. The modern thinking of Africa as a separate place from Europe simply did not exist in medieval times. This helps explain that the late-medieval explorer who "discovered" America in 1492, Christopher Columbus, named those he found there Indians. He was convinced that what he found had to be part of the unified world of the medieval mind.

Medieval Christian thought on slavery resembled that of Aristotle: some people were natural slaves. St. Augustine of Hippo (354–430) taught that slavery was a form of punishment for man's fall from grace in the Garden of Eden. St. Thomas Aquinas in his *De regimine principum* (1266) followed Aristotle closely in arguing that some people were natural slaves, to be viewed as mere extensions of their master's will rather than possessing a will of their own. Moreover, enslaving non-Christians could be interpreted as a divine act, since this would mean bringing the word of God to the infidels. The "just war" doctrine argued that warring against non-Christians was a service to God.

The specific infidels that many Christians had in mind when they argued for a just war were the Muslim inhabitants of the Iberian Peninsula (what are now Spain and Portugal). From 711 to 1492, Muslims inhabited the peninsula and Islam was the dominant religion. The Iberian Muslims developed an important precursor to racial thinking. By the ninth century, Muslims were distinguishing between their white and black slaves. White slaves, often called *mamluks*, had higher value because they could bring a substantial ransom from the Christian enemy. The common word for slave, *abd*, came to be used for black slaves. This differential value was reflected in the work assigned to each type of slave. White slaves were often house servants; black slaves often were given the most strenuous of outdoor labor—working in salt or copper mines, or on plantations in agricultural production.

As time went on, Muslim scholars justified this division between white and black slaves. The hot and humid climate of Africa was used as the explanation for the black skin and supposed weak minds of Africans. Africans came to be portrayed as savages who lived without laws, did not clothe themselves, and had

The slave market of Cairo (Library of Congress)

no civilization. Gradually these negative stereotypes came to be shared by both Christian and Muslim inhabitants of the Iberian Peninsula. Although they regarded each other as infidels, they shared contempt for Africans.

Yet this negative stereotype of Africans, which appears very early in Muslim thought and not long after in Christian thought, was not universally held. The bonds and divisions of faith were far more important than physical differences between different peoples. Christian Ethiopians, for example, were welcomed in Venice in 1402 and in Rome in 1408; regular missions to Rome followed throughout the fifteenth century. The Italians believed that the Ethiopians' physical differences meant little in the universal, spiritual realm where all were equal in the eyes of God.

The Iberian Muslims supplied two facets of racial ideology: that outer physical signs indicated a person's inner, moral worth and that races could be ranked in a social hierarchy. Yet these ideas were not held universally and were seen as rather minor facts in a world of faith. Moreover, the notion that race-based status is fixed and permanent, what Aristotle would call *essential*, was missing. Over the next few centuries, however, scholars would look more and more to the body rather than the soul for a person's essence. Once the body became a person's essence, a great barrier to racial thinking dropped away.

The Age of Exploration

Historians often mark the break between the medieval and modern worlds around the year 1500 because of several events that significantly changed the world. Europeans, starting with Prince Henry the Navigator of Portugal (1394–1460), expanded their control of territory beyond Continental Europe. The Christian expulsion of Islam from the Iberian Peninsula occurred in 1492, the same year as the "discovery" of the Americas by Christopher Columbus. The Age of Exploration created new economic ways of life that required new ideological and scientific justifications for European behavior.

The economic motor driving this enormous change was the European colonial system. Although it had its roots in the medieval world, the colonial economic system recreated the world after 1500. The basis of the system was establishment of an economic resource outside the mother country, for example, Spanish or English sugar plantations in the Caribbean islands or Portuguese mining operations in South America. The wealth generated from such operations, however, did not remain in the colony but was returned to the mother country. The result was the systematic stripping of resources from the colony for the benefit of the mother country. Centuries later, the "lesser developed" countries of the world are still feeling the economic effects of this arrangement.

An additional factor underlying this story is the new form of slavery that arose to generate this wealth. For the first time, Europeans systematically enslaved people with whom they had no territorial dispute—Africans. The "Atlantic system" of commerce had people of one continent, Europe, taking people from a second continent, Africa, to a third continent, the Americas, to serve as a labor supply to generate wealth for the first continent. This rather curious arrangement was a racial system. In fairly short order in the New World blackness and slavery became associated. To be black was to be a slave and to be a slave was to be black.

The eventual association of blackness with slavery underscores a very important point about how racial ideology developed in European thought. Race came to mean ever-larger groups of people. Europeans certainly did not believe that all Europeans were alike during this time—indeed, the Spanish, English, Portuguese, French, and other European nationalities were constantly competing with one another; often these competitions became open confrontations. Just as Europeans saw distinctions among different nationalities, they recognized that there were different African nationalities and different nationalities among the indigenous inhabitants of the Americas. Over time the distinctions between the ethnicities of different peoples were erased in European eyes, and they began seeing the white race, black race, yellow race, and red race. This is not a straightforward story—precisely who counted as a member of the white race was often contested. The roots of these differences in perceptions can be traced back to the discovery of the New World and the people who lived there.

Natural Philosophy and the Colonial Experience: The Sixteenth and Seventeenth Centuries

Europeans in the sixteenth and seventeenth centuries believed that the Bible explained many things about the natural world. Scholars and writers were monogenecists, meaning that they believed that all humans were the descendents of Adam and Eve in a singular act of creation. A few polygenecist writers, such as Giordano Bruno, who argued for a theory of multiple creations, were considered heretics. (Bruno was burned at the stake in 1600 for this and other heretical beliefs.) So when it came to explaining the differences between Europeans and American Indians or Europeans and Africans, scholars made sure that their explanations were consistent with monogenetic interpretations of the Bible.

In addition to their biblical beliefs about human origins, scholars of the sixteenth and seventeenth centuries relied on theories of organic growth and form as taught by natural philosophy. Natural philosophy's theories of physiology

The Wampanoags suffered high mortality rates related to smallpox during the 1600s. Hand-colored woodcut (North Wind Picture Archives)

were developed out of the teaching of the ancient medical writers Hippocrates and Galen who, in turn, had based their writings on Aristotle. Like Aristotle, natural philosophers taught that everything in nature was connected to everything else in nature. The celestial spheres of stars and planets were intimately connected to the earthly plane of existence, for example, and natural philosophers would explain these interactions with astrology. Physical nature was described through complex interactions of the four elements—earth, air, fire, and water. Health and disease and other matters of organic form were explained by the interactions of the four elements with the four humors of the body, each associated with a bodily substance, which would result in the disposition of the person. A simplified version of things could look like this:

Natural Philosophy's Four Elements and Human Differences

Humor	Bodily Substance	Dominant Temperament
Hot and Moist	Blood	Sanguine
Hot and Dry	Yellow Bile	Choleric
Cold and Dry	Black Bile	Melancholic
Cold and Moist	Phlegm	Phlegmatic

According to natural philosophy, people had different physical appearances because they came from different climates. Natural philosophy taught that there were different zones of climate on the earth that have different properties because they reside under different constellations. So natural philosophers routinely divided the world into temperate, torrid, and polar zones, and each zone had different plants, animals, minerals, and people because these things developed according to the peculiar interactions of the elements and stars in that zone. As natural philosopher Richard Eden wrote in 1561, "All the inhabitants of the world are formed and disposed of such complexion and strength of the body, that every [one] of them are proportionate to the climate assigned unto them" (Eden 1885, xlii).

The natural philosophical explanation for the ties between organisms and their climates should not be confused with modern, evolutionary notions about how the environment shapes organic form through natural selection. In the natural philosophical theory of organic form, the climate and stars had a *direct* connection to the shape and complexion of the organism. The doctrine of maternal impression, for example, held that the emotional or moral state of the mother during pregnancy had direct effects on the growing fetus. Moreover, natural philosophy taught that it was not just individual organisms that were affected by the climate but the entire population. Not too surprisingly, these climatic explanations were interpreted ethnocentrically. The English, for example, were convinced of their superiority because their climate was more temperate than the cold of Scotland or the heat of Spain.

The close connection between climate and organism had an implication: travel to and residence in a different climate would change the form of the organism. Moving to a different climate meant that the body had to adapt to the new climate and the new astral influences or it would die. When colonization of the New World started in the early sixteenth century, it was far from clear that Europeans could survive in this strange new place.

In North America, English views of the American Indians were not at all uniform. To begin with, there was considerable dispute as to the natural color of American Indians. Many American Indians wore little clothing, at least by sixteenth-century European standards, and travelers often noted their custom of painting their bodies. Perhaps these two factors could explain the apparent color difference? Dutch traveler Jan Huyghen van Linschoten argued in 1598 that for the North Americans: "When they first come into the world [they] are not so black but very white: the black-yellowish color is made upon them by a certain ointment . . . Their color likewise changeth because they go naked and with the burning heat of the sun" (Linschoten 1885, 220). Many travelers insisted that American Indians were not so dark, certainly no darker than Spaniards and probably no darker than the average Englishman.

Such arguments were not merely disinterested statements of fact for the English colonists in North America; they were attempts to persuade those left behind in England that living in the New World was not dangerous. Because organisms were peculiar to the climate, many English wondered if it would be possible to survive on a diet of American food and water. Many writings of the sixteenth century concern themselves with "seasoning" the English body to the American climate. The writers hoped that through discipline and a careful program of introducing New World foods slowly, the English body could adapt to the strange environment of America.

Because of the teachings of natural philosophy, many colonists suspected that they or their children would eventually come to resemble the American Indian. Natural philosophy did not allow that the English would continue to look like the English once they started living in the climate of the New World; thus, natural philosophy acted as a barrier to the development of racial ideology. Because climate would change bodies so readily, the notion that humanity could be divided into sharply divided races did not have a firm foothold in the sixteenth and seventeenth centuries. As during the medieval period, the soul, not the body, was essential.

The grounds for a racial ideology began developing in the seventeenth century in North America. The English colonists noticed that American Indians seemed especially prone to disease. A cold or flu that would cause an English person discomfort would kill Americans. Modern medicine explains this as a matter of immunity: Europeans brought with them a number of Old World diseases, the most virulent of which were smallpox and influenza, to which many Europeans had immunity but the American populations did not. The result was that those diseases had a terrible, nearly genocidal, effect on Native Americans.

Modern notions of disease and immunity, however, were unknown in natural philosophy. For the seventeenth-century English, diseases were part of the climate, just as the plants and animals were. This left natural philosophers asking how the English, foreign to the New World, could be hardier than the Americans, who belonged there? The answer to this puzzle was to postulate that the English were actually better acclimated to the environment than the American Indians were. Indians died of diseases—so the belief went—because of some internal constitutional failure within American Indian bodies. The reasons for this were not readily understood, but the notion of a natural difference internal to the body and not affected by climatic influences was an important stepping-stone toward the racial ideology that would come to fruition in the nineteenth century.

A parallel story developed for the Spanish colonists in South America in the sixteenth and seventeenth centuries. If anything, the Spanish settlers had a more difficult time than the English did convincing the mother country that the colonies were a livable place. After all, much of the equatorial region of South America is a true torrid zone and, to make matters worse, the Southern Hemisphere has entirely different constellations than the Northern. Many Spanish natural philosophers in Spain thought that the bad stars of the Southern Hemisphere combined with the hot, humid climate made it an exceedingly dangerous place to live.

The arguments about the habitability of the Spanish colonies introduced another important element to the development of racial ideology: the interaction between gender and racial thinking. Working off Aristotelian notions, natural philosophy taught that climates that were warm and dry were masculine and climates that were cold and moist were feminine. Hence, the American Indians had been emasculated by the humidity of the torrid zone, which explained why they could not grow beards (a notion that was very popular among the English in North America as well). To take up residence in such a place would be risk becoming effeminate. Indeed some Spanish authors maintained that American Indian women urinated while standing up, thus proving the unnatural ways of the land.

In the seventeenth century, Spanish natural philosophers in the South American colonies developed a number of arguments against these widely held beliefs about America. First, the colonial natural philosophers insisted that the constellations of the Southern Hemisphere were every bit as beautiful and the stars were as bright as those that controlled Europe. Moreover, the food found in the New World was nourishing for the male body and the colonists were every bit as masculine as those left behind in Spain. Indeed, Spanish colonists liked to portray themselves not only as healthy and vigorous but also as nobility: they were aristocrats who deserved better treatment from the Spanish crown.

Such colonial defenses of the climate of South America led to a paradox for the Spanish colonists. Simply put, if it were true that the southern stars were beneficial and the southern climate the paradise that colonists claimed, why did this not lead to the conclusion that the American Indians were superior, or at least equal, to Europeans? After all, the American Indians were born under the southern stars and were native to the climate. The problem for the colonists was that they were the beneficiaries of the portrayal of the American Indians as beardless, effeminate, and degenerate. The Spanish had enslaved a large proportion of the American Indian population by this time and were increasingly dependent on slave labor to maintain their economy. These violent actions were often justified under the Christian "just war" doctrines as necessary to bring the heathens to Christ. But eventually, that the American Indians were anything other than indolent and inferior was unacceptable to many Spanish colonists.

The answer the Spanish arrived at was very similar to that of the English in the Northern Hemisphere. Enrico Martinez, a scholar living in Mexico, postulated in an influential work published in 1606 that the weak constitutions of the Americans made them especially susceptible to the baleful influences of debilitating astrological phenomena. Spanish colonists, however, were constitutionally strong enough to withstand the astrological phenomena. As evidence Martinez pointed to a series of plagues that wiped out American populations while leaving the Spanish relatively untouched. Martinez's explanation, while offered in traditional natural philosophical terms, nonetheless drew a distinction between the weak bodies of Americans and the strong bodies of Europeans. Again, we have the beginnings of the notion that there were internal, *essential* differences between the bodies of different groups of people. No one in the seventeenth century was willing to postulate a mechanism for how these essential differences between people could be inherited. Nor did anyone claim that these different groups were different in a spiritual way—to do so was to run afoul of the church. But the beginnings of these ideas were in play.

The Science of Anthropology

In the European colonies such ideas were born and slowly worked their way back to the continent. There they joined with new sciences—taxonomy and anthropology—to form important building blocks for scientific racial ideology. Anthropology began as a branch of medicine; a form of anatomical study. In the seventeenth and eighteenth centuries anthropology became a science of classification of people and cultures. This was part of a larger intellectual change that often goes by the name the Enlightenment. How people should study nature and people's relationship to nature underwent profound changes during this time period.

Three key ideas underpinned the rise of anthropology as a science:

First, and perhaps the most significant, was removing the sacred as an explanation for natural changes. Scientists increasingly looked to explain natural phenomena on their own terms without postulating God as a direct cause. This did not mean that science suddenly became atheistic: most writers continued to offer scientific explanations that were consistent with Scripture and many scientists conceived of their work as sacred, as another way to understand the mind of God. In Great Britain and other Protestant countries in particular, the beliefs of "natural theology" were seen as an important religious supplement to the "revealed theology" of the Bible. Nonetheless, removing God as an active agent in scientific explanations was an important development in the sciences of the time.

Second was the concept of "progress." The medieval world, in many ways, was a static one. Not only was the world unified, but it was also unchanging. In the seventeenth and eighteenth centuries, by contrast, many believed that not only was the world changing, it was getting better. This was especially so in the realm of people and society. Europeans believed that their societies were more advanced, were *better* than those of other parts of the world. Part of their mission, therefore, was to help these "primitive" people progress toward the European ideal. The barbaric outsiders of the ancient Greeks, for example, became merely those who had not yet advanced to the "enlightened" stage of the Europeans. Although the European colonial powers may have doubted the racial inferiority of non-European peoples at times, they never doubted the superiority of their own society and way of life. This notion of superiority justified the European conquest of non-European peoples around the world—it was justified because of the superior religion and culture of Europe.

Third was the notion that people could be part of the natural world. In one sense, people had been part of the natural world since Aristotle. One of the ancient Greek conceptions was that of the Great Chain of Being in which everything in the universe was a link in the chain, ranked in its proper place. However, in the ancient and medieval conception of the Great Chain of Being, humans were someplace in the middle, poised between the natural world of animals, plants, and minerals and the divine realm of the angels and gods. During the Enlightenment, with the separation of humanity from the spiritual (at least in the scientific realm), humans were on the top of the Great Chain of Being— all else descended from them. Hence, the notion was that all of nature indicated progress toward humans in general and Europeans in particular.

One of the first figures to reflect these aspects of Enlightenment thought in terms of racial thinking was philosopher Francois Bernier (1625–1688), a traveler who spent time in Poland, Egypt, and India and was a close friend of John Locke, whose political ideas were the basis for the American and French Revolutions. In 1684, Bernier published *The New Division of the Earth,* one of the first attempts to classify humanity according to race. His arguments reflected all the basic themes of Enlightenment thought: separating the sacred from the natural, the notion of progress, and the need to make people part of the natural, not sacred, world.

Bernier argued that the fundamental way to divide people should be by physical types. He showed how Enlightenment thought focused on the material rather than the spiritual aspects of human beings; while Bernier's anthropology was *consistent* with the Bible, he did not *call upon* the Bible as evidence for his position.

Bernier postulated four basic divisions of humanity: the "first race" that included Europeans, North Africans, Middle Easterners, Asian Indians, and American Indians; second, Africans; third, East and Northeast Asians; fourth, the Lapps. Bernier's classification underscored a number of points that hold for nearly every anthropological classification scheme of the eighteenth century. Yet, Bernier was ignorant about some of the races in his categories. Although he admitted almost complete ignorance about the Lapps and had very little experience with this Arctic group, his judgment on them was uniformly negative. His experience with Africans was limited to seeing them in Turkish and Arabian slave markets. By modern standards, his judgment does not seem more accurate in those areas where he had greater experience. For example he spent twelve years in India, but thought that its inhabitants would be as white as the French except for the time they spent in the sun.

Bernier made explicit value judgments about the different races in his classification, especially aesthetic ones. A major part of his work was a detailed analysis of the women of different races in terms of their physical beauty. Although much of this discussion was a titillating description of what he witnessed in, for example, the African women he saw for sale in the slave markets, it nevertheless highlighted two important aspects of racial ideology. First, that discussion of race was nearly impossible to separate from discussion of gender and, second, that value judgments were built into the race concept from the beginning. In other words, racial classification never proceeded from a neutral discussion of physical principles, but had judgments concerning worth and beauty as well.

Francois Bernier (1625–1688)

French physician and traveler Francois Bernier was one of the first Europeans to classify people into human races. Trained as a physician at the University of Montpellier, Bernier achieved greater fame in his lifetime as a world traveler. In 1648, Bernier spent time in Poland. In 1656, Bernier spent a year in Cairo and then traveled to India where he spent twelve years as a physician for a high official. When he returned to France, Bernier published a number of accounts of his travels.

Bernier was a student of philosopher Pierre Gassendi, an important figure in the scientific revolution of the seventeenth century. Gassendi argued for a completely mechanistic philosophy of nature that excluded spiritual forces, including Christianity. Beginning in the 1670s and continuing until the end of his life, Bernier published Gassendi's writings in French; they had been available only in Latin before this time. Bernier's *Abrégé de la Philosophie de Gassendi*, published in seven volumes in 1684, became the definitive edition of Gassendi's work. Like Gassendi, Bernier maintained that humans had a dual nature, possessing both an eternal soul that gave us rationality and a second nonrational aspect that was also possessed by animals. The implication for Bernier was that different groups of people possessed different degrees of rationality and that some people were, therefore, natural slaves, just as Aristotle had described.

The cover of Bernier's Travels in the Mogul Empire *(Stapleton Collection/Corbis)*

Bernier also achieved a measure of fame for his accounts of his experiences in India. Bernier spoke highly of the Indian nobility in whose court he worked as a physician but condemned the lower castes of India as well as the Hindu and Muslim religions of the area.

Bernier's writings were persuasive to his European audience because he had firsthand experience with the people he described. He represents an important transition in science: he was partly the unsystematic world traveler, willing to indulge his audience's desire for exotic accounts of his travels; at the same time, he was a systematic thinker, who attempted to arrange his knowledge of the world in a system of thought that could be verified independently.

More influential than Bernier was Carl von Linné, who wrote under the Latin name Carolus Linnaeus (1707–1778). A professor of botany in Uppsala, Sweden, Linnaeus invented the modern classification scheme in which organisms are arranged in ever more specific categories from "kingdom" to "species" with a host of intermediate groupings. His *Systema Naturae* went through ten editions between 1735 and 1758 and his system of classification soon became the standard in all universities in Europe.

People were part of Linnaeus's natural order, under the order "anthropomorpha" in the genus "homo." All people were members of the same species for Linnaeus, which meant God created them to be distinct from other forms of life. There were, however, four basic "varieties," which meant that they had acquired some superficial differences from differing climates:

1. Americanus: Reddish skin, black hair, scanty beard, obstinate, merry, regulated by custom.

2. Asiaticus: Sallow skin, black hair, dark eyes, severe, greedy, covered with loose garments, ruled by opinions.

3. Africanus: Black skin, black, frizzled hair, indolent, women without shame, governed by caprice.

4. Europaeus: White, long, flowing hair, blue eyes, gentle, inventive, covers himself with close-fitting clothing, governed by laws.

Linnaeus's catalog of human varieties differed significantly from Bernier's. Linnaeus's varieties of humans were consonant with the modern understanding of divisions between continents. The physical features of the varieties were intermingled with moral and behavioral traits. Linnaeus's claims seem like ethnocentric judgments about moral capacities or styles of clothing. Linnaeus had not traveled as widely as Bernier but based his knowledge on travelers' accounts written by different people. That these early scientific works were based so heavily on hearsay contained in travelers' journals and books demonstrates the futility of claims that the science of race developed outside the social and political world, as the scientists based their judgments on the judgments of merchants, soldiers, and adventurers.

Each of Linnaeus's varieties contains an enormous variety of physical types, demonstrating how racial categories began to include ever-larger groups of people. The Swede, Linnaeus, might have seen that the Europeans around him had blue eyes and blonde hair, but had he been Greek he would not have claimed those traits as ones shared by all Europeans. By grouping all inhabitants of the continent under one variety, Linnaeus's system could gloss over physical differences within the group.

Although Linnaeus's system of classification was very successful it did have a few detractors, the most famous of whom was Georges-Louis Leclerc, Comte de Buffon (1707–1788). Buffon's chief objection was that Linnaeus cre-

HISTOIRE

NATURELLE,

GÉNÉRALE ET PARTICULIERE,

AVEC LA DESCRIPTION

DU CABINET DU ROY.

Tome Premier.

A PARIS,

DE L'IMPRIMERIE ROYALE.

M. DCCXLIX.

Title page of Comte de Buffon's Histoire Naturelle, Génèrale et Particuliere, *published in 1749 (Library of Congress)*

ated an inflexible system of classification because Linnaeus thought species were fixed and eternal. For Buffon, Linnaeus's system achieved its order because it was imposed on a messy natural world. Nature consists of groups of individual organisms, argued Buffon, that exist on a continuum and cannot be fit into Linnaeus's strict and unyielding classification system.

Buffon developed his objection to Linnaeus in his masterwork, *Histoire Naturelle* (1749). Where Linnaeus saw fixed species created and forever separate, Buffon saw a group of organisms from common lines of descent that could produce fertile offspring. Where members of the same species seemed to Buffon to be markedly different he called them a new species. Although this may appear to be sloppy work on Buffon's part, it should be understood as marking a deep philosophical break with Linnaeus. For Buffon no divisions that humans made in nature were "real," they were just labels humans use to understand nature. Unlike Linnaeus, Buffon's categories were not supposed to describe actual divisions of the natural world.

In his discussion of different groups of humans, Buffon dispensed with Linnaeus's concept of "varieties" and used a different word, "race." The word had two common meanings in the Romance languages of French and Spanish. First, it referred to a lineage of animals marked by common descent. Second, the word denoted the noble houses of Europe: a race of royalty. Buffon welcomed both connotations.

Buffon did not develop a permanent list of human races. As befitting his idea that categories were mere conveniences, he added and subtracted races throughout the course of his career. A typical list could include: Lapps, Tartars, South Asians, Ethiopians, and Americans. For Buffon these were groups of people of a common descent marked by physical markers that made them resemble each other. But these differences were not eternal, as Linnaeus taught, only transitory. Furthermore, Buffon argued that it was useless to assemble a list of specific traits for classification because one needed to gather general impressions and classify people according to groups of traits. Skin color, stature, intelligence, and face shape could be called upon or discarded according to the needs of the moment.

As with other racial writers, Buffon gave a central role to value judgments of the relative worth of the races in his writings. He argued that the original race was the European one and others could be understood as "degenerations" from that norm. Americans were perhaps the least degenerated by the climate in which they lived, Africans and Lapps perhaps the most. This was not a new idea with Buffon; after all Bernier had called Europeans the "first race" because he had believed that the other races had degenerated from them. Again, the value judgments about the moral worth of the different races were evident in Buffon's scientific work.

Georges-Louis Leclerc de Buffon (1707–1788)

Born into a wealthy family, Georges-Louis Leclerc de Buffon showed an early propensity for mathematics while a college student at the Collége des Jésuites in Dijon from 1717–1723. After a period of youthful wandering throughout Europe in his twenties, Buffon came to Paris in 1732 and soon ingratiated himself in French political and social circles. For a few years, he published a few scientific works on probability theory in mathematics and carefully built his personal fortune. He was

(Time Life Pictures/Mansell/Getty Images)

known in the scientific circles of Paris for his work in mathematics and engineering and was one of the first French defenders of Newtonian physics.

In 1739, he became the supervisor of the *Jardin du roi* or Royal Garden under King Louis XV. Under his leadership, the Royal Garden grew tremendously in size and reputation and the king eventually rewarded Buffon by making him a Count.

One of Buffon's duties as the administrator of the Garden was to catalog its collection of exotic plant life. However, Buffon set out to organize not just the Garden's holdings but rather the entire natural world in a monumental project that would consume the rest of his life, some five decades. The result was a thirty-six-volume work entitled *Histoire naturelle (Natural History)*.

Buffon's formal college education was in the law, and he set out to teach himself all there was to know about natural history in order to write his monumental work. Few works met his exacting standards for acceptable scientific work. Buffon thought the ancients, notably Aristotle and the Roman writer Pliny, were more reliable than many of his contemporaries who he thought suffered from the tendency to write without firsthand knowledge of their subjects. Buffon had at his disposal not only the contents of the Royal Garden, the largest in the world, but a worldwide network of correspondents who sent him specimens and accounts of what they had witnessed. The result of Buffon's lifelong effort to describe the natural world was a huge encyclopedia of the natural world, which, for Buffon, included the different races of human beings.

The most influential classifier of human races in the eighteenth century was the German professor of medicine Johann Friedrich Blumenbach (1752–1840). In his *On the Varieties of Mankind* (1775), he divided humanity into five races: first, Caucasians—that is the "European" race, for once including the Lapps; second, Mongolian—the residents of Asia; third, Africans; fourth, Americans; fifth, Malay—the newly discovered people of the South Pacific.

Blumenbach's work echoes many familiar themes found in his predecessors. The aesthetic judgment was obvious in his coining of the term "Caucasian" because Blumenbach considered the women of the Caucasus Mountains to be the most beautiful. He believed that the Caucasians were the most beautiful and the original race, the others having degenerated from them because of climatic influences. Like Buffon, Blumenbach did not see human races as fixed and unbridgeable; instead, he argued that the races faded into one another and that it was impossible to draw sharp lines between them. Moreover, Blumenbach maintained that even the African race, widely believed at the time to be hopelessly degenerate, could produce members that were the equal to Caucasians. Blumenbach even had a library of books written by Africans to prove this point.

The Atlantic Slave System

Blumenbach and other scientists wrote in a period of great economic and social change. The great Atlantic system of commerce was remaking the world and doing it with slave labor, the vast majority of it from Africa. How did this great change affect how people thought and wrote about race?

Nearly every culture had practiced slavery throughout history. But the great slave system that Europe developed in its colonies was different. Africans were not people with whom the Europeans had territorial disputes. Indeed, Africans were taken from their homes and across the ocean and, if they survived the brutal passage, lived out the rest of their lives in slavery. As previously mentioned, European encroachment into Africa was an extension of the just war doctrine. As early as 1415, the Portuguese justified an attack on citadels in Morocco on the grounds that these were infidels; and while they technically did not pose a threat to Christianity at the time they could in the future. Soon this doctrine was codified by Portuguese writer João de Barros in his *Asia* (1539) where he argued that "preventative" strikes at infidels denied them the ability to muster their forces against Christendom. Black slaves, who had first appeared in Portugal in 1441, were commonplace soon after.

The discovery of the New World by Columbus allowed for a great expansion in a traditional form of agriculture: sugar plantations. The cultivation of sugar in large plantations through the use of slave labor began on islands in the Mediterranean during the middle ages and worked its way westward onto islands in the Atlantic Ocean. Soon after Columbus, Europeans began cultivating sugar in the Caribbean islands and in Brazil. Because of the brutal and backbreaking labor required, slaves were necessary for sugar plantations to be profitable.

The existence of the economic need for labor on sugar plantations, however, tells only part of the story and does not explain why Europeans turned to Africa for slave labor. Economically, it made more sense to enslave American Indians or other Europeans. To be sure, the use of American Indians was not uncommon but they could plot revolts with their free countrymen and easily disappear if they escaped. Additionally, their susceptibility to disease made them a poor labor force. These issues were on the table in a famous debate between Bishop Bartolomé de Las Casas and Ginés de Sepúlveda in 1550. Las Casas had just returned from Spanish colonies where he had seen the terrible effect of slavery on the natives of the New World. He argued forcefully that the American Indians should be seen as people, possible brothers in Christ, and that they should not be enslaved. Sepúlveda argued that there were definite physical differences between American Indians and Europeans and therefore they could be considered Aristotle's natural slaves. Both agreed, however, that some people were natural slaves and that enslaving Africans was fully justified.

Africans had additional advantages as slaves in Europeans' eyes. They were less susceptible to many Old World diseases, just as the Europeans were; they had no friendly faces in the populace of the Americas, and they were easily marked as slaves by their skin color. Hence, Africa made an ideal source of slave labor from the European perspective.

African slavery came first to Brazil and the Caribbean Islands and much later to North America. Unlike the sugar plantations in the Caribbean and South America, there was no North American staple crop that benefited from the economies of scale afforded by plantation agriculture. Until the early eighteenth century the most common cash crop in North America was tobacco, which could be grown profitably by small farmers with the aid of a few indentured servants or slaves. It was not until the 1730s that rice was heavily cultivated in the area that is now South Carolina and Georgia.

There were definite economic benefits to growing rice in a plantation system, unlike the other crops grown in North America. English planters needed to grow rice in tidal areas where rivers flowed into the ocean; the plantations had a complex system of dams and gateways to irrigate the rice. The technology for this system was unknown in England but had been widely used in Africa for centuries. The technological system that made profitable rice plantations was largely an African one, and the English planters made sure that the slaves they bought knew the intricacies of rice cultivation. Therefore, the existence of rice plantations meant that the English colonialists did not think that "all Africans were the same" but were concerned to get Africans from specific tribes or ethnicities that had knowledge of rice cultivation. The notion that all Africans were the same race was actually not widely held by English colonists in the early eighteenth century. It was not until the close of the slave trade in 1808 and the discovery of a new staple crop, cotton, that the ideological belief in a "black race" served the interests of the dominant planter class in the American South.

Enlightenment Values and Racial Thought

The growth of the Atlantic system of slavery coincided with the growth of Enlightenment thought. This was the time when many great philosophical writers, such as John Locke, Montesquieu, and Condorcet, proclaimed the virtues of natural rights enjoyed by all, rather than reserved for the nobility. Democratic government was put forth as the most just and developed of all forms of government. How could these humanistic and egalitarian values have come to full development when slavery was growing in the New World and racist thought was beginning to take shape?

Part of the answer has to do with the notion of "progress" and the science of society. Many of these thinkers believed that societies develop and get better over time. There was a natural progress of society through various stages, beginning with hunting/gathering societies, moving on to animal husbandry, agriculture, and finally, commerce. Europeans believed that European capitalist society was the most developed of all societies in the world. For many of these thinkers, progress was *natural*—an inevitability. Just as the planets moved in their orbits according to fixed invariant laws, so too did societies progress through these stages of development.

The notion of societal progress seems, at first, to argue against essential racial differences between groups of people. A theory of societal progress presupposes a universal theory of human nature. If all societies are going to go through these stages, then all members of all societies must be essentially the same. Just as Europe had reached the pinnacle of societal development, so too would Africa because they shared in this universal human nature. The word "primitive" to describe Africa and Africans indicates this mode of thought—they were simply less advanced, not fundamentally different.

As the Atlantic slave system reaped huge economic rewards for Europe and the colonies, the argument that Africans (and American Indians) could not progress came to the forefront. Europeans had had contact with Africa for millennia and yet Africa remained backward and primitive. Perhaps there really was some essential difference between African people and European people. Just as the colonial administrators and physicians had posited bodily differences between themselves and their colonial subjects in the seventeenth century, many thinkers began to entertain that notion in the eighteenth century.

Perhaps no figure captures the tensions between Enlightenment notions of natural rights and universal human nature versus the growing racial ideology better than the third president of the United States, Thomas Jefferson. On the rotunda of Jefferson's memorial in Washington, D.C., are inscribed Jefferson's words, "Nothing is more certainly written in the book of fate that these people [the slaves] are to be free." What is not there is the conclusion of Jefferson's sentence, "nor is it less certain that the two races, equally free, can not live in the same government." The tension between the first and second phrases of Jefferson's sentence captures the profound ambiguity of Jefferson as an Enlightenment thinker.

Jefferson was a politician who penned in the opening sentence of the Declaration of Independence, "all men being endowed by their Creator with certain inalienable rights." He was also a learned naturalist who wrote of Negroes (a word that was increasingly popular in his time) that "one could scarcely be found capable of tracing and comprehending the investigations of Euclid; and that in imagination they are dull, tasteless, and anomalous." Jefferson reported his finding in his work, *Notes on the State of Virginia* (1787), the most extensive example of his naturalist thought.

Jefferson was a well-read, capable and brilliant man. His *Notes on the State of Virginia* was similar to the writings of Spanish and English colonists of the previous century: a defense of the New World using the science of the Old. In *Notes* Jefferson concocted an amalgamation of the thoughts of Linnaeus and Buffon. On the one hand, Jefferson spent a great deal of time refuting Buffon's contention that the natural history of the New World is merely a degenerate version of the Old. For example, Buffon had argued that the fossilized remains of mammoths found in the New World were a degenerate species of elephant that went extinct in the degenerate climate of North America. Jefferson, by contrast, argued that the mammoth was a distinct species still extant, though undiscovered by Europeans so far. Jefferson charged the famous Lewis and Clark expedition with finding a living mammoth on their travels in order to prove to the world his notions about the natural history of the New World.

Jefferson also defended American Indians against Buffon's charges that they were degenerate white men who had been affected by the excessive heat and moisture of the New World. Jefferson spoke highly of the American Indians, praising their inherent human propensity for improvement. Any weaknesses in the American Indians were not in their constitutions but in their unfortunate circumstance of not being long exposed to the civilization of Europe.

In other parts of *Notes* Jefferson embraced Buffon's ideas about the complexity and changing nature of the world. He spoke approvingly of what was called "catastrophist geology"—the notion that the geologic record showed evidence of huge floods and earthquakes. Many writers of the time shied away from catastrophist geology because it was associated with the heretical notions of polygenesis, the theory of multiple creations of humanity. Jefferson, freethinker that he was, was broaching the possibility of polygenesis without fully taking the plunge.

Nowhere are Jefferson's notions about the possibility of polygenesis more evident than in his discussion of Negroes. Here, he abandoned Buffon's idea regarding race as a mere organizing principle and seems to be closer to Linnaeus's notion of fixed, essential types. Though he couched his writings on the inferiority of Negroes in careful language, he clearly believed that they were fundamentally inferior to whites in intellectual and moral capacities.

Though he produced passionate antislavery writings, he also never manumitted his slaves. Though he urged that the slaves be freed, he also was quite consistent in his call that the "Free Negro" was an oxymoron. The Negroes should be freed, and then returned to Africa. Like James Madison, and others of the Founders, Jefferson was active in the American Colonization Society (founded 1817), a philanthropic organization dedicated to raising money to send Free Negroes to Africa rather than allowing them to remain in the United States. The conflict in Jefferson's writings between freedom and slavery, between equality and racial hierarchy, encapsulated the reality of life during the age of Enlightenment.

Conclusion

By the end of the eighteenth century, many elements of racial ideology were in place. Racial thought had no place in antiquity; the seeds of racial ideology were planted in the thought of Iberian Muslims in the medieval world, with their racialized hierarchy of slavery. During the Age of Exploration, the natural philosophy that saw no fixed types of organic form gave way to notions that there were some essential differences between the bodies of European colonists and those native to the occupied lands. Early taxonomists—Bernier, Linnaeus, Buffon, and Blumenbach—created the idea that humanity could be divided into categories. And Enlightenment thinkers such as Thomas Jefferson began writing that there were unbridgeable differences between black and white people. All these ideas would be given a firm, scientific footing in the nineteenth century as writers began justifying the slave societies that had been created in the wake of European expansion.

Bibliographic Essay

There are several excellent studies of racial ideas in Western thought. Among the older studies that are quite valuable are Winthrop D. Jordan, *White Over Black:*

American Attitudes Toward the Negro, 1550–1812 (Chapel Hill: University of North Carolina Press, 1968) and David Brion Davis, *The Problem of Slavery in Western Culture* (Ithaca, NY: Cornell University Press, 1966). Although containing much valuable information, both Jordan and Davis maintain that racial thinking is ancient in Western Civilization. An early example of someone who argues that race was "invented" around the sixteenth century was Dante A. Puzzo, "Racism and the Western Tradition," *Journal of the History of Ideas* 25 (1964): 579–586. More recent scholarship supports Puzzo's position, for example, George M. Fredrickson, *Racism: A Short History* (Princeton: Princeton University Press, 2002). Two works that informed much of chapter one are Ivan Hannaford, *Race: The History of an Idea in the West* (Baltimore: Johns Hopkins University Press, 1996) and Audrey Smedley, *Race in North America: Origin and Evolution of a Worldview*, Second ed. (Boulder, CO: Westview Press, 1999). For a recent statement by Davis that reiterates his views see David Brion Davis, "The Culmination of Racial Polarities and Prejudice," *Journal of the Early Republic* 19 (1999): 757–775.

Hannaford's book provided much of the information about Aristotle's racial beliefs and an excellent discussion of medieval racial thought. For an extensive treatment of the "Curse of Ham" see Benjamin Braude, "The Sons of Noah and the Construction of Ethnic and Geographical Identities in the Medieval and Early Modern Periods," *William and Mary Quarterly* 54 (1997): 103–142. On medieval Muslim racial thought see James H. Sweet, "The Iberian Roots of American Racist Thought," *William and Mary Quarterly* 54 (1997): 143–166. As the first of the maritime empires, Portugal is a useful example of the transition from medieval to early modern racial thought, especially the impact of the "just war" doctrine and the age of exploration. See A. J. R. Russell-Wood, "Iberian Expansion and the Issue of Black Slavery: Changing Portuguese Attitudes, 1440–1770," *American Historical Review* 83 (1978): 16–42.

The literature on the ideological and economic reasons for the growth of the Atlantic slave system is enormous. Major monographs include Ira Berlin, *Many Thousands Gone: The First Two Centuries of Slavery in North America* (Cambridge, MA: Harvard University Press, 1998); Robin Blackburn, *The Making of New World Slavery: From the Baroque to the Modern, 1492–1800* (London: Verso, 1997); Hugh Thomas, *The Slave Trade: The Story of the Atlantic Slave Trade, 1440–1870* (New York: Simon and Schuster, 1997). Works that explore the ideological tensions between the growth of slavery and the growth of Enlightenment ideology include Davis, *The Problem of Slavery in Western Culture*; David Eltis, "Europeans and Rise and Fall of African Slavery in The Americas: An Interpretation," *American Historical Review* 98 (1993): 1399–1423; and a pair of articles by Thomas Haskell: Thomas L. Haskell, "Capitalism and the Origins of the Humanitarian Sensibility, Part I," *American Historical Review* 90 (1985): 339–361; Thomas L. Haskell, "Capitalism and the Origins of the Humanitarian Sensibility, Part II," *American Historical Review* 90 (1985): 547–566. On the importance of African ethnicities in the slave trade see Daniel C. Littlefield, *Ethnicity and the Slave Trade in Colonial South Carolina* (Urbana: University of Illinois Press, 1991).

On natural philosophy and the problem of race in the European colonies in the sixteenth and seventeenth centuries see Joyce E. Chaplin, "Natural Philosophy and an Early Racial Idiom in North America: Comparing English and Indian Bodies," *William and Mary Quarterly* 54 (1997): 229–252; and Jorge Canizares Esguerra, "New World, New Stars: Patriotic Astrology and the Invention of Indian and Creole Bodies in Colonial Spanish America, 1500–1650," *American Historical Review* 104 (1999): 33–68. The work of Richard Eden is reprinted in Edward Arber, *The First Three English Books on America* (Birmingham, England: Turnbull & Spears, 1885). The work of Jan Huyghen van Linschoten is reprinted in *The voyage of John Huyghen van Linschoten to the East Indies [microfilm]: from the old English translation of 1598: the first book, containing his description of the East*, eds., the first volume by Arthur Coke Burnell, the second volume by P. A. Tiele (London: Haklyut Society, 1885).

On the continued growth of racial thinking in the colonies into the eighteenth century see Mark Harrison, "'Tender Frame of Man': Disease, Climate, and Racial Difference in India and the West Indies, 1760–1860," *Bulletin of the History of Medicine* 70 (1996): 68–93; and Sean Quinlan, "Colonial Bodies, Hygiene and Abolitionist Politics in Eighteenth-Century France," *History Workshop Journal* 42 (1996): 107–125.

On the modification of the Great Chain of Being in the Enlightenment see Francesca Rigotti, "Biology and Society in the Age of Enlightenment," *Journal of the History of Ideas* 47 (1986): 215–233. On the relationship between ideas of progress and racial degeneration see T. Carlos Jacques, "From Savages and Barbarians to Primitives: Africa, Social Typologies, and History in Eighteenth Century French Philosophy," *History and Theory* 36 (1997): 190–215. For the general argument that racism was an outgrowth of Enlightenment thought see George L. Mosse, *Toward the Final Solution: A History of European Racism* (New York: Howard Fertig, 1985); Richard H. Popkin, "The Philosophical Bases of Modern Racism," in *Philosophy and the Civilizing Arts*, editors Craig Walton and John P. Anton, 126–165 (Athens: Ohio University Press, 1974); and Richard H. Popkin, "Pre-Adamism in 19th-Century American Thought: Speculative Biology and Racism," *Philosophia* 8 (1978): 205–239.

On the racial ideas of seventeenth- and eighteenth-century taxonomists and anthropologists see Nicholas Hudson, "From 'Nation' to 'Race': The Origin of

Racial Classification in Eighteenth Century Thought," *Eighteenth-Century Studies* 29 (1996): 247–264; Londa Schiebinger, "The Anatomy of Difference: Race and Sex in Eighteenth-Century Science," *Eighteenth-Century Studies* 18 (1990): 347–405; Phillip R. Sloan, "The Idea of Racial Degeneracy in Buffon's *Histoire Naturelle*," in *Racism in the Eighteenth Century*, editor Harold E. Pagliaro, 293–322 (Cleveland: Case Western Reserve University Press, 1973); Nancy Leys Stepan, "Race and Gender: The Role of Analogy in Science," *Isis* 77, no. 287 (1986): 261–277; Siep Stuurman, "Francois Bernier and the Invention of Racial Classification," *History Workshop Journal*, no. 50 (2000): 1–21

For general treatments of the classification debates among Linnaeus, Buffon, and Blumenbach see Paul L. Farber, "Buffon and the Concept of Species," *Journal of the History of Biology* 5 (1972): 259–284; Paul L. Farber, *Finding Order in Nature: The Naturalist Tradition from Linnaeus to E. O. Wilson* (Baltimore, MD: Johns Hopkins University Press, 2000); Phillip R. Sloan, "The Buffon-Linnaeus Controversy," *Isis* 67 [1976]: 356–375).

For different views of the role of race on the North American continent see Barbara J. Fields, "Race and Ideology in American History," in J. Morgan Kousser and James M. McPherson, eds. *Region, Race, and Reconstruction: Essays in Honor of C. Vann Woodward* (New York: Oxford University Press, 1982) and Aldon T. Vaughn, *Roots of American Racism: Essays on the Colonial Experience* (New York: Oxford University Press, 1995). On the place of race in Thomas Jefferson's thought see Alexander O. Boulton, "American Paradox: Jeffersonian Equality and Racial Science," *American Quarterly* 47 (1995): 467–492; John P. Diggins, "Slavery, Race, and Equality: Jefferson and the Pathos of the Enlightenment," *American Quarterly* 28 (1976): 206–228; Nicholas E. Magnis, "Thomas Jefferson and Slavery: An Analysis of His Racist Thinking As Revealed by His Writings and Political Behavior," *Journal of Black Studies* 29 (1999): 491–509.

2

The Establishment of Racial Typology, 1800–1859

The first half of the nineteenth century was a watershed in scientific thinking about race. The concept of race was not a new invention of those decades; racial differences had certainly been noticed before 1800. Indeed, their cause had been a matter of speculation at least from the start of the Atlantic slave trade in the mid-fifteenth century, when Europeans began to think that Africans' skin color was a sign of their inferiority.

But if the concept of race itself was not new in 1800, what was? There were several basic shifts in scientific ideas about race as the eighteenth century became the nineteenth. One hallmark of the Enlightenment was its optimism—its belief that civilization, meaning European civilization, was an absolute value that all peoples were capable of achieving. But in the nineteenth century this hopefulness gradually gave way to a more pessimistic assessment—that one's position on the Great Chain of Being, the hierarchical ladder of life, was permanent and could not be altered. The Enlightenment assumption held that all peoples had sprung from a single origin, usually believed to be the biblical pair Adam and Eve, and that therefore all human beings belonged to a single species: a view referred to as monogenism. Given its biblical sanction, monogenism held strong sway. But in the nineteenth century this view was seriously challenged by the scientifically supported theory of polygenism: that the different races actually comprised different species, or different types, to use the polygenist term. Polygenists believed that these racial types had originated or been created separately, and that they were therefore essentially distinct. Though religiously heterodox, by the 1850s polygenism was firmly established as an alternative way of understanding differences among peoples.

The monogenists and the Enlightenment optimists had their own ways of explaining racial differences; as we saw in chapter one, they were hardly racial egalitarians. Degeneration by environmental influences could account for differing physical appearance and customs. Such a view allowed the environment a powerful shaping role, which observation seemed to support: white men who lived in the tropics turned brown, black men in England appeared to become lighter. But doubts about the efficacy of the environment grew with the growth of polygenism; environmentalism was gradually replaced by innatism, the view that differences between peoples were permanent and inborn. No matter how many generations white people lived in the tropics, the polygenists believed, the environment alone would not turn them black. This was because blackness for polygenists was more than simply a matter of skin color. Racial differences, lodged in one's inherent nature, literally in one's very bones, were fundamentally unchangeable—they were more than just skin deep. Finally, the monogenists held a diffusionist view: that the human species had migrated all over the earth from its one origin point. But the polygenists believed that each human race had originated in its own center of creation and that each therefore belonged in its own separate, natural homeland.

The shift in views can be characterized as a change from understanding man as a cultural, social, spiritual being, apart from the rest of nature, a product of the level of civilization, to man as a biological being. Biology, specifically race, was seen as the cause of cultural or behavioral differences. Culture or civilization was no longer something superimposed on an equipotential biological background; race and culture were yoked together because the one created the other.

The shift from monogenism to polygenism did not take place overnight. It was gradual, its progress was uneven, and it was never wholesale. It took decades to achieve, and even then certainly not everyone was converted. It was, nonetheless, a marked and important shift, one that constructed a view of race that began to get systematically dismantled only after the Second World War. Though greatly attenuated, the nineteenth-century understanding of race continues to exert its influence right up to the present day, and can help explain why the concept of race still wields such political and social power. The implications of nineteenth-century ideas about race are therefore profound. This chapter will explain what those ideas were, what kind of scientific backing they received, who advocated them, and why they began to take hold when they did. The cast of characters includes some of the most highly respected scientific and medical men of their day, from England, France, and the United States.

Two broad contexts, social and scientific, are relevant to our analysis. The first half of the nineteenth century was marked by the establishment of European colonial empires overseas, by the growth of slavery, and by abolitionist movements. This period was also one of enormous increase in scientific activity, especially in the life and human sciences.

Slavery and its abolition were critical parts of the context in which the science of race developed. The Atlantic slave trade grew to support European colonies and their sugar, cotton, tobacco, and rice plantations in the New World.

The slave deck of the Wildfire, *which arrived at Key West, Florida, on April 30, 1860 (Library of Congress)*

From 1451–1575, an estimated 175,000 Africans were brought as slaves into Europe itself and to plantations on the Atlantic islands off the west coast of Africa. Beginning in the mid-sixteenth century, slaves were taken to European possessions in the Americas. These included British North America, and later the United States; the Portuguese colony of Brazil; Spanish colonies in the

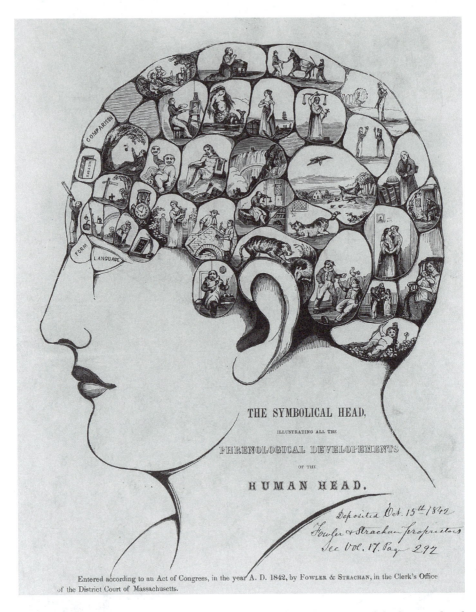

THE SYMBOLICAL HEAD,

ILLUSTRATING ALL THE

PHRENOLOGICAL DEVELOPEMENTS

OF THE

HUMAN HEAD.

Deposited Oct. 15th 1842
Fowler & Strachan proprietors
See Vol. 17. Pag 292

Entered according to an Act of Congress, in the year A. D. 1842, by FOWLER & STRACHAN, in the Clerk's Office of the District Court of Massachusetts.

The symbolical head, illustrating the phrenological developments of the human head (Library of Congress)

Americas; and British, French, Dutch, and Danish colonies in the Caribbean. This part of the slave trade, the infamous Middle Passage, reached its peak in the 1780s and brought more than nine million Africans to the Americas between 1662 and 1867.

Though the late eighteenth century represented the height of the slave trade, it was also the period during which abolitionist movements began to gain

WHAT MISCEGENATION IS!

—AND—

WHAT WE ARE TO EXPECT

Now that Mr. Lincoln is Re-elected.

By L. SEAMAN, LL. D.

WALLER & WILLETTS, Publishers,

NEW YORK.

Caricature of a white woman and African American man kissing adorns the title page of a book titled, What Miscegenation Is, *1864. (Corbis)*

momentum. Throughout the nineteenth century abolitionists made steady, if not always regular, progress. In 1787, the Society for Effecting Abolition of the Slave Trade was established in England, followed by a similar society in France. In 1792, after the French Revolution, slavery was abolished in France itself, and two years later in the French colonies, but in 1802 Napoleon restored slavery in the French possessions. In 1807 both Britain and the United States outlawed the trade in slaves, and by the mid-1820s, the British Navy began working to suppress the international slave trade. During this period slavery was abolished in the northeastern United States. In 1815 Napoleon outlawed the French trade, though it continued secretly. In 1833 slaves throughout the British Empire were emancipated, in 1848 in the French colonies, and in 1865 in the southern United States. From 1815 until well into the 1880s, slavery was also gradually abolished in South America.

Ironically, the nineteenth-century age of abolition was also the era of racial typology. Scientific obsession with racial differences took hold just as abolitionists were scoring their greatest successes. The racial theories to be described in this chapter were, therefore, produced not in the context of a slaveholding society, but rather by a society attempting to deal with the free intermixing of diverse peoples.

Developments in the life and human sciences, sciences that grew at an unprecedented rate in the early nineteenth century, were also key factors in encouraging the scientific study and classification of the races. A growing belief in materialism, that all life could be explained by matter in motion without resorting to vital spirits or a notion of soul, emboldened scientists to reject the Bible as the authoritative source for knowledge about nature.

Phrenology, the "reading" of head-shape, and its correlation with various abilities and propensities, supported the idea that mental activity could be interpreted in terms of the size and function of parts of the brain, an idea that long outlasted the popular fad of phrenology itself. Comparative anatomy, physiology, histology, and paleontology all experienced tremendous growth during the first half of the nineteenth century. Classification of life forms along lines established by Linnaeus continued to regard the ever-growing number of newly discovered species as immutable and divinely created. Statistics, as practiced by the Belgian astronomer Lambert A. J. Quételet (1796–1874), taught the measurement of human physiognomy, as well as of birth, marriage, and death rates. Quételet's concept of the "average man," an abstraction calculated from the measurements of a population, influenced the representation of racial groups in terms of ideal types. The Dutch anatomist Pieter Camper's (1722–1789) concept of the "facial angle" was superseded by the "cephalic index" developed by the Swedish anthropologist Anders Retzius (1796–1860). The index measured the ratio of the length to width of head, and as we will see, was supplemented by quantitative techniques designed to measure the volume of human crania. As the sciences of biology and anthropology grew in range and sophistication, the classification and characterization of human racial differences as innate, primordial, and permanent grew along with them.

The Reign of Monogenism:
Prichard and Lawrence

James Cowles Prichard (1786–1848), devout Christian, physician, and abolitionist, was the leading British monogenist and the most influential writer on race in
the first half of the nineteenth century. "On the whole," he wrote in his 1813
Researches into the Physical History of Mankind, "it appears that we may with
a high degree of probability draw the inference, that all the different races into
which the human species is divided, originated from one family" (155). Prichard
rejected the notion that all of nature was arrayed along a linear hierarchy—the
Great Chain of Being—and especially the idea that Negroes represented a connecting link between apes and white Europeans. He did not doubt that European
customs, culture, and physical appearance were superior to those of other
nationalities, which was a common assumption at the time. But he did believe
that all varieties of man were united and set apart from animals by their possession of culture, society, and the ability to learn. For Prichard it was especially
crucial that all peoples be considered capable of conversion to Christianity. And
for this, there could not be any essential differences among them.

But religion was not Prichard's sole motivation for propounding monogenism. Scientific studies supported the view as well. His books were detailed
ethnographic surveys based largely on travelers' accounts of all the known races
in the world. Prichard made comparisons among the customs and languages of
the different races and compared the bodily structures of the different races of
men with animals, combining ethnography, philology, and comparative anatomy.
He argued that as there were clearly different varieties within a single species of
animal, so there could be different varieties, or races, within a single species of
man. However, he emphasized that the varieties or races of man were themselves variable. All Negroes, according to Prichard, did not have the same skull
shape, which was precisely the idea to be later denied by polygenists. The human
species was, for Prichard, a unity, created on a biblical time scale within the preceding 6,000 years, and diffused throughout the world from the origin point.
Prichard theorized that that origin point was in Asia and that the original men
were Negro, leaving the pressing question of how the major races, the different
varieties of man, had been produced.

The production of racial diversity was a knotty problem for eighteenth- and
nineteenth-century naturalists. In the 1740s and 1750s, the Comte de Buffon and
Johann Blumenbach had concurred that differences in hair type, skin color, bodily stature, and constitution were the result of exposure to different climates,
foods, habits of life, and diseases. As the original race of men diffused over the
earth, contact with different conditions shaped each group differently. The group

of men that migrated to the tropics gained dark skin and other bodily changes, characteristics that were inherited by their offspring. Thus were differences among the races established and maintained.

By the early nineteenth century, this environmentalist position was gradually weakening. In 1813, when Prichard published the first edition of his *Researches*, he rejected it as an explanation for diversity and supported instead a twofold theory based in generation and heredity. First, Prichard argued that certain characteristics could suddenly appear as sports of nature and then, because they proved well adapted to the environment, and because they were heritable, would appear again in succeeding generations. Second, Prichard argued, members of different human groups might select for different characteristics in a mate that they consider beautiful; as a result, the different groups would diverge and diversify into different races.

In the second and third editions of the *Researches*, however, Prichard gave up these claims and adopted Buffon's and Blumenbach's argument that environmental influence and Lamarckian inheritance of acquired characters were the causes of racial diversity. Prichard's shift back to the older environmentalist reasoning was a response to the rise of polygenism. He remained the major British proponent of monogenism and environmentalism up to his death in 1848. Even in 1855, with polygenism in its ascendancy, the last edition of *The Natural History of Man* declared that "the same inward and mental nature is to [be] recognized in all the races of men. . . . [W]e are entitled to draw confidently the conclusion that all human races are of one species and one family" (page 714).

The problem that dogged Prichard and his contemporaries, and that would not be solved until Darwin's *Origin of Species* was published in 1859, was the meaning of "species." Prichard adopted Blumenbach's criterion, that the members of a species could produce fertile offspring. All human beings, then, were by this criterion clearly members of one and the same species. But this definition was increasingly called into question and dismissed by polygenists in the nineteenth century. Without any definite biological mooring, "species" became a free-floating and remarkably flexible concept, as narrow or as broad as one wished. In polygenist hands, the number of human species multiplied from two to more than a dozen. As each race became its own species, the term "species" became increasingly interchangeable with "type," and as such was used to indicate essential, biological, ineradicable difference.

Another leading British proponent of monogenism was the London surgeon Sir William Lawrence (1783–1867). In a series of lectures delivered before the Royal College of Surgeons in 1819, Lawrence outlined the questions that both he and Prichard were trying to answer: "Is there one species of men only, or are there many distinct ones? . . . How is man affected by the external influences of climate, food, way of life? Are these, or any others, operating on beings originally alike, sufficient to account for all the diversities hitherto observed; or must we suppose that several kinds of men were created originally, each for its own situation?" Indicating his own preference for monogenism, Lawrence continued: "If we adopt the supposition of a single species, what country did it first inhabit? And what was the appearance of the original man? Did he go erect, or on all fours? Was he a Patagonian, or an Eskimau, a Negro, or a Georgian" (Lawrence 1822, 103–104).

Like Prichard, Lawrence believed that all the various races of man comprised a single species, and like Prichard he believed that the human species was set apart from, over and above, the animals. Both postulated a definitive break between man and ape, and both dismissed the notion of a smooth, unbroken chain of being. But Lawrence also differed from Prichard in notable ways. For example, he always put more emphasis on racial difference than Prichard did. Thus while Lawrence rejected the traditional chain of being idea, he did adopt from the French comparative anatomist and monogenist Georges Cuvier a newly biologized concept of hierarchy. Lawrence correlated intellectual development with brain development, integrating anatomy, physiology, and mentality. He believed it possible to rank the species of animals and races of man along such a hierarchy, and in such a racial ranking, the Southern African race of Hottentots was at the bottom, closest to the ape, and the Europeans were at the top. The black races, according to Lawrence, were closer to the apes in both intellect and appearance. But though there were great differences between a Negro and a European, these were not enough to make them separate species. Like Prichard, Lawrence pointed to the continuous variation both between the races and within any single given race to argue against the idea that races were separate species. But Lawrence emphasized biological traits more than Prichard did. Instead of examining the customs and languages of different peoples, as Prichard had, Lawrence focused on anatomy and zoology, drawing comparisons between man and animals and among the different human races. He always managed to find an animal analogy for the various physical peculiarities of the races; even the protuberant buttocks of the so-called Hottentot "Venus" could be likened to a similar formation in sheep.

Finally, unlike Prichard, Lawrence rejected a literal reading of the Bible as a guide to natural history, calling the biblical account of the creation zoologically impossible and pointing out its many inconsistencies. As new developments in paleontology, geology, and archaeology in the first half of the nineteenth century opened up and expanded the biblical time frame, Lawrence took advantage of the newly discovered stretches of time to explain how racial diversity might have arisen out of primeval unity. There was still not any question of species arising out of prior forms; the original species, Lawrence believed, had been specially created as a unity, but then the different varieties or races could develop within those species limits. Even Prichard, in the third edition of his *Researches*, disjoined the biblical time scale from his ethnographic one and used the longer time to explain the development of diversity.

But Lawrence never considered the environment powerful enough to create racial diversity, even with a few extra thousands of years to work. Climate or customs could explain neither physical nor mental differences among the races, as Lawrence rejected the possibility of the inheritance of acquired characters. As proof he cited Prichard's example of Jewish male infants born with foreskins despite generations of circumcision. Moreover, "white people have distinguished themselves in all climates; every where preserving their superiority. Two centuries have not assimilated the Anglo-Americans to the Australian aborigines . . ." (Lawrence 1822, 420). So climate could not possibly have any powerful shaping role, especially not on morality or intellect, and even if it did, that influence impressed itself only on the individual and could not be passed on to the next generation.

Lawrence concluded, concurring with Prichard in the first edition of his *Researches*, that only variation and heredity could explain racial differences. Variations arose as a result of spontaneous sporting and were then maintained through isolation and inbreeding. Using the same analogy to the breeding of domesticated animals that Prichard did, and that Darwin also would in 1859, Lawrence argued that sports, or spontaneously occurring hereditary characteristics, appeared more frequently in domestic breeds than in wild ones. Since man, especially white European man, was a kind of domestic animal, it was to be expected that a range of hereditary variations would spring up and be maintained. Such a process could have produced racial diversification from the original stock or group. Lawrence thought it impossible to trace the human genealogy back to a single ancestral pair. Such a process could also explain why there was more mental, moral, and physical variation in the more domesticated breeds of man than in the savage races.

The monogenist position of Prichard and Lawrence was reflected in France by Joseph Marie de Gerando (1772–1842) and the members of the Société des Observateurs de l'Homme, and in the United States by the moral philosopher Samuel Stanhope Smith (1750–1819). Smith, a professor at Princeton and later its president, held a constellation of views typical of the reigning consensus of the early nineteenth century. Man was essentially an adaptable creature, susceptible to environmental and climatic influences; groups of men had all dispersed from a common center of creation; men's bodies were basically similar; the races represented a continuous range of variation and lines could not be drawn between them. Man was a cultural and social being, clearly set apart from animals. Though Stanhope Smith placed a higher value on white skin—he was not an egalitarian— he was, like Prichard, a devout Christian and an abolitionist. He was also a fierce critic of the views of Thomas Jefferson discussed in chapter one.

By the turn of the nineteenth century, however, cracks in this reigning consensus had appeared that would widen over the next four decades. The result was that by the 1850s, polygenism was an established though minority point of view in European science.

Steps toward Polygenesis

One of the earliest steps toward polygenesis was taken by the Scottish judge Lord Henry H. Kames (1696–1782). In his *Sketches of the History of Man* (1774), Kames averred that environment, climate, or state of society could not account for racial differences, so that the races must have come from distinct, originally separate stocks. In 1799, the Manchester physician and early polygenist Charles White (1728–1813) continued Kames's line of reasoning. Influenced by Thomas Jefferson, White made anatomical measurements of Negroes' bodies, concluding that Negroes comprised the lowest human link in the chain of being, closest to the apes, while Europeans were the highest, and other races were in between. For White each race was a separate species, divinely created for its own geographical region. Polygenism, clearly, was not a nineteenth-century invention, but before the nineteenth century its incursions could usually be kept at bay. By the 1820s, however, even certain monogenists were questioning environmentalism. Such open disagreements among monogenists and weaknesses in their position helped set the stage for the heterodox alternative, waiting in the wings for at least half a century, to make a grand appearance.

Polygenism had major proponents in France, the United States, and England. In France it was defended first by William F. Edwards and Victor Courtet de l'Isle, and later by Paul Broca, the brain anatomist. In the United States, first Charles Caldwell, then the quartet of Samuel Morton, Josiah Nott, George Gliddon, and Ephraim Squier, supported by the Swiss émigré naturalist Louis Agassiz, were outspoken and widely attended. In Britain, the anti-Prichardian banner was taken up by Robert Knox and James Hunt. By the 1840s polygenism was thriving in all these countries and its proponents were all in communication with one another.

Several important themes are apparent in the rise of polygenism. First, while the timeline of its ascendancy is similar in each country, there are some general cultural differences to bear in mind. Polygenism caught on more

Georges Cuvier examines an animal fossil. A print after an original painting by Chartran (Bettmann/Corbis)

quickly in France and the United States than it did in Britain, where powerful Christian traditions were reflected in the teachings of natural theology. Britain also had a strong abolitionist movement beginning in the late eighteenth century, though as we will see, one did not need to be a monogenist to be an abolitionist: polygenists could easily be abolitionists too. This points to a second important theme: there was no inevitable linking of scientific and political views, and they occurred in all sorts of combinations and permutations. Slaveholders appeared among the ranks of the monogenists as well as of the polygenists; abolitionists could also be found on both sides of the scientific fence. Finally, despite the divergences often emphasized between them, monogenists and polygenists shared many assumptions. They agreed that the history of the earth and of life had proceeded in a biblical or somewhat expanded biblical time frame. They held in common the idea that human, animal, and plant species had been created, ultimately, by God, some 6,000 years before the present. And they took for granted that the nonwhite races of man were inferior to the white. Where monogenists and polygenists most often disagreed was on whether the nonwhite races had the potential, given the proper environments, to "catch up" to the whites.

Aside from its expression by Lord Kames and Charles White, polygenism found its earliest exponents, and most secure institutionalization, in France. It was arguably in France in the 1820s that the permanence of racial types became established as a distinct viewpoint, spreading from there both to the United States and to Britain. Its early success in France was probably due in no small measure to the discrediting of Lamarck by his archrival, the comparative anatomist Georges Cuvier (1769–1832). For Cuvier, the animal kingdom was divided into four main types, or embranchments—vertebrates, mollusks, articulates, and zoophytes—each type an original and unalterable creation of God. Cuvier dismissed the Lamarckian notion that animals could evolve from simpler forbears by the inheritance of acquired characters. In contrast to Lamarck's theory, each of the genera and species within Cuvier's four main types were permanent biological variations not produced by environment and circumstance, and each was clearly set apart and distinguished from every other. There was no shading or graded transition between them. Each animal was a perfectly balanced and beautifully integrated example of its type, so the idea that any such organic form could undergo change, except of the most limited kind, was impossible.

Cuvier also believed that extinction was a result of natural catastrophes, like floods, a series of which had occurred to punctuate the history of the earth. Cuvier thought that some species were able to escape the catastrophe to repopulate the earth. Thus after the last catastrophe, about 5,000 years before the present, the three major races that had all originally descended from Adam escaped to different corners of the world, where they developed in isolation: Caucasian, Mongolian, and Ethiopian. Thus Cuvier, though a monogenist, developed a theory of distinct unchanging divinely created types that later gave strong support to polygenism.

Although he argued against the simplistic notion of a linear chain of being, which he associated with Lamarck, Cuvier arranged the genera and species hierarchically within each of his four embranchments. He ordered the animal and human races along a graded scale of intelligence based on their facial angle, an idea he borrowed from Camper and made more sophisticated with his own new comparative anatomical measurements and methods. By correlating facial and cranial measurements with perceived mental and moral qualities, Cuvier believed he had proved that the Ethiopian race was at the bottom of the scale, closest to the apes, and that its condition was foreordained and unchangeable.

French racial theorists largely followed Cuvier's lead in dismissing Lamarckism and arguing for permanence and hierarchy of types. Cuvier's work held all the key features of polygenism, developed in succeeding decades by those less tied to orthodoxy. These features included the strict limits on environmental influence, the notion of unchanging underlying type, the emphasis on anatomical and cranial measurement, and the correlation of physical differences and mental differences in defining racial worth. All that remained was for the human races to become distinct species, and for the singular origin of man to become plural.

This final step was taken in 1824 by the military physician and abolitionist Julien-Joseph Virey (1775–1846). An early polygenist, Virey argued for six races, among which there were strong, permanent distinctions. The two black races were closer to the apes in both physical and mental characteristics and formed a separate species. The physician-anthropologist Louis-Antoine Desmoulins (1796–1828), influenced by the phrenologists' correlation between anatomical structure and mental ability, ideas, and feelings, divided the human genus into sixteen species. These were in turn divided into races, which, despite interbreeding and population mixture, retained their typical characteristics.

The most influential of the early-nineteenth-century French racial theorists was William F. Edwards (1776–1842), who was born in the English sugar colony of Jamaica and spent his youth and early career in Belgium. He studied medicine in Paris and developed interests in biology, both in laboratory and in field, as well as in linguistics and racial physiology. In 1828, influenced by the historians Augustin and Amedee Thierry's division of Europeans into Gauls and Franks, Edwards drew a racial map of Europe. Although Blumenbach and Cuvier had grouped all whites as Caucasians and had focused on differences between the white and dark races, Edwards, like Desmoulins, looked for differences among European whites. Edwards has thus been called the founder of European ethnology, expressing his view in an 1829 essay in the form of a letter to Amedee Thierry. Relying on an assessment of facial features and head shape rather than the more technical craniological measurement of the 1850s, Edwards classified the races of Europe, linking nationality and perceived moral character with physical appearance. Each race had its own particular character; each had, like an individual, its own life history and followed its own line of progress; and each represented its own permanent type. As animal races retained their characteristics and behavior despite their environment, so too did the human races, Edwards argued, fixating particularly on the Jews as an example of racial permanence. He believed that the Jewish national countenance remained the same over time, pointing to Leonardo da Vinci's *The Last Supper* and to images of Jews on the tomb of an Egyptian king to demonstrate that Jews had evidently not changed in thousands of years, either physically, or consequently, mentally and morally. Edwards conceded that crossbreeding could modify a species but held that the types were ancient and could always be distinguished. His work therefore lent support and credibility to polygenism, convincing even the French monogenists to accept permanence of racial differences throughout history.

In 1839, Edwards founded the *Société Ethnologique de Paris*, which boasted a membership of some of the most distinguished naturalists, historians, geographers, and archaeologists in France, including some who were influential in French politics and colonial policy. A number of these were followers of the philosopher C. H. de Saint-Simon, who in his 1813 *Science de l'Homme* had argued that each race or racial type had its own particular powers and needed to be characterized so as to be properly situated in what he called the scale of civilization. The white race, for instance, might be characterized as rational and masculine, the black race emotive and feminine. According to Victor Courtet de l'Isle, for example, a Saint-Simonian politician and member of the *Société*, the native capacities of individuals and of peoples had to be properly understood and classified or political revolution would result. The Saint-Simonian notion of a place for everyone and everyone in his place lent support to the Edwardsian project of racial typology. The *Société*, involved as its members were in political activities, was disrupted by the revolutions of 1848, a year of uprisings all across Europe against hereditary wealth and power. But the *Société* maintained a nominal existence until the 1860s.

There are a number of noteworthy aspects of the *Société Ethnologique*. First, though the *Société's* founder helped make polygenism respectable, not everyone in the *Société* was a polygenist. There was in fact a good deal of heterogeneity to the members' views on race. Yet, as we have already seen in considering monogenists and polygenists, there were important areas of underlying agreement between them. The conservative end of the spectrum was occupied by Courtet, a hard-line polygenist who believed races belonged to different species, that blacks were intermediate between whites and orangutans, and that blacks were predestined for slavery. An intermediate position was held by Henri Milne-Edwards (half brother of William), a renowned biologist who argued for a hierarchical monogenism. On the liberal side, Eusebe de Salle, physician and Christian monogenist, believed polygenism led to exploitation. And on the radical fringe was Victor Schoelcher, an abolitionist who was partly responsible for the end of slavery in French colonies in 1848. The republican and egalitarian Schoelcher (1804–1893) went so far as to argue that the ancient Egyptians had been all or partly Negro. Courtet responded that they were white, and that the Caffirs and Ethiopians, the "advanced" Negroes, had benefited from Arab or Islamic contact and were therefore not truly black. True Negroes, for Courtet, were by definition irretrievably backward.

Yet in 1847, when the *Société* engaged in a discussion of slavery, most of the members, whether left, right, or center, looked forward to its abolition, and considered how the races should now behave toward and interact with each other. Gustave d'Eichthal, secretary of the *Société*, had proposed years earlier in a letter to his colleague Ismail Urbain, a man of color, that interbreeding with whites was necessary to improve the black race, which he called feminine. Stopping short of this solution in his report on the 1847 discussion, d'Eichthal nonetheless concluded that all, even Schoelcher, were in agreement that Europeans must educate blacks to bring them up to their standard. The report also included the consensus view that, since the subject of ethnology was the hierarchical classification of the races, absolute equality between them was out of the question.

A second notable feature of the *Société* was the fact that its members helped to shape and were in turn influenced by French colonial policy in Africa. Jean-Baptiste Bory de Saint Vincent (1778–1846), *Société* member and chief of the French scientific commission to Algeria, brought home a powerful argument against acclimatization when he saw French colonists die in great numbers, unable to accustom themselves to the foreign environment. Thus Edwards's notion of racial permanence was strengthened.

The *Société* also had connections both to American polygenism and to the Anthropological Society founded in 1859 by Paul Broca. Both the *Société* members and the American polygenist Samuel Morton agreed that interracial fertility, traditionally the criterion of species, did not prove that all humans comprised a single species. The Americans Josiah Nott and George Gliddon cited Virey's and Courtet's assertion that Egyptian mummies had been Caucasian, not Negro, and their 1854 *Types of Mankind* used plates from Courtet. Nott adopted Edwards's idea that racial diversity was permanent, that Negroes had not changed in 5,000 years, and that blacks required European contact to improve themselves, which they could do only to a limited extent.

Connections also existed between the *Société Ethnologique* and Broca's Anthropological Society of Paris, which was associated with the prestigious Paris Faculty of Medicine. Though the societies shared few members in common and though Broca intended his society to be strictly scientific and apolitical, Edwards's principle of the fixity of the races remained influential on him. Even after Darwin's *Origin of Species* was published in 1859, Broca continued to believe that human types did not share a common ancestry, that they formed a racial hierarchy, and that non-European races with inferior crania could never achieve full civilization.

American Polygenism: Morton, Nott, and Gliddon

The American School of Polygenesis had its first representative in Charles Caldwell (1772–1853), a physician trained at the University of Pennsylvania who taught natural history there and practiced medicine in Philadelphia and Kentucky. The first important American phrenologist, Caldwell attacked the already embattled position that environment was the cause of racial differences and argued instead that the four races, Caucasian, Mongolian, American Indian, and African, were four different species, created separately by God. The Indian and African were inferior, Caldwell believed, and were doomed to die out. Only interbreeding with whites could bring about improvement in these races.

In the 1830s, American polygenism was given sterling scientific credentials by Samuel George Morton (1799–1851), a Philadelphia physician and anatomy professor at Pennsylvania Medical College. Morton was interested in paleontology, geology, and especially in craniology, and built the largest collection of crania in the world at the Academy of Natural Sciences in Philadelphia. His hundreds of human and animal skulls were sent to him by other naturalists and army surgeons stationed in the Americas, India, Europe, and Egypt. For Morton, as for most nineteenth-century anatomists and natural historians with polygenist leanings, the human skull and its measurement revealed the essential quality, the mental worth, of its owner. Cranial size and shape directly reflected intellectual level and were considered particularly immutable, not at all susceptible to change by external influence. Morton believed that the skulls proved that the different human races showed different, essentially immutable head shapes. A wise Creator had from the beginning adapted each race perfectly to its own particular locale.

Like Blumenbach, Morton believed in five distinctly different races, Caucasian, Mongolian, Malay, American, and Negro, which he subsequently divided

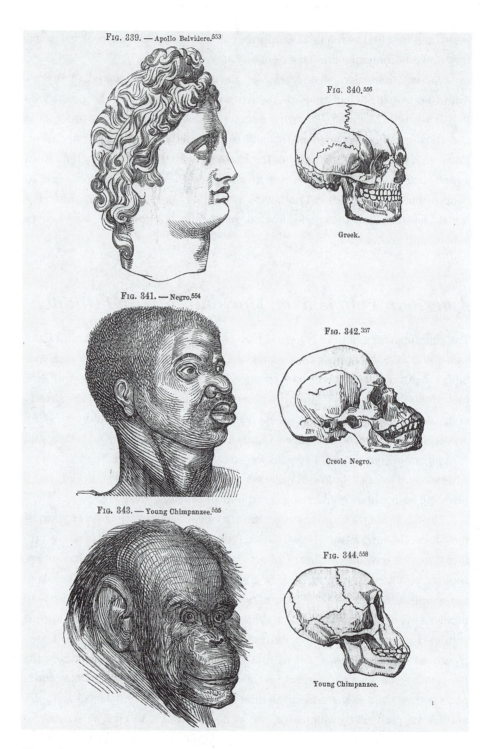

FIG. 339. — Apollo Belvidere.[553]

FIG. 340.[556]

Greek.

FIG. 341. — Negro.[554]

FIG. 342.[357]

Creole Negro.

FIG. 343. — Young Chimpanzee.[555]

FIG. 344.[558]

Young Chimpanzee.

Three faces with the skulls that underlie them. From Nott and Gliddon, Types of Mankind, *1854 (The British Library Institution/Heritage Image Partnership)*

into 22 families or groups of nations. Morton did not claim explicitly that the different races were different species, but he implied that their differences, given at the time of creation or shortly thereafter, were primordial. Morton's craniometric research consisted of plugging the openings of each of the skulls with cotton, filling the skull with white pepper seed through the large opening at its base, packing it until it was completely full, and then emptying its contents into a graduated cylinder. The cylinder readings gave the capacity of the crania in cubic inches. He made thirteen other measurements of each skull as well.

Morton published his results in his 1839 volume *Crania Americana*, a study of the large collection of American Indian skulls that he had gathered. His study gave their physical measurements and discussed the customs of the tribes from which they had come. Morton concluded that the American Indian race was different from all the others, including the Mongolian, and that the Eskimo tribes constituted a distinct family within that American race. He theorized that the so-called Mound Builders, responsible for the large rounded earthworks used for burial in the Mississippi valley, were also of that race.

Morton made comparisons among the skulls of the different races and concluded that the Causacian had the largest cranial capacity, followed by the Mongolian, the Malay, and the American, while the Ethiopian had the smallest. The physical measurements were supplemented by Morton's description of the moral characteristics of each race. The Caucasian possessed "the highest intellectual endowments"; the Mongolian was "ingenious, imitative, and highly susceptible of cultivation"; the Malay "active and ingenious" as well as "predaceous"; the American "averse to cultivation, and slow in acquiring knowledge; restless, revengeful and fond of war"; the Ethiopian "joyous, flexible, and indolent." "The Indian was 'incapable of servitude, and thus his spirit sank at once in captivity, and with it his physical energy,' while 'the more pliant Negro, yielding to his fate, and accommodating himself to his condition, bore his heavy burden with comparative ease'" (Morton 1839, quoted in Stanton 1960, 33–34). Morton's qualitative and aesthetic judgments about the worth of each race were supported by his seemingly objective quantitative measurements. An essay appended to *Crania Americana* by the phrenologist George Combe (1788–1858), a popular writer and lecturer, made connections between the national character of each race and its skull measurements as revealed by Morton. Morton himself, however, was never an advocate of phrenology.

Morton was slow to advocate polygenism. In 1839 he was not yet ready to endorse separate creations or pronounce on whether the races were separate species. He was aware that unions between Caucasians and American Indians could produce fertile offspring, thus members of these races were presumably descended from a common origin. Morton did, however, believe that racial differences were permanent, that they had been given by the Creator soon after the initial creation, that they were not created by environment, that neither intellect nor skin color was determined by climate. But by the late 1840s, perhaps under the influence of his less cautious followers, Morton had begun to advocate separate human creations in different areas.

Morton's followers included George Robins Gliddon and Josiah Nott. Gliddon (1809–1857), British-born vice-consul for the United States in Cairo, and a popular lecturer on Egyptology, corresponded with Morton and sent him nearly 100 Egyptian crania. From his studies of ancient Egyptian monuments and hieroglyphics, Gliddon concluded that the Egyptians had been white, and that even in that ancient world, the races had been distinctly different. Whites and Negroes had, even in that remote epoch, their characteristic present-day features.

Dating ancient Egyptian civilization to about 2000 B.C.E., two-thirds of the way back to the assumed initial Creation in 4004 B.C.E., Gliddon argued that neither environment nor climate could have produced the racial differences in a mere two thousand years. The races must therefore be primordial and permanent, their differences impressed upon them by the Creator himself. Moreover, even in ancient Egypt, Negroes, as portrayed on the monuments, had been slaves. Neither their appearance nor their social position had changed in thousands of years. Gliddon also made the distinctly unorthodox suggestion that the time frame of Creation must be expanded, since ancient Egyptian civilization was probably much older than traditional biblical chronology would allow. Racial differences were, then, of much longer standing than previously suspected.

Gliddon's findings impressed Morton, and in 1844 Morton published *Crania Aegyptiaca*, which reported the measurements of the Egyptian skulls Gliddon had collected for him. Here Morton argued, following Gliddon, that the races were of very great age. By the end of the decade he had made the shift from his original belief that racial differences came about through divine interposition at some point after the initial Creation, to a more radical belief that each race had been separately created, each in its own homeland. In *Crania Aegyptiaca* Morton also endorsed Gliddon's view that Negroes even in ancient Egypt had been slaves. He dedicated the 1844 volume to Gliddon.

While on the lecture circuit Gliddon introduced the arguments and evidence of Morton's book to the American South. *Crania Aegyptiaca* made a particular impression on one Southerner, Josiah Clark Nott (1804–1873), a physician in Mobile, Alabama, a leading surgeon, and a slaveholder. In 1842, Nott had published an article called "The Mulatto a Hybrid: Probable Extermination of the Two Races if Whites and Blacks are Allowed to Marry," arguing that Caucasians and Negroes were two separate species, and that hybrids were weaker, less fertile, and doomed to extinction.

There were, according to Nott, both mental and physical differences between whites and blacks, evidence for which he drew from the Negro's remarkable immunity to yellow fever during the epidemics of the late 1830s. Evading arguments that racial differences were environmentally caused or that they were divinely interposed after the initial Creation, Nott took the final, complete polygenist step of arguing that the races had been created separately. He was probably the first American scientist to go public with this view.

By 1844, Nott was arguing that Scripture could not provide an accurate account of the Creation, as it was too full of contradictions. He relied both on Gliddon's evidence that Negroes had been physically distinct in ancient Egypt and on what were thought at the time to be natural laws. As each genus of plants or animals was comprised of different species, so too was the human genus, and each species had been created for, and thus was particularly suited to, its own particular climate. The Negro was suited for hot climates and degenerated if removed from them. Blumenbach's traditional test of species, the ability to produce fertile offspring, had no place in Nott's science. By 1847, firmly convinced that the races had been created separately, each in its own environment, that Negro and Caucasian had been distinct at an early period, and that they were unable to change or adapt, Nott began openly to defend slavery as the only way to keep both races from deteriorating through interbreeding.

By 1851, the American school of polygenesis, led by Morton, Nott, and Gliddon, had gained several crucial allies. The archaeologist Ephraim George Squier (1821–1888) helped cement Morton's polygenism by excavating an ancient cranium from the midwestern mounds and sending a drawing of it to Morton. Morton found its similarities striking to Central and South American crania, confirming his belief that the American Indian nations had a common and indigenous origin. The nations were "so linked by similarity of conformation, mental endowments, moral traits and archaeological remains, as to constitute a vast homogeneous group of mankind . . . *aborigine*, distinct and separate from all the others" (Morton 1839, quoted in Stanton 1960, 83). Thus was Morton's polygenism, to which he came by gradual steps, explicitly stated. The Mound Builders were an American Indian race of great antiquity, they did not migrate from Asia, and their physical form had remained essentially unchanged in their descendants. Both Squier and Gliddon demonstrated for Morton the permanence of racial characteristics, and the suitability of each race to the region for which it had been created.

If Squier provided the American school of polygenesis with scientific evidence of racial inferiority, the second of its allies lent it a prestigious name. Louis Agassiz (1807–1873) had been professor of natural history in Neuchatel, Switzerland, a disciple of Cuvier, and an expert in fossil fishes. In 1847 he immi-

Louis Agassiz (1807–1873)

Agassiz was the leading representative of natural history to the American public from the mid-1840s until his death. Revered as a popular lecturer and author, he taught at the Lawrence Scientific School at Harvard University from 1847 to 1873. There, in 1859, he established the Museum of Comparative Zoology, a center for natural history instruction and research, as well as numerous other scientific institutions elsewhere. He made major contributions to marine biology and embryology, paleontology, and geology, and was the best known and most outspoken opponent of Darwinism in America.

Agassiz was born in Motier-en-Vuly, Switzerland. As a young man he attended college in Zurich, Heidelberg, and Munich, earning a doctorate in zoology in 1829 at the universities of Munich and Erlangen. His dissertation on the fishes of Brazil brought him to Cuvier's notice, and, after receiving an MD degree in Munich, Agassiz went to Paris to study with Cuvier. In 1832 Agassiz was appointed professor at the College of Neuchatel, in Switzerland; the same year he married Cecile Braun, with whom he had several children. Their son Alexander also became a scientist.

Over the course of the next two years Agassiz published his five volume *Fossil Fishes*, in which he described in painstaking detail over 1,700 species of ancient fishes and made illustrations of their reconstructions on Cuvierian comparative anatomical principles. As an antievolutionist, Agassiz saw modern species not as the genealogical descendants of ancient ones but both rather as fulfillment of ideal forms residing in the mind of God. In 1846 he accepted an invitation to lecture at the Lowell Institute in Boston, and in 1847, after the death of his wife, became a professor at Harvard. His second wife, Elizabeth Cabot Cary, was a member of one of Boston's

grated to the United States to take up a professorship at Harvard University. A compelling lecturer, Agassiz spoke in Boston, New Haven, and Charleston, and visited Morton in Philadelphia. Morton's collection of crania impressed Agassiz, but he was even more impressed, and viscerally disgusted, by the black waiters who attended him at his Philadelphia hotel. He wrote to his mother in December 1846 that

> I experienced pity at the sight of this degraded and degenerate race, and their lot inspired compassion in me in thinking that they are really men. Nonetheless, it is impossible for me to repress the feeling that they are not of the same blood as us. In seeing their black faces with their thick lips and grimacing teeth, the wool on their head, their bent knees, their elongated hands, their large curved nails, and especially the livid color of the palm of their hands, I could not take my eyes off their face in order to tell them to stay far away. And when they advanced that hideous hand towards my plate in order to serve me, I wished I were able to depart in order to eat a piece of bread elsewhere, rather than dine with such service. What unhappiness for the white race—to have tied their existence so closely with that of negroes

most socially prominent families.

Agassiz traveled widely, making journeys of exploration through central Europe, the Swiss Alps, the eastern and midwestern United States, and South America. In his studies of geology he formulated the concept of the Ice Age, which he believed was a catastrophe planned by God to exterminate the existing species, after which new species were divinely created. Agassiz believed that in the history of the earth there had been as many as twenty separate creations, each characterized by its own divinely produced set of life-forms. The species from one creation bore no genealogical relationship to that from any other—an idea that was easily adapted to Agassiz's theory of the separate origins of

(Library of Congress)

the human races. Despite his advocacy of polygenism, Agassiz was never a supporter of slavery, claiming that his views were those of a dispassionate scientist and had nothing to do with politics. His years at Harvard were marked by his controversy with his colleague Asa Gray, the Harvard botanist and friend of Darwin's. In 1873, the year of his death, Agassiz remained the only major scientific opponent of evolution.

in certain countries! God preserve us from such a contact! (Agassiz quoted in Gould 1981, 45.)

Earlier Agassiz had been a rather half-hearted defender of the doctrine of the created unity of the human species, but now he became convinced that the Negro and the white could not have shared a common origin. In 1850–1851 Agassiz wrote a series of articles for the Unitarian *Christian Examiner*, the second of which, "Diversity of Origin of the Human Races," showed his firm alliance with the American polygenists. Agassiz argued that although all human beings belonged to the same species, they did not share a common origin. The different races had been created separately, each in its own center of creation, specifically adapted to its own environment. Climate could not have produced the differences among them, and there had been no migration or diffusion from a common center. It was impossible to trace each race back to an original ancestral pair, as the races had been created as nations.

In an interesting variation on the anticlericalism of Morton, Nott, and Gliddon, Agassiz wrote that the Bible only reported on the origins of the white, specifically the Jewish, race; it made no mention of the origins of any other. Thus polygenism was not inconsistent with the biblical origin story. Still, the Bible should not be read literally because it was not a textbook of natural history and should not be expected to provide scientifically verifiable facts. The existence of the different races, Agassiz concluded, "presses upon us the obligation to settle the relative rank among these races, the relative value of the characters peculiar to each, in a scientific point of view." Asserting that absolute equality was out of the question, he continued:

> Such views would satisfy nobody, because they go directly against our every day's experience. And it seems to us to be mock-philanthropy and mock-philosophy to assume that all races have the same abilities, enjoy the same powers, and show the same natural dispositions, and that in consequence of this equality they are entitled to the same position in human society. . . . This compact continent of Africa exhibits a population which has been in constant intercourse with the white race . . . and nevertheless there has never been a regulated society of black men developed on that continent, so particularly congenial to that race. Do we not find, on the contrary, that the African tribes are today what there were in the time of the Pharaohs, what they were at a later period, what they are probably to continue to be for a much longer time? And does this not indicate in this race a peculiar apathy, a peculiar indifference to the advantages afforded by civilized society? (Agassiz 1850, 142–143)

In 1854, Nott and Gliddon collaborated on *Types of Mankind,* which they dedicated to the memory of Morton. Nott discussed types, including Caucasian, African, and Indian, with a section on Jews as a race unchanged over 4,000 years, in terms of their comparative anatomy and geographical distribution. Each type was distinct from the beginning, created separately, possessed of distinct capabilities and characteristics. Gliddon wrote on biblical chronology and Egpytology, and Agassiz contributed a chapter on the geographical distribution of animals and men. The book comprised a compendium of the existing evidence for polygenesis.

Polygenism in the Land of Prichard

In Britain, polygenism also had its independent and influential sources. The Christian monogenist position, strong into the 1840s and supported by Prichard and others, began to give way in the 1850s under the guidance of Robert Knox and his outspoken follower James Hunt. Knox (1791–1862), a friend of William

Edwards, was an Edinburgh anatomist whose reputation was damaged in an 1829 scandal involving the selling of murdered corpses for medical dissection. Knox subsequently moved to London where he wrote and lectured on physiology and anatomy. His 1850 *Races of Men* was based on his lectures and viewed history in terms of the racial struggle between Saxons, Celts, Gypsies, Jews, and the darker races, an outlook similar to that proposed by Count Arthur de Gobineau's *Inequality of Races* (1853–1854). Knox's theory gained an immediate impact in the wake of the uprisings of 1848, which he interpreted in racial terms and claimed to have predicted. His biographer Henry Lonsdale credited Knox with making race into a household word.

Knox explicitly rejected Prichard's monogenism and his historical approach that traced the races back to their original roots. It sufficed instead for Knox to focus on the biological and therefore also the mental and moral differences among the presently existing races. Racial natures, he argued, were unchanging over thousands of years, and were so different that they should be called different species. History was the result of each race attempting to dominate in its own geographical region and establish a government consistent with its own nature.

The Saxon race, for example, was by nature fair-haired and blue-eyed, tall, powerful and athletic, "the strongest, as a race, on the face of the earth" (Knox 1850, 43). Possessed of great self-confidence and an abstract sense of justice, the Saxon was for Knox "thoughtful, plodding, industrious beyond all the other races . . . large handed, mechanical, a lover of order, of punctuality in business, of neatness and cleanliness" (Knox 1850, 44–45, 47). This racial nature was unchanged either by environmental influence or by interbreeding with other races. Given the inalterability of race by any means, the Saxons were basically unsuited for life on continents other than the one on which they originated. There could be no healthy Saxon race in Africa, Australia, or the Americas; a constant influx of Saxons from the homeland and a reliance on native labor would be the only ways to maintain a colony. Such a view, a theory of "racial zones" similar to Agassiz's, led the politically radical, fiercely abolitionist Knox to an anticolonialist position. He thus provides a perfect illustration of the wide variety of political views held by those whom we would consider scientific racists.

Knox was influenced by the transcendental anatomy of Geoffroy Saint-Hilaire, a member of Edwards' *Société Ethnologique*, in his belief that the embryo acts as a kind of species reservoir, passing through developmental stages representing all the extinct, extant, and future species of its genus. Thus when a new species appeared, it was not the result of a totally new creation, nor the result of the transformation of a mature adult form of one species into another. Rather, the new species arose when one species form is replaced by another from out of the range of possibilities residing within the generic embryo. The

Robert Knox (1793–1862)

Knox was a wildly popular and successful teacher of anatomy whose career was compromised by scandal. His radical political views that became so much a part of his science were formed early in life. Knox's father was a schoolmaster in Edinburgh, Scotland, who had been sympathetic to and connected with liberal prorevolutionary groups during the French Revolution. The younger Knox was schooled at home and at Edinburgh high school, and attended medical school at the University of Edinburgh. He received his medical degree in 1814, specializing in anatomy, with a dissertation on the effects of alcohol and other stimulants on the human body.

(Mary Evans Picture Library)

Knox spent the next several years as an army physician and surgeon. He traveled to London to complete his medical studies and soon after was sent to Europe as a hospital assistant with the British army. In Brussels Knox tended to the wounded from the Battle of Waterloo. Upon his return to London in 1817 he voyaged as ship's surgeon to the Cape of Good Hope with the 72nd regiment. In South Africa he took part in a war against the Bantu, toward whom he was actually sympathetic, and the experience deepened his tendencies toward political radicalism and atheism. He also made scientific studies of the plants, animals, and people of South Africa.

Returning to Edinburgh in the early 1820s Knox published the results of his anatomical, zoological, and meteorological research from his journey and began a study of the anatomy of the eye. In 1825 he became the director of an independent school of anatomy in Edinburgh, where his dramatically performed lectures drew huge crowds of students and had to be supplemented by special Saturday lectures to the public. Knox's problems arose from his need for cadavers for his students to dissect. In 1827 he paid William Burke and William Hare for the dead body of a tenant found in their Edinburgh boarding house. By 1828, Burke and Hare sold Knox more than a dozen more corpses, but it was soon revealed that they had resorted to the murder of their tenants to keep up the supply. Burke was hanged (and afterward duly dissected), while Hare managed to flee the city. Knox took the brunt of the blame for their crimes, both from the Edinburgh citizenry and from some of his professional colleagues, though his name was officially cleared. Nonetheless his school of anatomy fell into decline, and in 1831 he was forced to resign as curator of the museum of anatomy of the Royal College of Surgeons. In 1842 he left Edinburgh for London, but the stain on his reputation prevented him from gaining any official position, either in England or in Scotland. He supported himself for the next fourteen years by medical journalism and public lecturing, presenting the series of lectures that eventuated in his 1850 *Races of Men*. In 1856, the cloud over his name having lifted somewhat, he was appointed anatomist at a cancer hospital in London.

genesis of new species from out of the generic embryo allowed Knox to reject any notion that species themselves might undergo change, or might blend continuously one into another. In a racial framework, the theory led Knox to argue that all the races, though each a permanently distinct species, were all of the same genus and shared a common humanity. Each race was a result of the embryonic possibilities developing in a different direction, a process he referred to as "deformation." The cuticular fold at the inner corner of the Eskimo's eye, for example, a feature absent in European adults, was shared by all human embryos. The feature was retained when that generic human embryo developed into one of its specific forms and lost when it developed into another.

"Race is everything," Knox wrote in 1850; "literature, science, art, in a word, civilization, depend on it" (Knox 1850, 7). As his views gained currency, Knox's basic message, about the immutability of racial character and its driving force in history, was invariably disjoined from his radical politics and put to conservative political ends. The Knoxian notion of racial struggle was used by Darwin and by Social Darwinists to justify European imperialism. Knox's polygenism was also adapted to very un-Knoxian purposes by Knox's devoted disciple James Hunt (1833–1869). In 1863, Hunt founded the London Anthropological Society as an alternative to the Prichardian Ethnological Society, which Hunt disparaged as dominated by monogenists, Quakers, and abolitionists. Hunt used the Anthropological Society, modeled on Broca's society of the same name, as a vehicle for Knox's polygenism, but combined it with reactionary politics.

In 1864, as the American Civil War raged, Hunt declared before his society that the Negro was a distinct species from the European. Intellectually inferior to the European, the Negro was more similar to the ape than the European was, and "more humanized when in his natural subordination to the European than under any other circumstances" (Hunt 1854, 23). Hunt did not want his listeners to believe that he was countenancing the horrors of the slave trade. Nonetheless, he could not help but note the degraded conditions of Negro slaves in Africa and how much better off they were as slaves in the Confederacy. In fact, slavery in America was, for Hunt, a boon to black people. "The highest type of the Negro race," Hunt concluded, "is at present to be found in the so-called Slave States of America, far superior in intelligence and physique to both his brethren in Africa and to his 'free' brethren in the Federal States" (Hunt 1854, 24).

Conclusion

The legacy of polygenism was the establishment of racial typology, the idea that the different races constituted different species, which in the period 1800–1859 meant that they were considered to be essentially, immutably, biologically distinct types. Though the most extreme forms of polygenism were often implied rather than explicitly endorsed, including the claim that the races had been separately created, the notion of racial type was a powerful and pervasive one. As doubts accrued about the efficacy of the environment to alter physical or mental traits in any lasting way, the reigning monogenist consensus was weakened, and polygenists solved the problem by arguing that racial differences were primordial and permanent. Once racial typology gained a foothold, it proved difficult to dislodge, persisting after Darwin and in fact well into the twentieth century. With the growth of new and quantitative sciences from 1800 to 1859, the polygenists' desire to categorize, classify, and measure gained unprecedented authority and respectability.

Though they assumed that the differences they observed indicated distinctly different racial essences, and that the dark races were unquestionably inferior to the white, the polygenists did not generally agree on the way the races should be classified. The actual number of races varied considerably from scientist to scientist. Nor did the polygenists hold a set of political beliefs in common. Indeed, they came from across the political spectrum in their views on abolition, slavery, and colonialism. It would therefore be a mistake to try to correlate any one particular political stance with a belief in polygenism.

Still, social context was clearly relevant to the rise of racial typology, and the relationship between scientific views and political developments is worth considering. For example, despite some notable exceptions, slaveholders in the American South did not use polygenism to defend their peculiar institution. Polygenism was too radical a doctrine for them, too far out of line with received biblical authority, and monogenism was perfectly adequate to maintain slaves in their subordinate position. The Reverend John Bachman of Charleston, South Carolina, a prominent naturalist, slaveholder, and antiabolitionist, was a monogenist and staunch defender of slavery on biblical grounds. In a sense, Bachman's slaveholding society scarcely needed a theory of different racial essences. It was rather the white abolitionists, faced with the prospect of black people moving freely among them, who used polygenesis to reinforce their own separateness and superiority.

Racial views also intersected with imperial interests in several different ways. The debate between the monogenists and the polygenists predated the late-nineteenth-century scramble for Africa among the major European imperial powers. In Britain, at least at that time, popular support for colonialism was low. Indeed, the colonial experiences of the British in India and the French in Algeria lent credence to the polygenist idea that whites were not well suited to hot climates. Ironically, Europeans' conviction of their essential difference, and therefore of their vulnerability, increased even as their colonial involvement deepened. And as it did, polygenist reasoning tracked it and explained it. When the colonial encounter was different, and it was instead the colonized peoples who died out, racial typology could again explain the experience. The colonized were clearly at the end of their racial life history and their vital principle was sapped. European invasion then only hastened an end that was already foreordained and inevitable. The American belief in Manifest Destiny, the white expansion into and capture of American Indian lands, thus had a clearly racial, and polygenically inspired, component to it.

These last few examples help expose the different aspects of racial typology, and the reasons for its remarkable success. With its contravention of biblical authority, polygenism stood for a new nineteenth-century scientific worldview, to which Darwin was about to make a major contribution. And with its possibilities for justifying European preeminence and oppression of colonial subjects, racial typology took on heightened significance in the imperialistic last decades of the nineteenth century.

Bibliographic Essay

On the shift from Enlightenment to nineteenth-century beliefs about race, see George W. Stocking Jr., *Race, Culture, and Evolution: Essays in the History of Anthropology* (Chicago: University of Chicago Press, 1982) and Nancy Leys Stepan, *The Idea of Race in Science, Great Britain, 1800–1960* (Hamden, CT: Archon, 1982). Both Stocking and Stepan agree that race was a concept characteristic of the nineteenth century. Audrey Smedley, *Race in North America: Origin and Evolution of a Worldview* (Boulder, CO: Westview Press, 1999) includes several chapters on scientific ideas about race. Stocking's editor's introduction to *Bones, Bodies, Behavior: Essays on Biological Anthropology* (Madison: University of Wisconsin, 1988) contains a useful summary of this transition period.

For a full chronology of slavery and its abolition, see Harry Harmer, *The Longman Companion to Slavery, Emancipation, and Civil Rights* (New York: Pearson Education, 2001). For numbers of slaves transported, see Philip Curtin, *The Atlantic Slave Trade: A Census* (Madison: University of Wisconsin Press, 1969). For a discussion of the relationship between slavery, abolition, and racial theories, see Seymour Drescher, "The Ending of the Slave Trade and the Evolution of European Scientific Racism," *Social Science History* 14 (1990): 415–450. David Eltis, in "Europeans and the Rise and Fall of African Slavery in the Americas: An Interpretation," *American Historical Review* 98 (December 1993): 1399–1423, argues that economic reasons alone cannot account for the enslavement of Africans. Joel Williamson, in *The Crucible of Race: Black-White Relations in the American South since Emancipation* (New York: Oxford University Press 1984) discusses the effect of the slave system in creating a hierarchical society in the South and provides a useful general framework for thinking about slavery.

James Cowles Prichard's *Researches into the Physical History of Mankind*, originally published in London by J. and A. Arch in 1813, was reissued in an edition edited by George Stocking (Chicago: University of Chicago Press, 1973). Stocking's introduction to this volume covers Prichard's biography, places his ideas in context, and considers their influence. The 1813 *Researches* grew to five volumes in subsequent editions in 1826, 1838, and 1851. It was supplemented by *The Natural History of Man: Comprising Inquiries into the Modifying Influence of Physical and Moral Agencies on the Different Tribes of the Human Family*, originally published in 1843 (London: H. Baillaire), with editions in 1845, 1848, and 1855. William Lawrence's *Lectures on Physiology, Zoology, and the Natural History of Man* were published in 1822 (London: Benbow). Stepan's *Idea of Race in Science* discusses Prichard's monogenism and compares it to Lawrence's and Samuel Stanhope Smith's. She also deals with the challenges to monogenism made by Henry Home Kames and Charles White. Kames's work is *Sketches of the History of Man* (Edinburgh: W. Creech, 1774, 2d ed. 1788). White's work is *An Account of the Regular Gradation in Man, and in Different Animals and Vegetables, and from the Former to the Latter* (London: C. Dilly, 1799).

Cuvier's contributions to polygenism are discussed in Michael Banton, *Racial Theories* (New York: Cambridge University Press, 1987). On polygenism in France, see Claude Blanckaert, "On the Origins of French Ethnology: William Edwards and the Doctrine of Race," pages 18–55 in Stocking's *Bones, Bodies and Behavior.* Martin Staum, "Paris Ethnology and the Perfectibility of the Races," *Canadian Journal of History* 35 (December 2000): 453–472, compares the *Société Ethnologique* with Broca's anthropological society and considers its connections to American polygenism.

On the American school of polygenism, see William Stanton, *The Leopard's Spots: Scientific Attitudes toward Race in America, 1815–1859* (Chicago: University of Chicago Press, 1960). Stephen Jay Gould, in *The Mismeasure of Man* (New York: Norton, 1981), argues that Morton, having unconsciously imbibed the prejudices of his time, fudged his cranial measurements so that his results would cohere with his preconceived notions about racial superiority. Gould repeated Morton's measurements and showed exactly where his apparently unconscious mistakes were. John S. Michael, in "A New Look at Morton's Craniological Research," *Current Anthropology* 29 (April 1988): 349–354, has in turn criticized Gould and stressed instead Morton's levelheadedness and caution, showing that in some cases Morton's results were not what he expected, still Morton reported them. Morton's original works are *Crania Americana; or, a Comparative View of the Skulls of Various Aboriginal Nations of North and South America* (Philadelphia: J. Dobson, 1839) and *Crania Aegyptiaca; or, Observations on Egyptian Ethnography, Derived from Anatomy, History, and the Monuments* (Philadelphia: J. Pennington, 1844). Charles Caldwell's work referred to here is *Thoughts on the Original Unity of the Human Race* (New York: E. Bliss, 1830). Nott's article "The Mulatto a Hybrid: Probable Extermination of the Two Races if Whites and Blacks are Allowed to Marry" appeared in *The American Journal of the Medical Sciences* 6 (1843): 252–256. Nott and Gliddon's *Types of Mankind* appeared in 1854 (Philadelphia: Lippincott, Grambo). Agassiz's article "Diversity of the Origin of the Human Races" appeared in the *Christian Examiner* in July 1850, pages 110–145. Agassiz's letter to his mother in which he described his reaction to seeing black people was translated and quoted in full by Gould in *Mismeasure of Man*, pages 44–45.

On the influence of polygenist theory on political and social policy, especially regarding Native Americans, see Reginald Horsman, "Scientific Racism and the American Indian in the Mid-nineteenth Century," *American Quarterly* 27 (May 1975): 152–168. See also Robert E. Bieder, *Science Encounters the Indian, 1820–1880: The Early Years of American Ethnology* (Norman: University of Oklahoma Press, 1986), which includes discussions of Morton and Squier.

On Robert Knox and James Hunt see Evelleen Richards, "The 'Moral Anatomy' of Robert Knox: The Interplay Between Biological and Social Thought in Victorian Scientific Naturalism," *Journal of the History of Biology* 22 (Fall 1989): 373–436. Knox's *Races of Men: A Fragment* was published in 1850 in Philadelphia by Lea and Blanchard. Hunt's *The Negro's Place in Nature* was published in 1864 in New York by Van Evrie, Horton, and Co. The relationship between racial theories and British imperialism is treated in Mark Harrison, "'The Tender Frame of Man': Disease, Climate and Racial Difference in India and the West Indies, 1760–1860," *Bulletin of the History of Medicine* 70 (1996): 68–93.

On John Bachman, see Lester D. Stephens, *Science, Race and Religion in the American South: John Bachman and the Charleston Circle of Naturalists, 1815–1897* (New York: Oxford University Press, 2000). Both Stanton and Stephens make the argument that polygenism was not of crucial importance in justifying slavery.

3

Race and Evolution, 1859–1900

1859, the year Darwin published *On the Origin of Species*, marks a convenient turning point for a history of scientific ideas about race. Darwin's work, while it did not persuade all scientists of the role of natural selection as the motor of evolution, did convince many that present-day life-forms had descended gradually over great stretches of time from a common ancestry. Whether a Divine Creator had been present from the beginning to start the process was an open question. But the belief that life had been produced in such a natural way without continuous divine intervention was widely held by 1870. Darwin's book helped make evolution respectable, and though there were holdouts against it, they became increasingly rare in the two decades after its publication.

1859 is thus convenient for marking this sea change in attitude. But in some ways isolating that year as the important one obscures as much as it reveals. It obscures the fact that Darwin was neither the first nor the only advocate of evolution. His influence in making evolution respectable and popular was matched, even exceeded, by that of Herbert Spencer. Spencer, a railroad engineer turned philosopher, began writing essays on evolution, though an evolution quite different from Darwin's, in the early 1850s. Moreover, *On the Origin of Species* focused on the evolution of animals and plants, and avoided directly discussing human evolution. One line was all it dedicated to the genealogy of the human species: "Light will be thrown on the origin of man and his history" (Darwin 1964 [1859], 488).

Fearing controversy, Darwin did not write publicly about human evolution until he published *Descent of Man* in 1871. But by that time, Darwin had been preceded not only by Spencer, whose evolutionary theory principally concerned human society, but also by the biologists Alfred Russel Wallace and Thomas Henry Huxley, as well as by the anthropologists John Lubbock, Edward Tylor, and John McLennan. In the 1860s, the evolution of human culture and of man's social behavior was a major focus for all these authors. We speak of "Darwin's theory," but we must be aware that he had predecessors, and that there were key areas of overlap between the pre- and post-Darwinian eras.

Charles Darwin, the British scientist whose theory of evolution created immense controversy in the mid-nineteenth century (Library of Congress)

Viewing the history of science in terms of continuity rather than in terms of radical revolutionary breaks helps reveal another feature of this period. Although evolutionary theories, particularly about human beings, circulated before Darwin himself advocated them, a host of pre-Darwinian notions about race continued to command broad assent even after Darwin published his work on natural selection. Evolution, thanks to both Darwin and Spencer, became the great organizing principle of the late nineteenth century, applied across the board in the sciences. Not only plants and animals, but human beings, the human mind, and human society were all imagined to have had an evolutionary history. But rather than overturning earlier scientific ideas about race, the new evolutionary framework accommodated and confirmed them, even those that seem at first glance to be in conflict with it. All the resources of the new evolutionary science were now brought to bear as organizing concepts, models, and metaphors on the preevolutionary goal of explaining and justifying the inferiority of Asian, African, and American Indian peoples. The hierarchy of the races now became an evolutionary hierarchy. In this sense the transition between the pre- and post-Darwinian eras was a seamless one indeed.

Darwin's Argument in On the Origin of Species

Charles Darwin was an unlikely revolutionary figure in the history of science. Darwin was born in 1809 into a socially prominent, wealthy family. His grandfather, Erasmus Darwin, was a naturalist of some repute, and his father Robert was a respected physician. As a young English gentleman, Darwin was expected by members of his social class to choose a profession that suited his class—he certainly could not be a merchant or a laborer as those occupations were unsuited for "gentlemen." His choices were limited: he could be a physician, attorney, or minister. Darwin was at best an average student at boarding school in Shrewsbury. Nonetheless, in 1825 his father sent his young son to the best medical school in the world, the University of Edinburgh in Scotland, expecting him to follow his illustrious father into the healing arts.

Darwin hated medical school. His gentle disposition rebelled against the blood, the dissections, and vivisections. He decided to leave medical school in 1827 and his professional options were narrowed even further. A legal career was out of the question, for he was shy and hated confrontations of any kind. The ministry was the only remaining option, so his father sent him off to Christ's College, Cambridge University to earn a theology degree. The plan was for Darwin to become a minister in a quiet country church somewhere, a respectable career for an English gentleman.

Even though he completed the training necessary to be a minister, he never became one, for Darwin had a secret vice: natural history. Since childhood he had been an avid collector of beetles, birds' eggs, minerals, and other natural specimens. His father considered the hobby a waste of time and berated the young man for his foolishness. Darwin, however, persisted in his pursuits. Both at Edinburgh and Cambridge, Darwin spent more time exploring nature with others who shared his interests than he did in the classroom, which partially explains why he was a mediocre student. The sciences were not part of the college curriculum in early-nineteenth-century England, so Darwin's interest in nature could never be anything more than a hobby. Most early-nineteenth-century naturalists were amateurs, English gentlemen who pursued natural history in their spare time between patient appointments or meetings with parishioners.

At Cambridge, Darwin met the clergyman and botanist John Stevens Henslow and the clergyman and geologist Adam Sedgwick, who both shared his passion for the natural world. In 1831, Henslow presented Darwin with an opportunity to join the crew of the HMS *Beagle*, which was embarking on a planned two-year survey of South America. The ship's captain, Robert Fitzroy, sought a respectable young gentleman to serve as a social companion for the long trip; the strict rules of ship's discipline and the class expectations of English society prevented the captain from socializing with any of his crew. A gentleman, however, could serve as a dinner companion for the captain.

On his voyage, Darwin noted a number of things about the natural world. He had with him a copy of Charles Lyell's *Principles of Geology*, which argued for uniformitarian geology, the view that the geological record was the product of the accumulations of small changes over incredibly long periods of time. Darwin's geological observations on his voyage seemed to accord with Lyell's ideas regarding uniformitarian geology.

Darwin also noted that organisms seemed to vary sequentially in time and space. In other words, he saw that in the fossilized remains of an animal, say an armadillo, there was a succession of organic forms over time. As one moved up the geologic strata, one could trace similar forms of armadillos that led to the present day armadillo of South America. Just as these similar organic forms appeared in the temporal fossil record, Darwin noted how similar organic forms appeared in space. The famous Galápagos archipelago, where each island had a different species of tortoise, all nonetheless very similar to one another, presented a puzzle similar to that of the fossil record. Why was it that there were similar, yet distinct, forms of these organisms? Darwin believed that he could explain these temporal and geographic successions of organic form by positing that a single species had been modified from the original type over a long period of time. For Darwin the question became, how was this modification accomplished? What was the mechanism that could change species in this way?

The planned two-year voyage of the *Beagle* stretched to five and when he returned, Darwin was a changed man. He had seen the world and established himself as a very promising young naturalist. Even his father recognized that his son could be a respectable gentleman and a practicing naturalist. A gift of money from his father allowed Darwin to abandon the ministry and focus on natural history. Darwin settled down to the comfortable life of an English gentleman.

In 1838, Darwin read the work of economist Thomas Robert Malthus (1766–1834). Malthus had suggested that there was a natural law that enabled

British economist Thomas Robert Malthus (Hulton Archive/Getty)

society to progress. He argued that population growth would always outstrip natural resources and that consequently there would always be competition for scarce resources in an economy. But, Malthus concluded, this seemingly dismal situation was actually beneficial to the economy, as the best people would rise to the challenge, gaining employment and wealth by virtue of their superior skills and energy. Malthus was critical of governmental attempts to change the natural social hierarchy, arguing that all such attempts must fail in the struggle for scarce resources. "No fancied equality," he wrote, "No agrarian regulations in their utmost extent, could remove the pressure" of the struggle for scarce resources "even for a single century" (Malthus 1798, 6). The natural law that dictated that population would always outstrip resources was the mechanism that guaranteed both a natural inequality of individuals and a natural drive toward social progress. Malthus was therefore a proponent of the laissez-faire theory of government that held that the proper role of government was to stay out of the economic affairs of the people altogether because the natural laws of society would create the best situation for all with maximum efficiency.

Darwin seized on Malthus's argument as the mechanism for organic change: just as people competed in an economy for scarce resources, so too did organisms compete in the environment for scarce resources. By the end of the 1830s, Darwin had formed his theory of "natural selection." Darwin's theory of natural selection seems simple on its face and can be stated in a few sentences. First, organisms vary within species with respect to their ability to compete for resources. Second, organisms compete for scarce resources. Third, organisms with those variations that better enable them to survive and reproduce *do* survive and out-reproduce organisms without those variations. Therefore, species are mutable as beneficial variations increase in frequency over generations.

Darwin knew he was on dangerous ground with his daring theory. For one thing, the theory of natural selection was completely materialistic and naturalistic; it outlined no role for God in the formation of organisms. Second, Darwin's theory was not progressive. For Darwin, organisms survived simply because they were better suited to their surrounding environment. There was no notion that organisms were progressing toward forms that were intrinsically better than the previous ones. Finally, these two notions together had profound implications for humans' understanding of their place in nature. Did Darwin mean that people were just another animal, not specifically created by God, not intrinsically better than other organisms?

Darwin knew that these questions were important. He knew that if he was going to publicly announce his theory he needed a lot of evidence. Consequently, he spent twenty years collecting evidence supporting his theory of natural selection. Darwin might have spent twenty more years if a young man, Alfred Russel Wallace, had not brought the same idea to the Royal Society in 1858. Wallace, equally nervous, had written to Darwin asking for advice, and they presented their findings jointly to the Royal Society in 1858. In 1859, Darwin published *On the Origin of Species*, which announced his theory to the world.

Darwin and Wallace on Natural Selection and Human Origins

Two interrelated questions confronted those who took up Darwin's theory: first, did natural selection apply to human beings, and second, if natural selection did apply to humans, how did it explain racial differences?

A key component of the first question was the nature of human origins. If, as Darwin argued in the concluding chapter of the *Origin*, "all the organic beings which have ever lived on this earth have descended from some one primordial form, into which life was first breathed," (Darwin 1964 [1859], 484), did this mean that humans evolved in the same way? Although he hesitated to say so publicly, Darwin was convinced that natural selection explained the evolution of humans. But it was not clear to him exactly how this process worked. Moreover, those human attributes that were traditionally explained by reference to a human soul, such as moral sense, speech, and intelligence, were not easily explained by a purely materialist version of natural selection.

Though his early notebooks and drafts show him pondering these issues, Darwin was not the first to take a public stand on them. In an 1864 paper Wallace used the new theory to explain the development of humans' characteristic mental traits as well as the origin of the human races. Wallace argued that human intellectual and moral capacities had shielded human bodies from the environmental pressures that would otherwise be operative in producing structural change. So, for example, if the environment suddenly changed and became much colder, this environmental pressure might, through the action of natural selection, cause an animal species to develop a thick layer of fur or blubber as protection against the cold. Humans, however, could adopt clothing and fire, technological fixes that would help preserve their physical bodies from modification. After human beings achieved a certain level of mental and moral sophistication, natural selection would not operate any longer on their physical form but on their intellect.

Wallace's argument was calculated to please and appease the polygenists and help reconcile them to the Darwinian view of evolution. In 1864, Wallace delivered his paper before Hunt's polygenist and racist Anthropological Society of London. The physical diversification of the races, Wallace reasoned, must have occurred at a remote time in the past before humans gained their characteristic sociality, morality, and intelligence, when natural selection was still operative on human bodies. The differentiation into separate races with distinct physical traits must have happened so soon after humans first appeared on the earth that, for all practical purposes, the races had always been distinct.

Wallace continued by arguing that once natural selection made the switch and began operating on man's intellect and moral sense, it continued to work to differentiate the races. More mentally and morally advanced and socially cohesive races would overtake, conquer, and ultimately exterminate the less advanced, just as in the animal and plant world, more fit varieties eliminated inferior varieties. Wallace's theory accounted for the development of humanity, both its physical peculiarities and its unique social/mental/moral traits, and was the first to do so entirely within the materialistic framework of natural selection.

When he first read Wallace's paper, Darwin was both pleased and anxious. He appreciated Wallace's attempt to apply natural selection to human origins but was anxious that Wallace was coming close to Darwin's own views on human origins. As it developed, however, Darwin had little to fear from Wallace overtaking him on natural selection and human origins because Wallace soon abandoned his idea.

By 1870, Wallace retreated from his materialist explanation of human origins. Wallace's new belief was that natural selection could not account for important human features. One of Wallace's more telling examples was brain size, a key indicator of humans' special nature. Wallace argued that the savage ancestors to modern humans possessed brains nearly as large as civilized humans, but savages obviously had no need of such an advanced intellect. Natural selection only selected for useful traits in a given environment and could not explain the large human brain. Wallace also argued against the usefulness of other uniquely human physical traits, such as the hand, hairless skin, erect posture, and the natural beauty of the human form.

Wallace cast his new argument in explicitly racial terms. When Wallace wrote of "savages" he meant Africans, aboriginal Australians, and other racial groups. For Wallace, such people had no need for intellect, for that was only needed in "civilization." Wallace also emphasized that human traits could be explained only by an internal spiritual drive that distinguished humans from animals. Wallace embraced spiritualism and had begun to believe in mesmerism, séances, and other attempts to contact the "spirit world." Although Wallace did not embrace traditional religion, he had abandoned the purely materialistic theory of natural selection that he had developed in parallel with Darwin.

Darwin on Human Evolution

When Darwin read Wallace's new views, he was horrified. Darwin was far less willing than Wallace to abandon natural selection as the explanation for human origins and human variation. He published his ideas on the subject in 1871 in *The Descent of Man.*

As developed in *On the Origin of Species,* Darwin's theory relied on tiny variations giving survival advantage to particular members of a species. Over time, these small advantages accumulated and species gradually transmuted into new forms. The *gradual* accumulation of traits over long periods of time was the key point. When Darwin took these basic ideas and applied them to human origins, he emphasized not the radical differences between humans and other animals but the similarities. Where Wallace and others stressed what they saw as enormous differences between human brains and animal brains, Darwin argued that the human brain, while larger and better developed, was not fundamentally different from those of other mammals.

In *The Descent of Man* Darwin maintained that even those mental and moral traits that make humans unique could be found in much more primitive forms in other animals. Darwin devoted two chapters of *The Descent of Man* showing that apparently stark differences between humans and animals were not so stark if one examined the actual behavior of social animals, from the well-developed ape to the lowly bee. The point, Darwin concluded, was to show that "The difference in mind between man and the higher animals, great as it is, is certainly one of degree, and not of kind" (Darwin 1871, 105). By these small gradations, which he believed were inherited, Darwin fashioned an argument that natural selection could account for humans evolving from animals.

Racial differences were central to his argument. To make his case, it helped that the very attributes that Darwin was struggling to explain with natural selection were the attributes tied most closely to race. Many polygenists believed that the races possessed different moral attributes, and even the monogenists were not necessarily willing to grant racial equality in that area. Darwin's own views, as revealed in his notebooks of the 1830s, later marked him as a moderate in these debates. He was not a confirmed racist—he was a staunch abolitionist, for example—but he did think that there were distinct races that could be ranked in a hierarchy.

In *The Descent of Man* these views of race helped Darwin fill in his gradualist picture of the origin of humans. Darwin admitted that the gap in intelligence and moral sense between civilized people and the animals was a great one. But one could look to the lower races to fill that gap. Ever the gradualist, Darwin came down on the side of the monogenists by treating races not as separate

A Victorian representation of the ascent from ape to human (Mary Evans Picture Library)

species, but as variations of a single species. "The most weighty of all the arguments against treating the races of man as distinct species," he wrote, "is that they graduate into each other, independently in many cases . . . of their having intercrossed" (Darwin 1871, 226). This graduation applied not only to their physical form but also to their mental and moral capabilities. Although Darwin maintained that there were established racial differences, these differences were a series of small gradations rather than large, unbridgeable chasms. What the naturalist confronted was not a stark break between humans and animals but a continuum from lower animals to higher animals, from higher animals to savages and barbarians, and finally from barbarians to civilized people.

Despite his evolutionary gradualism and argument for continuity, Darwin also clung to the idea that the human races were distinctly different and basically unchangeable, a legacy of the influence of polygenism on him. The differences were most obvious when one considered the racial extremes. When the *Beagle* arrived in Tierra del Fuego at the southernmost tip of South America, Darwin was astonished and horrified at the sight of the savages who ran out to meet the boat. "It was without exception," he wrote in his diary of the voyage, " the most curious and interesting spectacle I had ever beheld. I could not have believed how wide was the difference, between savage and civilized man. It is wider than between a wild and domesticated animal, inasmuch as in man there is a greater power of improvement" (Darwin 1989 [1839], 172). He recalled the same scene at the end of *The Descent of Man*, where he added that on seeing the Fuegians "absolutely naked and bedaubed with paint, their long hair . . . tangled, their mouths, frothed with excitement, and their expression . . . wild, startled, distrustful," the idea immediately occurred to him: "such were our ancestors" (Darwin 1871, 404). Darwin's experience with these savages provided him with further proof of their inalterable racial difference. When a party of Fuegian natives, Christianized and civilized in England, returned on board the *Beagle* as missionaries to their native land, the Fuegians reverted to their savage ways, convincing Darwin that racial habits and racial natures were entrenched and basically unchangeable. The conversion the savages had undergone had been superficial and fleeting, while their suitability to their native way of life, and their clear inferiority, were permanent. All that remained of racial evolution for Darwin, as for Wallace, was the extermination of the inferior races by the superior.

Darwin's theory of evolution from a common ancestor was a monogenetic one that, once it gained nearly unanimous assent, should have put the polygenetic alternative to rest. But this was not the case. Polygenetic concepts and assumptions continued to form the basis of much racial science in the late nineteenth century. The result was a curious synthesis of the evolutionary idea of ever-changing, ever-fluctuating populations and the polygenist belief in fixed, stable, racial categories. Both Darwin and Wallace, as we have seen, easily harmonized evolution by natural selection with polygenic notions; and they were not alone. The German Darwinian Karl Vogt, applying Darwin's evolutionary theory to man, argued, like Wallace had originally, that natural selection had formed the races so long ago that the differences between them had been rendered permanent (Vogt 1864). Vogt maintained, as did Darwin, that each race was so well adapted to its environment that it was incapable of change, even when moved to a new environment. For Vogt, as for Wallace and Darwin, racial evolution had essentially stopped. The polygenist idea of unbridgeable gaps between inalterable racial types thus found an honored place even in the new evolutionary science. The measurement and classification of the resulting distinct types became fodder for the burgeoning science of physical anthropology.

Physical Anthropology and the Persistence of Polygenism

Physical anthropology in the second half of the nineteenth century was dedicated to one major aim: the measurement of human bodies, particularly heads, in order to identify the stable racial types underlying human populations. The basic assumption of the science was that each race could be represented by its own essential set of traits, physical traits primarily, which were in turn associated with corresponding mental and moral characteristics. This set of traits defined the race, belonged properly only to it, and found expression in each and every one of its members. In reality, the physical anthropologists conceded that not every member of a given race possessed all of its proper racial traits. The essence of the race might not be perfectly represented in any single individual. But as an ideal, the racial essence could always be reconstructed, which is just what the physical anthropologists took their task to be. Though the mixing of populations, interbreeding, or immigration might conceal or disguise racial essences, the anthropologists believed they could always extract and identify the essences by techniques of careful measurement.

Broca developed over forty instruments, including various kinds of calipers, pelvimeters, craniostats, and torsiometers, to make the increasingly precise cranial and body measurements that his science demanded. His fellow physical anthropologists used Broca's tools and techniques to measure more than 25 million Europeans throughout the late nineteenth century. American anthropologists and physicians made similar measurements of thousands of soldiers and prisoners in the American Civil War. The idea that essential racial types existed beneath human variety and could be reconstructed, the assumption of underlying stable racial essences, was of course a polygenist one, traceable directly to Nott, Edwards, Knox, and Hunt. That Broca, an avowed polygenist and evolutionist, had such influence in anthropology in the second half of the nineteenth century, attests to the persistence of polygenist styles of reasoning in an era dominated by evolutionism.

In his 1856 work *Human Hybridity*, Broca followed polygenist tradition, arguing that there were degrees of fertility in human race mixing. Eugenesic crosses—matings between those races that were most closely allied in charac- ter—produced fully fertile offspring. Dysgenesic crosses, on the other hand— matings between the races farthest apart on the scale of humanity—were either sterile or produced only a few sterile offspring. For Broca it was as though nature herself was trying to prevent the racial essences from dissipating through mixing. But even in a fully eugenesic cross, the essential racial character would remain recognizable enough to be extracted by the anthropologist's calipers.

Such a polygenist idea was harmonious with evolutionism. The distinct racial essences developed over eons of divergent evolution. All humans may ulti- mately have had a common ancestor, but that singular origin point was so far back in time, the common ancestor was so remote, that to all intents and pur- poses the races had always been separate. By comparing modern skull meas- urements with the ancient ones discovered in the last half of the nineteenth cen- tury, anthropologists concluded that the races had evolved along their own separate lineages. Some anthropologists believed that the races descended from a common ancestor in the Pleistocene Era. Others, like Topinard and Vogt, traced the white, black, and yellow races each to a different ancestral species of ape. Polygenist thinking also surfaced in Topinard and Vogt's views on the impos- sibility of acclimatization. Racial types were so basically stable and so well suited to the environments in which they had evolved that they could not change or adapt even when placed in new conditions. Any racial transformation was out of the question. Evolutionary change had once occurred, but it occurred in the past, achieved its end, and was not ongoing.

The stability of types despite mixing, the separateness of different racial lineages, and the impossibility of acclimatization were all polygenist-inspired ideas that remained widely influential for the rest of the century. In the United States the anthropologist Daniel G. Brinton echoed them, even though he was nominally a monogenist. As late as 1896, Frederick L. Hoffman, peppering his "Race Traits and Tendencies of the American Negro" with references to Nott and Hunt, declared that a cross between a Negro woman and a white man would result in a mix that was inferior to either a full-blooded Negro or a full-blooded white. As for Negro men and white women, according to Hoffman, they were so disinclined to marry each other that the fertility of their unions was hardly a concern. So easily was Broca's polygenism combined with the new evolutionary anthropology that his most notable opponent, Armand de Quatrefages, was an anti-Darwinian monogenist who argued that all races were equally interfertile and that they could adapt to all environments.

For polygenically inclined physical anthropologists after Darwin, the traditional hierarchy of races remained unquestioned. Negro, Malay, American Indian, and Caucasian fell into their familiar positions on the human ladder. But these rough divisions were not the sole focus of interest. The drive for increasingly precise measurement allowed anthropologists to draw ever finer distinctions within these categories, especially within the Caucasian category. The idea that Europeans comprised different races was familiar from Edwards and Knox, and ultimately it goes back to Julius Caesar's divisions of Gaul.

Dividing the races of Europe, determining and measuring differences among European races, became a consuming interest too for late-nineteenth-century physical anthropologists. Following Knox, these anthropologists interpreted the political struggles of Europe in racial terms. To separate a Negro from a Caucasian, skin color would usually suffice, and anthropologists needed no elaborate anthropometric tools. But distinguishing a Saxon from a Celt, an Alpine from a Mediterranean, required precise measurements. Only Broca's arsenal of measuring techniques could reveal the minute differences in headform that anthropologists believed these races displayed. The interest in measuring types of Europeans was, then, both driven by and reflected in the anthropologists' increasing technical skill. The more they measured, the more their sense was reinforced that they were measuring something real. And yet the more they measured, the harder it became to clearly distinguish one type from another. Told by Otto Ammon that he could not provide a photograph of a pure Alpine type, William Z. Ripley wrote, "[Ammon] has measured thousands of heads, and yet he answered that he really had not been able to provide a perfect specimen in all details. All his round-headed men were either blond, or tall, or narrow-nosed, or something else that they ought not to be" (Ripley 1899, 108).

Measurements of the size and shape of head, summarized by the cephalic index, were the principal means of dividing European populations. Devised by Anders Retzius in 1844 as a refinement of Pieter Camper's facial angle, the cephalic index was a measure representing the ratio of length to breadth of skull. Retzius himself was interested in European races, and Broca, Topinard, and other physical anthropologists took up both his interest and his measure later in the century. In the post-Darwinian era, anthropologists treated the cephalic index as an especially important indicator of racial group since, as a relatively useless trait, headform would not have changed in response to selective pressures. Thus its purity as a marker of racial type would be unclouded, as would not necessarily be the case with such traits as stature or skin color. Anthropologists used the cephalic index to distinguish the dolichocephalic type, which had a long, oval-shaped head, from the brachycephalic type, which had a round head. Anthropologists associated other facial features with each type; for example, brachycephalic types were thought to have prognathous, jutting jaws.

By 1899, Ripley's *Races of Europe* summarized the consensus produced by Topinard and others during the preceding thirty years. There were three major divisions in Europe: the Teutonic, the Alpine, and the Mediterranean. The Teutonic, also called Aryan, or Nordic, was envisioned as a superior race originating in the East and bringing civilization to Europe. The beginnings of what would later become the Nazi myth of Aryan racial purity and superiority were therefore evident in this work. But Ripley's ties to pre-Darwinian racial theories were equally clear. For him the Aryans were, as they were for Knox, divided into the superior Saxon and the inferior Celt.. The Celtic type was represented by the Irish, who were commonly portrayed as monkeys in newspapers and popular journals. More fundamentally, Ripley's debt to polygenism manifested itself in his reduction of intermixed European populations to three basic types. Though he described himself as an "ardent evolutionist," evolution, for him, simply meant the mixing of these types, which the physical anthropologist then had to separate. Significantly, when considering the question of whether the types had descended from a single ancestor, Ripley refused to answer, calling the matter of origins too speculative to be a proper question for objective investigation.

The pre-Darwinian idea of stable racial types gained new force and acquired new evolutionary justification in the post-Darwinian era. In the second half of the nineteenth century, evolution became the guiding principle for the life and human sciences, helping to overhaul, rather than overturn, many older ideas that now took on a new scientific respectability. The evolutionary model that gained ascendancy during this period was a potent blend of the writings of Darwin and Spencer. Spencer was a prolific author and widely read before and after the publication of Darwin's works. The result was that, especially for Anglo-American audiences, Darwin was read through a Spencerian lens, the Darwinian emphasis on struggle combined with Spencer's emphasis on progress, and their two rather different theories of evolution conflated into a single worldview.

According to that view, evolution occurred in society just as it did in nature. Society could achieve evolutionary progress only by a fierce struggle for survival, with the losers unapologetically relegated to the bottom of the heap. Scholars often call this view social Darwinism, though it owed as much to Spencer as it did to Darwin. It came in many different varieties depending, as we will see, on which particular aspects of the Spencer-Darwin mix the writer chose to emphasize. As they conceived the struggle for existence taking place not only between individuals, but also between groups of people, many social Darwinists reserved an honored position for race in their evolutionary worldview. Just as the newly scientific physical anthropology helped legitimize the older concept of racial type, social Darwinism lent new respectability to the well-worn notions of racial hierarchy and interracial struggle. To understanding the evolutionary framework in which social Darwinism was embedded, and the key role of race in that framework, we have to understand the life and philosophy of Herbert Spencer.

Spencer and Evolution

Herbert Spencer (1820–1903) was born in Derbyshire, in the English provinces, into a family of modest means. Both his parents, who were of Methodist and Quaker backgrounds, fostered Spencer's skepticism toward religion and toward church authority and encouraged him to dissent from the doctrines of the high Anglican Church. Spencer received his education at home from his schoolmaster father and at his uncle Thomas Spencer's school in Somerset. Spencer did not attend a university and throughout his life was mostly self-taught. After a stint as a railway and civil engineer, in 1841 he resigned his position and began writing for various periodicals.

As a young man Spencer developed the set of ideas that remained with him for the rest of his life. In his 1842 pamphlet "The Proper Sphere of Government," for example, Spencer argued that government should be strictly limited in function to protecting property and person and should not be responsible for educating, building roads, or administering charity. State-sponsored charity prevented the poor from trying to improve themselves. It encouraged them to marry and have children even though they lacked the ability to support those children. It militated against voluntary charity, thus blunting the development of the finer feelings of sympathy and generosity in the well-to-do. Self-improvement, Spencer believed, came only through struggle and free individual competition, also called laissez-faire, without government interference or support, except of the most restricted kind. Progress came only through the struggle to achieve, with every person responsible for his or her own interests. In this early radical phase of his thinking, Spencer envisioned government eventually withering away, as each member of society, including women and children, enjoyed full rights and full freedoms without infringing on any other. In 1848 Spencer moved to London to become subeditor of the *Economist*, a liberal journal, where he continued to champion his individualist, free trade, and laissez-faire policies. In 1853 he left the *Economist* to write full time.

In the 1850s, Spencer fit his ideas about government and society into an

English sociologist Herbert Spencer is credited with developing the phrase "survival of the fittest." (Library of Congress)

evolutionary framework. In such works as *Social Statics*, "The Development Hypothesis," and "Progress: Its Law and Cause," Spencer defined and popularized the concept of evolution and argued deftly the absurdity of the creationist alternative. For Spencer, evolution was synonymous with progress, development from the simple to the complex, the increasing specialization of an undifferentiated mass to a complex, ordered whole. Note that this was a very different type of evolution from Darwin's, which implied no such progress. Evolution for

Spencer meant increasing diversification and differentiation of structure and function. Evolution was also a universal principle, an all-encompassing process that could explain equally the formation of galaxies, the transmutation of species, and the history of human societies. The organic, mental or psychological, and social realms were therefore all united by this developmental master plan.

Spencer argued that higher biological organisms and more advanced societies showed the same characteristics. Both displayed greater individuation, progressively greater specialization, and differentiation. In both there was a complex division of labor, a concept exported from economics to physiology, in which different parts specialized for different functions. In fact, Spencer referred to societies as social organisms, and his analogy between organisms and societies was nearly perfect. Each had a head, a ruling portion, responsible for the sensitive and intelligent functions, as well as subsidiary members that did the mechanical work.

The analogy was so exact for Spencer that he spoke of the tissues of the body as "communicating" with each other, and of society as needing to "excret[e] its unhealthy, imbecile, slow, vacillating, faithless members" (Spencer 1851, 324). Any influence that interfered with this process was therefore evil and to be combated. Each person was to work according to his own abilities, to find his rightful place in the social organism, while society purified itself of its waste products. The suffering that this would cause for those earmarked for excretion might seem unkind at the moment but was ultimately working toward the greater good. "The poverty of the incapable, the distresses that come upon the imprudent, the starvation of the idle, and those shoulderings aside of the weak by the strong, which leave so many 'in shallows and in miseries,' are the decrees of a large, far-seeing benevolence" (Spencer,1851, 323). Spencer called this struggle for existence "the survival of the fittest," failure and death to the unfit "social selection," concepts he framed almost a full decade before Darwin borrowed them for his own evolutionary purposes.

Spencer believed that the struggle and the suffering necessarily had a good outcome. Not only would a more highly differentiated social organism result, but also one that showed the greatest interdependence of its members. Ultimately struggle would cease and harmony would reign. Just as in a perfectly adapted and efficiently functioning biological organism, in the most highly evolved society all conflict would end, and cooperation and interdependence would take over, a state he referred to as "equilibration."

For Spencer, the progressiveness of the evolutionary process was ensured by his belief in the Lamarckian inheritance of functionally acquired traits. As the members of a society, or the parts of an organism, specialize and take up their different stations in the division of labor, the modifications in mental or physical structure that they acquire will be passed to the next generation. There was never any possibility that the process would reverse or stagnate, since Spencer's Lamarckian mechanism kept it moving in a progressive direction. Perfectibility was guaranteed by this mechanism. Those who survived the process of social selection were the fittest of their generation, and they passed their achievement via Lamarckian inheritance to their offspring. The evolution of a society for Spencer meant that intelligence, morality, and perfectibility increased, along with fitness, cooperation, and interdependence. In an interesting reversal of Malthusian reasoning, Spencer insisted that increasing morality would bring decreasing fertility, so that unchecked population growth would not stand as an obstacle to the realization of his harmonious utopia.

Spencer developed the two aspects of his progressive evolutionism, struggle and cooperation, in voluminous writings. Following on the essays he wrote in the 1850s, in 1862 he published *First Principles*, a prologue to his next ten volumes, which dealt with biology, psychology, sociology, and ethics. His *Principles of Sociology* threatened to grow so large that he had to supplement it with *Descriptive Sociology*, a compilation in more than a dozen volumes of facts about different cultures. Spencer used these facts, which he had his secretaries cull from books of travel, to support his *Principles. Descriptive Sociology* is a prime example of what is sometimes called armchair anthropology, which means that Spencer did not conduct any fieldwork or experiments but simply speculated on sociology based on others' descriptions.

In his *First Principles*, as well as in the writings that followed, Spencer emphasized that struggle and survival of the fittest could be only a contributing cause to the advance of society, but never the whole story. Struggle might be important in the early stages of civilization to eliminate the weaker races and produce the rougher traits. But for more advanced civilizations, struggle, brutality, and violence lost their effectiveness, and war became disadvantageous. Cooperation and adaptation via a Lamarckian mechanism were more important in bringing about the dynamic equilibrium of organism and environment that Spencer envisioned as the endpoint of evolution. The higher traits, including man's delicate mental structures, his refined social habits, and his sense of justice, could not have been produced by struggle and selection, Spencer believed, since these traits have no apparent survival value. Only a Lamarckian mechanism, driving the increasing interdependence of society's members, could account for the appearance and persistence of these higher traits.

Evolution as progress, struggle and survival of the fittest eventuating in cooperation and interdependence, and the concept of society as an organism were the building blocks of Spencer's philosophy. It was a capacious and highly adaptable philosophy, and a rich resource for social thinkers in the late nineteenth century. Spencer's followers often took what elements they liked, many of them emphasizing the struggle for existence at the expense of his other principles. Indeed, the social Darwinists are perhaps more accurately called "social Spencerians," since they saw unfettered individualistic competition and raw struggle as the key elements of social progress, and these are the ideas often identified with Spencer. When Spencer was at his peak, his philosophy was more complex and more nuanced than that. But as he grew older, as the British economy worsened in the 1880s and 1890s, and as Marxism gained ascendancy, Spencer became increasingly conservative, distancing himself from the socialist aspects of his own philosophy, emphasizing laissez-fare struggle, and downplaying his vision of the harmonious utopia.

Spencer on the Savage Mind

Spencer believed that the hierarchy of races that he and most of his fellow Victorians observed was an evolutionary hierarchy. The lower races were less evolved, stuck in the past, biologically and culturally simpler than Caucasians. As one moved from the savage to the civilized, one advanced in evolutionary time. Society became increasingly complex and specialized, and primitive homogeneity diversified into modern heterogeneity. Civilized people showed increasingly complex physiological and psychological organization and had a correspondingly more complex relationship to their environments.

Spencer's evolutionary scale was, crucially, a unilinear one. Mankind was a unity, not because all human beings were the same, but because the different human groups stood at different steps in the same process. All human groups progressed along the same scale and all could be measured by the same standard. Spencer expected the savage to come up to a European standard, and to do so by progressing through the same stages that European society had presumably passed through. More than metaphorically, the savage showed the European what his own past, his own racial history, had been. Sociocultural evolutionists would develop the idea that the savage was a clue to the Caucasian past.

Spencer took the idea of increasing specialization quite literally. Brain mass, he believed, was a direct indication of position on the evolutionary scale. Because their ancestors had used their brains more effectively, through a process of Lamarckian inheritance the higher races inherited a larger brain mass. This put the lower races, inheriting a smaller brain mass, at a disadvantage from the outset. Spencer was far from believing that all people entered the world with equal potential. Brain mass varied directly with mental complexity, and those with less of both showed a correspondingly smaller range of behavior. The lower races tended to be guided by reflex action and irrational mimicry. Their behavior was characterized by rigid customs that could not be modified to suit changing circumstances. "Many travelers comment on the unchanging habits of savages," Spencer wrote (Spencer 1979, 192). "The semi-civilized nations of the East, past and present, were, or are, characterized by a greater rigidity of custom than characterizes the more civilized nations of the West. The histories of the most civilized nations show us that in earlier times the modifiability of ideas and habits was less than it is at present."

This lack of plasticity in the lower races was due not only to their small brains but also to the fact that their children's period of development was shorter than that of children of advanced races. Infancy and childhood were key phases in development, and the more extended they were, the more they allowed impressions from the environment to shape the brain. The more environmental influence, the greater the departure from ancestral forms, and the more civilized the race. The savage child was considered precocious, developing at a faster rate than the civilized child, but with puberty came mental arrest, an abrupt shutting down of the developmental process. Thereafter the savage nature became fixed. An American popularizer of Spencer, John Fiske, provided an anatomical explanation for this mental arrest. Fiske believed that the cranial sutures of the savage skull closed when the child reached puberty, stopping all further brain growth and mental development. The idea was pre-Darwinian, traceable to Gratiolet, Broca's colleague, and the polygenist Hunt, but for Fiske it was entirely amenable to an evolutionary framework.

Spencer's writings on the comparative psychology of man amounted to an attempt to characterize the savage mind. Members of all the races lower than the Caucasian had minds that were rigid and unadaptable, automatic or reflex in character, impulsive and uncontrolled. The savage showed persistence in the lower intellectual faculties, spending hours carving a stone tool, for example, but little aptitude for anything requiring higher thought. His emotional responses were impulsive, showing how little they were controlled by any higher part of the nervous system. The lack of the cardinal Victorian virtue of self-control demonstrated for Spencer the evolutionary distance between the savage and the civilized.

But Spencer did not believe that all savages were identical. Like everything else in his progressive scheme, different savage natures possessed different qualities in degrees and could be arrayed hierarchically. Although they all may have lacked self-control, rational curiosity, and the capacity for abstract thought, in other traits their natures differed widely. They showed various emotional specialties: some savage tribes were gregarious, others indifferent to society; some

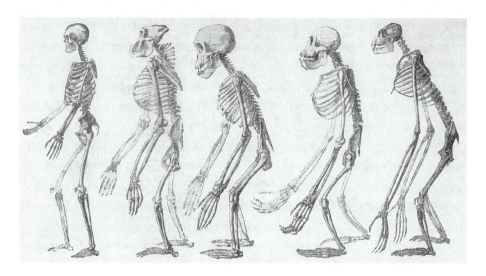

The skeletons of five primates: human, gorilla, chimpanzee, orangutan, and gibbon based on Ernst Haeckel's The Battle of Evolution, *1905 (Bettman/Corbis)*

were ungovernable, while others submitted easily to external restraint; some sought praise eagerly, others less so; some desired property, others did not.

Some savage races possessed peculiar aptitudes. For example Spencer recounted the musical ability of Negroes who could sing harmonies to complex tunes upon their first hearing of them. He noted that each savage tribe treated its women differently. In keeping with his idea that evolutionary progress means increasing specialization, Spencer maintained that the higher the race, the greater the contrast between men and women in physical appearance and social role. Significantly, however, when discussing the altruistic sentiments, which he considered the highest, including pity, generosity, and justice, Spencer did not provide any savage examples. The implication was that the lower races had not yet evolved to those levels. Whether they would ever so evolve was highly doubtful.

For Spencer and Fiske, the lower races—African, Polynesian, American Indian—were arrested in a state of savagery, from which only direct intervention could remove them. The ancient Egyptians and the Chinese had moved out of savagery, but only into an immobile, nonprogressive type of civilization. The Spencerians, however, doubted that Asians, Africans, and other lower races could be brought onto a progressive course, for reasons having directly to do with Spencer's evolutionary philosophy.

In Spencer's laissez-faire evolutionary framework, Caucasians achieved civilization by self-development and individualistic struggle. Struggle was essential for progress, but the problem with the lower races, according to Spencer and his followers, was that they seemed to have little ability for it. Their behavior was circumscribed largely by their imitativeness, a tendency toward irrational or automatic mimicry that suppressed any more rational or critical response. But imitation was superficial and no substitute for real striving. A savage might imitate a civilized man, but such imitation stood in the way of his becoming truly civilized and was in fact a dangerous thing to encourage, for the savage could throw off the guise and revert at any moment. Imitation could not overcome the ingrained habits of the race. The behaviors carved into the savage's system by Lamarckian inheritance would overpower his puny attempt to imitate his betters. The steps of evolutionary progress were gradual and deliberate and could not be hurried over or supplanted by being sped up artificially. Neither imitation nor education, then, could really solve the race problem because the problem was a consequence of the savage's very nature.

Impulsive and irrational, mirthful and intolerant of discipline, the savage was stuck in a permanent childhood and lacked the capacity to grow out of it. As the ability to learn self-restraint and self-discipline eluded him, so did the ability to develop into a civilized adult. For Spencer, the resemblance between savages and children came as no surprise. Since the savage represented the past, literally, the childhood, of the civilized race, the similarity between adults of the lower races and Caucasian children was an essential outcome of Spencer's evolutionism. And since all peoples progress through the same intellectual and moral stages, those who have not, or not yet, reached the top of the ladder must therefore share common traits.

The equation between the savage and the Caucasian child was one outcome of this reasoning. But it was not the only one. Women, the lower classes, and criminals were also childlike, or savage, in certain ways. All were subordinates in different realms of life, all lacked the ability to look after or control themselves, and all represented lower positions on the unilinear scale. These were powerful analogies. Victorian philosophers, scientists, and social thinkers equated and spoke in similar terms about women, children, peasants, laborers, criminals, madmen, Irishmen, and savages. The American Spencerian sociologist William I. Thomas, for example, made parallel arguments about the dangers of educating Negroes and women. These lower orders of humanity were not completely interchangeable, nor did Spencerians treat them as exactly identical. But they did share certain basic traits that marked them as primitive.

The German biologist and social Darwinist Ernst Haeckel generalized the Spencerian analogies among primitive groups into the biogenetic law. Encompassing all of nature, this law stated that ontogeny recapitulates phylogeny, that the stages of individual development repeat the stages of racial development, or, more simply, that the individual while growing into an adult climbs all the steps of the evolutionary ladder. Thus Haeckel believed that the human fetus at various points in its development resembled an adult reptile and an adult amphibian before progressing to mammalian status. As the infant grew into an adult, and by adult Haeckel of course meant the northwestern European male adult, it recapitulated not only the physical stages, but just as crucially the mental and moral stages of its ancestors, represented by apes, savages, and women. For Haeckel as for Spencer, the hierarchical chain of being was entirely compatible with an evolutionary framework.

Social Darwinism and Its Variants

For the Spencerians, evolution provided a many-sided justification for domination, a paternalistic philosophy that could control the childlike outsider, whether that outsider was a member of a lower race, gender, or class. But social Darwinist arguments varied and underwent subtle shifts depending on which aspects of the Spencer-Darwin blend the writer chose to emphasize. The idea of individualistic struggle was often replaced by a collectivist ideal, meaning that the races themselves were in competition. The American sociologist William Graham Sumner, for example, argued for unrestricted competition among individuals and survival of the fittest; success in the struggle belonged to the industrious, the frugal, and the temperate. But the English Spencerian Walter Bagehot envisioned the competition as between nations or civilizations, the important forces being those, like religion, that bound the individual members of a nation together, kept them subordinate to their government, and molded their national character. For Bagehot, the struggle took place on a national or racial rather than on an individual level.

When it came to racial relations and interracial struggle, British and American Spencerians tended to lessen Spencer's original laissez-faire emphasis. There were now reasons that all the races could not compete equally on a level playing field, reasons that struggle, and therefore progress, had to be restricted to Caucasians. For what were considered the lowest races of men—Africans, Polynesians, and American Indians—there could be no question of racial struggle with Caucasians. Domination by Europeans was inevitable, as the lower races could never progress on their own and so required such domination. As the ideal of direct intervention provided a rationale for imperialism, it also virtually assured the extinction of these lower races, which was in some cases already happening.

Whether Negroes or Chinese immigrants to the United States should be allowed to compete in society was a slightly more delicate issue. According to American Spencerians, the Negro needed to be exposed to struggle in order to progress. But efforts to help the Negro had to be strictly limited, as too sudden an uplift could be dangerous. Here the efficacy of intervention was thrown into doubt. A race that needed constant prodding by compulsory education could never compete in a truly fair manner. Moreover, such exposure to the struggle would ultimately prove the Negro's demise. Common medical opinion held that freedom was unhealthy for Negroes, that they deteriorated mentally, morally, and physically as freedmen, a belief bolstered by supposedly high rates of Negro insanity reported in the 1870, 1880, and 1890 census. Chinese immigrants, on the other hand, possessed an unhealthy advantage in competition with whites. Though considered tradition-bound and rigidly unable to adapt, many Americans also believed the Chinese to be hard workers and all too willing to help one another. The Chinese had to be excluded from the racial competition because their racial habits could potentially make them a little too successful.

Spencer's evolutionism could thus provide a rationale not only for imperial expansion but also for subordinating African Americans and for restricting the flow of immigrants into the United States. In this last area social Darwinism overlapped with the eugenics movement, which helped put policies of immigration restriction into practice. Both ideologies aimed to maintain the integrity of the white race. The homogeneity of society should not be compromised by an influx of unassimilable elements. Its health as a smoothly functioning organism depended on the full integration of its parts, and those that refused assimilation, especially groups that did not behave according to Euro-American standards, should be excluded or eliminated or society would break down. Spencer valued heterogeneity in the division of labor as the mark of an evolved society, but never racial heterogeneity. When it came to the races, both Spencerians and eugenists believed that all parts of a society must be homogeneous in race and character, and whether they relied on the organic analogy or on beliefs in the purity of the blood, Spencerians and eugenists came to the same conclusion, both believing that race mixture must be resisted. Rome fell, they argued, because of an influx of unassimilable elements, and in the late nineteenth century, the fear was that the United States was taking the same path.

Social Darwinism in Germany

Anglo-American ideas about racial hierarchy and interracial struggle derived from a mixture of Spencerian and Darwinian theories. In other contexts, however, the blending of these two evolutionary philosophies was not as complete. In Germany, for example, they were almost entirely pried apart. Here Spencer's influence was slight, although the notion of struggle, both on an individual and on a racial or national level was traceable in the writings of German scientists directly to Darwin. In Germany, we can speak accurately of social *Darwinism,*

Ernst Haeckel (1834–1919)

Haeckel was Germany's premier zoologist and one of the earliest champions of Darwinism. Born in Potsdam, he received an M.D. degree in 1858 but never practiced medicine, as he was always more interested in pure biology. He received a doctorate in zoology from the University of Jena in 1861 and remained a professor of zoology and comparative anatomy there for the rest of his life. He was an important teacher at Jena, where a chair and Zoological Institute were created for him, and where he

(Library of Congress)

counted many important German scientists among his students. In the mid 1860s Haeckel became an enthusiastic convert to Darwinism and integrated humans into an evolutionary framework before Darwin himself dared to do so. Haeckel embraced Darwinism not only as an evolutionary theory but as a cosmic philosophy, applicable to the entire universe. He saw evolution as a kind of religion that revealed beauty, design, and meaning in nature. Becoming close to nature, and understanding and celebrating man's animal origins, were for Haeckel the goals of the evolutionary religion that he called "Monism." Monism meant that matter and mind were everywhere conjoined in nature, and was opposed to traditional Christian dualism—that soul and body were separate entities.

In his 1866 *Generelle Morphologie*, Haeckel placed all of the organic and inorganic worlds into a Darwinian evolutionary framework, and this work, combined with the highly detailed biological treatises that followed, most of them dealing with problems of classification of invertebrates, made their author famous. In addition to being an

although the Germans kept an important place for progress and for an organic conception of society stemming from Romantic nature-philosophy.

Darwinian theory strongly influenced and spread rapidly through the German intellectual community. By the 1860s, many German biologists, sociologists, philosophers, theologians, ethnologists, and economists converted to Darwinism, applying it easily to the natural and social realms. At first many of these thinkers used Darwinism to support a liberal ideology of progress, opposing socialism and favoring laissez-faire. But in succeeding decades, as Bismarck consolidated power and the former liberals became part of an entrenched elite, the social Darwinist movement became increasingly conservative and wedded to the status quo. This political shift was common to the history of the movement in Britain and France as well.

Ernst Haeckel was one of the earliest and most powerful of these German

original researcher, Haeckel was an indefatigable popularizer of the theory of evolution, which he did in part by drawing gnarled and detailed evolutionary trees. He also held to several speculative theories, all of which he saw as more important to evolution than Darwin's mechanism of natural selection—spontaneous generation, the notion of pan-psychism (which holds that all things, living and nonliving, possess some form of mind or soul), the Gastraea theory (that there is a common ancestral form for all many-celled creatures), and, perhaps most famously, the biogenetic law (that ontogeny recapitulates phylogeny, or that individuals, as they grow, pass through the evolutionary stages of their ancestors). Haeckel was also a committed Lamarckian throughout his career.

From the 1880s, Haeckel turned increasingly to the social, moral, and religious implications of evolution. His 1899 *Riddle of the Universe* popularized his Monist philosophy, as did the German Monist League, which he founded in 1906. Members of the League included some of the most prominent scientists in Germany in the early twentieth century. There was much in Haeckel's Monist worldview that endorsed social Darwinism, indeed, that was proto-Nazi in character. In keeping with their religion of nature, Haeckel and his Monists believed that the Germans needed to revitalize their inner racial essence by renewing their contact with nature. True Germans were Aryans, the highest race, but they faced biological deterioration and decay unless they applied nature's law unimpeded in society. This meant that the weak and sickly must be destroyed at birth, that the needs of the individual must be subordinated to the state, particularly to the state's authoritarian power, and that a harmonious organic community, pure in racial essence, must be evolved as a result. A supporter of polygenism and of conflict and struggle between higher and lower races, Haeckel helped make racism scientifically respectable. A strong nationalist his entire adult life, he died deeply disappointed in Germany's defeat in World War I, but he was celebrated for his scientific work and for the religion he made out of it.

converts to Darwinism. As a professor of biology at the University of Jena, Haeckel began applying Darwin's theory to humans before Darwin himself did. In his 1868 *History of Creation*, which appeared in over twenty editions before World War I, Haeckel argued for unfettered struggle as the motor of progress. He saw all of nature as a struggle of organism against organism in an unending war. There was no reason, Haeckel argued, to think that human beings were any different from the rest of nature.

For Haeckel the struggle took place not only among individuals but between nations or races as well. In the *History of Creation* Haeckel divided human beings into ten races, of which the Caucasian was the highest and the primitives were doomed to extinction. His beliefs in militarism and nationalism, racial competition and imperialism were manifested in his founding of the Monist League, with its emphases on the union of spirit and matter and the dominance of superior races. Members of the Monist League later became important in constructing Nazi ideology.

Haeckel's views were echoed by the paleontologist Friedrich Rolle, who argued that Malthusian population pressure would precipitate a war between the races. The biologist Heinrich August Ziegler declared in 1893 that the clearest lesson Darwin taught was the preeminent role that war played in spurring progress in human evolution by the elimination of inferior types. The zoologist Oskar Schmidt wrote that society should stop seeing savages through the rose-colored glasses of the missionary and adopt the objective view of the scientist wherein savages became slated for destruction in the struggle for existence. Among sociologists the same views prevailed. Both Max Weber and Otto Ammon justified national and racial competition in Darwinian terms. Weber spoke of the struggle for "elbowroom," while Ammon glorified war as a progressive force.

The German social Darwinists believed that an aristocracy of talent, identified across the board with the white race, would prevail in these interracial struggles, and that within European society, brisk competition would prepare the race for these inevitable conflicts. The ethnographer Friedrich von Hellwald justified brutal struggles on both individual and racial levels in the most extreme terms, untempered by any ethical concern for the weak. The collectivist struggle among the races was also justified by several other thinkers who in the latter decades of the nineteenth century made the shift from radicalism or liberalism to conservatism. Ludwig Gumplowicz, Austrian professor of sociology at the University of Graz, wrote in his 1883 *Racial Struggle* that war between the races was inevitable, that peace was only temporary, and that Africans and Asians would be exterminated in any struggle with Europeans. Imperialism was part and parcel of this scheme, since the conquering of the weak and inferior was necessary for social progress. Gumplowicz's follower, Gustav Ratzenhofer, an Austrian military officer, echoed his teacher's belief in racial war and imperialism, arguing that such struggles strengthen the conquering nation and improve its internal harmony, its civilization and culture. And the geologist and geographer Friedrich Ratzel, in his 1901 *Lebensraum*, defined the Darwinian struggle for existence specifically as the struggle to control territory, not only among animals and plants but also among human races. For Ratzel, the primitive races, of which he considered the American Indians one example, would continuously be displaced by the cultured races.

Sociocultural Evolutionism in Britain

The evolutionary framework did not rise to prominence unchallenged. Even after evolution was accepted as a fact for nonhuman animals and plants, the place of human beings in the Darwinian evolutionary picture was contested, primarily by religious thinkers. In the late 1860s, the Duke of Argyll and Archbishop Richard Whately both lodged objections to the idea that man had arisen from lower forms. Instead, they argued, man had degenerated from a higher, more perfect state endowed by God in the Garden of Eden. Argyll and Whately claimed that there were distinctive human traits and that these helped deny any genealogical relationship between man and the animals.

Such challenges did not, however, weaken the evolutionary framework. To the contrary, Argyll and Whately's assertions helped strengthen that framework by setting the research program for a group of evolutionary anthropologists. Known as the sociocultural evolutionists, this group came of age in the generation just after Darwin's and took on Darwin's own problem of anthropogenesis. Meeting the religious challenge, they asked how these distinctively human characteristics could be explained in a natural, developmental way without recourse to divine origin or causation. The three anthropologists who, in different but complementary ways, answered this question were John Lubbock, Edward Tylor, and John McLennan. Together they created a powerful framework to explain the evolution of human culture and customs. Lubbock, Tylor, and McLennan were not social Darwinists in the sense of advocating or justifying individual or collectivist struggle. But in much the way that Spencer's ideas had, their theories of anthropogenesis placed savages below Europeans on the evolutionary ladder.

In his 1865 book *Prehistoric Times, as Illustrated by Ancient Remains and the Manners and Customs of Modern Savages*, Lubbock argued for the great antiquity of man. The subtitle summarizes one of the major methods of sociocultural evolutionism: the comparison of ancient remains to the material culture of present-day savages in order to illuminate what Stone Age people must have been like. Now of course extinct in Europe, the representatives of the Stone Age were to be found among those living fossils, the primitive races of the world. In *Prehistoric Times*, Lubbock characterized savages, whether found in South Africa, North or South America, India, or Australia, not as noble in any way but as enslaved by their own limitations, needs, passions, and ignorance.

In 1867 and 1868, Lubbock responded directly to the challenge posed by Argyll and Whately. In order to oppose the view that human characteristics were divinely given, Lubbock had to show that savages could indeed provide clues to the missing link between the European and the ape. He had to argue that there was continuity between the savage and the Victorian, that there were indications of the ability to progress among the primitives, and that there were residues of barbarism among the civilized.

In his 1870 *Origin of Civilization*, Lubbock expanded on this view by tracing each of the major social or cultural institutions or forms up from savagery to

Sir John Lubbock (1834–1913)

Sir John Lubbock had careers not only as an anthropologist and archaeologist, but also as a science popularizer, financier, and politician. Born in London, he was the eldest son of a prominent banker who was also distinguished as an astronomer and mathematician. When Lubbock was young the family moved to an estate within one mile of Darwin's home in Kent, and Lubbock grew up with Darwin as a surrogate father and as a member of Darwin's inner circle; he was one of the few to learn of Darwin's theory of natural selection before 1859. A regular churchgoer his whole life, Lubbock nonetheless early on lost all orthodox belief, in which he was doubtless influenced by Darwin.

Lubbock had only a few years of formal schooling and entered the family banking business at the age of 14. But his entry into the world of science was helped along by Darwin and Lyell, and through them Lubbock became acquainted with many of the most important scientific men of the day. In the 1850s, upon his discovery of the first fossil musk ox in England, he gained admission to two of the most prestigious British scientific societies, the Geological and the Royal, even as he pursued his banking career. In 1865 his *Prehistoric Times* was published, presenting the archaeological, geological, and paleontological evidence for man's antiquity and introducing to the public the idea of four prehistoric ages: Paleolithic, Neolithic, bronze, and iron. The same year he ran for a seat in Parliament but lost (a loss one of his biographers attributed to his still controversial views on man's antiquity). In 1870, however, the same year that his second major anthropological work appeared, *The Origin of Civilization*, Lubbock ran again for Parliament and won. As a member of Parliament he introduced numerous bills to reform education and labor, including one that established

its highest flowering in modern Europe, imagining the stages through which civilization might have developed. Instead of arguing, as he had earlier, for a diffusionist view, that civilization had spread from East to West, Lubbock now shifted his strategy to propounding the independent invention of cultural forms. To counter the religious degenerationists, Lubbock had to show that the savage could progress on his own, could in effect think himself out of savagery without help, divine or otherwise. By arguing that the savage shared in a core of common human traits, that the races developed in parallel from the same primitive beginnings and passed through the same stages, Lubbock could claim that Stone Age man could have progressed to present-day Victorian gentleman completely naturalistically. The diffusionist view implied that a primitive race needed outside intervention to evolve. But if savages could invent various cultural forms independently, just as Stone Age man must have, then no such intervention was necessary. Lubbock's view of the savage in 1870 was therefore somewhat different from his earlier work. Though still portrayed as inferior, the savage was now basically rational, capable of progress, and shared in a common human nature.

Edward Burnett Tylor took up Lubbock's argument against the diffusionist

the first secular bank holiday, a day popularly known as "St. Lubbock's Day." In 1871 he became the first president of the Anthropological Institute of Great Britain and Ireland. In addition to his study of prehistoric remains in Britain and on the Continent, Lubbock also published extensively in botany and entomology.

Lubbock served in Parliament for thirty years, from 1870 to 1900; during the same period he held such prominent positions as vice-chancellor of the University of London and president of the Institute of Bankers. In 1900 in recognition of his public service he was given a peerage and chose his title, Lord Avebury, to commemorate a prehistoric site he had studied. His later works were popularizations, books of travel and of uplifting quotations on "The Pleasures of Life," but even his major anthropological works, which were issued in numerous editions into the 1910s, were intended to introduce scientific themes to the general public and were widely successful in doing so.

(Library of Congress)

Lubbock remained until his death in 1913 in many ways a typical Victorian: absolutely secure in his privileged place in the world, wishing to help the worthy working poor help themselves, and certain of the Englishman's superiority to the savage races—a notion he saw as clearly connected to the civilizing project of British imperialism.

view. To make the case for the naturalistic evolution of man, Tylor argued, as Lubbock had, that savages could progress unassisted and that the development of culture was not the result simply of diffusion. Tylor's contribution to solving the problem of anthropogenesis was to classify the phenomena of culture and arrange them in probable order of evolution. He reconstructed the general course of human development as progressing through the stages of savagery, barbarism, and civilization. To reconstruct this order, Tylor introduced the doctrine of survivals, by which the anthropologist looked for surviving forms or relics of the past.

John McLennan (1827–1881) used a version of Tylor's doctrine of survivals to reconstruct the naturalistic evolutionary development of marriage customs. In *Primitive Marriage*, McLennan traced human marriage to its origins in primitive promiscuity and polyandry. Rather than having degenerated from some higher state, marriage had instead evolved from lower forms of association. The symbols of the present-day Victorian marriage ceremony were relics of what must have been the realities of the Stone Age past. Once McLennan reconstructed the causal developmental sequence of marriage customs, he could trace all similar present day symbols to the same primitive realities. Inspired by Lyell's yielding to Darwinism in 1863 and his subsequent work on *The Antiquity of Man*, McLennan argued for the long stretches of time during which humanity had evolved. In an article "The Early History of Man," McLennan summarized the tenets and methods of sociocultural evolutionism. These included a belief in human antiquity and opposition to biblical chronology, an argument for progressive development and against degenerationism, the comparative method, and the doctrine of survivals.

None of these three major sociocultural evolutionists interpreted human history or human progress in terms of racial conflict, as did the social Darwinists. In fact their idea of evolution was not even particularly Darwinian. Darwin favored connecting similar forms as branches of an evolutionary tree, tracing their diffusion from common origins. But the sociocultural evolutionists assumed the separate and independent origin of cultural forms and their advancement in parallel through time, all to prove that the development of humanity had occurred unassisted. At its base, such a set of assumptions reflects polygenism. The invention of human cultural forms occurred many times in many different places, the result of like minds responding to similar circumstances, and without divine help. The sociocultural evolutionists' vision of the human past was one of regular, continuous, gradual, unidirectional progress, excluding all divine intervention. It was a vision they shared with Spencer. Indeed, Lubbock, Tylor, and McLennan firmly endorsed Spencer's view of the stages of human progress represented by the various savage races of the world. This evolutionary framework was, as we will see, the paradigm against which early-twentieth-century cultural anthropology, led by Franz Boas, constituted itself.

In the meantime, however, the evolutionary worldview was entrenched in the institutions of Victorian anthropology. In 1871, after a decade's worth of struggle, the two major British anthropological societies, the liberal Darwinist Ethnological Society and the Anthropological Society of London, founded by the polygenist James Hunt, combined to form the Anthropological Institute of Great Britain and Ireland. Its establishment reflected the growth of anthropology as a profession that was no longer the exclusive domain of amateurs like Darwin and Spencer but now a field for specialists. The Institute's founding demonstrated that a reconciliation had been made between the two formerly warring societies on such previously divisive issues as monogenism and polygenism. Although many of the former Ethnologicals had strenuously objected to Hunt's polygenism and the conservative outlook of his society, indeed to the very name "anthropology" itself, the joining of the societies signaled that they had come to consensus. With polygenism explicitly in retreat, though its influence was subtly incorporated into the evolutionary worldview, and with the predominance of that world-view itself, there was now agreement on what the important issues were.

Bibliographic Essay

The material for this chapter was drawn from several different historical litera-tures, and the treatment of a complex period and topic was made even more dif-ficult by the fact that the literatures were almost entirely mutually exclusive. Writings by historians on Spencer and social Darwinism generally treat the topic of race only briefly. Meanwhile writers on the history of the race concept have largely ignored or given very short shrift to social Darwinism. There are a few exceptions to this larger pattern, and those are the works that have formed the basis for this chapter.

There is a library of writing on Charles Darwin himself. One of the best sources is the two-volume biography by Janet Browne, *Charles Darwin: Voyag-ing* (New York: Knopf, 1995) and *Charles Darwin: The Power of Place* (New York: Knopf, 2002). The best single-volume biography is Adrian Desmond and James Moore, *Darwin: The Life of a Tormented Evolutionist* (New York: Warner Books, 1991). Readers seeking a short introduction to Darwin and his times would be well served by Michael Ruse, *The Darwinian Revolution: Sci-ence Red in Tooth and Claw* (Chicago: University of Chicago Press, 1979). *On the Origin of Species* is available widely, usually in the sixth and final edition. A facsimile of the first edition is available as *On the Origin of Species* (Cambridge, MA: Harvard University Press, 1964).

The works above touch on Darwin's views of race (Ruse excepted). For the original, there are several editions of *The Descent of Man*. This chapter relied on Charles Darwin, *The Descent of Man and Selection in Relation to Sex* (Prince-ton: Princeton University Press, 1981). For a detailed look at Darwin's racial views see Nancy Stepan's *Idea of Race in Science* (Hamden, CT: Archon, 1982). On Darwin's dispute with Wallace over human origins see Malcolm Jay Kottler, "Alfred Russel Wallace, the Origin of Man, and Spiritualism," *Isis* 65, no. 227 (1974): 145–192.

There is a voluminous literature on social Darwinism, its history and its meaning, most of it conceived in reply to Richard Hofstadter's classic work, *Social Darwinism in American Thought* (originally published 1944 by Univer-sity of Pennsylvania Press, reissued in 1955 by Beacon Press). Subsequent histo-rians have taken issue with Hofstadter's definitions and generalizations, specifi-cally to his claim that social Darwinism was widespread throughout Anglo-America. Such rebuttals can be found in Robert C. Bannister, "'The Survival of the Fittest is Our Doctrine': History or Histrionics?" *Journal of the History of Ideas* 31 (1970): 377–398, also his *Social Darwinism: Science and Myth in Anglo-American Thought* (Philadelphia: Temple University Press, 1979); in R. J. Halliday, "Social Darwinism: A Definition," *Victorian Studies* 14 (1971): 389–405; and in Donald C. Bellomy, "'Social Darwinism' Revisited," *Perspectives in American History, New Series I* (1984): 1–129. Most of these have very little to say about the role of racial thinking in the work of social Darwinists, however, and the historiographic debates over the term will probably strike a noninitiate as hair-splitting, inconclusive, and confusing. For those seeking a path through them, the debates over social Darwinism have been clearly summarized and a newly inclusive definition for the term set out by Mike Hawkins in *Social Darwinism in European and American Thought, 1860–1945* (Cambridge: Cambridge University Press, 1997).

For the purposes of this chapter, and for those wishing to understand race and social Darwinism, the best sources remain Hofstadter's chapter on racism and imperialism; Greta Jones's *Social Darwinism in English Thought* (Brighton, Sussex, UK: Harvester, 1980), which includes a discussion on race and class (although Jones unhelpfully conflates social Darwinism with eugenics); and Gregory Claeys, "'The Survival of the Fittest' and the Origins of Social Darwinism," *Journal of the History of Ideas* 61 (2000): 223–240. On the German social Darwinist ideas of racial competition and struggle, and for insightful commentary on the role of collectivism in social Darwinism, see Richard Weikart, "The Origins of Social Darwinism in Germany," *Journal of the History of Ideas* 54 (1993): 469–488. On Ernst Haeckel, see Daniel Gasman, *The Scientific Origins of National Socialism: Social Darwinism in Ernst Haeckel and the German Monist League* (New York: American Elsevier, 1971). On Herbert Spencer's evolutionism and his racial views, see John S. Haller, *Outcasts from Evolution: Scientific Attitudes of Racial Inferiority, 1859–1900* (Urbana: University of Illinois Press, 1971), especially the chapter "From Biology to Sociology: Spencer and his Disciples." Haller's book, however, is repetitive and poorly written; his explanations of Spencer's philosophy are unclear and neglect the larger social Darwinist context. The best source on Spencer's racial views remains Spencer himself; his 1876 article on "The Comparative Psychology of Man," included in Michael Biddiss's anthology *Images of Race* (Leicester, UK: Leicester University Press, 1979) helped inform the discussion in this chapter. Background on Spencer and his science of society can be found in Robert L. Carneiro and Robert G. Perrin, "Herbert Spencer's Principles of Sociology: A Centennial Retrospective and Appraisal," *Annals of Science* 59 (2002): 221–261. Readers should be warned, however, that Carneiro and Perrin take the peculiar and distinctly ahistorical view that Spencer's science, its method, its theory, and even the facts he collected, should be revived and put into use by sociologists today. A more historical treatment of Spencer's philosophy can be found in Robert Richards's *Darwin and the Emergence of Evolutionary Theories of Mind and Behavior* (Chicago: University of Chicago Press, 1987). On Spencer's shift toward conservatism, see Mark Francis, "Herbert Spencer and the Myth of Laissez-Faire," *Journal of the History of Ideas* 39 (1978): 317–328.

The equally voluminous literature on the science of race in the latter half of the nineteenth century pays only glancing attention to social Darwinism. Nancy Stepan's *Idea of Race in Science* (Hamden, CT: Archon, 1982) contains a thorough discussion of physical anthropology and race in this period, on which the section in this chapter drew, but astonishingly mentions neither social Darwinism nor Spencer. The argument that there were "polygenist survivals" post-Darwin, and that these are evident in the physical anthropology of the late nineteenth century, comes from George Stocking, *Race, Culture and Evolution: Essays in the History of Anthropology* (Chicago: University of Chicago Press, 1982), especially the essay "The Persistence of Polygenist Thought in Post Darwinian Anthropology." Stepan concurs with and further develops Stocking's argument. Stocking treats Spencer's evolutionism, Lamarckianism and ties to social Darwinism in essays in *Race, Culture, and Evolution*, especially "The Dark-Skinned Savage: The Image of Primitive Man in Evolutionary Anthropology" and "Lamarckianism in American Social Science, 1890–1915." Stocking discusses Spencer and especially the sociocultural evolutionists Lubbock, Tylor, and McLennan at more length in George Stocking, *Victorian Anthropology* (New York: Free Press, 1987). An overview of Lubbock's life and work can also be found in the editor's introduction to John Lubbock's *Origin of Civilization and the Primitive Condition of Man* (originally published 1870), ed. Peter Riviere (Chicago: University of Chicago Press, 1978). Roger A. Pauly, Jr., makes the case for Lubbock's connection to the imperialist project in his unpublished Ph.D. dissertation, "Unnatural Selections: British Evolutionary Anthropology and the Civilizing Mission" (University of Delaware, 2000). On the debate between the degenerationists Argyll and Whately and the sociocuulutral evolutionists, see also Neal C. Gillespie, "The Duke of Argyll, Evolutionary Anthropology and the Art of Scientific Controversy," *Isis* 68 (1977): 40–54.

Too often historians are willing to exempt Darwin from the racial ideology and social Darwinist views held by his contemporaries and attribute these "perversions" of Darwin's thought to Spencer or to less "objective" social thinkers. Hofstadter's is a prime example of this argument: to him Darwinism was simply a "neutral tool" that could be put toward a number of different political ends, both conservative and liberal. Fortunately this kind of excision of Darwin from his social context is now being thrown into serious doubt by, among others,

Robert Young, in "Darwinism *is* Social," in *The Darwinian Heritage*, ed. David Kohn (Princeton: Princeton University Press, 1985, 609–638), and Jim Moore, "Socializing Darwinism: Historiography and the Fortunes of a Phrase," in *Science as Politics*, ed. Les Levidow (London: Free Association Books, 1986, 38–80).

4

The Hardening of Scientific Racism, 1900–1945

Despite Darwin's idea that there were no fixed divisions between species, let alone races, polygenist notions of race, which assumed that the divisions between races were ancient and fixed, thrived in the new evolutionary thought. Moreover, the idea articulated by Spencer, that evolution was a struggle between races rather than between individuals, became a dominant fixture of twentieth-century racial thought. Finally, the notion that there were several European races, such as those sketched by William Z. Ripley, would begin to loom large in the twentieth century.

Evolutionary thought grew into a significant ideology that can be called "scientific racism" at the end of the nineteenth and beginning of the twentieth century. Scientific racism was the result of two lines of scientific thought merging. First, new ideas about heredity provided an explanation of the way traits could be held stable for generation after generation. Second, ideas flowered about the supremacy of the north European races—what was called Aryanism or Teutonicism in the nineteenth century and Nordicism in the twentieth. These two lines of thought were conceptually distinct. That is, one could firmly believe in the notion that heredity was fixed and immune from environmental influences while rejecting the idea that the Nordics were the supreme race. Alternatively, one could believe in Nordicism and reject the findings of modern science regarding heredity. However, among some thinkers these two ideas joined in the eugenics movement and changed how the Western world thought about race.

The Problem of Heredity

After the publication of *On the Origin of Species*, Charles Darwin needed to answer a strong objection to his work: how were the characteristics that allowed organisms to survive transmitted from generation to generation? Natural selection turned on the idea that tiny advantages could accumulate in an organism's line of descent, but Darwin had no mechanism that could explain this process. Indeed, most ideas about heredity argued that it would be impossible for characteristics to be transmitted down the generations.

There were two fundamental problems. The first was "blending" inheritance. Darwin's theory depended on a beneficial trait in a parent generation being transmitted, more or less intact, to the offspring generation. The problem was that the dominant theory of inheritance did not allow for the survival of a trait in this fashion; rather, in succeeding generations a favorable trait would eventually be obliterated by other traits over time. So, if tallness of a plant was a beneficial trait, and two tall plants crossed to produce offspring, the offspring would not be as tall as the taller of its two parents but would be midway in height between the two. In artificial selection, the breeder could control crosses to ensure that a specific trait was selected for. However, Darwin's natural selection did not allow for a guiding hand in this manner. Hence, it was not clear exactly how an advantageous trait could be passed down without being swamped by random crosses with inferior types.

In a famous review of Darwin's *On the Origin of Species*, Fleeming Jenkin put the case for blending inheritance in explicitly racial terms. Jenkin argued that a white man who was shipwrecked on an island inhabited by Negroes would naturally rise to become their king. However his natural superiority over the savages would not last through generations as the superior white qualities would be swamped by the inferior Negro stock. "Can any one believe" asked Jenkin, "that the whole island will gradually acquire a white, or even a yellow population, or that the islanders would acquire the energy, courage, ingenuity, patience, self-control, endurance, in virtue of which qualities our hero killed so many of their ancestors, and begot so many children; those qualities, in fact, which the struggle for existence would select, if it could select anything?" (Jenkin 1867, 289–290)

To deal with the problem of blending inheritance, natural selection needed a mechanism that would allow for beneficial traits to be passed to succeeding generations intact and there was no clear idea what that mechanism could be.

The second problem natural selection faced was the inheritance of acquired characteristics. In the late twentieth century and continuing now into the twenty-first, the accepted idea is that heredity is largely isolated from environmental influences. In the nineteenth century, most ideas about heredity did not distinguish so sharply between heredity and environment. Indeed, such a distinction made little sense given widespread ideas about how an organism's characteristics were formed by the environment and passed along to subsequent generations. Most learned people of the nineteenth century believed in the doctrine of "inheritance of acquired characteristics." Most often associated with the

French evolutionist Jean Baptiste de Lamarck (1744–1829), the doctrine taught that environmental pressures change the physical nature of an organism and that these acquired characteristics were inherited by subsequent generations.

In this view, an organism acquired traits through interactions with the environment and passed those changes to offspring. Thus, there was no sharp distinction between heredity and environment. Even Darwin argued for a version of the doctrine of the inheritance of acquired characteristics when he put forth "pangenesis" as the mechanism by which characteristics were passed from generation to generation. Darwin argued that there were tiny particles that cells dissipated through the body and passed into the offspring. Because each part of the body manufactured its own particles, the environment could directly affect heredity as changes in bodily form that owed to the environment would be transmitted to the offspring. Darwin's theory of pangenesis gained few adherents and quickly disappeared as a mechanism for heredity after Darwin's death; however, most scientists continued to accept that traits acquired through environmental influences could be inherited biologically.

As early as the 1830s, the inherited nature of some mental diseases was widely understood in Great Britain. Early statistical measurements helped hospital administrators track the prevalence of certain diseases and conditions in certain families and lineages. Such knowledge of "good" and "bad" families was disseminated widely in marriage advice manuals. Although there was no clear idea that such conditions were immune from environmental influences, there was also a general belief that heredity and destiny were intertwined. There was also a notion that such pathological conditions were increasingly a matter of public concern. Utopian writers, such as William Lawrence and Thomas Edwards, claimed that the state should take control of marriage more firmly to insure that good lines propagated and poor ones were eliminated. William Farr, in a series of writings beginning in the 1830s, argued that the state should take an active role in guaranteeing the health of the British population by quarantining those with undesirable traits. Farr pointed to the success of stockbreeders and others in agriculture who controlled the breeding of their animals and crops to guarantee the best possible product.

Francis Galton

Most British intellectuals in the 1830s dismissed the utopian schemes of Farr and others who argued for controlled breeding, but they were taken up by Darwin's cousin, Francis Galton (1822–1911). Galton coined the phrase "nature versus nurture" and he came down strongly on the side of nature. Galton's early life and

Nineteenth-century British anthropologist Francis Galton (Library of Congress)

upbringing was much like his cousin's. He was born into a wealthy family and expected to become a physician. Also like Darwin, he was miserable at medical school. He was spared from completing his medical education by his father's death in 1844. Upon inheriting the family fortune, Galton was free to pursue his interest in natural history.

The kind of science Galton produced exemplified a widespread understanding in Great Britain about what counted as good science. Galton claimed to be a strict adherent to induction, the form of reasoning that moves from specific instances to a general rule. Following the philosophy of science laid down by Francis Bacon (1561–1626), most nineteenth-century British scientists argued that a good scientist proceeded by induction, gathering as many facts as possible without any theory or general principle that might prejudice a neutral and objective view of these facts. Darwin, for example, made much of his inductivist principles in *On the Origin of Species* although historians have shown that Darwin clearly had his theory of natural selection in mind and he set out to find examples to help him prove it.

Galton, however, seemed to be an avid inductivist who was convinced that the road to science was collecting and tabulating as many examples as possible. For Galton, the inductivist method helped him sidestep the central problem of the mechanism of heredity. Galton argued that we did not need to know the mechanism of heredity to see its effects. We could observe and enumerate how traits passed from generation to generation while remaining agnostic on the actual mechanics of how this occurred. In other words, as long as we could see the effects of heredity, we could control its deleterious social impacts.

The most gifted protégé of Galton, and a key figure in promoting Galtonian views of heredity and science, was Karl Pearson (1857–1936), who set out his views about science in an influential work, *The Grammar of Science* (1882). For Pearson, a good scientist avoided all speculation about unobservable entities and focused only on directly sensed evidence. Pearson argued that there was no point in trying to uncover the "real" causes of anything in science; they were, in principle, unknowable. However, the scientist could apply mathematics, in particular statistics, to scientific phenomena without actually committing to the existence of an underlying causal agent. In other words, if statistics showed that heredity worked in a particular manner, then the scientist's work was done.

The idea that the scientists should focus only on biological traits that could be directly measured and tabulated became known as biometrics. Pearson founded the journal, *Biometrika*, in 1901, which became the main outlet for statistical studies of the physical traits of organisms. This view of the sufficiency of statistical constructs to explain scientific phenomena would continue on into the twentieth century, particularly in psychometrics and IQ testing. Galton and Pearson are correctly seen as the founders of this approach and both contributed key ideas to the science of statistics.

One of Galton's most famous works makes his approach clear and underscores the social motivations of his work. In *Hereditary Genius*, published in 1869, Galton undertook a statistical analysis of "men of genius" in the United Kingdom. His book attempted to rank the geniuses in the country in order to determine if mental ability was inherited and concluded that it was. For Galton, society should take steps to ensure the emergence of more geniuses and fewer of lower intellectual ability. Galton believed that improving the race meant that the government should encourage breeding among the best people and take steps to keep the superior stocks from mixing with inferiors. The death of classical Greek civilization, for example, owed to the lax morality that discouraged marriage and to women of high ability refusing to become mothers. Additionally, "in a small sea bordered country, where emigration and immigration are constantly going on, and where the manners are as dissolute as were those of the Greeks . . . the purity of a race would necessarily fail" (Galton 1869, 331).

Galton did not shy away from racial interpretations of his data. He believed that Negroes were at least two grades below Anglo-Saxons in ability and intelligence. "Every book alluding to Negro servants in America is full of instances" of the half-witted nature of the race, he wrote, "I was myself much impressed by this fact during my travels in Africa" (Galton 1869, 328). Like Spencer, Galton believed that the inferior races were losing the evolutionary battle for existence in the face of their superior European conquerors. Galton also argued for a social program that would prevent the same fate for England, and he was very concerned about the low level of the common English population. "It seems to me," he concluded, "that the average standard of ability of the present time should be raised" because "the needs of centralization, communication, and culture, call for more brains and mental stamina than the average of our race possess" (Galton 1869, 332-333).

Hereditary Genius drew mixed reviews from the English press in the 1870s. Many scientists appreciated Galton's sophisticated statistical technique but many religious reviewers objected to his unapologetic naturalism, which seemed to leave no room for God's grace or people's control over their own salvation. Many reviewers criticized Galton's assumption that heredity and not environmental factors was the cause of genius, an idea that cut against most of the common thinking of the time. Galton argued that the numbers showed that the hereditary material was somehow immune from environmental influences, an idea that belied widely held ideas about the inheritance of acquired characteristics. But evidence for Galton's view would soon be forthcoming from German cytologists—scientists who study cells. However, Galton and Pearson would not necessarily appreciate the new evidence.

Hard Heredity

The move from "soft" heredity, which drew no sharp distinctions between heredity and environment, and "hard" heredity that did, had two scientific components. First, by the 1880s, advances in the microscope led cytologists, particularly German ones, to many new scientific discoveries: the nucleus of cells, for example, and the process of mitosis, wherein cells divide. In the 1880s, several German cytologists, including August Weismann, Moritz Nussbaum, Oscar Hertwig, and Albert Kölliker put forth a number of new ideas that joined these discoveries in cytology to inform scientific understanding of *Vererbung* or heredity.

Although most late-nineteenth-century German cytologists had similar findings and arguments, the most famous contribution was that of August Weismann, who argued that the body actually contained two kinds of cells. Most of the body was made up of somatic cells. Germ cells, by contrast, were found only in the gonads and produced the sperm and egg. Germ cells were the units of heredity and, unlike somatic cells, were immune to environmental influences. This separation of germ cells from somatic cells required a drastic reorientation of the common attitudes toward the body and reproduction. In Weismann's view, the body and all of its somatic cells were merely the conveyers of germ cells. The body did not really produce germ cells, it just transmitted them, unaltered, from generation to generation. This Weismann called the continuity of the germ plasm.

Weismann believed that his theory meant the death of the theory of acquired characteristics. In a rather grisly experiment, he cut the tails off mice, generation after generation. Yet each time a new generation of mice was born from mutilated parents, they were born with tails. Weismann pointed to this as proof that germ plasm was immune from environmental influences and acquired characteristics could not be transmitted from generation to generation.

The second major contribution to the new notion of heredity came from the work of the Austrian monk Gregor Mendel (1822–1884). In the 1860s, Mendel published a paper that argued that characteristics of pea plants were preserved as they passed down through generations. When he crossed tall pea plants with short pea plants, the resulting offspring were not medium in height but were almost uniformly tall. Mendel could calculate the ratio of tall with short pea plants and found that inheritance was always in a 3:1 ratio. Mendel argued that this could be explained by supposing that the units of inheritance, what he called "factors," existed in pairs in the plants. Crossing these factors brought mathematically precise and very predictable patterns of inheritance. Mendel published his work but it was ignored in the 1860s and for three decades afterward. But on the eve of the twentieth century, when many scientists were looking for a new theory of heredity they found Mendel's explanation very promising. Mendel's ideas dealt a serious blow to the theory of "blending" inheritance just as Weismann's work had to the theory of acquired characteristics.

There was no firm consensus over these issues at the dawn of the twentieth century. The biometricians, Galton's followers, did not immediately appreciate Mendelism because biometrics focused on continuous rather than discontinuous variations. Pearson, in particular, objected to Mendelism because of its

Austrian botanist and geneticist Gregor Mendel, ca. 1880 (Bettman/Corbis)

focus on discontinuous variations. It also violated his views on the place of unobservable entities in science with its talk of unobservable "factors" that caused these variations. Additionally, Lamarckians, particularly in France, resisted Weismann's theories of the continuity of germ plasm.

Nonetheless, the new scientific ideas had important implications for the development of racial ideologies. The notion that heredity was everything and environmental factors could not change the essence of a person's talents and abilities certainly resonated with racist notions that there was some inherited racial essence that could not be erased by education or civilization. To see how racial themes blended with the new ideas about heredity, we first need to look at the developing ideas about race among social thinkers.

The Rise of Nordicism

Nordicism and Civilization

William Z. Ripley's tripartite division of Europeans into Teutonic, Alpine, and Mediterranean races in 1899 was widely accepted even though no one could find a pure example of any of these races. A significant group of writers believed the most superior of the three was the Teutonic race, which was also called the Aryan race in the nineteenth century and came to be called the Nordic race in the twentieth.

The Nordicists added several important ideas to racial ideology. First was the notion that civilization itself was the product of race, and many Nordicists devoted their work to discovering the Nordic nature of all great civilizations of the past. The belief in Nordic superiority was not new at the end of the nineteenth century. Many writers in the United States before the Civil War trumpeted the superiority of the Teutons. The ancient Roman historian, Tacitus (ca. 55–120), expressed admiration for the Teutonic tribes who lived north of what Tacitus considered a decadent Rome. Many writers in the United States in the early nineteenth century took Tacitus's writings as proof that democracy as a form of government was actually an ancient practice that began in the woods of ancient Germany. These writers used this theory of the "Teutonic origin" of democracy as proof against conservative critics who argued that democracy was an inherently unstable form of government. Not so, they argued: democracy originated in the German tribes with their primitive parliaments and protorepresentative government and was therefore an ancient form of governance rather than an untested theory. The Teutonic tribes of Angles and Saxons brought this heritage to England; it then crossed the Atlantic to the United States. Hence, democracy was in some sense part of the racial heritage of the Germanic people who settled in the United States.

The second contribution of the Nordicists to racial thought was the claim that race, not nation or political alliance, was the basis of social order. In the late nineteenth century, the defense of democracy became deemphasized in favor of more general arguments that the very capacity for civilization was racial in nature. In the 1880s, during a lecture tour of the United States, writer Edward A. Freeman argued that there were three homes of the Teutonic race: the United States, England, and Germany. These nations, Freeman argued, should put their differences

Comte Joseph-Arthur de Gobineau, nineteenth-century French diplomat and proponent of racism (Harlingue-Viollet)

behind them, for they could surely rule the world. The division between superior Anglo-Saxons and inferior Celts as well as other lower races was succinctly stated by Freeman: "The best remedy for whatever is amiss in America would be if every Irishman killed a Negro and be hanged for it" (Freeman 1882, 200).

Comte Joseph-Arthur de Gobineau (1816–1882) gave one of the most widely read and elaborate defenses of the Teuton. Gobineau was from an aristocratic French family and was a firm believer that the aristocratic elite had always ruled the masses through their protection of virtue and honor, as had the ancient Teutons. In the modern age, the masses had risen and destroyed the natural order. Gobineau pointed to the political turmoil of the French Revolution wherein the ruling classes had been overrun by the masses.

Both the central ideas of Nordicism—that race was the basis of all civilization and that race must be the basis of political order—came together in Gobineau's most extended treatment of race, the *Essay on the Inequality of the Races* published in four volumes between 1853 and 1855. Gobineau was not concerned with biology as much as history and linguistics. He affirmed the widely accepted division of the races into white, black, and yellow, and introduced the idea that civilization itself was based on race. The white race, which Gobineau called the "Aryan" race, was the only one capable of creative thinking and civilization building. The downfall of such great civilizations as Egypt and Greece owed to the commingling of Aryan blood with that of the lesser races.

The Supremacy of Nordics

Houston Stewart Chamberlain (1855–1927) followed and extended Gobineau's theories. Although he was English by birth, Chamberlain was a fervent admirer of Germany, moving to Bayreuth, Germany, at the end of the nineteenth century. In 1899, Chamberlain published *Foundations of the Nineteenth Century*, which laid out his racial ideas in full. Like Gobineau, Chamberlain believed that race was the key to all of history and the only truly creative race was the Aryan. Much of the *Foundations* is devoted to showing that all great historical figures were, on close examination, Aryan. For example, Marco Polo, Copernicus, Galileo, and especially Jesus Christ were Aryans in Chamberlain's account.

Both Gobineau and Chamberlain were, in some significant sense, "racial mystics." Their discussion of the great Teutonic race was shot through with talk of German blood that mystically bound all Teutons together with a racial soul. Although Chamberlain accepted all the anthropological evidence for the existence of the Teutonic/Aryan/Nordic race, for him the reality of race turned on a spiritual sharing of the "race-soul." Hence, the importance Chamberlain placed on the supposed Aryan identity of Christ can be understood as an embrace of a mystical racism that had a spiritual, not materialistic, core.

A French writer, Vacher de Lapouge (1854–1936), firmly and forcefully rejected racial mysticism. Lapouge was the founder of a science he dubbed "anthroposociology." He was a tireless correspondent and organizer within the scientific community (he provided William Z. Ripley with photographs for Ripley's *Races of Europe*, for example). Lapouge was one of first to successfully develop a full-blown version of scientific racism. Lapouge grounded his theories of race firmly in Darwin rather than in some mystical "racial soul" and this would have profound influence on twentieth-century racial theories.

Lapouge's theories were developed most fully in two works: *Social Selection* (1896) and *The Aryan and His Social Role* (1899). For Lapouge, the key racial marker was the cephalic index, which anthropologists had used to divide the European population into different races based on the shape of their heads. Lapouge tied the index, not just to head shape, but also to a range of socially desirable characteristics. He was the champion of the dolichocephalic Aryans, long-headed, blond, blue-eyed, creative, strong, and natural leaders. By contrast, brachycephalic types were round-headed, dark-skinned, and timid. "Brachies," as Lapouge called them, were natural followers who did not have the imagination necessary to create and lead. Lapouge's "Dolichos" dominated northern Europe, England, and Germany. Additionally, Lapouge followed Gobineau in arguing that the French Revolution had destroyed the ancient aristocracies, which, according to Lapouge, had been dominated by Dolichos.

An outspoken atheist, Lapouge had no patience for Chamberlain and Gobineau's emphasis on a "race soul." Anthroposociology was completely materialist and rejected any and all appeals to any sort of quasi-religious mysticism. For Lapouge, the science spoke for itself and had no need for any other concepts— certainly not for any religious or moral ideas. He called for the elimination of all moral sentiment that would stand in the way of a massive breeding program that would eliminate racial inferiors. In his writings, Lapouge demanded that sentimentality, especially religious faith, blocked the necessary social reforms for the elimination of racial inferiors through selective breeding. Like Ernst Haeckel in Germany, Lapouge rejected all religion and all morality. He did not attempt to replace traditional morality with any other view and tipped into nihilism in pursuing the perfect breeding population.

Lapouge was also unusual in his embrace of "hard heredity." Most of his fellow French scientists still embraced versions of the inheritance of acquired characteristics, Jean Baptiste Lamarck being something of a national hero. Not so Lapouge, whose strict breeding program left no room for environmental improvements. For Lapouge, the only solution to the racial crisis would be the elimination of the inferior races. This cavalier attitude toward human life would be one of the key "contributions" that Darwinism made in Germany. By the dawn of the twentieth century, these ideas were in the air: the notion of a heredity immune from environmental influences and a notion of Nordic supremacy. These two views would be combined in the early twentieth century in the United States and Germany as part of a larger eugenics movement.

The Rise of Eugenics

Between 1900 and 1945 nearly every modernizing society had some form of eugenics movement. Recent work on the history of the eugenics movements underscores how diverse the ideologies and policies were that went under that name. Popular understanding of eugenics is often restricted to the horrors of Nazi Germany, but, in fact, leftists proclaimed their adherence to eugenic doctrines as much as those on the political right. In many countries, eugenics was confined to what we might think of as prenatal care, focusing on the "future generations" carried by pregnant women. In other countries, particularly those where Lamarckian doctrines were still scientifically respectable, eugenics focused as much on environmental improvement as it did on selective breeding.

Still, despite the diversity of eugenic doctrines, there were some commonalities. Eugenics was the idea that good people should be encouraged to reproduce and bad people should be discouraged from it. Taken in this light, eugenic thinking was a way to think about social problems in scientific terms. The decades between 1870 and 1939 were confusing and exciting times. Industrialization spread throughout western society; the focus of life was no longer the small town or the farm. The dawn of the twentieth century brought with it large, industrial cities and attendant labor unrest, urban poverty, and slums. The worldwide economy experienced a number of economic shocks, the largest of which was the Great Depression that began in 1929. This new social order included a new belief in the responsibility of the government to take an active part in solving social problems. The old, laissez-faire, free-market solutions proposed by writers like Herbert Spencer were seen as increasingly inadequate, even while many accepted his notions concerning racial struggle.

Eugenics and Race in the United States

In the United States, for example, the idea of an activist government in the early part of the twentieth century is often called "Progressivism." In the Progressive era, an increasing number of leaders called for the government to take action to regulate a capitalism that could no longer be controlled by Adam Smith's invisible hand. This view led to many governmental interventions such as the Sherman Anti-Trust Act (1890), the Food and Drug Act (1906), and the Federal Trade Commission (1914). The aim of legislative acts like these was to put issues of public concern under expert control so that the deleterious effects of industrialization could be predicted and the impacts minimized. If food, water, housing, and health care could be put under governmental control to make them safer, why not our breeding as well?

Although not all eugenicists in the United States were racists, certain key figures certainly were. In the United States, the doctrine of Nordic superiority had one of its most eloquent and forceful voices in Madison Grant (1865–1937). Much like Charles Darwin, Grant was not a scientist by training. Trained as an attorney, Grant was wealthy and had no need to practice his profession in order to make money and could therefore indulge his passion for natural history.

Like his close friend, President Theodore Roosevelt, Grant was very active in the nascent conservationist movement. He was a great organizer of causes for the environment and was an active member of the Save the Redwoods League and president of the Bronx Parkway Commission, which created the Bronx Zoo. Grant was instrumental in saving from extinction the American bison, whales, pronghorn antelopes, and bald eagles. He was a key figure in preserving pristine wilderness for future generations to enjoy. Just as he wanted to preserve the environment, Grant wanted to preserve the race; for him these were two sides of the same coin. Grant's racial *magnum opus* was published in 1916 as *The Passing of the Great Race or the Racial Basis of European History.*

Like Lapouge, Grant offered his racial theories as grounded in materialist science rather than on race mysticism. This was no accident, since Lapouge had read the entire book and offered his advice to Grant before publication. Grant celebrated the Nordic stock that made the original colonial population of the British colonies. The Nordics created the United States, according to Grant, but were in danger of being swamped by the inferior races in what he called the "survival of the unfit"(Grant 1916, 82). Grant blamed "sentimentalists" who held the "fatuous belief in the power of environment . . . to alter heredity." Not so, Grant declared: "Speaking English, wearing good clothes, and going to school does not transform a Negro into a white man."

Immigration was a similar threat. "We shall have a similar experience with the Polish Jew," Grant warned, "whose dwarf stature, peculiar mentality, and ruthless concentration on self-interest are being engrafted upon the stock of the nation" (Grant 1916, 14). The danger, Grant warned, was allowing more than one race in the same geographical area under the common "melting pot" notion that

Madison Grant (1865–1937)

American lawyer, conservationist, and eugenicist, Grant was a key figure in the pop- ularization of Nordic supremacy in the United States and Europe. Born into a wealthy and established New England family, Grant was educated at Yale (B.A. 1887) and Columbia (LL.B., 1890). A substantial inheritance, however, relieved Grant from the burdens of everyday work, leaving him free to pursue his interest in political reform and natural history.

Grant was a member of many exclusive and established private clubs in the Northeast and it was his membership in one of them, the Boone and Crockett Club, that brought his first substantial project to life. Grant proposed to fellow member, Theodore Roosevelt, that the Club create a wildlife sanctuary just out- side New York City. Roosevelt, like Grant, was a big-game hunter and was very con- cerned with the rapidly disappearing American wilderness. The wildlife sanc- tuary eventually became the Bronx Zoo and was the first of many triumphs Grant had as a leading figure of the American conservationist movement.

For Grant, the conservation of nature and the conservation of the Nordic race went hand in hand. Like many upper-class Americans of his generation he was deeply concerned with the growing immigration of "undesirable stocks" into the United States. Grant's *magnum opus, The Pass- ing of the Great Race* published in 1916

(Courtesy of the Save the Redwoods League)

was an unapologetic defense of what Grant considered the "pioneering type" that made the country great: the Nordic. For Grant, the Nordic race was in danger of being swamped by the inferior racial types that were coming to the country from southern and eastern Europe. Grant's book became a touchstone for Nordicists both here and abroad, most notably for Adolph Hitler who wrote approvingly of Grant's book in his 1924 autobiography, *Mein Kampf.*

Well-connected politically, Grant was a key figure in orchestrating the passage of the 1924 Immigration Restriction Act, which prevented further immigration from those races he considered inferior. However, the increased internal migration of African Americans out of the Deep South and into the North led him to further despair that he might be losing the battle to maintain the racial purity of the United States. His last book, *Conquest of a Continent* reiterated the Nordic supremacy of *The Passing of the Great Race.* However, Grant's time had passed and *Conquest* was roundly criticized for its racism. Grant died of nephritis in 1937.

the environment would erase racial differences. Grant argued, "Whether we like to admit it or not, the result of the mixture of two races, in the long run, gives us a race reverting to the more ancient, generalized and lower type. The cross between a white man and an Indian is an Indian . . . and the cross between any of the three European races and Jew is a Jew" (Grant 1916, 15–16). The solution, Grant declared, was two-fold: man "can breed from the best, or he can eliminate the worst by segregation or sterilization" (Grant 1916, 47). Grant believed that it would be very difficult to increase breeding of the best types, so, "under existing conditions the most practical and hopeful method of race improvement is through the elimination of the least desirable elements in the nation by depriving them of the power to contribute to future generations" (Grant 1916, 49).

Grant's call for a eugenically pure United States merged with wider concerns about the degeneration of inferior social types. This view was cast in terms of the new thinking about heredity, epitomized by Richard L. Dugdale's 1874 *The Jukes: A Study in Crime, Pauperism, Disease, and Heredity*. Dugdale's work on the Jukes was a family study in which the researcher studied an impoverished family in order to discover how social problems were transmitted through generations. Dugdale found that the family of Jukes, a fictional name for a real family, was predisposed toward a life of crime and poverty. But, in keeping with commonly held views of heredity of the time, Dugdale argued that by providing education and medical care, this hereditary tendency toward crime in the Jukes family would be reversed. In other words, Dugdale argued that environmental changes could lead to changes in an inherited condition.

In 1915, eugenicist Arthur Estabrook published a second edition of Dugdale's classic work, *The Jukes in 1915*, which reflected the new thinking about heredity. Estabrook called for eugenic segregation and sterilization as the solution to the problem of the Jukes, claiming that environmental changes would do nothing to change their inherited tendency toward crime. This change in the evaluation of the Jukes family indicated that the eugenic proposals of the late nineteenth century differed from those of the early twentieth century, which came in the wake of Mendelism and Weismannism.

The first eugenics organization in the United States was the Eugenics Committee of the American Breeder's Association (ABA) formed in 1906. The ABA was dedicated to the development of American agriculture, fostering cooperation between farmers and ranchers, who had been developing their stocks of animals and crops through selective breeding for some time, and the growing number of academic biologists interested in developing the mathematical and theoretical understanding of heredity.

The Eugenics Committee of the ABA was chaired by David Starr Jordan, the president of Stanford, and included a number of prominent biologists: Vernon L. Kellogg, William E. Castle, and Luther Burbank. Eventually the work of the Committee became so wide-ranging that the ABA reorganized into the American Eugenics Association in 1913, and they began publishing the *Journal of Heredity* that same year.

Among those involved with the Eugenics Committee was Charles B. Davenport (1866–1944). Davenport had been trained as an engineer as an undergraduate and received his Ph.D. in biology from Harvard in 1892. He was a professor at the University of Chicago until 1904, when he convinced the Carnegie Institution to underwrite a biological laboratory at Cold Spring Harbor in New York. The laboratory was the Station for the Study of Experimental Evolution and leaped to the forefront of the scientific study of heredity with Davenport firmly in control.

Davenport was an established scientist; he had served on the editorial board of Karl Pearson's *Biometrika* and had published some of the first papers by an American scientist on Mendel. Davenport embraced both the biometric approach and Mendelism, even though the two schools of thought were in the midst of a feud over the nature of continuous versus discontinuous variations. This reflected Davenport's plan for Cold Spring Harbor, where he aimed to unite theories of heredity, evolution, and cytology. Davenport himself contributed studies of heredity in mice, poultry, canaries, and horses using both biometrical and Mendelian approaches. But Davenport was also interested in human heredity. He published papers on the Mendelian inheritance of human eye color and a paper on the complex inheritance patterns in human skin color.

Davenport's interest in human heredity translated into a branch of the Station at Cold Spring Harbor. Davenport petitioned Mary Harriman, heir to her husband's railroad fortune, to underwrite the Eugenics Records Office (ERO) at Cold Spring Harbor in 1910. Davenport chose Harry H. Laughlin (1880–1943) as the administrator of ERO. Laughlin was teaching biology in the agriculture school of the Missiouri State Normal School and had been corresponding with Davenport on matters of heredity since 1907. In 1910, Davenport hired Laughlin to overtake the administrative needs of ERO. Laughlin was dedicated to the twin purposes of the ERO: to undertake serious research in human heredity and to educate the public about eugenics.

Unlike researching heredity in farm animals or insects, scientists could not experiment on human beings, and the long generations of humans made tracing lineages difficult within the lifetime of a researcher. To avoid these problems, Laughlin and Davenport set out to collect family histories by sending specially trained eugenics fieldworkers out to question families about their history of disease, feeblemindedness, or other eugenic disabilities. The fieldworkers would visit families with questionnaires and try to collect information

relevant to the goals of the ERO. They would then take the collected information and create family histories that could yield useful information for inherited traits. Some traits actually followed a strict pattern of Mendelian inheritance. By the mid-1910s, researchers at the ERO had discovered a number of
them including polydactylism (having more than 10 fingers or toes) and Hunt-
ington's chorea, for example.

But the family histories went far beyond these physiological traits and
included characteristics such as "feeblemindedness"—a catch-all phrase that
covered not only what we might consider mental retardation but also any failure
in scholastic performance—pauperism, alcoholism, criminality, musical ability,
and other social traits interpreted as owing entirely to heredity. One famous
example was a 1919 report Davenport prepared for the Navy on "thalassophilia"
or love of the sea. Davenport argued that the tendency for naval officers to come
from the same family owed to a Mendelian trait for the love of the sea. Ignoring
possible environmental pressures for sons to follow in their father's footsteps,
Davenport reasoned that since the "tendency to wander" was a racial trait, as it
appeared in Gypsies, Comanches, and Huns, the tendency to wander on the sea
must also be an inherited trait.

Eugenics, however, was never just a science destined for the ivory tower:
another part of its mission was to translate scientific truths, like thalassophilia,
into public policy. Eugenicists called for two different kinds of social programs.
A 1926 popularized pamphlet, "A Eugenics Catechism," published by the American Eugenics Society, spelled out the two approaches. Negative eugenics dealt
"with the elimination of the dysgenic elements from society. Sterilization, immigration legislation, laws preventing the fertile unfit from marrying, etc., come
under this head." By contrast, positive eugenics dealt "with the forces which tend
upward, or with the furtherance of human evolution. Encouraging the best
endowed to produce four or more children per family, encouraging the study of
eugenics by all, etc., are positive eugenics" (American Eugenics Society 1926,
n.p.). These policy options had no greater champion in the United States than
Laughlin, who tirelessly promoted eugenic policies throughout the nation.

Although both positive and negative eugenics were possible, Laughlin, like
his friend Madison Grant, concentrated on the negative aspects. As the "Eugenics Catechism" made clear, there were three policy choices for proponents of
negative eugenics: sterilization, immigration control, and laws preventing marriage of eugenic undesirables. Eugenicists had various degrees of success with
these programs of action.

As far as race was concerned, the option of preventing eugenically undesirable marriages was a nonissue. Marriages between whites and blacks were
legally prohibited long before eugenics became a popular doctrine. Laws against

miscegenation, interracial marriage, were a mainstay of American legal culture beginning in the eighteenth century and were not declared unconstitutional by the US Supreme Court until 1967. Even the authoritarian Madison Grant admitted that "in a democracy" it would be "a virtual impossibility to limit by law the right to breed to a privileged and chosen few" (Grant 1916, 47).

Although eugenicists had limited impact on the racial aspect of marriage laws they were much more successful in limiting immigration, mainly because their concerns dovetailed with widespread anxieties about increased immigration into the United States after World War I. Although the United States has long proclaimed itself a nation of immigrants, such a view waxed and waned according to economic and social concerns. In the late nineteenth century, for example, concerns that cheap labor from China was swamping out "white" jobs in California led to the Chinese Exclusion Act of 1882, which cut off all immigration from China. Beginning around the same time, the nature of immigration from Europe began changing as more and more immigrants arrived from southern and eastern Europe, many of them Jewish and Catholic.

By the 1910s immigration had touched off a reaction from many circles. Labor leaders worried about the new immigrants taking jobs from their traditional constituencies, and many conservative Americans were concerned that the new immigrants were political radicals espousing Marxist ideas. Many Americans worried that the immigrants were Jewish or Catholic, and thus unable to assimilate into the traditionally Protestant United States.

Eugenicists expressed concern that the new immigrants were from inferior racial stock and would bring with them the biological degradation of the United States. Madison Grant was especially concerned with the influx of eastern and southern European immigrants, for example the "swarm of Polish Jews" who were coming to New York City. "While he is being elbowed out of his own home," Grant despaired, "the American looks calmly abroad and urges on others the suicidal ethics which are exterminating his own race" (Grant 1916, 81). His chief disciple Lothrop Stoddard agreed: "even within the white world," Stoddard wrote in *The Rising Tide of Color* in 1921, "migrations of lower human types like those which have worked such havoc in the United States must be rigorously curtailed. Such migrations upset standards, sterilize better stocks, increase low types, and compromise national futures more than war, revolutions, or native deterioration" (Stoddard 1921).

The eugenicists presented their concerns about immigration before Congress in the early 1920s. Representative Albert Johnson, who chaired the House Committee on Immigration and Naturalization and was also an honorary president of the Eugenics Research Association, brought Harry Laughlin before the committee's 1922 hearings on immigration reform as an "expert eugenic witness." Laughlin came prepared with an elaborate statistical analysis that tracked the relationships between social ills and race. As early as 1914, Laughlin had worked with Judge Harry Olson of the Psychopathic Laboratory of the Municipal Court of Chicago on a study that showed that immigrants were hereditarily predisposed to crime; over 75 percent of the juvenile delinquents in Chicago had foreign-born parents, predominantly Slavic or Italian. Pointing to poverty as the cause of crime was mistaken, Laughlin and Olson argued, because poverty was created by poor genetic constitution.

In his testimony before the House Committee, Laughlin extended this kind of analysis to include not just crime, but a host of "inadequacies" such as feeblemindedness, insanity, epilepsy, tuberculosis, blindness, deafness, deformity, and pauperism. "The outstanding conclusion," Laughlin declared for the committee, "is that . . . the recent immigrants, as a whole, present a higher percentage of inborn socially inadequate qualities than do the older stocks" (Laughlin 1922, 755).

In 1924, Laughlin added another arrow to his quiver: the intelligence test. Alfred Binet had developed intelligence tests in France in 1904 as a way to help the French government educate children, especially those who had trouble learning in the regular curriculum. In 1908, psychologist Henry H. Goddard brought the tests to the United States. As the director of the Vineland Training School for Feeble-Minded Boys and Girls, Goddard sought a tool to help him classify his charges to provide them with an education fitting their abilities. Goddard eventually published a eugenic family study of his own, *The Kallikak Family: A Study in the Heredity of Feeblemindedness* in 1912.

Intelligence testing received an enormous boost during World War I when Stanford psychologist Robert M. Yerkes and others developed a series of tests to help the Army with the induction process. The aim of the Army tests was not to detect the feebleminded but to sort draftees into appropriate positions in the military. The Army did not want to have highly intelligent applicants assigned to ditch-digging and dull draftees sent to Officer Training School. After the war, intelligence testing generally, and the Army tests in particular, took on new life. The Army tests showed that black soldiers were far less intelligent than white solders. This surprised no one and created little stir in the academic community until these conclusions were challenged in the 1930s. Of more immediate importance during the 1920s and the great immigration scare were the results that pointed to racial differences among the white inductees. One of the staff psychologists who had worked with the Army, Carl Brigham, published a volume in 1923 from the Army data. Brigham declared that only applicants from the Nordic countries fared well on the intelligence tests and recommended strict laws forbidding race mixing and radically curtailing immigration of Alpine and Mediterranean stocks. In the meantime, Henry H. Goddard gave a series of intelligence tests to recent immigrants on Ellis Island and declared that two out of five were feebleminded.

The result of this widespread intelligence testing together with all of Laughlin's other data and the enormous political popularity of immigration restriction caused Congress to pass the Immigration Restriction Act in 1924. Under the 1924 Act, immigration quotas would be set according to the population ratios that existed in the United States according to the 1880 census. The reason for choosing the census from four and a half decades before the Act was passed was explicitly racial: that year predated the waves of immigration from southern and eastern Europe. Hence, immigration was encouraged from the Nordic countries and discouraged from the Alpine and Mediterranean countries, just as Madison Grant had hoped.

The 1924 Immigration Restriction Act had an important effect on racial theorists in the United States. Madison Grant's *Passing of the Great Race* paid almost no attention to "the Negro Problem" in the United States, instead focusing on the dangers of inferior white racial types overtaking the heroic Nordics. However, the 1924 Act solved the problem of inferior white races coming into the country. Additionally, World War I brought with it the "Great Migration" of blacks from the rural south to the urban north as they attempted to leave the authoritarian Jim Crow system, the crushing poverty of the tenant farming system, and systematic disenfranchisement. Grant, and others, despaired at the growing number of dark faces they saw on the city streets and declared that something must be done about it. In his last book, *Conquest of a Continent*, published in 1933 Grant declared that, "The Negro problem must be taken vigorously in hand by the Whites without delay. States which have no laws preventing the intermarriage of white and black should adopt them" (Grant 1933, 288). Consequently, beginning in the 1930s American scientists lost sight of the different white races and focused increasingly, if not exclusively, on the "black" and "white" races.

The third program of negative eugenics was sterilization. Madison Grant had proposed mass sterilization, "beginning always with the criminal, the diseased, and the insane, and extending gradually to types which may be called weaklings rather than defectives, and perhaps ultimately to worthless race types" (Grant 1916, 47). However, unlike immigration restriction, in the United States sterilization was not targeted racially as Grant had urged. The involuntary sterilization of individuals who had become public charges, especially those institutionalized, was a patchwork affair in the United States, varying widely from state to state and from institution to institution. The first law requiring compulsory sterilization of criminals, idiots, rapists, or imbeciles was passed in 1907 in Indiana. By 1922, seventeen other states had similar statutes on the books. These laws were not racially targeted but were aimed at institutionalized people

Harry H. Laughlin (1880–1943)

Born in Oskaloosa, Iowa, Harry Laughlin was raised in Missouri. He received a college degree in 1900 from North Missouri State Normal School in Kirksville, Missouri. He went onto to Iowa State College where he studied for a short time without receiving an advanced degree. Between 1900 and 1907, he taught high school biology and served in various administrative posts in the school system in Kirksville. In

(Courtesy of Harry H. Laughlin Collection/Pickler Library/Truman State University)

1907, he took a post in the agriculture school at North Missouri State Normal School where he had received his degree.

In 1907, Laughlin began corresponding with Charles B. Davenport, who had founded the Station for Experimental Evolution at Cold Spring Harbor. Davenport was impressed with Laughlin's enthusiasm for matters concerning heredity and offered Laughlin an administrative post in 1910, directing the Eugenics Record Office (ERO) at Cold Spring Harbor.

At ERO, Laughlin trained eugenics fieldworkers who collected vast amounts of data on the family histories of individuals they had interviewed. Laughlin worked hard to organize and present the data on the dangers of inferior breeding that emerged from the fieldworkers' efforts. He also worked hard to present the case for eugenic sterilization. By 1919, Laughlin had amassed a thirteen-hundred-page document on the scientific and legal case for the eugenic sterilization of undesirable individuals but was unable to find a publisher. Laughlin, undaunted, continued to collect data, working closely with Judge Harry Olson of the Chicago Psychopathic Laboratory on the inherited nature of crime.

In 1922, Laughlin published a meticulous and detailed study entitled *Eugenical Sterilization in the United States*, which catapulted him into the first rank of eugenic experts in the United States. His stature was such that he was asked to serve as an expert witness on the eugenic dangers of immigration in the 1920s in a series of hearings that led to the passage of the Immigration Restriction Act of 1924. Laughlin also served as an expert witness for the state of Virginia in the case of *Buck v. Bell* that eventually led the Supreme Court to find that involuntary sterilization was not a violation of the Constitution.

In 1936 the University of Heidelberg, by then under firm Nazi control, awarded Laughlin an honorary doctorate for his tireless efforts at promoting eugenics. However, in the United States, Laughlin's star was fading. Eugenics was increasingly seen as a political campaign with scientific dressing rather than as a pure scientific program. The overt racism of the Nazi regime, moreover, made eugenics increasingly unpopular as a political program. The Carnegie Foundation, which had underwritten Laughlin's efforts at ERO, withdrew its support in 1938 and he moved back to his hometown of Kirksville where he died in 1943.

who had, for one reason or another, become charges of the state. The reasons for these laws, moreover, were not exclusively eugenical: some physicians believed that sterilization lowered the sex drive, making it easier to manage people under institutional care. Others simply did not want those who had shown a propensity to become public charges to have children for whom they could not care.

As with immigration reform, the champion of compulsory sterilization was Harry Laughlin, who believed that at least ten percent of the population was defective and needed sterilization. He published a number of works between 1914 and 1922 that outlined the legal aspects of involuntary sterilization. The key legal problem was that sterilizing people against their will faced the constitutional objection of denying people their rights without due process of law. Laughlin drafted, and urged states to adopt, a "Model Sterilization Law," designed to withstand constitutional challenges.

In 1927, Laughlin played a key role in the Supreme Court decision in *Buck v. Bell*, which held that involuntary sterilization was constitutional. The state of Virginia had attempted to sterilize Carrie Buck, feebleminded mother of a feebleminded child, under a sterilization statute based on Laughlin's Model Sterilization Law. At the trial to determine the constitutionality of the measure, Laughlin served as an expert witness, testifying that Carrie Buck's immorality and feeblemindedness were hereditary in nature. In 1927 the Supreme Court decided that Virginia's actions were constitutional. The renowned jurist, Oliver Wendell Holmes, Jr., in issuing the court's opinion wrote, "It is better for all the world if, instead of waiting to execute degenerate offspring for crime or to let them starve for their imbecility, society can prevent those who are manifestly unfit from continuing their kind. The principle that sustains compulsory vaccination is broad enough to cover cutting the Fallopian tubes. . . . Three generations of imbeciles are enough" (*Buck v. Bell*, 208).

Despite the triumph in *Buck*, sterilization in the United States remained a haphazard affair. The nature of the American federal system left the enactment of sterilization statutes in the hands of state governments, which meant there was no central authority for making sterilization decisions. Moreover, despite *Buck*, there were legal concerns as laws needed to be carefully drafted in order to pass constitutional muster. Moreover, the guarantees of freedom of speech meant that involuntary sterilization was always open to public criticism. The Roman Catholic Church was a powerful critic of involuntary sterilization and many scientists, including geneticist Herbert Spencer Jennings and political scientist Joseph Gilman, took public stands against Laughlin's policy recommendations. Despite the controversies surrounding involuntary sterilization, however, between 60,000 and 90,000 Americans were sterilized under various state programs in the twentieth century.

German Rassenhygiene

For many the very term "eugenics" is equivalent to Nazi racism and the genocide of Jews, Gypsies, and others under the Nazi regime. However, it bears repeating that nearly every industrialized country embraced eugenic doctrines in the early twentieth century. Only in Nazi Germany, however, did eugenical thinking play a substantial role in genocide. There was no inevitable relationship between eugenics, even racist eugenics, and genocide, but this does not change the fact that under the Nazi regime, genocide was the result.

Just as the United States had Madison Grant, Germany had its own champion of Nordicism in Hans F. K. Günther (1891–1968). His most popular work, *Rassenkunde des deutschen Volkes* (*Racial Studies of the German People*) was published in 1922 and went through fourteen editions by 1930. Günther drew on all those who went before him, including Gobineau, Chamberlain, and Grant, but his greatest influence was Lapouge. Like Lapouge, Günther presented himself as a pure scientist, unaffected by sentimentality and race mysticism. For Günther, like Lapouge and Grant, science had proven that the Nordic was the best race

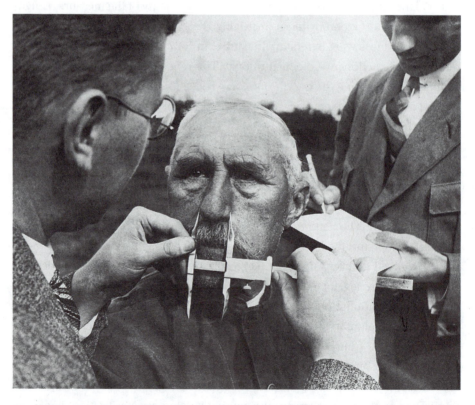

Nazi officials use calipers to measure an ethnic German's nose. The Nazis developed a system of facial measurement that supposedly determined racial descent. (Hulton-Deutsch Collection/Corbis)

and the Nordic's natural home was Scandinavia, Germany, Britain, Holland, and the United States. Günther accepted Lapouge's estimate that there were 25 million Nordics in the United States and 10 million in Britain.

Günther joined the Nazi party in 1932, a year before Hilter's rise to power. In 1933, Günther was given a chair at the University of Jena, Ernst Haeckel's old university. Although the faculty at the university objected to his appointment, Lapouge, who wrote a stirring letter of recommendation, guided it along. In fact, Günther's position was professor of anthroposociology, the field named by Lapouge. Wilhelm Frick, the Nazi official in charge of the region, eventually appointed Günther over faculty objections. Hitler himself attended Günther's inaugural address.

Günther was the most famous of the Nordicist writers in Germany, but Nordicist doctrines also appeared from other scientists who embraced eugenics. One of the most important was Alfred Ploetz (1860–1940). Ploetz's book *The Fitness of Our Race and the Protection of the Weak*, published in 1895, underscored the same question that Darwin had faced: does the modern world protect the weak from extermination and thus operate against natural selection? Herbert Spencer's solution to this problem was to embrace unfettered competition and a minimalist government. Ploetz was a socialist and rejected Spencerian laissez-faire in favor of governmental programs to improve the environment and to improve human breeding: improving hygiene not only for individuals, but also for the race. Ploetz coined a new term for his program: *Rassenhygiene* or "race hygiene."

What Ploetz meant by "race" was not always clear in his writing. At times he wrote as if the Germans were a race, at other times as if all white people were a race, and still other times he wrote as if he meant the entire "human race." That being said, there is no doubt that he considered the white race, and the Nordic race particularly, to be superior to all others. Ploetz was a member of a secret Nordicist organization called the Mittgartbund. In 1905 Ploetz and others founded the Society for Racial Hygiene, and Ploetz organized a secret Nordic society within that group. By 1909, the secret became public when membership in the Society for Racial Hygiene was limited to "whites" or "Nordics." However, and unlike the Nazi theorists who would follow him, Ploetz believed that German Jews were included in the broad category of "Aryan" since they had intermingled with the Germans for so long.

Another important founder of German eugenics was Wilhelm Schallmayer (1857–1919), whose first eugenic work was published in 1891 as *Concerning the Threatening Physical Degeneration of Civilized Humanity*. Here, Schallmayer warned of the increasing drag that "defective individuals" had on the selection process and the welfare of the German nation. Schallmayer achieved a certain measure of fame when he won a prize in a contest sponsored by Friedrich Alfred Krupp, heir to an arms-manufacturing fortune amassed by his father. Krupp had sponsored an essay contest, judged by Ernst Haeckel, on the question, "What can we learn from the theory of evolution about internal political development and state legislation?" Schallmayer's answer rejected capitalism and minimalist government, just as Ploetz had earlier, and called for state management of both economic resources and racial stock through restriction of marriage of criminals, the insane, the feebleminded, and others who suffered from hereditary defects. Schallmayer rejected Nordicism and spoke out frequently against mixing the mysticism of Nordicism with the scientific program of eugenics.

In the Weimar Republic, the democratic government established after World War I and eventually replaced by the Nazi regime, eugenics was a topic of national concern. In 1927 the Kaiser Wilhelm Institute for Anthropology, Human Genetics, and Eugenics (KWI) was established and soon became an important center for the study of *Rassenhygiene*. KWI was a direct response by Weimar officials to the support the United States provided to eugenics and was dedicated to the study of hereditary diseases, crime, mental illness, and the race. The Institute had three divisions: Eugen Fischer (1874–1967) was the head of the institute as a whole and also of the department of anthropology, Hermann Muckerman (1877–1962) was the head of the eugenics department, and Otmar von Verschuer (1896–1969) was the head of the department of human heredity.

Fischer was a pioneer of a new kind of anthropology. Traditionally, anthropology was confined to the measurement of physical features and classification of people into racial types. Fischer, however, embraced the new thinking about heredity and expanded anthropology to include the study of heredity, especially as it related to mental and social traits. He was a follower of Günther's teachings about racial purity and the danger of race mixing.

Muckerman was a former Jesuit priest and did not take race as a particular object of study. His Catholicism forced him to abandon his advocacy of sterilization after the Pope condemned the procedure in 1930. When the Nazis came to power in 1933, he was replaced by Fritz Lenz (1887–1976) who was more reliably racialist in his outlook, although he did not share the rabid anti-Semitism of the Nazi regime.

Verschuer was an outspoken anti-Semite and an important figure in the development of "twin studies." Identical twins, because they share identical genetic composition, had been recognized as key instruments in the study of heredity at least since Galton. Verschuer published an extensive study of hundreds of pairs of twins in 1933 to sort out the relative effects of heredity in relationship to the environment. This work would take on grotesque forms under the Nazi regime. Verschuer arranged for his student, Joseph Mengele, to be the camp doctor at Auschwitz. Mengele sent back body parts, particularly eyes, from twins who were shipped to the camp. Mengele also conducted studies at Auschwitz by injecting Jews, Gypsies, and others with typhus and typhoid to determine if resistance to disease was racial in nature.

As the careers of the directors of KWI show, some scientists suffered under Nazi rule, while others flourished. When Adolph Hitler came to power in 1933, Nazi Germany overtook the United States as the leading eugenical state. Rudolph Hess, a high-level Nazi functionary, made the phrase "National Socialism is Nothing but Applied Biology" famous, but it actually originated in the medical literature that embraced National Socialism even before 1933.

Historians have conceptualized the applied biology of the Nazis in two ways. The first is the "selectionist" metaphor, which viewed the world as engaged in a struggle of race against race, and the survival of the fittest demanded racial purity and the elimination of racial inferiors. This view is clearest in Nazi propaganda calling for the elimination of Jews, Gypsies, and Slavs as a Darwinian imperative. The second is the "organicist" metaphor in which society is like an organism and each group within society needed to keep in its place for the organism to function correctly. In Nordicist terms, this meant that the Nordics would be the leaders, the brain, and the Alpine and Mediterranean races would be the workers, the hands or feet. This view accounts for Nazi propaganda that painted Jews as "parasites" on the Aryan body. Rats were a common Nazi metaphor for Jews; the Nazis argued that such parasites needed to be eliminated.

Eugenic laws came quickly under the Nazi regime. A few months after coming to power, the Nazi government passed the Law for the Prevention of Genetically Diseased Offspring, aimed at sterilizing those carrying hereditary defects. The Nazis instituted an elaborate system of "Genetic Health Courts" to ensure that all whom they sterilized had adequate legal protections. Across the Atlantic, American eugenicists were delighted. Harry Laughlin boasted that the German law was based on his own Model Sterilization Law. Indeed, Laughlin received an honorary doctorate from the University of Heidelberg in 1936 for his work in eugenics. Paul Popenoe editorialized in the *Journal of Heredity* that the German law was not racist in origin and the legal safeguards in place would prevent any possible abuse. A few months later, American eugenicists greeted with joy the extension of the sterilization laws to cover "habitual criminals." American eugenicists admired the German system which, unlike the frustrating patchwork state-by-state system in the United States, enjoyed a strong central authority to guarantee the eugenic purity of the country. Further laws followed the sterilization law. In 1935, Hitler signed into law three measures often called the "Nuremberg Laws." These laws stripped non-Aryans of citizenship, prohibited the marriage of Jews and Aryans, and required all couples wishing to marry to submit to medical examinations to ensure the purity of the race. By 1939, the urge to purify the race would take another step beyond preventing the conception of inferior children: the elimination of children whose lives the Nazi government deemed not worth living.

In 1939 Hitler signed an order directing physicians to determine if institutionalized patients who were incurably ill should be granted a mercy killing by the state. This would relieve the state and the German people of carrying the load of "racially valueless" people. By 1941, the Nazis had euthanized over 70,000 hospitalized people under this program. The Nazis tested and improved many of the technical aspects of the Shoah, or Holocaust, in the medical elimination of lives deemed not worth living: the gassing, the transport of prisoners so as to not induce panic, and the use of these deaths to advance medical knowledge.

The Nazi regime, of course, culminated in the paroxysm of destruction called the Shoah. Scholars have written literally thousands of books on the Nazi genocide of Jews, Gypsies, and others in the search for an explanation for these atrocities. Scientific ideas about race certainly were not solely responsible for all the horrors produced by Nazis, but it is worth noting two aspects of science that were significant and tell us something about the relationship between science and society. One of the lessons of Darwinian racism was that not all lives were equal in value and hence society should not fear the death of some inferior individuals. Certainly that was the lesson of Lapouge and Haeckel. Ploetz and Schallmayer argued that the eugenic imperatives of Darwinism trumped traditional moral inhibitions against killing because these were inferior lives. This view was not limited to European Darwinists. "The laws of nature," Madison Grant declared, "require the obliteration of the unfit, and human life is valuable only when it is of use to the community or race" (Grant 1916, 45). The United States, however, never wed this ideology to political power as happened under Hitler.

The second way that science contributed to the Nazi genocide was by providing the appearance of a value-neutral judgment on the worth of some human lives. Science reported "the facts" about human inequalities, and to object to "the facts" on sentimental grounds was foolish. As an illustration, consider the fates of the two chief ideologues of the Nazi regime: Alfred Rosenberg and Hans F. K. Günther. Rosenberg was part of the Nazi inner circle and his racial writings, notably *Foundations of the Twentieth Century*, echoed the race mysticism of Houston Stewart Chamberlain. After the war, Rosenberg was hanged as a war criminal. Günther, by contrast, lived a full life after the war and continued to publish until his death in 1968. Because he was a scientist, and science was divorced from political concerns, he was immune from the ramifications of his writings. A more chilling example is that of Otmar von Verschuer, the direct beneficiary of the immense human suffering at Auschwitz, who continued to serve on the boards of scientific journals until his death in 1969.

After World War II, the science of race would undergo a stunning transformation. Science, which had provided a substantial underpinning for racist doctrines before the War, would be enrolled against racist concepts afterward. Even as the Nazis rose to power in the 1930s, the fundamental doctrines of scientific racism were under attack. After the War the objectivity of science would be dedicated to denying the truth of racial differences, a complete reversal of orientation.

Bibliographic Essay

For an encyclopedic treatment of ideas about heredity and their interplay with Darwinism see Peter J. Bowler, *Evolution: The History of an Idea* (Berkeley: University of California Press, 1984). Fleeming Jenkin's review of Darwin was published as Fleeming Jenkin, "(Review of Darwin's) *'The Origin of Species'*," *North British Review* 46 (1867): 277–318.

Specific monographic studies on the late-nineteenth-century views of heredity include Kathy J. Cooke, "The Limits of Heredity: Nature and Nurture in American Eugenics Before 1915," *Journal of the History of Biology* 31 (1998): 263–278; Phillip Thurtle, "Harnessing Heredity in Gilded Age America: Middle Class Mores and Industrial Breeding in a Cultural Context," *Journal of the History of Biology* 35 (2002): 43–78; John C. Waller, "Ideas of Heredity, Reproduction, and Eugenics in Britain, 1800–1875," *Studies in the History and Philosophy of Biology and the Biomedical Sciences* (2001): 457–489.

On Weismann see Bowler, *Evolution*, and Frederick B. Churchill, "From Heredity Theory to *Vererbung*: The Transmission Problem, 1850–1915," *Isis* 78 (1987): 337–364. There is now a full-length biography of Francis Galton: Nicholas W. Gillham, *A Life of Sir Francis Galton: From African Exploration to the Birth of Eugenics* (New York: Oxford University Press, 2001). Important monographic studies include Ruth Schwartz Cowan, "Nature and Nurture: The Interplay of Biology and Politics in the Work of Francis Galton," *Studies in the History of Biology* 1 (1977): 133–208; John C. Waller, "Gentlemanly Men of Science: Sir Francis Galton and the Professionalization of the British Life Sciences," *Journal of the History of Biology* 34 (2002): 83–114. On the reception of *Hereditary Genius* see Emel Aileen Gökyigit, "The Reception of Francis Galton's *Hereditary Genius* in the Victorian Periodical Press," *Journal of the History of Biology* 27 (1994): 215–240. For Galton in his own words see Francis Galton, *Hereditary Genius: An Inquiry into Its Laws and Consequences* (New York: Horizon Press, 1952 [1869]).

Several good discussions exist on Nordicism. Ivan Hannaford, *Race: The History of an Idea in the West* (Baltimore: Johns Hopkins University Press, 1996) sketches the thought of all the Nordicists discussed in this chapter. For Nordicists in the United States see Thomas F. Gossett, *Race: The History of an Idea in America* (Dallas: Southern Methodist University Press, 1963). For European Nordicists see George L. Mosse, *Toward the Final Solution: A History of European Racism* (New York: Howard Fertig, 1985). The life of Houston Stewart Chamberlain is profiled in Geoffrey G. Field, *Evangelist of Race: The Germanic Vision of Houston Stewart Chamberlain* (New York: Columbia University Press, 1981). On Vacher de Lapouge see Jennifer Michael Hecht, "The Solvency of Metaphysics: The Debate Over Racial Science and Moral Philosophy in France, 1890–1919," *Isis* 90 (1999): 1–24; and Jennifer Michael Hecht, "Vacher de Lapouge and the Rise of Nazi Science," *Journal of the History of Ideas* 61 (2000): 285–304. The latter also includes a good discussion of Hans F. K. Günther that should be supplemented by Geoffrey G. Field, "Nordic Racism," *Journal of the History of Ideas* 38 (1977): 523–540. The best work on Madison Grant is Jonathan P. Spiro, "Patrician Racist: The Evolution of Madison Grant," (Ph.D. Dissertation at University of California–Berkeley, 2000). Also valuable on Grant is Mathew Pratt Guterl, *The Color of Race in America, 1900–1940* (Cambridge: Harvard University Press, 2001). Madison Grant's masterworks were published as Madison Grant, *The Passing of the Great Race or The Racial Basis of European History* (New York: Scribner's, 1916) and *Conquest of a Continent or The Expansion of Races in America* (New York: Scribner's, 1934). The other key work on American Nordicism was Lothrop Stoddard, *The Rising Tide of Color Against White World-Supremacy* (New York: Scribner's, 1921).

Eugenics is also extensively documented. For a brief primary source see The American Eugenics Society, *A Eugenics Catechism* (New Haven, CT: American Eugenics Society, Inc., 1926). The best book-length treatment remains Daniel J. Kevles, *In the Name of Eugenics: Genetics and the Uses of Human Heredity* (New York: Knopf, 1985). A briefer introduction is Diane B. Paul, *Controlling Human Heredity: 1865 to the Present* (Atlantic Highlands, NJ: Humanities Press International, 1995). A recent review that captures the complexity of the historiography of eugenics is Frank Dikötter, "Race Culture: Recent Perspectives on the History of Eugenics," *American Historical Review* 103 (1998): 467–478. Specific monographs that address Harry Laughlin, Charles Davenport, and the Eugenics Record Office are Garland E. Allen, "The Eugenics Record Office at Cold Spring Harbor, 1910–1940: An Essay in Institutional History," *Osiris* 2 (1986): 225–264; Garland E. Allen, "The Biological Basis of Crime: An Historical and Methodological Study," *Historical Studies in the Physical and Biological Sciences* 31 (2001): 183–222; Philip K. Wilson, "Harry Laughlin's

Eugenic Crusade to Control the 'Socially Inadequate' in Progressive Era America," *Patterns of Prejudice* 36 (2002): 49–67. On involuntary sterilization in America see Philip R. Reilly, *The Surgical Solution: A History of Involuntary Sterilization in the United States* (Baltimore: Johns Hopkins University Press, 1991). On the intricacies of *Buck v. Bell* see the decision itself, *Buck v. Bell* 274 U.S. 200 (1927), and Paul A. Lombardo, "Three Generations, No Imbeciles: New Light on *Buck v. Bell*," *New York University Law Review* 60 (1985): 30–62. For Laughlin's testimony before Congress see Harry H. Laughlin, "Analysis of America's Melting Pot," in *Hearings before The House Committee on Immigration and Naturalization, House of Representatives*, 67th Cong., 3d sess. (Washington, DC: Governmental Printing Office, 1922).

The role of science in the eugenics movement in Germany is enormous. Begin with Robert N. Proctor, *Racial Hygiene: Medicine Under the Nazis* (Cambridge: Harvard University Press, 1988) and Benno Müller-Hill, *Murderous Science: Elimination by Scientific Selection of Jews, Gypsies, and Others, Germany 1933–1945*, translated by George R. Fraser (New York: Oxford University Press, 1988). A useful guide to the complex literature on the subject and an explanation of both the "selectionist" metaphor and the "organicist" metaphor is Paul Weindling, "Dissecting German Social Darwinism: Historicizing the Biology of the Organic State," *Science in Context* 11 (1998): 619–637. On the relationship between the German eugenics movement and the American eugenics movement see Stefan Kühl, *The Nazi Connection: Eugenics, American Racism, and German National Socialism* (New York: Oxford University Press, 1994).

On the history of pre-Nazi eugenics in Germany see Paul Weindling, "Weimar Eugenics: The Kaiser Wilhelm Institute for Anthropology, Human Heredity and Eugenics in Social Context," *Annals of Science* 42 (1985): 303–318, and Sheila Faith Weiss, "Wilhelm Schallmayer and the Logic of German Eugenics," *Isis* 77 (1986): 33–46. On the effect of the Nazi government on scientific institutions and eugenic thought in Germany see Peter Weingart, "German Eugenics between Science and Politics," *Osiris* 5 (1989): 260–282, and Sheila Faith Weiss, "The Race Hygiene Movement in Germany," *Osiris* 3 (1987): 193–236. On the disturbing career of Otmar von Verschuer see Benno Müller-Hill, "The Blood of Auschwitz and the Silence of the Scholars," *History and Philosophy of the Life Sciences* 21 (1999): 331–365. On the effect Darwinism had on evaluating the worth of human life see Richard Weikart, "Darwinism and Death: Devaluing Human Life in Germany, 1859–1920," *Journal of the History of Ideas* 63 (2002): 323–344. On the interactions of science and values see Robert N. Proctor, *Value-Free Science? Purity and Power in Modern Knowledge* (Cambridge MA: Harvard University Press, 1991).

5

The Retreat of Scientific Racism, 1890–1940

By the 1890s, race had become the major organizing principle of the biological, human, and social sciences, and the scientific study of race was afforded widespread ideological and institutional sanction. We have explored the reasons that a worldview based on race became established. What is remarkable is that, given its solid establishment, this worldview ever got undermined. Why should it have fallen into disrepute and eventually have vanished almost completely? So entrenched were its assumptions about racial types, racial hierarchy, and racial struggle that its retreat and ultimate decline come as nothing short of a surprise. We need to ask why and how those assumptions ever began to be questioned, and why the racial theories that had served the sciences so well for a century or more began even at the peak of their influence to break down.

The retreat of scientific racism began in the 1890s and had multiple and complex causes—scientific, political, and social. Among the scientific reasons was the rise of cultural anthropology and of population genetics, both of which helped to question the notion of fixed and stable racial types. Ethnography in particular, the central method of cultural anthropology, threw doubt on the Eurocentrism by which those types had been ordered. With the breakdown of the racial hierarchy, the denigration of Africans, Asians, Native Americans, and Latinos began to look less like a rational scientific conclusion and more like a pathology, and sociologists and social psychologists—influenced by the ethnographers' egalitarian ideals—studied it as a new phenomenon they called racism. Both the term and the concept of racism were inventions of the 1930s. Meanwhile the new population genetics and a new, more subtle, liberal eugenics allowed for important environmental influences on all manner of traits and questioned the older eugenic influence on single genes as causes of complex mental and moral characteristics. The new genetics, with its focus on populations as continuously varying groups of individuals, directly opposed the nineteenth-century ethnologists' search for unchanging racial essences.

But the rise of new sciences, and of new directions in established sciences, cannot alone account for the retreat of scientific racism. Political and social causes were also crucial. The composition of the scientific elite was changing: leftists of all types, from moderate liberals to socialists and Marxists, found representation among the geneticists, while women, African Americans, and Jews, many of whom were also leftists, made up a significant fraction of anthropologists, sociologists, and psychologists. The changing demography of the sciences, the increase in female and minority members in their ranks, had a definite impact on theoretical perspectives and methods. Moreover, the political contexts in which these sciences were done were broadly influential. In the wake of World War I, there were race riots in more than twenty American cities, and a revived Ku Klux Klan terrorized the African American population throughout the 1920s. These clear evidences of racial antagonism shaped the efforts of liberal social scientists to use their science to work for justice and democracy. In the 1930s the Great Depression proved that poverty could happen to anybody and was not an outcome of bad genes; and late in that decade the Holocaust showed the horrible extremes to which scientifically sanctioned racism could go.

Though World War II and its aftermath marked the official end of scientifically sanctioned racism and the establishment of a new liberal orthodoxy on race, the decline of the race concept began decades earlier. That decline was not the automatic consequence of any single political, social, or scientific cause, but resulted from a complex of causes in combination—scientists with new professional goals, working in changed political and social circumstances, and slowly becoming aware of the power of their sciences to effect social change. The retreat of scientific racism was thus an incremental process. There was no definitive break from the past or sudden overthrow of reigning ideas but rather a gradual chipping away at a grand and imposing edifice. The questioning of nineteenth-century racial assumptions grew out of the very sciences that those assumptions had supported. The new ideas that replaced the traditional ones appear radically different in retrospect because we know the outcome to which they ultimately led. But at the time they were intended as variations or improvements on well-established themes. This kind of continuity can be seen in nearly all the scientific developments discussed here, in anthropology, psychology, sociology, and genetics. Nowhere is it more clearly demonstrated than in the career and work of the anthropologist Franz Boas.

Boas and the Culture Concept

No one person in the first half of the twentieth century did more to defeat scientific racism than Boas. Of course he did not do so single-handedly. Even more important, he was definitely a Janus-faced figure, strongly rooted in the traditions of nineteenth-century anthropometry even as he laid the foundations of a new science of culture and a new approach to race. Boas could not have foreseen the ends to which his critique would lead, and he would not have always agreed with them. Still, his critique was an essential starting point. Boas's anthropology basically broke apart the link between race, language, and culture that the nineteenth-century ethnologists held dear. He thus separated biology from culture, and placed culture on its own autonomous level—looking at cultures as independent, integrated wholes that must be understood on their own terms and judged only by their own values, not by a Eurocentric standard. In doing so, Boas cast serious doubt on the validity of the concept of race and established a relativistic view of culture that became paradigmatic not only in anthropology but in all the other social sciences as well by the mid-twentieth century. Boas rejected the evolutionary racial hierarchy of the nineteenth century that arrayed the races of man in singular linear hierarchical sequence of savagery, barbarism, and civilization.

Boas (1858–1942) was born in Minden, Germany, into a family of Jewish liberals and freethinkers. Though Boas always strongly identified himself as German both before and after his immigration to the United States, his Jewishness made him culturally marginal in both places. In 1881 he received a Ph.D. in physics, with a minor in geography, after studying at the universities of Heidelberg, Bonn, and Kiel, with a dissertation on laboratory studies of the color of seawater. These early studies raised the problem of the extent to which the subjective perception of the observer determined what was considered to be reality.

To pursue the problem of the relationship between observer and reality, the psychological and the physical, knowledge of nature and nature itself, Boas traveled to Baffinland in the Arctic Circle in 1883. There, living among the Inuit, he studied how the members of an entirely foreign culture understood and perceived the physical world around them. In the notebook he kept during his ethnographic fieldwork, he expressed the relativistic view of culture that would become a hallmark of his cultural anthropology. He questioned the notion that his own society could be considered more advanced than that of the so-called savages. He concluded that the idea of a cultured individual was a relative one: while the Inuit were not cultured according to the Europeans, the Europeans were not cultured according to the Inuit.

In 1886 and again in 1888 Boas traveled to Vancouver, British Columbia, to live among the Kwakiutl, the Native Americans whose way of life, folklore, traditions, and beliefs he spent years studying, collecting, and interpreting. These travels and studies resulted in an 1894 article, "Human Faculty as Determined by Race" (in *Proceedings of the AAAS*), which was his earliest public expression of

Inuit killing salmon with spears, Canada (Library of Congress)

antiracism. Here he specifically attacked Herbert Spencer's notion of the inferior mental capacity of the so-called lower races, using the Kwakiutl as an example to disprove Spencer's claim that savages were inattentive. This use of ethnographic examples to counter sociocultural evolutionism formed the basis for Boas's 1911 volume, *The Mind of Primitive Man*.

In 1887 he emigrated from Germany to the United States. After some difficulty he obtained a position at Clark University, in Worcester, Massachusetts, and later at Columbia University, where he spent the remainder of his career. From 1896 to 1906 he was also associated with the American Museum of Natural History in New York City.

In 1887, Boas became involved in a controversy with Otis Mason and John Wesley Powell, the dominant American ethnologists, which shows Boas's developing views on cultural relativism. Mason and Powell, both unilinear evolutionists, believed that each material object—from whatever culture it originated—should be classified according to type—tool, weapon, or musical instrument—and arranged according to the evolutionary stage of cultural development that it typified. Boas, on the other hand, grouped all the items from a single tribal culture and argued that each culture must be represented as a whole, as neither higher nor lower than any other, with objects displayed in their original cultural contexts. His impulse was historical and descriptive, rejecting Mason and Powell's evolutionism.

In the 1890s Boas pursued two lines of inquiry. The first, while he was at Clark, was a study of growth in the schoolchildren of Worcester, Massachusetts, concluding that physical differences between them were due to differences in the pace of their development, which was a mixture of hereditary and environmental influences. The second was his study of Native American populations, particularly his focus on the "Half Blood Indian," in which he found that race mixing did not impair fertility, that in some cases it had "a favorable effect upon the race," and that the "half bloods" tended to be taller (Boas, 1894/1940, 140). Both of these studies show Boas as a physical anthropologist working within a Galtonian tradition of anthropometry. In this tradition, in 1903 Boas began his studies of headform, and from 1908 to 1910 he carried out a major anthropometric project—"Changes in Bodily Form of Descendants of Immigrants"—for the United States Congress Immigration Commission. This was the same commission that supported the Immigration Restriction Act of 1924, but Boas managed to get funding from it to pursue his own project. His findings were not in keeping with the rest of the Commission's, though Boas himself, a creature of his era, was not entirely opposed to immigration restriction.

In his study Boas, assisted by his graduate students at Columbia, took body measurements on nearly 18,000 people, in schools, private homes, and at Ellis Island, representing what were believed at the time to be the major European types: Nordic, Alpine, and Mediterranean. He noted the differences between the body and headforms of the immigrant parents—Neapolitans, Sicilians, eastern European Jews, Poles, Hungarians, and Scots—and their U.S. born children. Neither body type nor cephalic index remained stable once the second generation was removed to a new environment. The American surroundings and upbringing, Boas concluded, produced changes even in those aspects of bodily form thought to be most unchangeable and considered therefore the best indicators of racial type. Boas's findings directly challenged the assumption of the stability of headform and therefore of the entire type concept. As he wrote in a paper based on his report for the Commission, when discussing race, "we must speak of a plasticity (as opposed to permanence) of types" (Boas 1912/1940, 71).

Boas found that changes in physical type varied directly with the length of time elapsed between the arrival of the mother in the United States and the birth of her child, a result that showed the effect of environment. A population could not be reduced to a pure type, nor could any one individual be definitely identified as one type or another, because types overlap, and individuals falling within the overlap could belong to either type. Such a finding shows that Boas was at this point still trying to clarify the type concept—still, that is, working very much within the framework of nineteenth-century physical anthropology and formulating criticisms that had occurred to the likes of Otto Ammon. But in the years afterward, Boas's critique became increasingly radical as his skepticism of the type concept grew. Type, he argued, is only an arbitrary classification, not indicative of a natural kind. Variation within the type is greater than between types, and in a local population isolated from other groups, subtypes could develop. All of these criticisms of the type concept and emphasis on the variability of populations were later echoed and expanded by population geneticists during the evolutionary synthesis of the 1930s.

Boas's critique of the type concept helped him to undercut the traditional assumption of the hierarchy of races, and in *The Mind of Primitive Man* he set out his theoretical alternative. The main theses of the book were that race must be separated from language and culture, which were to be treated as independent variables; that the racial superiority of Anglo-Saxons has no basis; that the observer must adapt his mind to the culture observed; and that there is no unbridgeable gap between primitive and civilized cultures. Many of the differences between so-called primitive and civilized men were in fact not racial but environmental and cultural. If types could no longer be reliably defined, and if hereditary and environmental influences could not be easily distinguished, then the idea that one race was superior to another in mental ability must also be abandoned. Individuals must be treated as individuals and not as members of a type. These were new ideas for the time, but even in them Boas showed his debt to an earlier era. He still spoke in terms of civilized and primitive and believed that the latter was the true subject of ethnography. And though he argued for egalitarianism, he still believed that on the whole Negroes were inferior to whites—though many of them were just as capable as whites.

The Mind of Primitive Man set out Boas's anthropological definition of culture as historical (changing and developing over time), relativistic (taking cultures on their own terms, and fostering a respect for difference and diversity), integrated, determinative of behavior, and plural. In the first generation of Boas's students, in the 1910s, one finds frequent use of the word "cultures," in the plural. This use is in striking contrast to the sociocultural evolutionists Tylor, Lubbock, and McLennan, who used "culture" in the singular and as present to a greater or lesser extent in all peoples. In *The Mind of Primitive Man* Boas argued that seemingly similar phenomena might stem from diverse cultural causes and not be the result of the mind passing through linear evolutionary stages. He constantly emphasized local ethnographic study and the histories of individual cultures and critiqued evolutionary hierarchies of marriage forms, myth, and religion. His focus was always on the differences among peoples rather than on their commonalities. Taken together, these ideas represented a radical departure from nineteenth-century evolutionism, even if Boas himself was formed in that mold and it was really his students who fulfilled his radical suggestions. For example, in 1911 Boas still made reference to the "genius of a people," a phrase reminiscent of the nineteenth-century typologists. Boas meant it in a cultural rather than racial way, but it does show that he was not always consistent in his individualist emphasis and still sometimes thought in terms of types.

The anthropological concept of culture—fully worked out by Boas's students—rejected the Spencerian idea of evolution from simple to complex, from savage to civilized societies progressing along a single line and judged by a single, European, standard of value. In the Boasian framework, values were relative and ethnocentrism was rejected. Talk of plural *cultures* replaced that of cultural *stages*. Behavior was determined not by heredity or race but by the culture in which a person lived. And the folklore or mythology of a people was particularly important for getting to the heart of their culture.

Boas and his students represented not only a theoretical departure from the armchair evolutionary anthropologists of the nineteenth century but a professional one as well. The Boasians saw themselves as scientific professionals, made so by their ethnographic fieldwork, and looked down on their armchair predecessors as speculative amateurs. Spencer's culling of facts about savages from travel books in his study could not have been more different from the Boasians living for extended periods as participant-observers among the peoples whom they were studying. In 1905 the Boasians took over the major professional anthropological society—the American Anthropological Association—and by the 1920s they were a dominant force in anthropology.

The Boasians' impact on and relationship to physical anthropology was a complex one. How much direct impact the Boasians' cultural anthropology had on physical anthropology is an open question; for the most part the two branches of the science seem to have worked in parallel, rather than in direct confrontation. In the 1920s and 1930s physical anthropology was a discipline in crisis, with little agreement among its practitioners on its proper subject matter or methods—and the Boasians seized on and critiqued such perceived weakness. On the other hand, despite the disciplinary chaos, the physical anthropologists were more mainstream and more conservative than the Boasian cultural anthropologists and held positions of power and prestige in scientific institutions. The Boasians therefore had to accommodate to them, coexist, and in some cases even cooperate with them. The coexistence of these two groups of anthropologists that were at a basic level deeply opposed to each other—the typologists and racists of physical anthropology and the relativists and egalitarians of cultural anthropology—demonstrates well the politics of a divided discipline and also shows the limits of the Boasian critique. Such a critique could never become too radical lest it lose the support of representatives of mainstream institutions and funding sources. The examples of Ales Hrdlicka, Earnest A. Hooton, and Clark Wissler clearly demonstrate how this coexistence worked.

Hrdlicka (1869–1943), an M.D. and physical anthropologist, was curator of anthropology at the Smithsonian Institution in Washington, D.C.—a central and powerful location for the science. He was an immigrant from Bohemia, but in contrast to Boas's situation there were no liberal politics associated with his ethnic status. Hrdlicka cooperated with the notorious racist Madison Grant on the measurement of World War I army recruits and was a member of the racist and eugenist Galton Society. Hrdlicka's best known work, *Old Americans*, argued that the most recent immigrants to America were beginning to resemble the "old Americans" (those with four grandparents born in the U.S.) in stature and body type, but he never used these findings to combat immigration restriction, on which question he always remained neutral. He represented the immigrant outsider who adopted mainstream racist attitudes—or at least an attitude of scientific neutrality—in order to be accepted in powerful scientific circles. And yet Boas supported and encouraged Hrdlicka, especially in Hrdlicka's editorship of the *American Journal of Physical Anthropology*.

Earnest Hooton (1887–1954) was even more central to the discipline of physical anthropology and cooperated even more closely with Boas. Hooton was professor of physical anthropology at Harvard for forty years and held views on race reflecting the racist conventions that prevailed in the sciences up to World War II. The four great groups of mankind—Negroids, Mongoloids, Whites, and Composites—were divided into races, and the different physical qualities of each race were associated with different mental and temperamental characteristics. Hooton rejected Boas's conclusion that changes in skull shape reflect changing environmental conditions and from the mid-1920s on turned to the study of the biological basis of criminality. Hooton's work in this area definitely hearkened back to an earlier tradition of criminal anthropology, arguing that criminals contribute to the degeneration or de-evolution of humankind and that patterns in crime were associated with different races and nationalities. That his work in this area was largely ignored by the scientific community signifies the change in opinion on the legitimacy of biological determinism on the eve of World War II.

Yet Hooton and Boas worked together in the mid-1930s to try to draft a statement to define race scientifically in response to the Nazi program of racial hygiene that the Germans were making public. The anthropologists whom Hooton and Boas consulted never came to any consensus on the matter of race, reflecting the lack of consensus in the discipline as a whole. Public opposition to racism by anthropologists speaking as a community did not appear until after 1938. But despite their failure with this initial statement, Hooton continued to support Boas in the latter's attempts to reach a wide public audience, and in 1936 Hooton himself published his own statement on race in which he criticized the crimes committed by whites in the name of racial purity. Yet he was also both openly and privately critical of Boas, calling him an environmental extremist on matters of race whose views were shaped by the fact that Boas was Jewish. Hooton's support for antiracism was thus tempered by his political conservatism and his general pessimism about humankind, and throughout his long and powerful career he both supported and criticized Boas.

The third example of a physical anthropologist who worked with Boasians even while disagreeing with them is Clark Wissler (1870–1947). Wissler studied psychology and anthropology at Columbia, in part with Boas. He succeeded Boas as curator of anthropology at the American Museum of Natural History in New York City, yet never became a Boasian. Wissler was a member of the Galton Society's inner circle and believed in such traditional ethnocentric ideas as the marginality of dark-skinned peoples, the superiority of Nordics, and the passage of each culture through rigid stages from primitive to civilized. Yet because of Wissler's central position at the Museum, the Boasians who worked there had to cooperate with him. Moreover, Wissler was a member of the Committee on Scientific Problems of Human Migration, one of a number of such government-funded scientific committees that served as clearinghouses for grants and support of research. The Migration committee was set up to work for immigration restriction, yet it funded at least one Boasian, Melville Herskovits. On this committee and others like it, scientists of markedly different opinions on race had to cooperate and coexist. Wissler's cooperation with and support of his Boasian opponents demonstrates the importance of this professional coexistence.

Boasian Anthropology and Black Folklore

Boas and a number of his students took major strides in the fight against scientific racism through their theoretical contributions and by cultivating a professional demeanor that they contrasted to the speculative evolutionists. They also established and maintained contacts and associations with African American intellectuals. Boas, for example, allied himself professionally and personally with W. E. B. Du Bois (1868–1963), a leader in the struggle for black equality and a major thinker on matters of race in the first half of the twentieth century. Even before he began his association with Boas, Du Bois had developed a line of thought similar to the anthropologist's, arguing that race must be distinguished from culture and that race is not a biological category. Boas, for his part, sympathized with Du Bois's radical arguments for equality and integration. Boas opposed the case made by Du Bois's rival Booker T. Washington, who advocated a slower program of progress in which black people must accommodate themselves to the inequities of American society and focus on gaining technical and industrial training rather than higher education. In 1896, Du Bois, who had received a doctorate in sociology from Harvard University, published *The Philadelphia Negro*, an ethnography based on his participant-observation in that community; the following year he became a professor of economics and history at Atlanta University. At Atlanta, Du Bois initiated an ambitious project to study all aspects of Negro life and culture and imagined each aspect being revisited and updated every ten years for a century.

In 1906, Du Bois invited Boas to participate in one of the conferences organized around the longitudinal study, and also to give the commencement address at Atlanta University. Boas used the opportunity to heighten the students' awareness of and pride in their African ancestry. Du Bois later described the impact that Boas's speech made on him: "Franz Boas came to Atlanta University where I was teaching History in 1906 and said to the graduating class: You need not be ashamed of your African past; and then he recounted the history of black kingdoms south of the Sahara for a thousand years. I was too astonished to speak. All of this I had never heard and I came then and afterwards to realize how the silence and neglect of science can let truth utterly disappear or be unconsciously distorted" (Du Bois, *Black Folk Then and Now*, 1939, vii). Du Bois also wrote that "Dr. Boas has done more to clear away the myth of inherent race differences than any living scientist" (Du Bois 1941, 190).

In 1910 Du Bois left Atlanta to focus on social activism, becoming an officer of the newly organized National Association for the Advancement of Colored People and editor of its journal *The Crisis*. He invited Boas and the Cornell zoologist Burt G. Wilder to the first conclave of the NAACP, where they delivered the opening addresses. Boas also spoke at the meeting the following year, publishing his talk in *The Crisis*. He maintained his alliance with Du Bois, the NAACP, and their fight for integration and equality until his death.

Boas also encouraged and helped to institutionalize the study of Negro folklore. He had always considered the investigation of folklore a key method of understanding a culture and had founded the American Folklore Society (AFS) in 1888. In the 1920s Boas and Elsie Clews Parsons (1875–1941), an independently wealthy anthropologist who trained with Boas and worked with him at the *Journal of American Folklore* (JAFL), made an intensive effort to recruit and train black graduate students both to collect Negro folklore and to take anthropometric measurements on black people. The JAFL dedicated fourteen issues between 1917 and 1937 to studies of Negro folklore by such prominent black anthropologists as Arthur Fauset, Zora Neale Hurston, Arthur Schomburg, Alain Locke, and Carter Woodson.

Fauset (1899–1983)—the younger brother of Jessie Redmon Fauset, a Harlem Renaissance novelist and the literary editor of *The Crisis*—was an

THE CRISIS

A RECORD OF THE DARKER RACES

Volume One   NOVEMBER, 1910   Number One

Edited by W. E. BURGHARDT DU BOIS, with the co-operation of Oswald Garrison Villard, J. Max Barber, Charles Edward Russell, Kelly Miller, W. S. Braithwaite and M. D. Maclean.

CONTENTS

PUBLISHED MONTHLY BY THE

National Association for the Advancement of Colored People

AT TWENTY VESEY STREET   NEW YORK CITY

ONE DOLLAR A YEAR   TEN CENTS A COPY

Cover of the first issue of the NAACP journal The Crisis *(Bettmann/Corbis)*

Zora Neale Hurston (1891–1960)

Writer and anthropologist Zora Neale Hurston was born in Eatonville, Florida, the first African American town incorporated in the United States. Her father, John Hurston, was a three-time mayor of the town, and she was educated in an all-black community that emphasized self-reliance. As a teenager, she left home and worked in various

menial positions in Baltimore, Maryland, before getting a high school diploma from a preparatory school operated by Morgan College in 1918. Hurston then moved to Washington, D.C., and became a part-time student at Howard University from 1919–1924. There she worked with philosopher Alain Locke, one of the leaders of the New Negro Movement, which celebrated the literary and artistic accomplishments of African Americans. With Locke's encouragement, Hurston began writing fiction, publishing in both Howard University's literary magazine and in *Opportunity*, a major outlet for New Negro writers.

(Library of Congress)

In 1925, Hurston moved to the heart of the New Negro Movement, New York City, where she continued to publish. She enrolled as a student at Barnard College and in 1928 became the first African American graduate there. While at Barnard, Hurston took classes from Franz Boas, which increased her interest in African American folklore. Between 1927 and 1932, Hurston made several ethnological trips through the American South to collect folklore under the sponsorship of Charlotte Osgood Mason, a white patron of folklore activities. Hurston's fiction increasingly demonstrated her

anthropologist trained at the University of Pennsylvania. Though not a Boas student, Fauset published in the JAFL and was supported financially by Parsons in his fieldwork in the American South, the Caribbean, and Nova Scotia. Fauset's work clearly demonstrated the diversity of the African American experience and pointed out the problems with stereotypes about black people. In his collection of *Folklore from Nova Scotia* (1931), Fauset wrote that, despite common stereotypes, Negroes who lived in Nova Scotia did not want to move further south because they did not like hot weather. Nova Scotia Negroes also did not share common folktales that were well known among black populations of the southern United States. Fauset's emphasis throughout was on the variability of Negro cultures (in the plural) and the great extent to which they adapted and changed in new contexts—a thoroughly Boasian theme.

Another example of a folklorist and anthropologist supported by Parsons

interest in African American folklore as evidenced by her first novel, *Jonah's Gourd Vine* (1934), which was criticized for letting the folklore overwhelm the plot. Hurston's fiction was also criticized for underplaying or ignoring white oppression.

In 1934, with a Rosenwald Fellowship, Hurston enrolled in graduate school, studying anthropology with Franz Boas at Columbia. Frustrated with the extensive library research required for Ph.D. study, Hurston never completed the Ph.D. degree. However, she did publish numerous works on her fieldwork in folklore, notably *Mules and Men* in 1935, which focused on gender relationships within the African American community.

African American folklore also played a role in Hurston's most celebrated novel, *Their Eyes Were Watching God* (1937), a celebration of African American folkways. In the 1940s, Hurston continued to do fieldwork and publish novels and stories. However, she was increasingly frustrated by the reception of her work within the anthropological community. White scholars often objected to her work as lacking objectivity and many questioned whether African Americans had sufficient distance from their communities to be reliable recorders of their own culture. Her fiction also began to suffer poor reception, and a scandal involving false charges that Hurston had seduced a sixteen-year-old retarded boy shook her reputation in the African American community.

By the 1950s, Hurston had been reduced to working as a domestic servant for rich white people. Her celebration of African American folkways and her refusal to condemn white oppression brought her a different kind of notoriety. Increasingly bitter, her criticisms of the *Brown* decision and the civil rights movement were eagerly publicized by segregationists. She died penniless in Fort Pierce, Florida, in 1960. In the years since her death, however, her work recording African American folklore and her innovative methodology of deep involvement in the lives of her subjects are increasingly seen as pioneering and scientifically valuable.

and active in Boas's AFS was Zora Neale Hurston (1891–1961). Hurston used her interest in Negro folklore to promote African American cultural pride—a hallmark of the 1920s "New Negro Movement"—and also to stress continuities from Africa throughout the diaspora. Hurston studied at Howard University and then transferred to Barnard College where she met Boas. Carrying out Boas's ideal of fieldwork, Hurston became a participant-observer of black communities in New Orleans, Florida, Haiti, and Jamaica. Like Fauset, Hurston used her fieldwork to debunk stereotypes about black people and to dismiss the idea that black cultures were inferior. Like Melville Herskovits, a white Jewish student of Boas's, Hurston noted the African cultural patterns that were retained in African American cultures. Like Margaret Mead and Ruth Benedict, two other Boasians, Hurston was interested in the ways that culture shapes personality, as demonstrated in her fieldwork in Jamaica. Hurston's study of Negro folklore in rural

Florida, *Mules and Men*, emphasized its connections to African ancestry and argued that it had a rich and complex tradition that helped blacks adapt to the New World. Hurston also studied Haitian Voodun, stressing its complexity and its associations with Africa, and stripping it of its negative connotations.

Hurston and Fauset both contributed to an anthropological literature on African Americans that was aimed at destroying stereotypes and at reconstructing the richness, complexity, and diversity of their cultural traditions; Boas and Parsons supported their work both intellectually and financially. Meanwhile others among the Boasians also worked in antiracist directions.

One of the most notable of these was Melville Herskovits. Born in Illinois to a family of Jewish immigrants, Herskovits (1895–1963) received his Ph.D. in anthropology in 1922. Under the influence of Boas and Parsons, Herskovits made anthropometric measurements of blacks both in Harlem and at Howard University, where he taught for several years, as well as throughout the American South. His physical measurements showed that blacks in America were becoming more homogeneous and even forming a new physical type. This conclusion was quite similar to Boas's study of bodily form in immigrants, as both constituted a critique of the notion of a pure race. In Herskovits's work, the blacks he studied were of mixed ancestry, yet their physical form was strikingly homogeneous. At this point in his career, Herskovits was an assimilationist, a believer that justice and equality for African Americans would come only through acculturation to white society and its values. The assimilationist argument held that slavery had destroyed any remnants of African culture among black people. Herskovits's anthropometric study supported the possibility of assimilation; in fact the assimilationist argument was always present in Boasian discourse, evident in Boas's own study of immigrant headform, and in his claim that race mixing—leading to the eradication of all racial difference—was the ultimate solution to all racial conflict. The assimilationist strand stood in stark contrast to the equally Boasian stress on relativism and created an important inconsistency in cultural anthropology that would play itself out in later decades.

Under the influence of certain African American intellectuals, like W. E. B. Du Bois and James Weldon Johnson, however, Herskovits had a change of heart. From the late 1930s on, he gave up on assimilationism and began to argue the cultural pluralist and relativist line that there existed among African Americans strong ties to an African heritage. Continuities to an African past could help African Americans develop a distinctive culture. Herskovits's fieldwork in West Africa, the West Indies, and in North America confirmed his relativist position: he found vestiges of African culture especially among blacks in Harlem—in their folklore, religion, music, and language. In adopting this stance, Herskovits, like Hurston, contributed to the New Negro Movement of the Harlem Renaissance, which celebrated African culture and noted its persistence among African Americans. Herskovits believed in encouraging ethnic pride in African Americans by attributing the positive features of their culture to their African heritage and the negative ones to their oppression in American society. In *The Myth of the Negro Past* (1941) Herskovits argued that it was myth to believe that the Negro had no civilization and no history. That belief, Herskovits argued, "validate[d] the concept of Negro inferiority" (Herskovits, 1941, 1). By contrast, Herskovits emphasized the richness of the cultural traditions he had encountered in his fieldwork in the West Indies and West Africa. Such emphasis, he believed, would increase the pride of African Americans and the respect of whites for their rich and complex traditions.

But Herskovits's emphasis on African cultural continuities brought him into conflict with the sociologists at Howard University, who were thoroughgoing assimilationists—taking up the other strand of Boasian discourse. Showing that African cultural traditions were so persistent, tenacious, and slow to change, the sociologists argued, would constitute an argument against the full Americanization of blacks, against their full integration, and against their fully equal treatment. Thus the underlying contradiction in Boasian anthropology contained the makings of a major disagreement about the best way to make black people a part of American society.

Arthur Schomburg well expressed Herskovits's side in the controversy: "The Negro has been a man without a history because he has been considered a man without a worthy culture. But a new notion of cultural attainment and potentialities of the African stocks has recently come about, partly through the corrective influence of the more scientific study of African institutions and early cultural history" ("The Negro Digs Up His Past" in *The New Negro*, ed. Alain Locke, 1925/1968, 237). But Herskovits's view was considered radical for the time, not only by the Howard sociologists, whose beliefs became mainstream, but even by most of the other Boasians as well, including Boas himself. As a result, Herskovits's and Hurston's New Negro view of African cultural continuities was marginalized, while the assimilationist perspective became orthodox social science and formed the basis for much social policy in the decades to come. The emphasis on African cultural continuities did not reemerge until it was taken up by black nationalists in the 1960s.

The alliances—personal, professional, and intellectual—forged between white and black anthropologists benefited both sides in important ways. For the black scholars like Hurston, Fauset, Schomburg, and Du Bois, connections to powerful white scientists like Boas gave them access to mainstream universities and institutions from which they otherwise would have been excluded because of the segregated nature of American science and society in the first half of the twentieth century. The black scholars accepted Boas's anthropological framework and expanded it to study Negro life and culture, and the alliance gave them a legitimacy and a professional clout that they otherwise would have lacked. For the white scholars, black colleagues like Du Bois gave them access to activist political outlets, and black students like Hurston, who would be accepted more readily into black subject populations, allowed them an entrée into the African American cultures and populations they wanted to study. Recruiting black students and black collectors of folklore helped Boas fulfill his research agenda in anthropometry and cultural analysis, and the black anthropologists expanded the range and quality of Boasian ethnographic fieldwork.

Psychologists and the Critique of IQ Testing

The anthropologists' concept of culture formed one line of attack in the battle against scientific racism. A second line emerged from psychology, specifically out of the critique of IQ testing in World War I. As with the anthropologists, alliances were forged here too between white and black scientists. The best known and most influential of these attacks on the eugenically inspired IQ tests was by Otto Klineberg (1899–1992), a white Jewish psychologist trained at Columbia in the 1920s, where he came under the influence of Franz Boas. Klineberg's critique built on those made by lesser-known black psychologists, particularly Horace Mann Bond and Howard Hale Long.

For his dissertation research, Klineberg administered IQ tests to Yakima Indian children, African American children, and white children and used the anthropological concept of culture to explain the results. Klineberg argued that "speed" was a relative, cultural notion, and that the Yakima and African American children understood it in a different way from the whites. They tended to value it less, took their time with the tests, and as a result did less well. When the time variable was controlled for, the Yakima and African American children did better than the whites. Thus Klineberg showed that a supposedly neutral test could be compromised by cultural factors.

In his 1935 book *Race Differences*, Klineberg attacked the selective migration thesis, an argument used by scientific racists to point out innate racial differences in intelligence. According to the thesis, the higher IQ scores of northern blacks resulted from the fact that the more intelligent blacks migrated north, leaving the less intelligent ones behind in the South. Klineberg, however, showed that there was actually no superiority in IQ scores of recent migrants over those who stayed behind. He interpreted his results in environmental and cultural terms. The better educational opportunities in the North raised IQ scores in blacks and whites, and wherever the blacks lagged behind the whites, this too was due to the environmental effects of unequal opportunity.

By the 1930s the idea of mental differences between the races, a hallmark of the eugenists' program of IQ testing, had fallen into decline. Several psychologists underwent well-publicized reversals. Carl Brigham (1890–1943), a psychologist who had been a strong proponent of racial differences in IQ in 1923, recanted his former claims in 1930. Howard W. Odum (1884–1954), who wrote a strongly racist psychology textbook in the 1920s, turned through the study of sociology to a much more egalitarian position, and eventually became a proponent of the study of southern black life. Thomas Russell Garth (1872–1939), an educational psychologist affiliated with the applied branches of psychology and social work, and therefore always more moderate than Brigham or Odum, also underwent a shift. From his work in the field with Native Americans and Mexicans, Garth grew sympathetic to their cultures, in the manner of a Boasian anthropologist. As the major race psychologist of his day, Garth had originally been certain of racial differences in mentality but thought that further scientific effort was needed to uncover them. After his research in the field, and in the context of the shifting emphasis within psychology on environmental conditioning of behavior, Garth concluded in the late 1930s that nurture, in the form of educational opportunities and other environmental factors, was in fact more important than nature, in the form of heredity.

Black psychologists also played an important role in the rejection of the hard-line eugenic emphasis on hereditary racial inferiority. Horace Mann Bond (1904–1972), an educator, sociologist, and university administrator, emerged in the 1920s as a strong critic of racist interpretation of IQ tests. He showed that the scores of blacks from the northern states of New York, Ohio, and Pennsylvania were higher than those of southern whites and explained the difference in environmental terms. Such an argument flew in the face of innatist explanations, as did Bond's demonstration that the scores of northern whites, including large numbers of European immigrants, were higher than those of southern whites, who were always held up by eugenists as the ideal of racial purity. If a mixed population scored better than a supposedly pure race, the IQ testers' emphasis on white racial superiority was thoroughly shaken. Nonetheless, despite his criticisms of hereditarian interpretations of the tests, Bond never condemned the tests outright and in fact used them in his work as a college administrator. Intelligence tests could, he argued, be used to remedy the subjectivity of individual teachers' judgments. If used properly—that is, for the diagnosis of learning problems—and if interpreted in an environmentalist way, Bond believed that the tests could actually subvert bias. Such an argument shows Bond's faith in the objectivity of science, its detachability from moral judgments, and its capacity to right the wrongs of racism. By the mid-1930s, Bond's evidence and arguments had severely damaged the hereditarian interpretation of IQ test results.

One reason for the dominance of hereditarian interpretation of the tests in the 1920s was the exclusion of black researchers from the mainstream social sciences. As in anthropology, in psychology black scholars forged alliances with whites, like Klineberg, Herskovits, Garth, and Odum, who had, or came to have, environmentalist sympathies, and relied on those alliances to break through the color barrier. By the 1930s educational opportunities in all the social sciences, but particularly in psychology, were opening up slightly for African Americans. When black social scientists turned their attention to the critique of IQ tests they focused on several areas of research.

Howard Hale Long, an educational psychologist trained at Clark and Harvard universities, studied the relationship between socioeconomic status and length of residence in northern cities and scores on IQ tests—in all cases showing that environmental and educational opportunities strongly affected test performance. Horace Mann Bond and Martin D. Jenkins, a psychologist trained at Northwestern, examined the "mulatto hypothesis," according to which lighter-skinned blacks performed better on IQ tests because of their admixture of white blood. Jenkins debunked this claim, which had been used to argue against race mixing as compromising the quality of the white race. He investigated the numerous cases he had discovered of black children without any white ancestry who made exceptionally high scores on the tests. Like Long, Jenkins concluded that higher socioeconomic status produced higher scores, and he emphasized these students' intellectual gifts as individuals.

A third area of research pursued by black social scientists was the influence of testing methodology on IQ test performance. Herman Canady, also trained as a psychologist at Northwestern, asked whether it mattered if the person administering the test was black or white and designed experiments to answer the question. He found that the effect of the tester's race on the students' scores was negligible, but criticized the use of culturally biased tests. His colleague A. S. Scott, at West Virginia State College, showed that familiarity with testing situations and with standardized tests produced markedly improved IQ scores.

From Race Psychology to Studies in Prejudice

As the idea of inherent mental differences between the races fell into decline during the 1930s and the races came to be viewed as fundamentally similar, new ways of explaining racial antipathies had to be invented. Hatred of and disdain for the members of other races—so much a part of the race psychology of the

1910s and early 1920s—could no longer be seen as a rational response to the facts of racial hierarchy. With notions of superiority and inferiority largely abandoned, racial antagonism came to be explained as a basically irrational attitude—a *prejudice*—unreflective of reality. Studies of prejudice in the 1930s were pursued along two lines. Psychologists, particularly social psychologists, tended to focus on the irrationality of prejudice and its disconnection from any actual experience with members of the despised race.

Meanwhile sociologists, especially those associated with the highly influential Chicago school of sociology, tended to argue that racial antagonism and prejudice were necessary parts of the assimilation of a minority group into the mainstream, but that they could also cause severe social pathologies in the group being discriminated against. The sociological approach was favored by University of Chicago sociologist Robert E. Park and his students, who worked in the 1920s and 1930s on the problems of assimilation. Park formulated a social pathology model of the assimilation of minorities as occurring in four stages: competition, then conflict , followed by accommodation of the minority to the dominant way of life, and finally complete assimilation. For example, Emory Bogardus, a Park-trained sociologist, presented race prejudice as an inevitable feature of the stages of assimilation—of the progress of minority groups up the social scale—and therefore as an essentially benign force that preserved the distance between ethnic groups and maintained the social order. Many of the sociologists who trained at the University of Chicago took recent immigrants to the United States as the subjects of their assimilation model and argued that the experience of Negroes would eventually follow the same path as that of European immigrants.

The psychologists developed a different approach to the study of prejudice. Goodwin Watson (1899–1976), a Columbia-trained psychologist, made tests of racial animosity assuming that it arose from the actual experience of unfriendly contact between members of different races. Watson's view of prejudice made it less benign than Bogardus's but still treated it as a phenomenon based in real experience. Psychologists who followed Watson, however, began to cut its moorings in reality. Floyd Allport (1890–1970), an experimental social psychologist, and his students Daniel Katz and Kenneth Braly argued that prejudice was instead a matter of cultural stereotypes, inherently irrational and not based in any actual experience with individuals of the despised group. For Katz and Braly, race prejudice was a psychological phenomenon, a problem with people's internal mental states, a disorder of the mind. In this same vein, Gardner (1895–1966) and Lois Barclay (1902–2003) Murphy, and their students at Columbia University, Eugene (1912–2002) and Ruth Horowitz (1910–1997) (both pairs of psychologists were married couples), studied the racial attitudes of white children toward

Mamie Phipps Clark (1917–1983)

Mamie Phipps was born in 1917 in Hot Springs, Arkansas. She enrolled at Howard University at age 16 as a mathematics major where she met Kenneth Clark, who was majoring in psychology. Kenneth convinced her that psychology, rather than mathematics, would help her teach children, which is what she wanted to do with her degree. Kenneth and Mamie were married in 1938, when he was working on his doctorate in psychology at Columbia University and she was working as a secretary in the law offices of William Houston. Houston's brother was Charles Hamilton Houston, the dean of Howard Law school and lead attorney for the National Association for the Advancement of Colored People.

(Library of Congress)

For her Master's thesis in psychology at Howard, Mamie Clark collected data on racial identification in nursery school children in Washington D.C. In a number of articles based on the data collected for her thesis, Mamie and Kenneth argued that children are aware of their skin color at a relatively young age. The Clark's next project set out to test the "wishful thinking" hypothesis. Do black boys and girls wish they were white? In 1940 a grant from the Julius Rosenwald Fund allowed Mamie Clark to enter Columbia's Ph.D. program in

blacks. Their project was to try to understand the development of prejudice early in life, the assumption being that it was a learned behavior and not an innate trait. The Horowitzes showed that white boys (the sample included only males to avoid the extra variable of gender) from both the north and the south, and in segregated and in mixed groups, held prejudiced attitudes toward black people. Only those children who were raised in a communist commune in New York City showed no prejudice. The Murphys and the Horowitzes concluded that prejudice arises from stereotypes—from the negative beliefs and stories that circulate in a community—and not from actual contact with members of the other race.

Kenneth (1914–) and Mamie (1917–1983) Clark—another married couple—changed the focus of psychological examination to the attitudes of black children, rather than of whites toward blacks. Kenneth Clark received a Ph.D. in psychology from Columbia under Otto Klineberg in 1939. Mamie Clark studied at Howard University for her master's degree and earned a Ph.D. at Columbia in 1944. Both of the Clarks were African American. In one of the earliest studies of black children, the

psychology and begin gathering data for this project. At the same time, Kenneth was collecting data from selected northern and southern states. The Clarks found that black children, when presented with dolls identical in every way except for skin color, would often identify the brown doll as the "bad" doll and the white doll as the "good" doll. When asked to color pictures of children, black children often preferred to color them as lighter than their own skin color. The Clarks argued that racism had psychologically damaged these children to the extent that many of them rejected their own skin color.

In her Ph.D. work at Columbia University, Mamie Clark chose to work with the head of the psychology department, Henry E. Garrett. Garrett was the author of one of the first textbooks on statistics in psychology so he was a logical choice for Clark, a former mathematics major. However, Garrett was a notorious racist and Clark also chose him to prove to him that an African American student could perform as well as a white student. She received her Ph.D. from Columbia in 1944 but was unable to find employment. Her husband had found a position at the City College of New York, but an African American woman with a Ph.D. was an anomaly in the 1940s. After a year of being passed over for various research positions in favor of far less qualified whites, in 1946 she founded her own organization, the Northside Center for Child Development. The Northside Center was designed to offer psychological services to the community and provide them without regard to race. For more than half a century, the Northside Center has been a fixture in New York City, heavily involved in education, urban renewal, community action, and psychological services. It represents the dream of both Mamie and Kenneth Clark: a socially active and involved science that is part of the larger community in which it is located.

Clarks used projective psychological tests to gauge the attitudes of 150 African American nursery school students. Based on the ways these students identified and represented themselves on open-ended tests, the Clarks showed that the children were basically satisfied with their skin color and did not wish that they were white—contrary to some results that Ruth Horowitz had produced earlier.

Although the social psychologists emphasized the irrationality of prejudice and devised experiments to demonstrate its lack of basis in real experience, the Chicago sociologists and their radical variant, the Howard University circle, developed a social pathology model of African American culture. These sociologists, while maintaining Park's original stress on the inevitability of prejudice as a part of the cycle of assimilation, turned their attention to the impact of prejudice and discrimination on the formation of African Americans' personalities. They argued that racist attitudes created pathological social structures and malformed personalities in the members of the hated group. The sociological studies proceeded along two lines.

One was the ethnographic work on southern society pursued by Allison Davis (1902–1983), an African American Ph.D. in sociology from the University of Chicago and later a professor there, and John Dollard (1900–1980), a white anthropologist trained at Chicago and a professor at the Yale Institute of Human Relations. In *Caste and Class in a Southern Town* (1937), Davis and Dollard maintained that whites and blacks in the American South formed two separate castes, and that within those castes status was determined by membership in a social class. The authors conducted life-history interviews with African American families in Louisiana, concluding that class status within caste affected the personalities of African American youth even more significantly than caste itself did. But the organization of southern society based on caste and the race discrimination that caste sanctioned were definitely harmful for African American youth, frustrating their needs, impulses, and ambitions and causing them to act aggressively. Davis and Dollard argued that the belief, commonly held by white southerners, that "childlike" African Americans were content with "caste controls" was a fallacy designed to "prevent general human recognition of the basic deprivations and frustrations which life in a lower caste involves. But it is certain that the sting of caste is deep and sharp for most Negroes" (Davis and Dollard 1940, 245).

The second type of sociological study was pursued by Charles S. Johnson and E. Franklin Frazier, both associated with the radical Howard University variant of Chicago sociology. Johnson (1893–1956), an African American sociologist and student of Park at Chicago, studied the skin color preferences of rural African American children. He found that the children tended to reject the extremes of black and white skin, and to identify themselves as brown-skinned, which Johnson interpreted to mean that African Americans saw themselves as becoming a new brown race. Like the Clarks, Johnson argued that the children did not wish to be white—that in fact African American children preferred on the whole not even to associate with whites. As Johnson put it:

> The Negro community is built around the idea of adjustment to being a Negro, and it rejects escape into the white world. Community opinion builds up a picture of whites as a different kind of being, with whom one associates but does not become intimate. Without much conscious instruction the child is taught that his first loyalties are to the Negro group . . . . This doctrine is reinforced by stories of the meanness and cruelty of white people. To wish to be white is a sacrifice of pride. It is equivalent to a statement that Negroes are inferior and, consequently, that the youth himself is inferior. (Johnson 1941/1967, 301).

As a result of this view, segregation, according to Johnson, was not a pressing problem, since African Americans seemed to prefer it. In Park's four-stage model of race relations, accommodation to the dominant white culture and attitude adjustment in the face of the societal norms of discrimination and segregation were central parts of minority assimilation. Johnson's study showed African American youth to be completely adjusted to their segregated status, a finding in keeping with his Chicago training. The one place where African American youth did not accommodate well was the segregated southern school system. Here, Johnson argued, the completely inferior schools—the product of segregation—created "misshapen personalities" in black children (Johnson 1941/1967, 134).

Johnson's social pathology argument—that segregation had harmful effects on the black personality—was taken in more radical directions by his fellow member of the Howard circle, E. Franklin Frazier. Frazier (1894–1962) was an African American sociologist who earned a Ph.D. from the University of Chicago under Robert Park and who taught at Atlanta University, Fisk University, and Howard University. For Frazier, as for Johnson, African Americans seemed not to reject their own skin color, and Frazier saw them as striving toward a brown-skinned ideal rather than wishing to be white. Unlike Johnson, however, Frazier stressed the pathological state of the African American family, a state that was the result not of the inherent degeneracy of the black race but was the outcome of slavery and segregation. Although Johnson's subjects appeared relatively well adjusted to their segregated status, Frazier's subjects— African American children whom he interviewed in Kentucky and Washington, D.C.—were being actively harmed by it. Segregation pervaded black life, Frazier wrote, and the "pathological feature[s] of the Negro community" resulted from "the fact that the Negro is kept behind the walls of segregation and is not permitted to compete in the larger community . . . . Since the Negro is not required to compete in the larger world and to assume its responsibilities and suffer its penalties, he does not have an opportunity to mature" (Frazier 1940, 290).

The Chicago school, led by Robert Park and the Howard circle that it deeply influenced, including the sociologists Johnson and Frazier, rejected the idea of African cultural continuities that the Boasians, notably Herskovits, had emphasized. Instead, the Howard sociologists argued that African Americans, because of their heritage of slavery, segregation, discrimination, and poor environmental conditions, had developed a pathological variant of mainstream American society. Their lives were shaped not by a culture but by cultural deprivation. The sociologists compared African Americans to a white-American standard and found that their deviations from the norm included high numbers of female-headed households and a greater incidence of divorce, both helping to produce crime, poverty, and delinquency in their communities. The more African Americans deviated from the standard, the more they would be prevented from achieving the fulfillment of Park's race relations cycle—the development of normative patterns that would allow them to assimilate.

Segregation was not only psychologically harmful in its creation of social pathologies, it was considered physically harmful as well. The psychological toll of racism noted by the Howard sociologists had a physical parallel in the work of W. Montague Cobb (1904–1990). Cobb was a Howard University-trained M.D. who returned there to teach anatomy and physical anthropology. In the 1930s he worked with the NAACP National Health Committee to shape national health care policy. Cobb's work contravened ideas about African American infertility—a stereotype dating from the era of polygenism that the black race was inherently sickly and doomed to extinction. Cobb demonstrated instead the deleterious physical effects that segregation had on African Americans. He argued that ending segregation of hospitals and improving health care for African Americans would help solve the whole nation's public health problems. Similarly, effective public health policies would also help end the segregation and racism of the nation's medical institutions. Cobb was a political activist as well as a doctor and scientist, working on Capitol Hill to bring about health care reform and fight segregated institutions.

Park's social pathology model was highly influential not only among the Howard sociologists, especially Frazier. It also formed the basis for Gunnar Myrdal's *An American Dilemma*, a 1944 book on the problem of race relations, and for legal arguments in the 1954 *Brown vs. Board of Education* decision desegregating the public schools. According to the social pathology argument, African Americans could and should assimilate to Western white culture—any emphasis on their African heritage or African cultural roots would only get in their way. The means to achieve racial equality was through assimilation into the mainstream by overcoming whatever social pathologies prevented African Americans from becoming just like whites. Full integration and assimilation into white society would mean both psychological and physical health for African Americans. Anyone arguing for preservation of the unique culture that an African heritage created, according to those connected to or influenced by Howard sociology, was an apologist for inequality.

Another central aspect of the sociological and social-psychological study of prejudice was the degree to which it made prejudice a psychological problem. These scientists perceived prejudice as a problem of individual people's attitudes—a problem, specifically, of irrational attitudes, of attitudes not based in reality. It became a problem that could be solved only by understanding the inner workings of people's psyches, of their hearts and minds. As a psychological problem, the concept of prejudice became detached from broader sociological causes, like economics, relationships of power, or institutional organization. The scientists discussed here psychologized the problem of prejudice, and, in doing so, depoliticized it.

Genetics and the Critique of Eugenics

The retreat from scientific racism among American and British geneticists was more measured than among the social scientists. Biologists repudiatied eugenics and its typological and hierarchical assumptions in several gradual but distinct steps that were not complete until after World War II. At first, during the1910s and 1920s, eugenists and geneticists—at this point there was no distinction between them—generally condemned race crossing as a central plank of their eugenist stance. Racial purity had to be maintained, and that meant avoiding race mixture. In the United States, antimiscegenation laws were on the books in 41 states in order to prevent interracial sex and marriage. No published opposition by geneticists to arguments about the dangers of race crossing existed before 1924. Such works as *Race Crossing in Jamaica* (1929) by the American eugenists Charles Davenport (1866–1944) and Morris Steggerda (1900–1950) condemned the practice.

Davenport and Steggerda divided the Jamaican population into three groups: blacks, whites, and the mixture of these two—browns or mulattoes. The authors believed that disharmonies appeared in the hybrid race of mulattoes. In a few cases the disharmonies were physical: for example, the long legs of the Negro combined with the short arms of the white to produce a poor physical specimen. But in most cases the different mental traits of the races produced mental disharmonies in the mixed offspring. Davenport and Steggerda used their study to argue against race mixture since one could never tell if a disharmony, either mental or physical, would result, and one could not control breeding thoroughly enough to prevent disharmonious combinations. Under such conditions it was best to avoid the mixing of two races altogether.

This argument resonated in the genetics community of the 1920s. Edward M. East (1879–1938), a Harvard University geneticist and, from 1919 to the mid-1930s, the most influential American scientific spokesman on the social and political impact of genetics, thoroughly agreed with Davenport and Steggerda's conclusions, placing them on a more secure scientific footing. East was a population geneticist and a political liberal, an advocate of civil rights for all people. Nonetheless, he argued that race mixing caused the breakup of a harmoniously integrated genotype. The interbreeding of different races would destroy the genetic composition of a race, which had been selected for, maintained, and coadapted over generations. Physical, mental, and temperamental disharmonies would be the result. Crosses between blacks and whites, East concluded, should be avoided, as the Negro is inferior to the white and would disrupt his integrated genotype.

East's Harvard colleague and fellow population geneticist, William Castle (1867–1962), provided one of the earliest arguments against the notion of the deleterious effects of race crossing. In 1916, Castle presented a general critique of eugenics, arguing that society could not be managed like a farm, even though he accepted contemporary eugenist views on the segregation and sterilization of the feebleminded. By the mid-1920s he had developed and expanded his critique to argue that genes do not determine social status. The higher average ability of the wealthy is an unproven assumption and probably due to the environment and, therefore, the differential birthrate is not necessarily dysgenic. Moreover, Castle concluded, negative eugenics interferes with individual liberty. Against East, Castle argued that there was absolutely no scientific evidence that biological disharmonies would result from wide race crosses. In a move that shows the basic conservatism of his critique, however, Castle felt that there could be social objections to the mixture of widely different races. And he had no hesitation in pronouncing his view, like that of many in the white scientific elite, that whites were as superior in intelligence to blacks as blacks were in amount of melanin to whites.

Herbert Spencer Jennings (1868–1947), an American zoologist and anatomist, also demonstrates, as Castle does, the distinctly mixed character of these early critiques of eugenics. In a 1923 article published in *The Survey* magazine, Jennings presented a solid, if measured, critique of eugenic immigration restriction policies, arguing that most mental or physical defects observed in immigrants resulted from environmental handicaps and not from racial degeneracy. Therefore, discrimination on the basis of race or nationality was unjustified. Nonetheless, in 1930 Jennings accepted Davenport and Steggerda's conclusions about the physical and mental disharmonies of hybrid Jamaicans and applied the same argument to dogs—that widely different breeds should not be mated lest biological monstrosities result. Under the influence of Castle's critique, Jennings later modified his view, arguing in 1941 that either hybrid vigor or hybrid weakness could possibly result from race mixing, and distinguishing biological reasons from social prohibitions against miscegenation.

The examples of East, Castle, and Jennings show that training in mathematical population genetics, and adoption of its antitypological stance that populations are comprised of continuously varying individuals, did not necessitate antieugenist or antiracist positions. Although both Castle and East were population geneticists, measuring gene frequency and flow in ever-fluctuating populations, their views on race crossing differed widely. The new science, particularly in its early days, did not link up to only one sort of racial belief. More important than scientific theories in determining a stance on race were the social and political developments of the 1930s.

In response to the Nazi race doctrines that were being implemented in the 1930s before the start of World War II, the genetics community shifted from an earlier condemnation of racial mixing to a belief that more scientific investigation of the matter was needed before definite conclusions could be reached. This agnostic stage is represented by two influential and popular works published by prominent geneticists in the 1930s: *We Europeans: A Survey of "Racial" Problems* (1936) by Julian Huxley (1887–1975) and Alfred C. Haddon, and *Heredity and Politics* (1938) by J. B. S. Haldane (1892–1964). Both books concluded that the evidence for or against race mixing was inadequate and more scientific study was necessary.

Huxley, a geneticist, ethologist, embryologist, and popularizer of Darwinism, and Haddon, an anthropologist, attacked Nazi race doctrines, using genetics to show that Nazi claims about race were pseudoscience. The focus of the book was German racism with its doctrine of Aryan or Nordic superiority and Jewish racial inferiority. Huxley and Haddon argued that the idea of a pure race was a fallacy and that there was no way to reliably classify the races of Europe. All traits were a combination of nature and nurture; division of humankind by blood type bore no relation to racial classifications based on headform; nor did intelligence correlate in any way with physical type. Race, the authors concluded, was a confused term, especially when it came to the European races, and it should be replaced by ethnicity. But *We Europeans* stopped short of an outright denial of hereditary mental differences between the races or of condoning all race mixing.

In *Heredity and Politics*, Haldane, a major contributor to the evolutionary synthesis (the integration of evolution and genetics), argued the agnostic line that until a scientific study on the effects of race crossing was done, no dogmatism about it one way or the other should be countenanced. A similar shift toward agnosticism took place among geneticists on the issue of hereditary mental differences between the races. In the heyday of eugenics geneticists had been certain that such differences existed; between 1924 and 1939 they began to argue that, as with race crossing, there simply wasn't enough evidence to prove it one way or the other. Both privately, however, and in some published writings throughout the 1930s most geneticists continued to believe that racial differences in intelligence certainly did exist. Julian Huxley exemplifies this attitude well: for him racism combined with the awareness that the scientific jury was still out. He argued in 1931 that further study would probably show that racial differences existed and that Africans were inferior to Europeans in desirable traits. However, these differences would be slight and the overlap between the races would be great.

After the war, as the next chapter will explore in more detail, the genetics community underwent yet another shift, from the agnostic position to the outright condemnation both of Nazi racial doctrines and of the notion of hereditary mental inequalities. Similarly, the agnostic tone about race crossing that many geneticists maintained before the war shifted during and after the war to a more positive endorsement of the practice. Now race crossing was—at the very worst—biologically harmless. There could be no scientific justification whatsoever for arguing against it. But this last position led geneticists into the postwar dilemma that faced them in the drafting of the UNESCO Statements on Race. As geneticists they knew that, even if racial mental differences were nonexistent and strictures against race mixing scientifically unjustified, all people were not absolutely equal in genetic endowment. Biological differences among individuals were clear. The geneticists' problem in the 1950s was to detach this view, which they identified as scientific, from any moral considerations. People should be treated equally and afforded equal opportunities even if—and especially if—it was a scientific fact that they were not genetically equal. Science was to be disconnected from moral values; social views of equality need not be, and should not be, derived from or dependent on genetic or biological equality. To what extent this argument could be maintained—and to what extent it fell apart in the wake of the UNESCO Statements—will be taken up in the next chapter.

Haldane and Huxley were both politically liberal—Haldane, a socialist and communist, always more so than Huxley—but neither was as consistently leftist or as consistent a critic of racism and eugenics as Lancelot Hogben (1895–1975). Hogben was trained as a mathematical population geneticist at Cambridge, where he also became a feminist and a socialist. After being jailed as a result of his refusal to fight in World War I, he took up an academic appointment in South Africa, where he was horrified by apartheid, the state-sanctioned segregation and disenfranchisement of blacks. Upon his return to England he became professor of social biology at the London School of Economics, and throughout the 1930s published critiques of eugenics and its simplistic formulations. His critiques made three basic points. First, Hogben emphasized the role of the environment in forming traits, expanding the meaning of environment to include not only education and training but also the prenatal environment of the womb, which affects the way that the genotype, or genetic makeup, will be expressed in the phenotype, or appearance. Hogben cited the work of the geneticist Lionel Penrose, who showed in a famous set of experiments that Down's syndrome, known in the early twentieth century as "Mongolian idiocy," was a genetic defect caused by the environment of the womb of older mothers, not passed down the generations by defective germ-plasm, as the eugenists had argued earlier. Second, Hogben showed that most pathological or abnormal conditions in human beings were caused by recessive genes, that is, those that were carried but not expressed because they were masked by a normal dominant gene. In the heterozygous condition, in which a dominant and a recessive were paired, the recessive trait would be hidden. Such defective recessive traits would be difficult to eliminate through eugenic sterilization, Hogben argued, because they do not show up regularly in the phenotype. Thus he questioned the efficacy of negative eugenics. Third, social biologists—of which Hogben was officially the first in Britain—must improve the precision of their definitions. Feeblemindedness, he said, was a grab bag, a catchall term that covered many different conditions caused in myriad different ways. No single gene lay at the bottom of it, and the environment was crucial in creating it. Thus Hogben questioned a central conceptual category of the eugenists.

None of these critics of the older eugenics, neither Hogben, nor Haldane, nor Huxley, ever actually gave up on the eugenic ideal. Hogben, for example, along with his wife, a demographer by the name of Enid Charles, became concerned with the declining birthrate in England and the uncertain future that the British population faced. To combat what they viewed as a growing crisis, Hogben and Charles wanted to encourage the development of what was called in later decades "medical genetics"—a science of medicine that focused on prevention—on the elimination of disease before it occurred by the elimination of those genetic defects that caused it. Though medical genetics was billed as pure science, as neutral in contrast to the open social agenda of the eugenists, its continuity with eugenic themes was clear.

Similarly, Haldane and Huxley always kept a place for eugenics. Haldane, like Hogben, argued that recessive genetic conditions were difficult to detect because they were often hidden, thus difficult to treat by sterilization. Moreover, Haldane noted, mutations, spontaneous changes in the genetic makeup, were constantly introducing new traits into the population, most of them harmful, and because of the unpredictability of their occurrence they were largely beyond control by sterilization. Haldane argued that the human population had not changed in genetic endowment in hundreds of thousands of years, so changes introduced by eugenists in a few generations could have little effect. And yet Haldane also believed that the sterilization of those with dominant sex-linked traits like deaf-mutism was thoroughly scientifically justified, as was the prevention of immigration of people who were not up to par physically or mentally. In the socialist state that Haldane envisioned, eugenics would have a central place, and a uniquely fair one, because the state would have equalized the effects of the environment. Huxley never took Haldane's socialist position, but he too held to an enlightened eugenics, which he thought ought to become part of religion. Huxley also believed, even as he argued against hereditary racial differences, that class differences in England had a genetic basis. Thus the class biases of the older eugenics lived on even among its critics, and even as race was losing its power as a classificatory tool.

The example of these geneticists shows that the crucial combination of their science with a leftward shift in politics accounts for their critique of the older eugenics and the scientific racism that supported it. Population genetics alone could not have accounted for the development of this critique. Indeed, the geneticist Ronald A. Fisher (1890–1962)—along with Haldane and the American geneticist Sewall Wright, an architect of the evolutionary synthesis—was as steeped in population thinking as the others, but his politics were decidedly right-wing and he was an advocate of old-fashioned social selection of the "fittest." As a result, Fisher did not play the role in the retreat of scientific racism that Haldane did. On the contrary, Fisher and his fellow members of the conservative Eugenics Society looked with interest upon the Nazi sterilization campaign of the early 1930s. It was only as news of the Nazi atrocities spread that the members of the Eugenics Society had to retreat with some awkwardness from their eugenical views.

From this review of racial science in the first four decades of the twentieth century, a number of important themes emerge. First, in their most definitive break from the traditions of social Darwinism and eugenics, the scientists discussed here fully recognized the importance of the environment as a determining factor—a factor as important as, or even more important than, inborn biology. This was recognized by scientists in genetics, anthropology, sociology, and psychology. Geneticists began to treat nature and nurture as complex and interdependent, as mutually influential and constantly interacting. Anthropologists recognized the importance of environment by stressing the role of culture as the essential determinant of behavior. Cultural anthropology, social psychology, and sociology formed themselves during this period around the study of the environment as sciences of the environmental impact on behavior. Psychologists recognized the determining influence of socioeconomic status on IQ test scores, and sociologists studying prejudice came to see treatment by the dominant white culture as a central factor in forming African American behavior and identity. The environmental turn in all of these sciences helped to break apart the entrenched paradigm of race.

The second major theme here is that the critique of scientific racism, in whatever form, was a basically conservative one up to the beginning of World War II. None of the critics we have encountered here represented a complete overthrow of the traditions that produced them. Even as they rejected links between race and society, culture, and mentality, they shared important beliefs with their predecessors. The Boasians, for example, cooperated with and accommodated themselves to the conservative physical anthropologists. The critics of IQ testing never gave up on the tests. The geneticists continued to cling to a eugenic ideal. And the sociologists used norms of white society as their standard, rejecting the radical relativism of the cultural anthropologists.

Finally, a combination of political, social, and scientific developments produced the critique of scientifically sanctioned racism. Science did not do it on its own; it took science shaped by the political motives of political actors. Practitioners of both the biological and especially the social sciences turned toward political activism, toward the dream of achieving a just society. That commitment, combined with the fallout from the Great Depression, with revulsion at the lynching of African Americans, and with horror at the Nazi campaigns, helped shape their critique of racism in the sciences. We have seen here the roots of this critique and its gradual development during the 1930s. World War II radicalized the critique. The conservatism that was countenanced earlier and the ties to earlier racial ideas lost their acceptability during and after the war. Only after the war was the liberal orthodoxy on race definitively established.

Bibliographic Essay

The title for this chapter, and the concept of a "retreat" that it describes, are drawn from Elazar Barkan, *The Retreat of Scientific Racism: Changing Concepts of Race in Britain and the United States between the World Wars* (Cambridge: Cambridge University Press, 1992). Barkan's study is especially strong on the British and American biologists' critique of eugenics and racist biology. It also covers Boas and the Boasians, though to a lesser extent. For further details on the life and work of Franz Boas, see George Stocking, *Race, Culture, and Evolution* (Chicago: University of Chicago Press, 1968), especially the essays "From Physics to Ethnology," which charts Boas's development as a cultural anthropologist, "The Critique of Racial Formalism," which discusses Boas's studies of headform, and "Franz Boas and the Culture Concept in Historical Perspective," which describes what was new about the Boasian definition of culture. Also useful in this last regard is Stocking's introductory essay to the *Shaping of American Anthropology (1883–1911): A Franz Boas Reader* (New York: Basic Books, 1974). Boas's work on headform is also treated in John S. Allen, "Franz Boas's Physical Anthropology: The Critique of Racial Formalism Revisited," *Current Anthropology* 30 (1989): 79–84. On the Boasians, see Richard Handler, "Boasian Anthropology and the Critique of American Culture," *American Quarterly* 42 (1990): 252–273. On the Boasians' relationship to the conservative branches of anthropology and to eugenics, see Dwight D. Hoover, "A Paradigm Shift: The Concept of Race in the 1920s and 1930s," *Conspectus of History* 1 (1981): 82–100. For the inherent contradictions in the Boasians' definition of culture and the way court cases capitalized on those contradictions, see Peggy Pascoe, "Miscegenation Law, Court Cases, and Ideologies of 'Race' in Twentieth-Century America," *Journal of American History* 83 (1996): 44–69. Some of Boas's major papers, including the ones quoted in this chapter, are collected in Franz Boas, *Race, Language, and Culture* (New York: The Free Press, 1940).

The relationship of Boas to W. E. B. DuBois and the study of black folklore was drawn from Lee D. Baker, *From Savage to Negro: Anthropology and the Construction of Race, 1896–1954* (Berkeley: University of California Press, 1998). On a view different from Baker's of Boas and the Boasians, especially regarding their attitudes toward African American culture, see E. L. Cerroni-Long, "Benign Neglect? Anthropology and the Study of Blacks in the United States," *Journal of Black Studies* 17, No. 4 (1987): 438–459. W. E. B. Du Bois's comments quoted in this chapter are from W. E. B. Du Bois, "A Chronicle of Race Relations," *Phylon* 2 (1941): 172–190. On Herskovits, see Walter Jackson, "Melville Herskovits and the Search for Afro-American Culture," in *Malinowski, Rivers, Benedict, and Others: Essays on Culture and Personality*, ed. George W. Stocking, Jr. (1986): 95–126; and Mark Helbring, "Feeling Universality and Thinking Particularistically: Alain Locke, Franz Boas, Melville Herskovits, and the Harlem Renaissance," *Prospects* 19 (1994): 289–314. The primary source is Melville J. Herskovits, *The Myth of the Negro Past* (New York: Harper and Brothers, 1941).

The subtitle for the section on scientific studies of prejudice is taken from Franz Samelson, "From 'Race Psychology' to 'Studies in Prejudice': Some Observations on the Thematic Reversal in Social Psychology," *Journal of the History of the Behavioral Sciences* 14 (1978): 265–278. The discussion on the sociological and social-psychological studies of prejudice was based on John P. Jackson, Jr., *Social Scientists for Social Justice: Making the Case Against Segregation* (New York: New York University Press, 2001).

On the assimilation vs. cultural pluralism issue, see R. Fred Wacker, "Assimilation and Cultural Pluralism in American Social Thought," *Phylon* 40 (1979): 325–333, which focuses on the Chicago assimilationists. Park and the Chicago school of sociology are also treated in John H. Stanfield, "The 'Negro Problem' Within and Beyond the Institutional Nexus of Pre-World War One Sociology," *Phylon* 43 (1982): 187–201 and in Stanfield, "Race Relations Research and Black Americans Between the Two World Wars," *Journal of Ethnic Studies* 11, No. 3 (1983): 61–93. A discussion of the methods of the Chicago school can be found in Jennifer Platt, "The Chicago School and Firsthand Data," *History of the Human Sciences* 7 (1994): 57–80 and Stow Persons, *Ethnic Studies at Chicago,*

1905–45 (Urbana: University of Illinois Press, 1987). The primary source documents quoted in this chapter are Charles S. Johnson, *Growing Up in the Black Belt: Negro Youth in the Rural South* (Washington D.C.: American Council on Education, 1941; reprint, New York: Schocken Books, 1967); and E. Franklin Frazier, *Negro Youth at the Crossways: Their Personality Development in the Middle States* (Washington, D.C.: American Council on Education, 1940).

On the critiques of IQ testing, see William B. Thomas, "Black Intellectuals, Intelligence Testing, and the Sociology of Knowledge," *Teachers College Record* 85, No. 3 (Spring 1984): 477–501. For a somewhat different interpretation, see Wayne J. Urban, "The Black Scholar and Intelligence Testing: The Case of Horace Mann Bond," *Journal of the History of the Behavioral Sciences* 25 (1989): 323–334. On Thomas Russell Garth, see Graham Richards, "Reconceptualizing the History of Race Psychology: Thomas Russell Garth (1872–1939) and How He Changed His Mind," *Journal of the History of the Behavioral Sciences* 34 (1998): 15–32. Nancy Stepan's *The Idea of Race in Science: Great Britain, 1800-1960*, (Hamden, CT: Archon, 1982) includes a chapter on race science before the Second World War that gives a comprehensive overview of the whole period and treats particularly well the British critique of eugenics and the fate of eugenics in Britain at that time. The discussion of genetics was largely informed by William B. Provine, "Geneticists and Race," *American Zoologist* 26 (1986): 857–887, and by Provine, "Geneticists and the Biology of Race Crossing," *Science* 182 (1973): 790–796. Bentley Glass, "Geneticists Embattled: Their Stand Against Rampant Eugenics and Racism in America During the 1920s and 1930s," *Proceedings of the American Philosophical Society* 130 (1986): 130–154, is a response to Provine and provides a slightly different view.

6

The Liberal Orthodoxy, 1940–1960

By the early 1930s, scientific racism was in retreat, the outcome of several decades of steadily building critique. Even before the rise of Nazism, the idea that the races were different and unequal in mental and moral capabilities was falling into disrepute among scientists in all fields. The criticisms presented by such geneticists as Jennings and Castle of Davenport and Steggerda's work showed that the racial hereditarian position was weak and easily questioned. Under the influence of Thomas Hunt Morgan's research program on the genetics of the fruit fly Drosophila, biologists began to argue the difficulty, if not the impossibility, of applying such technical results in any meaningful way to the culture and mentality of human racial groups. A fully new view to replace scientific racism—the view that understanding humankind in terms of shifting populations rather than fixed racial types—had not yet come into focus, and would not until after 1950. And of course there were always such conservative holdouts against the building critique as Reginald Ruggles Gates, the British geneticist who continued to believe well into the 1930s that the races were fixed and distinct biological species. But by and large even before 1933 a pervasive doubt had set in among biologists that racial differences and racial hierarchies could be clearly defined.

Meanwhile, among social scientists, environmental interpretations were becoming paramount and a more radical critique was building. Psychologists, particularly social psychologists who occupied the left-leaning branches of their discipline, stressed the role of nurture, upbringing, and experience in shaping behavior. Physical anthropologists, who once relied on race as the cornerstone of their science, were becoming aware of their disciplinary and methodological anarchy and beginning to drop the term race from their textbooks and theories. Cultural anthropologists using their ethnographic methods, studied cultures and societies, which they defined as separate from the notion of race. They tended to criticize race as a concept without meaning or restrict it entirely to physical characteristics. The sociologists had, from the 1920s on, ignored biology—and race along with it—as irrelevant to their concerns.

World War II poster of two men in hard hats, one an African American (Library of Congress)

These trends toward doubt—some of a mild and agnostic variety, some already comprising a thoroughgoing critique—were accelerated by the rise of Nazism in 1933 and 1934. Scientists in these years came under increasing public pressure to renounce "Aryan science," which most of them did, again except for the conservatives. Boas, for example, worked on behalf of German Jewish refugees to the United States, and spoke publicly against Nazism and racism. But until 1938, there was little organized response among scientists. They tended to object, when they did, as individuals, and the scientific community did not yet speak with a unified voice.

This mode of individual response, however, changed dramatically into a community response in 1938 with the outbreak of war. In that year, for example, both the American Anthropological Association and the Society for the Psychological Study of Social Issues publicized antiracist statements. In 1939, the Seventh International Congress of Genetics in Edinburgh issued the Geneticists' Manifesto, a document intended to refute Nazi doctrines of scientific racism. None of these statements yet contained the egalitarian, cultural critique of scientific racism that would be represented by the UNESCO (United Nations Educational, Scientific, and Cultural Organization) statements on race of the 1950s. But they do show how definitively the tone of the scientific community shifted with the outbreak of war. The building critiques of earlier decades now turned into a wholesale and nearly unanimous refutation of scientifically justified racism. The retreat had become a rout. The revulsion against Nazi racial doctrines was so strong that no scientist wanted, even by his silence, to be associated with them. Scientists built international coalitions across the board to refute the scientific legitimacy and sanction of racism.

The Geneticists' Manifesto

An examination of one of these international antiracist documents—the Geneticists' Manifesto—shows, however, that even though the revulsion against Nazism and the critique of scientific racism were fully in place, no consensus yet existed about what should replace race as an organizing principle, or how to treat race so that it was separate from racism. Among biologists and physical anthropologists, ignoring the biological basis of traits and behaviors was never an option as it was for the social scientists. Geneticists rejected what they saw as the extremes of the sociologists' and cultural anthropologists' environmental determinism on the one hand and the scientific racism of the traditional eugenists on the other. Geneticists were nonetheless loath to give up on the idea that traits in individuals were hereditarily determined, at least in part.

Moreover, many geneticists and physical anthropologists—even as they renounced scientific racism—believed that the races were not wholly identical and that some distinctions had to exist among them. Thus the biologists' agnosticism about what the *real* racial differences were coexisted uneasily with the social scientists' outright environmentalism. These disagreements about what should be substituted for the rejected racial typologies led to problems following the drafting of a statement on race by a UNESCO-appointed committee of scientists.

The geneticists' middle ground—what they saw as their reasonable compromise—was represented in the 1939 Manifesto. The American Marxist geneticist Hermann J. Muller was the principal author of the document, which was signed by twenty-two other geneticists with socialist or Marxist allegiances. The Manifesto made the case for the substantial hereditary determination of intellectual, moral, and psychological traits in individuals—if not, perhaps, in nations or races—and consequently for a socially responsible eugenics. For these left-leaning geneticists, the only way eugenics could become rational was if the state equalized environment and opportunity for all by turning to socialism. Only in a socialist state such as the Soviet Union, which had leveled all class differences, could scientists tease apart the environmental and hereditary components of traits and fully understand the genetic determination of intelligence, character, and personality. Only under such conditions could eugenics be responsibly applied.

Muller came to the drafting of the statement as a dedicated feminist. He believed that scientists should learn to control reproduction artificially, leaving women free to love and work as they chose. In the projected socialist state, which he described in his 1935 book *Out of the Night*, Muller imagined the artificial insemination of women with the sperm of men of high intelligence as the means to raise the intellectual level of the whole population and discourage the unfit from breeding. Thus Muller wrote in 1935 that "it would be possible for the majority of the population to become the innate quality of such men as Newton, Leonardo, Pasteur, Beethoven, Omar Khayyam, Pushkin, Sun Yat-sen, Marx (I purposely mention men of different fields and races), or even to possess their various faculties combined" (Muller 1935, 113). Clearly this was not the class- and race-based eugenics of Davenport and Steggerda, nor of the Nazis, but Muller's hereditarianism remained unquestioned.

The Geneticists' Manifesto reflects the signers' belief that there were certainly differences among individuals—hence the possibility of and need for eugenics. About differences among nations, races, or classes the geneticists were less certain. Those who signed on, among them such leftists as Haldane, Hogben, Huxley, Theodosius Dobzhansky, and Conrad H. Waddington, agreed that a radical change in social conditions toward socialism would make possible the genetic improvement of mankind. "The most important objectives," of such an enlightened eugenics, they wrote, were

> the improvement of those genetic characteristics which make (a) for health, (b) for the complex called intelligence, and (c) for those temperamental qualities that favour fellow-feeling and social behavior rather than those (today most esteemed by many) which make for personal "success," as success is usually understood at present.
>
> A more widespread understanding of biological principles will bring with it the realization that much more than the prevention of genetic deterioration is to be sought for, and that the raising of the level of the average of the population to nearly that of the highest now existing in isolated individuals, in regard to physical well-being, intelligence, and temperamental qualities, is an achievement that would—so far as purely genetic considerations are concerned—be physically possible within a comparatively small number of generations. Thus everyone might look upon "genius" combined of course with stability, as his birthright. (Geneticists' Manifesto 1939, 521).

Through the early 1940s, the consensus therefore existed among geneticists that intellectual, psychological, and moral traits were genetically determined. Though they differed among themselves about the relative contributions of nature and nurture, none doubted that nature played a significant role. Both positive and negative eugenics therefore made sense: unfitness should be eliminated and desirable traits enhanced through rational breeding. Not all of the geneticists who signed the Manifesto shared Muller's idea that the important genetic diversity was mainly among individuals and that the best among individuals must be cultivated. Haldane, for example, who also became a Marxist, held to racial and even class differences, and he was not alone. But the unified front presented by the Manifesto emphasized individual and not group differences.

In the two decades that followed the publication of the Manifesto, however, the consensus it represented collapsed. The middle ground it occupied disappeared. The postwar antiracist liberal orthodoxy shifted the tone even further in the environmentalist direction than during the 1930s. After the revelation of Nazi atrocities, advocating eugenics of any kind became more than unfashionable: it became morally abhorrent. Even outright hereditarianism, seemingly unbalanced by a belief in the power of nurture, came in for critique. In addition, many people like Muller—who was so enamored of the Soviet system that he immigrated to the Soviet Union in 1934—became disenchanted with the Soviet experiment. The state-sponsored rise of Lamarckian Lysenkoism, the attack on Western chromosome-based genetics as "bourgeois," and the hounding and murder of geneticists inspired a general revulsion. As they saw capitalism persist even after the Great Depression, Muller and his leftist colleagues came to believe that the Soviet model had failed.

The socialist eugenists were therefore compelled to give up, at least in public, their advocacy of hereditarianism and their hopes for a scientifically rational eugenics. But these geneticists never really completely abandoned hereditarianism and eugenics—their beliefs only went underground: Muller, for example, remained a closet eugenist into the 1960s. By the early 1940s, their fragile middle ground had disappeared, but geneticists and those they inspired continued quietly to hold to hereditarian beliefs. And they continued quietly to assume that such beliefs were entirely separate from racist doctrines. The tensions such beliefs created when they came into contact with the outspoken environmentalism of the social scientists were clear in the postwar attempts to establish a new liberal consensus on race.

The subtle but important point to understand here is that even though scientists repudiated scientific racism, especially in its Nazi formulations, they did not necessarily repudiate the concept of race. They tried to salvage and reenvision the concept, to separate its new meaning from the old political misuses, and to define race so that it would no longer mean hierarchy or typology. Race no longer occupied its former keystone position in the human sciences but the concept did not vanish entirely. Scientists rejected racism, but they did not reject race.

Wartime Antiracism: Benedict, Montagu, and Dunn and Dobzhansky

Three popular books on race published during the war and in the immediate postwar period illustrate especially well the scientists' challenge: to redefine race while rejecting racism. Each one argued, in its own way, against any scientific justification for racism.

The first of these books was Ruth Benedict's *Race: Science and Politics* (1940). A cultural anthropologist trained by Franz Boas, and herself a professor of anthropology at Columbia, Benedict took the Boasian perspective on race, separating it from language and culture. Race was not in any way equivalent to nationality; national and linguistic differences between people were entirely cultural and social and had no racial or biological basis. She thoroughly debunked the notion of pure races or pure types, arguing instead that the world's population was composed of "areas of characterization"—groups of people that inbred for a while, forming a set of stable hereditary characteristics. That stability was then undermined by migration, mixture with other groups, and interbreeding. Thus areas of characterization broke up and new ones formed, and the whole cycle repeated itself. This pattern was typical of the history of the human race, Benedict claimed. There was no way to trace the innumerable present-day areas of characterization back to a few aboriginal races or essential types. Throughout history there had been only shifting populations. Benedict did not deny that there were races, or that those races differed in physical or even mental and emotional traits. But she did deny that those differences provided any grounds for claims of superiority or inferiority, and she relied in part on Klineberg's influential studies of IQ tests to argue her point that differences could exist without hierarchy.

Benedict distinguished carefully between race and racism. The former, she argued, was a scientific term, capable of scientific investigation and definition. Racism, however, the dogma of the superiority of one people over another, she deemed "the modern superstition" (Benedict 1959, 98). She provided a history of racism, from ancient Rome to the Third Reich, in order to show that racism never had any scientific basis but was instead always used for political ends. Racism was "a politician's plaything" used "to condemn the enemy of the moment" (Benedict 1959, 138). The solution to racism, according to Benedict, was not to get rid of the notion of race but to provide equal political rights and thereby eliminate conflict between people. Full citizenship and equal rights extended to all would negate the cause of racial hatred and racial persecution. Benedict did concede, however, that most African Americans needed improvement in their social conditions before they would be ready for full citizenship.

The antiracist conclusions of the book were publicized even more widely in a pamphlet entitled "The Races of Mankind" that Benedict wrote with her Columbia colleague Gene Weltfish and published in 1943. The pamphlet ended with a challenge to Americans to rid themselves of prejudice so that the United States "could stand unashamed before the Nazis and condemn, without confusion, their doctrines of a Master Race" (Benedict 1959, 192). But the pamphlet became controversial when conservative advocates of racial typology and hierarchy objected to it as Communist propaganda.

The second of these wartime antiracist books was Ashley Montagu's *Man's Most Dangerous Myth: The Fallacy of Race* (1942). Montagu was a physical and cultural anthropologist, trained in the latter field by Boas, and though his book appeared only two years after Benedict's, it took a much more radical position. Race, Montagu stated at the outset, was a myth. The myth of race held that physical traits were somehow linked with mental, social, and emotional characteristics, and that this linkage was supposedly transferred wholesale from generation to generation within distinct human groups. The notion of such a linkage and the idea of distinctly separable human groups were both fallacies, Montagu claimed. First of all, anthropologists should learn from population geneticists, who study gene frequencies and distributions, not congeries of traits transferred wholesale. Second, any classification of humanity, even the seemingly self-evident division of people into four major racial groups, is arbitrary. Races, if they are to be defined at all, must be defined in populational terms—as groups of people in which the incidence of certain genes occur. And if they are to be so defined, it must be understood that races can then be differentiated only on the basis of physical traits, not mental or moral ones, which are entirely cultural in origin. The nineteenth-century notion that race could apply to physical, mental, and moral traits and was determinative of behavior was completely unscientific. Further, there were no grounds for claiming superiority of one group of people over another. The genetic differences between blacks and whites were, for instance, very small, and there was no basis to alleged black biological inferiority. The Negro type—a blending of many other peoples—was perfectly harmonious and biologically well adapted.

The notion of racial purity, Montagu argued, was a myth. There were no pure races: every group of people was a mixture. Not only was race mixture not harmful, but it had a creative power, as hybrids showed a definite vigor. In fact—and here Montagu displayed his radicalism clearly—the term "race" ought to be

Ashley Montagu (1905–1999)

Montagu was born in London's East End to a family of recent Jewish immigrants from Eastern Europe. His original name was Israel Ehrenberg, which he changed during college to Montague Francis Ashley-Montagu, and later shortened to Ashley Montagu, an amalgam of names drawn from literary figures whom he admired.

As a teenager Montagu met and befriended the physical anthropologist Sir Arthur Keith whose interest in skulls Montagu shared, but whose beliefs in racial hierarchy and innate human aggressiveness he did not. Montagu attended college at University College, London and at the London School of Economics, studying psychology with Charles Spearman, statistics with Karl Pearson, physical anthropology with Grafton Elliot Smith, and cultural anthropology with Bronislaw Malinowski.

In 1927 Montagu immigrated to New York City, where he taught anatomy at New York University Dental School, and developed an interest in comparative primate anatomy. He also became involved with the circle of Boasian anthropologists at Columbia University, ultimately receiving a Ph.D. in cultural anthropology under Franz Boas and Ruth Benedict. His dissertation, *Coming into Being among the Australian Aborigines: A Study of the Procreative Beliefs of the Native Tribes*, was published in 1937 as his first major book.

In the 1940s, Montagu's three major academic supporters (Boas, Benedict, and Malinowski) died, and he had trouble finding an academic appointment. He taught anatomy at Hahnemann Medical College in Philadelphia and anthropology at Rutgers, but by the early 1950s was forced to leave Rutgers because of its conservative political climate. After leaving the academy, Montagu wrote full time, producing dozens of popular and scientific works on physical and cultural anthropology, psychology, and history of science. Probably best known for his forward-thinking works on race, he also wrote on women's issues and on mothering. His *Natural Superiority of Women* (originally published 1953, with its latest edition in 1999) and *Touching: The Human Significance of Skin* (1972) combined evolutionary anthropology and popular psy-

banished altogether, and ethnic group used instead. Similarly, the term "miscegenation"—which he called " a remarkable exhibit in the natural history of nonsense"—should be dropped (Montagu 1974, 445).

Man's Most Dangerous Myth went on, in Montagu's characteristic witty and erudite fashion, to consider and debunk all the major supports of scientific racism. Throughout, Montagu showed his strong environmentalist tendencies. The mental capacities of humans were everywhere at the same level, though of course not everyone was exactly the same. The distinguishing feature of humans was their ability to be educated, and Montagu recommended education, along with equal opportunity, as the most important solutions to race prejudice. He argued that psychological theories, like the frustration-aggression hypothesis, could be applied to explain race prejudice, but that such prejudice always func-

chology in an extremely readable way. Though his views on women angered some feminists who considered him old-fashioned, Montagu thought of himself as an advocate of the nurturant values usually associated with women. He also wrote about the adaptability and educability of human beings, against the idea of a human instinct for aggression, and against sociobiology, which became popular after 1975. His work in the history of science included a biography of Edward Tyson, the anatomist who published the first anatomical description of a chimpanzee in 1699. Another of Montagu's books inspired the 1980 David Lynch movie *The Elephant Man*.

As a popular, accessible writer on scientific issues with a remarkably humane perspective and an irrepressible sense of humor, Montagu was unmatched during his lifetime.

(CBS Photo Archive/Getty Images)

As a scientist he wrote technical papers in anatomy and anthropology and two definitive textbooks on physical anthropology and genetics. As a popularizer, in addition to the books mentioned above, he wrote a regular column in the 1950s for the *Ladies' Home Journal*. In all he wrote over 80 books and thousands of articles, reviews, book chapters, letters, and commentaries. Cultivating an image as the sophisticated and witty British professor, Montagu was a frequent guest on television talk shows, especially *The Tonight Show with Johnny Carson* and the *Phil Donahue Show*, in an episode of which in the early 1970s he debated the Harvard psychologist Richard Herrnstein on the genetic basis of violence.

tioned within an economic, political, and social framework that made it profitable to a certain group or to a certain individual. Race and culture were in no way connected: the Jews, for example, did not constitute a race or physical type, and their traits resulted from their shared cultural traditions, not from their biology. The basic biological potentialities, of which the most important was the capacity to learn, were the same in all people. From the mixings of cultures and peoples—not from a false purity—the greatest achievements of civilization have come. Montagu dismissed eugenics outright, arguing that what mankind requires is improvement of social environment, not improvement in biological makeup. Not enough is known about human heredity to "meddle" with it (Montagu 1974, 247). Finally, he made an argument for the importance of cooperation, rather than aggression, both in the history of the human species and in its present-day condition. In a ringing declaration that would later prove highly controversial, Montagu asserted, "not nature red in tooth and claw but cooperation is the primary law of natural conduct" (Montagu 1974, 294).

If Montagu's book represented the radical environmentalism of the early 1940s, *Heredity, Race and Society* (1946), by the geneticists Leslie Clarence Dunn and Theodosius Dobzhansky, took a more moderate position. Dunn and Dobzhansky sought very self-consciously to provide a balanced view that both nature and nurture were important in forming human beings. They never considered the importance of heredity without also arguing for the crucial role of environment. Like Benedict and Montagu, Dunn and Dobzhansky acknowledged that there certainly were differences among people, but maintained that the existence of those differences should not deny democracy or access to equal opportunity, and that it did not imply any kind of superiority or inferiority.

The two geneticists reviewed the laws of heredity and of evolution, explaining in clear terms what was meant by Mendelism and by such concepts as gene pool and mutation. They detached the notion of fitness from its Social Darwinist connotations and defined it as the ability to live within the society of which one is a member and as the ability to learn. Educability was the mark of the whole species. Where they departed from Montagu was in not dismissing eugenics entirely, but in arguing instead that—though eugenics had its difficulties—deleterious dominant genes could indeed be removed from the gene pool by the voluntary sterilization of the affected individuals. Dunn and Dobzhansky also acknowledged the problems of racial classification, but claimed that such problems did not mean that race was an imaginary entity and should be dismissed. On the contrary, they explained that geneticists could often draw sharp distinctions between races where geographical boundaries separated one racial group from another. Where there was interracial contact, the distinctions were less clear. Like Montagu, they noted that the trend toward race fusion was not a bad one, though here too they were more measured in their claims. Dunn and Dobzhansky said that among the closely related races, heightened vigor might follow from interbreeding, while among the more widely separated ones, neither good nor bad effects necessarily resulted.

Like Montagu, Dunn and Dobzhansky defined race in terms of population genetics: as a population that differed from others in the relative frequency of its genes. They left the possibility of hereditary psychological or mental differences between the races an open question, rather than denying them outright as Montagu did. But Dunn and Dobzhnsky did acknowledge that cultural factors influenced racial differences more than biological factors. Moreover, differences among individuals, even among individuals of the same race, were always greater and more important than differences between racial averages. In endorsing the outlook of population genetics, Dunn and Dobzhansky emphasized the importance of individual differences and individual variability.

Dunn and Dobzhansky's views, which developed upon and expanded Benedict's, came to represent the liberal consensus among biologists and anthropologists, while Montagu, in his outspoken environmentalism, remained an outlier. According to this liberal stance, nature and nurture existed in balance. Race still had some reality, and hereditary racial differences were still a matter for scientific investigation. Racism, but not race itself, was dismissed.

Experts in Prejudice

While the geneticists and anthropologists developed a populational definition for race and struck a balance between nature and nurture, social scientists were establishing their own liberal orthodoxy. World War II did more than reveal the horrors of Nazi science and Nazi racism. It also exposed the American racial dilemma and brought it into sharper focus than ever before. Here was a nation fighting for freedom and democracy and against the state-sanctioned ideology of Aryan superiority, yet doing so with a military in which African American soldiers were kept segregated from their white counterparts. The cruel irony of a segregated military fighting against racism was not lost on African American soldiers and their white sympathizers, and the military was desegregated shortly after the war. The fact that the United States interned its Japanese American citizens in concentration camps also exposed American racial hypocrisy, as did the anticolonial revolutions throughout the third world, where it often seemed that racial justice would be achieved faster than in the segregated Jim Crow American South.

The conflict between American ideals of democracy and equality and the reality of racial segregation brought the problems of black-white relations in the United States to international attention. To solve its racial dilemma, the U.S. government and powerful private foundations turned to the expertise of social scientists. Social scientists had already proven their usefulness during the war. They had used psychological, sociological, and anthropological methods to help the military probe the depths of the enemy mind, use propaganda effectively, formulate battle plans, and maintain citizen morale. World War II was fought as much in social scientific, especially social psychological, terms as it was pursued militarily. During the war, as attention was drawn to America's racial problems, social scientists expanded the focus of their expertise to those problems. They had already come to the belief that the races were substantially equal in intellect and morality and that nurture was much more important than nature in determining traits and behaviors. Moreover, they saw that in wartime they could really

Tuskegee airmen at Tuskegee Army Air Field, ca. 1941–1945. The Tuskegee Airmen were the only African American Air Corps officers during World War II. (Library of Congress)

make a difference and could be perceived as powerful experts—a professional motivation added to the already pressing political reasons for action. They combined their environmentalism with an activist, interventionist stance, newly honed in a wartime context, to address America's most pressing wartime problem: racial injustice.

In this wartime context, social psychologists expanded their studies of prejudice, this time aiming to show that prejudice was not simply irrational, as the prewar studies of prejudice had shown, but that it was in fact dangerously antidemocratic. This approach to prejudice was expressed in the social-psychological work of the early 1940s, which focused on three major issues: morale in wartime, race riots, and anti-Semitism.

In 1942 Resnis Likert, a Columbia-trained social psychologist working at the Office of War Information (OWI), hired Kenneth Clark to study the first of these issues: wartime morale of African Americans. Clark—at this point an assistant professor of psychology at City College of New York—argued that if African Americans were expected to participate fully in the war effort, the barriers created by discrimination would have to be torn down. The OWI report concluded, "[Negro] enthusiasm for the war is dampened by the resentment of discrimination at home. Many feel no burning urge to go 'all out' for a victory that may perpetuate the present way of life to which they are being subjected—a way of life, as they see it, based on the undemocratic premise of white supremacy" (Likert 1942). The problem was neither that minorities existed in American society, nor that the minorities were disloyal. It was, rather, that minorities were not treated as equals. The country would have to ease its racial tensions in order to unite behind the war effort and get the full support of African Americans for the war. The following year, 1943, Clark argued for the elimination not only of race prejudice but of its legalized expression in segregation as well in order to improve African American morale. Moreover, the promise of equality must last beyond the war and be a real promise.

Social psychologists' approach to race riots, the second major wartime issue, took a similar direction. As African Americans came to the cities looking for wartime employment, racial tensions increased and, in the summer of 1943, violent riots erupted in Detroit, Harlem, and other cities. In a 1943 study of the Detroit riot, sociologists Alfred McClung Lee, Jr., and Norman Humphrey argued that the ultimate cause of the riot was the uneasy state of race relations in that city and the social isolation of the races from each other. The resulting riot weakened the promises of democracy and equality of a country at war with fascism. Elimination of segregation and discrimination in housing, the schools, and the workplace was the recommended solution. As Lee and Humphrey put it, "people who live near each other or go to school together feel none of the alleged 'natural animosity' that so many people claim exists between the races—a 'natural animosity' that scientists have disproved a thousand times" (Lee and Humphrey 1943, 17). The sociologists claimed that in integrated situations there were no racial antagonisms and consequently no cause for rioting behavior. In his own 1943 study of the Harlem riot, Kenneth Clark looked at the psychological ill effects on a single African American individual of the social isolation imposed by race prejudice. The individual developed a warped personality, rejected legitimate authority, and was all too ready to participate in the riot.

The third area in which social scientists made wartime arguments about the dangerous and antidemocratic effects of race prejudice was in studies of anti-Semitism. Refugee scientists fleeing a Nazi-dominated Europe were prominent in this area.

One of the first actions of the Nazi government after Hitler's rise to power was passing the "Law for the Reconstitution of the Professional Civil Service" in April 1933. The law called for dismissing all non-Aryans from governmental service. Among those Jews who were dismissed under the law were approximately 2,000 academics, including physicists, chemists, biologists, and social scientists. Many other Jewish academics fled Hitler's regime on their own, resulting in an influx of academic talent to other parts of the world, including the United States.

To their shock, many of the Jewish social scientists who came to the United States found echoes of Hitler's anti-Semitism there. Anti-Semitism was, to a large degree, intellectually respectable in the United States of the 1930s and 1940s. Scientific racists, such as Madison Grant and Lothrop Stoddard, were openly critical of what they claimed were the inferior racial traits of Jews. Powerful popularizers of anti-Semitic doctrines included the automobile manufacturer Henry Ford and radio-preacher Father Charles Coughlin. As hostilities grew in Europe, with the Nazi Anschluss in Austria in 1938 and invasion of Poland in 1939, anti-Semitic Americans became more outspoken in their opposition to America's involvement in what they claimed was a war to save the Jews of Europe. Aviation hero Charles A. Lindbergh proclaimed in a speech in 1941 that Jewish control of radio and motion pictures meant that Jews had the power to push the United States into a war with Hitler.

For Jewish social scientists, recent arrivals from Hitler's Germany, the danger that the United States could follow Germany down the path of totalitarianism was all too real. The transplanted European social scientists soon set out to prevent the United States from suffering Germany's fate, often joining with American social scientists in the process. At the University of California at Berkeley, for example, two refugee scholars, Else Frenkel-Brunswik and Theodor Adorno, collaborated with two American social psychologists, R. Nevitt Sanford and Daniel Levinson, in work funded by the American Jewish Committee. The Berkeley team conducted psychological tests on individuals, looking for signs of anti-Semitism, which they interpreted as part of a broader personality type, the protofascist. They saw anti-Semitism not simply as a negative attitude toward the Jews but as a larger and more important threat to American democracy. According to the Berkeley researchers, if anti-Semitic prejudice was allowed to gain a foothold in a society, that society was well on its way toward fascism and authoritarian dictatorship—well on its way to becoming just like the Nazi state. The Berkeley group concluded that race prejudice was not just an aberrant psychological condition but closely associated with authoritarianism. In the fever of World War II, when some of the original research was published, the point was driven home in a May 1944 conference on anti-Semitism. The participants in the conference included not only Theodor Adorno but also Gordon Allport, Charles S. Johnson, Paul Lazarsfeld, Alfred McClung Lee, Kurt Lewin, Talcott Parsons, and Goodwin Watson, a veritable *Who's Who* of researchers in racial prejudice during the 1940s. The conclusion of the conference was that race prejudice, and anti-Semitism in particular, was a danger to liberty and democracy for all, not just Jews and Negroes. "Anti-Semitism in the United States of America," the conference participants concluded, "is tied with Nazism, Fascism, dictatorship, and is a concealed attack on American liberty" (Younker 1945, 697).

An American Dilemma

Social scientists' emphasis in the early 1940s on integration and equality to raise morale and stop rioting and on the ties between anti-Semitism and fascism helped set the stage for the definitive wartime study of race relations in the United States: Gunnar Myrdal's *An American Dilemma: The Negro Problem and Modern Democracy*, published in 1944. This definitive book established the postwar liberal orthodoxy, building on the earlier arguments that race prejudice was dangerously undemocratic and basically un-American.

The Carnegie Corporation, a private foundation, underwrote the research for the book. To direct that research the Carnegie's leaders chose Gunnar Myrdal (1898–1987), a Swedish economist and politician and one of the architects of Sweden's welfare state. They considered Myrdal, a European from a country without a colonialist tradition, sufficiently detached from America's racial problems to be objective about them. Myrdal began work on the project in 1938 with a grant of a quarter of a million dollars, with which he hired researchers, many of them young African American scholars. He saw the project as an opportunity to solve social problems through social engineering, to further liberal values, and to reject any notion of social science as value-free. The seventy-five researchers whom Myrdal hired for the project, including such scientists as Kenneth Clark, Franklin Frazier, Charles S. Johnson, Ira De Augustine Reid, Ralph Bunche, and Otto Klineberg, wrote monographs on every aspect of American race relations. The book that resulted was huge—1,500 pages and 46 chapters, supplemented by six appendices—and four technical monographs were spun off from it and published separately. Myrdal himself traveled around the United States and reported in the book his impressions, as a foreigner, of American racism. When World War II broke out, research for the book was interrupted, as Myrdal went back to Sweden. When he returned to the United States in 1941, he was assisted in writing the book by a Swedish associate, Richard Sterner, and an American sociologist, Arnold Rose, both of whom were listed as coauthors. Myrdal was also assisted by the unofficial collaboration of his wife, Alva Myrdal, who was an intellectual, activist, and politician with strong interests in the social sciences.

The American dilemma, Myrdal argued, lay in the conflict between what he called the American Creed—the guarantee of life, liberty, the pursuit of happiness, and equality before the law for all people—and the reality of racial discrimination and segregation. Reflecting the distinctly psychological turn of American social science, Myrdal saw this conflict in psychological terms, as a conflict in the minds and hearts of Americans. The conflict between the ideals of democracy and the reality of racial discrimination was giving white Americans a guilty conscience. It was a conflict about which, Myrdal believed, whites felt acutely uncomfortable. The American Creed, revitalized as it was during World War II, was entirely at odds with the disenfranchisement of part of the population. Racial discrimination was a nineteenth-century aberration from the democratic ideals upon which the United States was founded.

Myrdal's book fell squarely within the tradition—associated before the war with such Chicago school sociologists as Franklin Frazier—of the social pathology of African American life and culture. Myrdal presented the case (drawn from the work of Otto Klineberg) against innate racial differences in intelligence. He showed how discrimination functioned in the economy and in the political and justice systems. He analyzed the competing strategies within the black protest movement, which he argued was weaker than comparable labor movements in Scandinavia. But his focus was always on white attitudes, which he argued were poorly understood; on the conflict between prejudice and the American democratic creed; and particularly on the damage that such attitudes caused in blacks. Indeed, Myrdal argued that black life and culture were wholly determined by white attitudes—by oppression, discrimination, and prejudice. The African American was a victim of white society, and the "Negro problem" was really the white man's problem. As Myrdal put it, "The Negro's entire life and, consequently, also his opinions on the Negro problem, are, in the main, to be considered as secondary reactions to more primary pressures from the side of the dominant white majority" (Myrdal 1944, li).

Thus, when it came to the concept of race, Myrdal sided with Boas. Race was entirely a social construct and had no biological meaning. The notion of types or pure races made no biological sense, and Myrdal stressed that the concept of race itself was being replaced in the scientific literature by the concept of population. Geneticists and anthropologists were now studying the frequency and distribution of traits in a population and the overlap of traits between groups and no longer searching for the underlying type. Though sharing egalitarian ideals, Myrdal otherwise rejected the Boasian cultural pluralist approach. Myrdal rarely used the term "culture" in the Boasian sense, and he rejected the relativism of such Boasians as Herskovits and Hurston. Instead, Myrdal stressed the social pathology of black life—the warping effects on black personality and culture of white racial discrimination. Black life was more than simply determined as a secondary reaction to prejudiced white attitudes; blacks were literally made sick by these attitudes, and the ways in which blacks lived clearly demonstrated their sickness. In a passage in his book that became infamous in the 1960s, Myrdal wrote:

> *In practically all its divergences [from dominant white society] American*
> *Negro culture is not something independent of general American culture.*
> *It is a distorted development, or a pathological condition, of the general*

American culture. The instability of the Negro family, the inadequacy of educational facilities for Negroes, the emotionalism in the Negro church, the insufficiency and unwholesomeness of Negro recreational activity, the plethora of Negro social organizations, the narrowness of interests of the average Negro, the provincialism of his political speculation, the high Negro crime rate, the cultivation of the arts to the neglect of other fields, superstition, personality difficulties, and other characteristic traits are mainly forms of social pathology which, for the most part, are created by the caste pressures. (Myrdal 1944, 928–929)

Myrdal ignored the strengths of black life emphasized by Herskovits and Du Bois, and stressed instead the damage to black life caused by segregation. Myrdal used Dollard's term "caste" to underscore the argument that the status of African Americans was entirely determined by their relation to whites. Like Frazier, Myrdal was unimpressed by historian Carter Woodson's movement to uncover Negro history and by other aspects of black nationalism in the 1930s and 1940s. Although the African American nationalists and the cultural pluralists emphasized the uniqueness of the black church and its origins in preslavery African culture, Myrdal stressed its pathological deviance. The cure for the social pathologies of black life, he argued, was complete integration and assimilation into the white American mainstream. Emphasis on difference and irreducible diversity worked only to the detriment of African Americans, since it could potentially be used against them to deny them equal rights. As assimilation was the ultimate aim of all ethnic groups in the United States and a central part of the American Creed, so it must also be the goal of African Americans. Adjustment to the norms of white society was necessary for blacks if acceptance as equals was to follow. *"We assume,"* Myrdal wrote, *"that it is to the advantage of American Negroes as individuals and as a group to become assimilated into American culture, to acquire the traits held in esteem by the dominant white Americans"* (Myrdal 1944, 928–929). Myrdal rejected Robert Park and Howard Odum's thesis that cultural change in race relations must be gradual and long-term, passing through several well-defined stages. Myrdal was optimistic that blacks could soon overcome the peculiar social and cultural patterns they developed as accommodations to the caste system and that integration and assimilation would thereafter proceed apace.

An American Dilemma evinces, then, two important themes. First, in focusing on racism as a problem of white attitudes, and on the pathological behaviors and personalities that such attitudes produced in blacks, Myrdal reflected a strong trend in American social science toward psychologizing problems that might otherwise be interpreted in political, economic, institutional, or social terms. Myrdal's focus, like Dollard's and Clark's, was on personalities and on the moral struggles that took place within individuals. *"The American Negro problem is a problem in the heart of the American,"* Myrdal wrote. *"It is there that the interracial tension has its focus. It is there that the decisive struggle goes on . . . . The moral struggle goes on within people and not only between them"* (Myrdal 1944, xlvii-xlviii).

As a corollary to this argument, Myrdal followed a long tradition of emphasizing the social pathology of black life and the need to overcome the peculiarities of black culture in order to assimilate. The pathologies could ultimately be traced to the damage brought on by racism.

The second major theme of Myrdal's study was social engineering. Myrdal argued that the problems of racial discrimination were interlocking, so that addressing one required addressing them all and, consequently, none could be isolated from the others. All the social problems caused by racism were amenable to the planning of the social engineer. Myrdal argued that institutional change toward integration was necessary in schools, churches, trade unions, and housing. He made specific policy recommendations for the federal government to assist blacks in migrating to areas with job opportunities, particularly to the cities of the northern and western United States.

He analyzed the economic situation of African Americans, whose poverty he termed pathological, and called for full employment of blacks and for educational campaigns to reduce prejudice. He pointed to racism as the primary cause of the backwardness of the southern economy, and recommended that blacks be fully integrated into the economy of both the North and South. He assumed, optimistically, that greater contact between white and black workers would lead to the lessening of racism, and, as it turned out, greatly underestimated the amount and severity of racial prejudice among northern white workers. Myrdal appealed to well-off whites as the natural allies of poor African Americans, who were in direct competition with poor whites. Poor whites, he argued, were a textbook case of Dollard's frustration-aggression hypothesis, according to which frustration is translated into aggression. Drawing on his own travels around the United States, particularly in the South, Myrdal argued that racial hatred was strongest among poor whites who, frustrated at their own destitute situation, acted aggressively toward blacks.

In keeping with campaigns by the NAACP to publicize lynching, Myrdal stressed not only lynching but the entire array of extralegal controls that southern whites used to keep blacks in their place. "The Negro's person and property are practically subject to the whim of any white person who wishes to take advantage of him or punish him for any real or fancied wrongdoing or 'insult.' A white man can steal from or maltreat a Negro in almost any way without fear of reprisal, because the Negro cannot claim the protection of the police or courts, and personal vengeance on the part of the offended Negro usually results in organized retaliation in the form of bodily injury (including lynching), home burning, or banishment" (Myrdal 1944, 530).

Myrdal's outlook as a social engineer caused him to see the problems of racism in America as solvable. He made specific recommendations, but never restricted his book to the realm of policy. Rather, a moralizing tone pervaded the book. Racism conflicted with the values of the American Creed, and individuals experienced the conflict as intensely personal. Myrdal appealed to the sense of the rightness of democracy that he believed was secure within every American, even the most bigoted. And he thought that once the conflict was exposed it could be resolved. So influential was Myrdal's work—not only on several decades' worth of social science, but on national policy as well—that it defined what has been called the liberal orthodoxy on race relations for the postwar era. This liberal orthodoxy called for desegregation, full civil rights for blacks, and the integration and assimilation of blacks into all realms of white society. It demanded equalization of economic opportunity, educational campaigns to reduce prejudice, and social engineering through the state's policymaking apparatus to lessen psychological damage in blacks—in effect to bring them up to speed. Finally, the liberal orthodoxy underscored the necessity of assimilation, the integration of blacks into mainstream America, and rejected the arguments of the cultural pluralists and the African American nationalists for black difference and black separatism.

The Post-Myrdal Liberal Orthodoxy

Myrdal's book, and the liberal orthodoxy it established, had a tremendous influence on social scientists, on policymakers, and on presidents for twenty years after its publication. Liberal scientists and politicians alike argued that establishing civil rights was not merely important for its own sake but necessary to maintain America's commitment to democracy in the face of fascist and communist threats both at home and abroad. Pervading this liberal orthodoxy were Myrdal's moralizing stance and emphasis on the psychological costs of racism.

In 1947, after postwar demobilization and at the very beginning of the Cold War, President Harry S Truman responded to a rash of lynchings the previous year by engaging an interracial and interreligious committee of citizens to draw up a report on civil rights. The report, *To Secure These Rights*, presented racial prejudice as causing a moral conflict with the American democratic ideal of equality for all. The report surveyed the effects of discrimination and recom-

Psychoanalyst Bruno Bettelheim (UPI-Bettmann/Corbis)

mended an end to segregation, and it cited social science studies of interracial contact as a way to end prejudice. It linked prejudice against blacks to prejudice against Catholics, Jews, and Japanese and Mexican Americans and argued that ensuring civil rights was crucial in the Cold War against totalitarianism. Through-out the report Myrdal's psychological perspective was evident. "It is not at all surprising that a people relegated to second-class citizenship should behave as second-class citizens," the report said. "This is true, in varying degrees, of all minorities. What we have lost in money, production, invention, citizenship, and leadership as the price for damaged, thwarted personalities—these are beyond estimate" (Myrdal 1947, 139).

In the 1940s and 1950s the intercultural education movement sponsored much social scientific research on race prejudice. Intercultural education (again showing the influence of Myrdal's program for change) was supported by civic and religious institutions, as well as by private foundations, and was designed to teach the public, through radio programs, public school programs, interethnic luncheons, and the like, to tolerate ethnic diversity. In the scientific arena, the American Jewish Congress's (AJCongress) Commission on Community Interrelations, an intercultural education initiative, supported the work of social psychologist Kurt Lewin, a Jewish refugee from Nazi Germany. Lewin founded the Society for the Psychological Study of Social Issues in the mid-1930s as an activist alternative to the American Psychological Association and advocated action-oriented research to destroy prejudice and to help people change. In Lewin's program, social psychologists were to work with communities to diagnose their problems and propose solutions. He emphasized raising the self-esteem of members of minority groups through ethnic pride and rejected Myrdal's assertion that assimilation was the desirable end. Lewin applied his ideas mostly to Jews; he died in 1947 before he could turn his attention to African Americans.

In 1947, Robin M. Williams, Jr., a social psychologist at Cornell, summarized the perspective of the intercultural educators in his book *The Reduction of Intergroup Tensions*. Williams emphasized the conflict between the American Creed and racial and religious hostility and recommended education as the key to lessening hostility. Prejudice and aggression, he argued, were deeply rooted in human nature and could be rerouted through education, but never entirely removed. Though less optimistic than Myrdal, Williams took a generally assimilationist view, recommending ways that the oppressed minority could lessen the prejudice of the majority. His recommendations for minorities included not displaying traits that the majority finds objectionable and participating as individuals—not as a group—in the larger community's activities.

The "Studies in Prejudice" series, funded by the American Jewish Committee's (AJC) Department of Scientific Research, thoroughly reflected a psychological or psychoanalytic perspective on prejudice, rather than emphasizing the social, economic, or institutional roots of racism. In their 1950 *Dynamics of Prejudice: A Psychological and Sociological Study of Veterans*, émigré psychoanalyst Bruno Bettelheim and sociologist Morris Janowitz focused on World War II veterans to understand the source of racial hostility toward blacks and Jews.

Bettelheim was a concentration camp survivor who had argued that the German national character was psychologically disturbed, while Janowitz was an American intelligence expert during World War II. Together they concluded that prejudice reflected a fundamental aggression with roots in childhood deprivations and anxiety about future economic deprivations. The veterans they studied controlled their aggression poorly and rather than channeling it in productive directions discharged it in irrational ways. Bettelheim and Janowitz found prejudice in all socioeconomic classes, not only in the poorest. They suggested changes in public policy to reduce intergroup hostility, but their central recommendations were to educate and to reorganize personality structures by changing parenting methods, family dynamics, and the socialization of children. Forming tolerant personalities by changing parental attitudes—focusing on the family as the locus of change—had more of a chance of success, Bettelheim and Janowitz believed, than eliminating racism through radical economic reforms.

The Authoritarian Personality was also published in 1950 as part of the same series, the book a product of the collaboration between Nevitt Sanford, Daniel Levinson, Theodor Adorno, and Else Frenkel-Brunswik. These four scholars began working together in Berkeley, California, in 1944 on a study of anti-Semitism. Their project was an innovative combination of empirical American research methods, which included new techniques for the quantitative scaling of attitudes, opinion research, and clinical interviews, with theoretical and abstract European insights into social theory. The end result of the project was a thousand-page book.

The Berkeley group wanted to understand what went wrong in Nazi Germany and what they believed could potentially go wrong in the United States. They sought to explain in psychological terms how a totalitarian regime with racial hatred at its core could overtake a civilized country like Germany. What sort of person would follow a madman like Hitler? As they wrote in the introduction to their book, "If a potentially fascistic individual exists what, precisely, is he like? What goes to make up antidemocratic thought? What are the organizing forces within the person? If such a person exists, how commonly does he exist in our society? And if such a person exists, what have been the determinants and what was the course of his development?" (Adorno, Frenkel-Brunswik, Levinson, and Sanford 1950/1969, 2).

For the Berkeley group, anti-Semitism was part of a larger problem that threatened not just Jews, but all of American society. The four scholars viewed anti-Semitism as part of a larger personality type: the "proto-Fascist." The group developed a scale, called the E (for ethnocentrism) Scale, to measure the degree to which an anti-Semitic person is also prejudiced against other minority groups. They then correlated the E scale to the likelihood that a highly prejudiced person would succumb to the lure of fascism—the F (for fascism) scale—as measured by the degree to which the person would obey authority, not question orders, and despise the weak.

After the war was won, and as the 1950s progressed, the work of the Berkeley scholars came under increasing scrutiny. One critique emerged from the changing political climate of the 1950s. The political critique, put forth by sociologist Edward Shils and psychologist Hans Eysenck, was that the authors of *The Authoritarian Personality* were concentrating on the wrong group: instead of focusing on the dangers of the political right wing, they should have focused on the dangers of the political left wing, or the Communists. In the wake of Hitler's defeat in World War II, many Americans and western Europeans viewed the Soviet Union not as the valuable ally it had been during the war but as a dangerous adversary bent on taking over all of Europe. Additionally, Germany's sins were quickly forgiven as western Europeans began to view West Germany, not as the perpetrator of World War II, but as an important bulwark against Soviet expansion. The Soviet Union was the new totalitarian menace and *The Authoritarian Personality* was criticized for ignoring the dangers of the left.

In the new anti-Communist climate, the elaborate theoretical apparatus designed by the Berkeley scholars was increasingly stripped of its political underpinnings. Psychologists adopted the tools, such as the F Scale, as a measure of conformity and a useful way to generate data sets on personality, but the specific critique of fascist ideology was abandoned as unscientific and politicized. Such a move demonstrates the extent to which problems of prejudice in the 1950s became psychological problems, removed from political contexts.

In 1954, Gordon Allport, a senior social psychologist at Harvard, endorsed the liberal orthodoxy on race in his influential book *The Nature of Prejudice*, which became the definitive psychological treatment of the subject for a generation. Allport solidified a number of arguments about race and race prejudice that social scientists had been developing over the previous three decades. Allport argued that differences in groups, even racial groups, were not as important as the interpretations society placed on those differences. "Facts are one thing," he wrote, "the significance people place upon them is something else" (Allport 1954/1979, 104). The differences between the races, Allport claimed, were slight and could not serve as justifications for racial prejudice. Pointing to anti-Semitism, Allport argued, "Our findings thus fall far short in establishing objective grounds to justify the hostility. Even when slight ethnic differences appear, they are never large enough to warrant the prediction that any given Jew will possess the qualities in question" (Allport 1954/1979, 125).

After establishing that prejudice was an irrational attitude that was not based on real traits possessed by any ethnic groups, Allport argued that preju-

Gordon W. Allport (1897–1967)

Allport was a psychologist whose influential theorizing about personality stressed the uniqueness of the individual and rejected both the approaches of Freudian psychoanalysis and the mechanistic and quantifying impulses of behaviorism. Allport also possessed a deep dedication to social justice, combining a Progressive belief in social

change with a religious belief that required Christians to work for a better world. Born in Montezuma, Indiana, into the deeply religious (Methodist) family of the physician John Allport and his wife Nellie Wise, a former schoolteacher, Allport received his early education in Cleveland, where his father maintained a medical practice. In 1915 Allport joined his elder brother Floyd (1890–1978) at Harvard, where the latter was a graduate student and later an instructor in social psychology. The elder Allport published a pioneering textbook in social psychology in 1924 and spent his career, after Harvard, at Syracuse University. The younger Allport received his A.B. degree from Harvard in 1915, majoring in philosophy and economics. For a year fol-

(Walter Sanders/Time Life Pictures/ Getty Images)

lowing graduation Gordon Allport taught sociology and English at the religiously inspired Robert College in Istanbul, Turkey.

Allport returned to Harvard after his stint abroad to pursue graduate work in psychology, under the influence of his brother Floyd, who suggested he work on personality, and Hugo Munsterberg. Allport's first publication, "Personality Traits: Their Classification and Measurement" was coauthored with Floyd in 1921. Allport

dice had deleterious psychological consequences for both the prejudiced person and the person who was the target of the prejudice. Victims of stereotyping suffered from impaired personalities, including denying membership in the hated group, and developing self-hate, increased prejudice toward the dominant group, and aggression.

Allport also outlined what society could do to reduce racial prejudice. One of the pressing concerns for many social scientists was the contact hypothesis: did interracial contact increase or decrease racial prejudice? There was some evidence that interracial contact increased racial prejudice but there was also some evidence to the opposite effect. Allport summarized a number of studies of interracial contact, including those of the recently desegregated armed forces,

received an M.A. in 1921 and a Ph.D. in psychology in 1922, with a dissertation (directed by Herbert S. Langfeld) on the testing of personality traits. He spent several postdoctoral years studying in Berlin and Hamburg, Germany, and in Cambridge, England, before returning to Harvard in 1924 as instructor in social ethics. In 1925 he married Ada Gould, a fellow psychologist, who, despite the fact that she never attained a full-time university position, collaborated unofficially with Allport on his major works. Allport taught at Dartmouth College for four years from 1926 to 1930, returning to Harvard for the last time in 1930. He spent the rest of his career there. In 1937 he became associate professor, and full professor in 1942. After World War II, Allport joined with sociologist Talcott Parsons and anthropologist Clyde Kluckhohn to create a Department of Social Relations at Harvard dedicated to teaching students a socially active social science.

Allport's definitive book on personality *Personality: A Psychological Interpretation* (1937) distinguished between the traits that human beings share in common and those distinctive to the individual. He also pursued the problem of the development of self-awareness through childhood and adolescence. Upon entry into World War II by the United States, Allport became involved in a host of projects for the government, including organizing a seminar at Harvard devoted to topics useful to the war effort: analyses of rumor, of Hitler's character, and of rioting behavior. Allport's study of the problem of spreading rumors eventuated in a 1947 book, *The Psychology of Rumor*, written with Leo Postman. Allport later recalled that the Harvard seminar "had a long-range consequence. It continued year after year, with a gradual focusing on what seemed to be the most urgent problem of national unity, namely, group conflict and prejudice" (Allport 1968, 396). In addition to his 1954 book on prejudice, he also wrote a book in 1950 called *The Individual and His Religion: A Psychological Interpretation*, which warned against the harmful effects of prejudices fostered by institutionalized religions.

In 1956 he served as visiting consultant to the University of Natal in South Africa, where he predicted the overthrow of the racist societies of both South Africa and the southern United States.

new interracial housing projects, and desegregated labor unions. Allport found that interracial contact increased racial prejudice, unless the contact was between two groups of relatively equal status and the two groups shared a common goal, in which case interracial contact decreased prejudice. He concluded that the sanction of such interracial contact by law or custom would decrease racial prejudice to an even greater extent. Allport's conclusions on interracial contact resonated with Myrdal's program of social engineering and with intercultural education. According to Allport, society did not need to wait for prejudice to decrease before pushing for interracial contact. Rather, interracial contact could, in and of itself, decrease racial prejudice, especially if the interracial contact had the authority of law. Even though the law affected only "outward manifestations of intolerance" Allport argued, "outward action, psychology knows, has an eventual effect upon inner habits of thought and feeling. And for this reason we list legislative action as one of the major methods of reducing, not only public discrimination, but private prejudice as well" (Allport 1954/1979, 477). Like Myrdal, Allport advocated desegregation, equal economic opportunity, and assimilationalism and emphasized America's guilty national conscience. Like his Swedish predecessor, he placed the issue of tolerance in an international context. Finally, like Myrdal, Allport focused on white attitudes rather than on the black community, granting blacks scarcely any role in his recommendations for intercultural education.

The Damage Argument

The social science research on prejudice, then, in the two decades after Myrdal, focused almost entirely on white attitudes and on white-against-black racism and on the parallel case of anti-Semitism. The source of the hatred and prejudice among white people interested these scientists, not the oppressed and victimized groups. In studies of antiblack and anti-Jewish prejudice, scholars attempted to understand hatred of an entire group of people in psychological terms and interpreted such hatred in a global context as a threat to American democratic values. Both the psychologizing and the emphasis on the creed of democracy reflected the approaches enshrined by the liberal orthodoxy. The psychologization of prejudice, in particular, was a popular approach during this conservative era in which radical social and political changes were rarely options.

In other ways, however, the social scientific studies of antiblack racism and of anti-Semitism differed from each other. In both cases, scientists emphasized the racist attitudes of whites but viewed black and Jewish victims of hatred differently. Black and white scholars alike interpreted black people to be damaged by the effects of racism. The harm done to the black psyche was a major focus of research during and after the war. By contrast, neither scientists nor the American public perceived Jews as damaged in the same way. In fact the anti-Semitism of such public figures as Father Coughlin and Charles Lindbergh often invested Jews with a greater power than they actually possessed. Jews were seen as strengthened as a community and as a people by being outcasts. Blacks, on the other hand, were widely perceived as weakened by the effects of racism, both in their personalities and in the structures of their community. Along with the attitudes of white racists, the ways in which blacks were damaged was a key part of social scientific research in the framework of the liberal orthodoxy.

Social scientists who focused on the damage argument paid little attention to African American social behavior, culture, or communities. African American culture was thought to be disappearing through assimilation anyway, so there seemed little point in studying it. Black social pathologies, and not their independent culture or communities or their strategies of resistance, were the central focus of this research.

Building on the prewar tradition of black social pathology to which he had contributed, Franklin Frazier developed the damage argument both during the war and afterward. In his 1939 *Negro Family in the United States*, Frazier argued that slavery had destabilized the black family, depriving black men of economic opportunity and forcing them out of their natural roles as breadwinners and heads of the household. Matriarchal families—strikingly out of keeping with the dominant white patriarchal culture—and social pathology were the result. The solution was male employment, ensuring that black men regained their rightful place in the black family. (In this prefeminist era, there was little question about what was natural for men and women.) In his 1940 *Negro Youth at the Crossways*, Frazier explored the epidemic of low self-esteem among black urban youth. In his 1949 *Negro in the United States*, he looked at the damage that a heritage of slavery and racism had done to blacks, as well as the ways they had accommodated to white society. In his 1957 *Black Bourgeosie*, he argued that social pathologies were present in middle-class blacks, not just in the poor. But like Myrdal, Frazier ended optimistically, predicting that an interracial alliance would form in support of equality and civil rights.

Psychiatrists Abram Kardiner and Lionel Ovesey supported Frazier's social pathology argument with clinical data. In their 1951 *The Mark of Oppression: Explorations in the Personality of the American Negro*, they discussed life history interviews and psychological tests on twenty-five African Americans. They concluded that the normal patriarchal pattern was reversed in black families, where women were in control and men were either absent or in a subordinate position. Such an unnatural pattern caused personality damage in blacks, which was revealed in aggression and self-hatred. Racism thus left a mark of oppression on all of its victims, producing dysfunctional families headed by "loveless [female] tyrants" and men unable to fulfill their role as economic providers (Kardiner and Ovesey 1951, 65). Changing the attitudes of whites—thereby ending the damage to blacks—was Kardiner and Ovesey's recommended solution.

The high-water mark of the damage argument came in the early 1950s when it was used in court cases to support the cause of public school desegregation. In research on racial preference conducted between 1947 and 1950, Kenneth and Mamie Clark had demonstrated that segregation caused psychological damage in children, and the plaintiffs' lawyers relied largely on their evidence. One of the Clarks' experiments consisted in giving 160 African American children, aged five

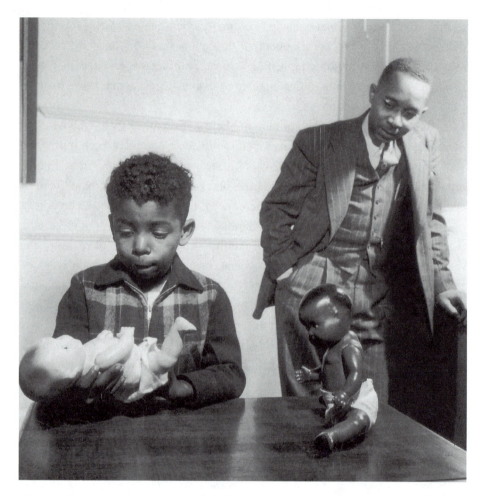

Kenneth Clark conducting the doll test with a young male child (Library of Congress)

to seven years, a coloring test, asking them to color a sketch of a child the same color that they were. The Clarks found that the children consistently portrayed themselves as lighter than they actually were, and that the disparity was greatest in those children whose skin color was darkest.

In an even more famous experiment—the so-called doll tests—the Clarks showed African American children three to seven years old a white doll and a brown doll and asked them which doll they would like to play with and which doll was a nice color. The Clarks found that most of the children chose the white doll in answer to both questions, and they interpreted their evidence to mean that the children suffered from low self-esteem.

According to the Clarks, racism did not simply conflict with abstract notions of justice. Instead, they managed to show in a particularly graphic way that children even at a very early age were painfully conscious of the racial hierarchy, that they already knew that they were at the bottom of it, and that their own developing sense of identity was damaged by this awareness. The Clarks concluded, "It is clear that the Negro child, by the age of five, is aware of the fact that to be colored in contemporary American society is a mark of inferior status . . . . This apparently introduces a fundamental conflict at the very foundations of the ego structure" (Clark and Clark 1950, 342). They made practical recommendations for education and mental hygiene to reduce this deep sense of inferiority.

The argument that racism caused damage to children's sense of self-worth played an important role in court cases for desegregation. In 1951, as part of the National Association for the Advancement of Colored People's campaign to end public school segregation, Thurgood Marshall, an attorney for the NAACP's Legal Defense Fund, filed the case of *Briggs v. Elliott*. The case was brought to desegregate the public schools in South Carolina. Marshall decided on a strategy of proving injury to schoolchildren and used the Clarks' doll tests as evidence that racism and segregation cause psychological damage. Kenneth Clark, called as an expert witness on behalf of the plaintiff, said in his testimony before the court in South Carolina:

> I have come to the conclusion that discrimination, prejudice, and segregation have definitely detrimental effects on the personality development of the Negro child. The essence of this detrimental effect is a confusion in the child's concept of his own self esteem—basic feelings of inferiority, conflict, confusion in the self-image, resentment, hostility toward himself, hostility toward whites . . . [or] a desire to resolve his basic conflict by sometimes escaping or withdrawing (*Briggs v. Elliott*, quoted in Herman 1995, 196).

Such testimony made clear that the product of racism was damaged, deviant personalities. Though the NAACP lost the case, it used the same strategy of proving damage, relying on the evidence of liberal, activist social science, in the 1954 *Brown v. Board of Education of Topeka, Kansas*. Here the damage argument prevailed. Chief Justice Earl Warren of the United States Supreme Court cited the work of social scientists, including Clark, Myrdal, and Frazier, in ordering states to desegregate their public schools "with all deliberate speed." Warren's decision said, in part:

> To separate them [black students] from others of similar age and qualifications solely because of their race generates a feeling of inferiority as to their status in the community that may affect their hearts and minds in such a way unlikely ever to be undone . . . . A sense of inferiority affects the motivation of the child to learn . . . . Whatever might have been the extent of psychological knowledge at the time of *Plessy v. Ferguson* [the 1896 case upholding

the doctrine of separate but equal facilities for blacks and whites], this finding is amply supported by modern authority (*Brown v. Board*, quoted in Herman 1995, 198).

The *Brown* decision marked the beginning of a trend in which the use of social scientists as expert witnesses pointing to the psychological damage that

not refused admission to any school where they are situated similarly to white students in respect to (1) distance from school, (2) natural or manmade barriers or hazards, and (3) other relevant educational criteria.

5. On remand, the defendant school districts shall be required to submit with all appropriate speed proposals for compliance to the respective lower courts.

5. Decrees in conformity with this decree shall be prepared and issued forthwith by the lower courts. They may, when deemed by them desirable for the more effective enforcement of this decree, appoint masters to assist them.

7. Periodic compliance reports shall be presented by the defendant school districts to the lower courts and, in due course, transmitted by them to this Court, but the primary duty to insure good faith compliance rests with the lower courts.

Draft of the Supreme Court decision in Brown v. Board of Education, *1954 (Library of Congress)* segregation wreaked became a routine matter. Warren's phrase "with all deliberate speed" provided an excuse for white southern resistance to the decision, but notably the southern segregationists had few scientists on their side. By the mid-1950s only a few scientific racists were left who would speak openly for race differences in intelligence and other psychological traits. Psychologist Henry Garrett—who had advised Mamie Clark's graduate work while she was at Columbia—was among them. But outspoken racists like Garrett had little impact on the mainstream social science community, so completely had the liberal consensus become orthodoxy.

The Breakdown of the Liberal Orthodoxy

The ideals of the liberal orthodoxy were also evident in the civil rights movement during the early 1960s. In his 1963 "I Have a Dream" speech, Martin Luther King, Jr., appealed to the guilty conscience of white Americans, asking them to resolve the moral problem that segregation caused. In the wake of nonviolent protest marches led by King, President John F. Kennedy began to advocate a strong civil rights program, using Myrdal's moralizing arguments for desegregation and equal opportunity. Kennedy placed the problem of racism in an international context, pitting America's democratic values against fascist ones, and declared that only the color of their skin—not the content of their culture—prevented African Americans from joining mainstream America. In 1964, under President Lyndon B. Johnson, Congress passed the Civil Rights Act, desegregating such public venues as restaurants, theaters, and hotels; it passed the Voting Rights bill the following year. In 1965, Johnson's assistant secretary of labor, Daniel Patrick Moynihan, gave the damage argument and the logic of African American social pathology pride of place in his report on the black family. *The Negro Family: The Case for National Action* shows the extent to which the social science discourse of Myrdal, Frazier, the Clarks, and others had become a central part of public policy. And the response to the report shows that by 1965 their liberal orthodoxy was starting to fall apart.

The Moynihan report made the same social pathology argument prominent social scientists had been making for some three decades. Influenced by the psychological turn in the social sciences, Moynihan focused on the black family, arguing that a heritage of slavery and racism had twisted that family structure into aberrant matriarchal patterns. The black personality suffered from low self-esteem, especially the black male personality. Restoration of black men to their rightful place as breadwinners and heads of the family was Moynihan's solution to the black community's social problems:

At the heart of the deterioration of the fabric of Negro society is the deterioration of the Negro family . . . . In essence, the Negro community has been forced into a matriarchal structure, which, because it is so out of line with the rest of American society, seriously retards the progress of the group as a whole, and imposes a crushing burden on the Negro male and, in consequence, on a great many Negro women as well . . . . Given the strains of the disorganized and matrifocal family life in which so many Negro youth come of age, the Armed forces are a dramatic and desperately needed change: a world away from women, a world run by strong men of unquestioned authority. . . . " (Moynihan 1965, 5, 29, 42–43)

In addition to demonstrating Moynihan's gendered perspective, such a comment shows the psychological tenor of the report. Indeed, critics attacked the report chiefly for psychologizing and personalizing the problems of racism— making them into questions of individual, personal analysis rather than addressing them at an institutional or structural level. According to the critics, Moynihan saw changing the family as somehow easier than changing the structures of society. Psychological therapy, rather than equal economic opportunity, he perceived as the answer to racism. The critique was somewhat ironic, since Moynihan advocated full employment for African Americans to bring them out of the underclass and into the working class. But Moynihan couched the argument about employment in terms of social pathology, and in 1965 charges of social pathology had a much different ring to them than they did in 1944.

By the mid-1960s, African Americans were beginning to tire of seeing themselves consistently portrayed as victims and as pathological. With the advent of the Black Power movement in 1966, critics of Myrdal's liberal orthodoxy began to emphasize black nationalism, separatism, and pride in their cultural heritage. Black studies programs grew, allowing black scholars to be the spokespeople for their own culture, history, and social issues. The cultural pluralist argument, sidelined for decades by the assimilationist school, gained new force among sociologists and anthropologists, who began to develop innovative and strongly relativist approaches to the study of black life and culture. Increasing protests against the Vietnam War, the assassinations of Martin Luther King, Jr., and Robert F. Kennedy—among the public figures who helped hold a liberal consensus together—and violent urban race riots from 1965 to 1968 helped to consolidate the new militant approach of black leaders and to fragment both the civil rights movement and the liberal orthodoxy on which it was based.

Black nationalists like Stokely Carmichael and Malcolm X envisioned a black movement orchestrated by blacks, free of white interference and influence. Their critique of a racist American society involved a concerted shift from

Martin Luther King Jr. waves to the crowd gathered at the Lincoln Memorial during the delivery of his famous speech at the March on Washington in 1963. (AP/Wide World Photos)

the psychologizing of the 1950s to an emphasis on institutional racism, on the lack of black political power, and on the poverty of the black underclass. In such an environment, the Moynihan report came in for a radical critique. The report contended that the black family was pathological because it was matriarchal in a patriarchal white society, that black culture represented a poor approximation of white norms, and that family disorder was the key issue. All these claims were criticized as attacks on the victim, as deflecting attention from issues of power and equal opportunity to issues of family and from issues of economics and possible change of the economic system to issues of deviant individuals.

Since they perceived the problems of racism to be institutional and pervasive, black nationalists and their sympathizers completely lost the optimism and faith in the American Creed that had marked the liberal orthodoxy. The novelist James Baldwin claimed in a 1964 roundtable discussion in New York City that the American Creed was hypocrisy, and rejected the assumption that blacks longed to join the white American mainstream. Participating in the same discussion, even Kenneth Clark concluded that white Americans lacked a strong ethical commitment to equal rights for blacks.

Such comments were echoed in a burgeoning social scientific critique of Myrdal's idea of an American moral dilemma. In 1949, sociologist Robert K. Merton had argued that allegiance to the American Creed was not a constant in American society and that racists held their prejudice up as a kind of creed. In 1962, social psychologist Nahum Medalia accepted and expanded Merton's argument, asserting that there was in fact no unifying creed in the United States, only individual whites who adapted their behavior to different situations—liberal in some, racist in others. Social scientists and radical scholars alike rejected the optimistic assumption of the liberal orthodoxy that racism was out of keeping with the American Creed. Instead they saw racism as endemic in American society. They rejected Myrdal's stress on social pathology and assimilation in favor of African American cultural distinctiveness. They replaced his faith in the power of education to change people's minds with more radical arguments for economic restructuring and institutional change. They criticized him for having greatly underestimated the power and persistence of white racism. Myrdal's emphasis on the American Creed seemed naïve in the face of southern white opposition to desegregation. In the wake of rioting in the Watts section of Los Angeles in the mid-1960s, his prediction of an orderly and peaceful end to desegregation seemed tragically wrong. Meanwhile, as the Black Power movement was galvanized, many whites turned to the Moynihan report for help with the problems. Moynihan became their prophet, his report expressing a basic truth: perhaps blacks were disordered after all.

In this way, the liberal orthodoxy fragmented. In the loss of the consensus that it represented, conservative and radical sectors of American society each adopted widely differing perspectives on the problems of racial minorities.

The UNESCO Statements on Race

Like psychologists and sociologists, biologists and physical and cultural anthropologists attempted to construct a postwar consensus on race—a consensus that also subsequently fragmented, though in a somewhat less spectacular way than Myrdal's liberal orthodoxy. Geneticists and anthropologists were, with the exception of a few conservatives, strongly committed to repudiating any scientific basis for racism. They agreed that racial typologies were nonsense and that the notion of superior or inferior races had no biological justification. The revelations of Nazi ideology and Nazi atrocities united the community in this antiracist stance.

Where they disagreed was how to settle on something to put in the place of scientific racism, to reach a positive conclusion rather than simply reject racist assertions. Was there, after all, something called race, and could it be defined in a nonracist way? If scientific racism was rejected in its most virulent forms, did that mean that race itself has no biological meaning? If it did have some meaning, how much of what might be called racial difference was hereditary, and how much due to environment? Or was race entirely useless as a scientific concept, and should it be rejected along with scientific racism? The divergent answers scientists gave to these questions at midcentury were demonstrated by the drafting of and the responses to the UNESCO Statements on Race.

In the wake of World War II the United Nations Educational, Scientific, and Cultural Organization passed a resolution to provide up-to-date scientific information on race problems and an educational campaign to distribute that information. UNESCO's Director General, Mexican poet Jaime Torres-Bodet, and Arthur Ramos, the Brazilian anthropologist who was head of UNESCO's social science department, convened a committee to draft a statement on race. The committee's mandate from UNESCO said that the committee was "(1) to collect scientific materials concerning problems of race; (2) to give wide diffusion to the scientific information collected; (3) to prepare an educational campaign based on this information" (Montagu 1951, 1). Moreover, the constitutional purpose of UNESCO was to "harness the forces of education, science, and culture in order to contribute to peace, security and international understanding" (Montagu 1951, 3).

The mandate, in other words, asked the committee to base a moral position—the removal of race prejudice—on scientific facts about race: to derive ethics from science. The scientists were to assemble those scientific facts that would support the desired moral position. But the problem was that many of the scientists involved, particularly the geneticists and physical anthropologists, believed in a biological or genetic basis for differences in mental and psychological traits among individuals. Many of them were still—even in the egalitarian racial atmosphere of the 1950s—agnostics about the possibility of hereditary mental differences between the races. Could such beliefs in the reality of race, and the importance of heredity, coexist with a moral commitment to egalitarianism?

The committee of scientists selected to draft the statement, including the sociologist Franklin Frazier and the anthropologist Claude Levi-Strauss, convened in Paris in December 1949 and chose Ashley Montagu as its rapporteur. Montagu, both a physical and a cultural anthropologist, was a strong environmentalist and had made his views of race known in his 1942 book, *Man's Most Dangerous Myth: The Fallacy of Race*. Indeed, Montagu was chosen as official author of the statement because of his prominence in racial matters. In his book, Montagu had defined race solely in physical and physiological terms, as a genetically distinguishable population. Cultural and social differences among people were in no way related to racial differences. Moreover, he believed that it was UNESCO's duty to further egalitarianism and educate the public, rather than simply to review the scientific facts. This belief, combined with his environmentalism, inspired him to make some claims in the statement that went beyond what mainstream scientists accepted as the facts about race. In addition, sociologists and cultural anthropologists dominated the committee; it included no geneticists, and Montagu himself was the only representative of physical anthropology.

The statement that resulted, released in June of 1950, was accordingly controversial. The outright environmentalism expressed by the social scientists in the statement clashed with the critiques of the biologically and physically oriented scientists, whose views on race were always more measured and cautious, who believed in biological differences between individuals and remained agnostics about racial differences. The 1950 statement on race that Montagu drafted made several major claims. First, it defined a race as a population or group in which certain gene frequencies occurred. Second, it asserted that these genetic differences among populations were unconnected with any perceived cultural or social differences among races. The classification of mankind should be based entirely on physical and physiological characteristics, not mental, temperamental, personality, or character differences. Third, the statement argued that the range of mental capacities in all groups of mankind was the same, and that in all people educability was the key trait. Fourth, it declared that there were no problems of any kind resulting from the mixture of different races. Montagu summarized the outlook of the committee with two controversial claims. In an echo of his 1942 work, he wrote, "for all practical social purposes, 'race' is not so much a biological phenomenon as a social myth" (Montagu 1951, 10). And, he asserted toward the end of the statement, "Biological studies lend support to the ethic of universal brotherhood; for man is born with drives toward cooperation, and unless these drives are satisfied, men and nations alike fall ill" (1951, 12).

The criticism from geneticists and physical anthropologists came swiftly. They lamented their absence from the committee that drafted the statement. They said that contrary to the statement's claims, there might indeed be some biological reality to the races and to the differences among them, not only in physical traits but in mental characteristics as well. Finally, they recoiled from the suggestion that cooperation was an innate drive in human beings. Such objections detracted from the credibility of UNESCO and its mandate, and its leaders decided that a second statement needed to be drawn up, but presented as a supplement, rather than as an outright critique of the first. A second committee was accordingly convened. Montagu was the only holdover from the first committee. The second group of scientists consisted entirely of geneticists and physical anthropologists, including L. C. Dunn, who acted as rapporteur, J. B. S. Haldane, Theodosius Dobzhansky, and Solly Zuckerman, with Julian Huxley offering advice on the wording.

The second statement, titled "Statement on the Nature of Race and Race Differences" by "Physical Anthropologists and Geneticists," was issued in 1951 and represented in some ways a definite retreat from the first. The more radical claims of the first—the point about innate cooperativity and the idea of race as a social myth—were both omitted from the second statement. Dunn wrote that the committee was "careful to avoid saying that, because races were variable and many of them graded into each other, therefore races did not exist. The physical anthropologist and the man in the street both know that races exist" (Montagu 1951, 140). But the basic egalitarianism of the first statement remained. The second statement defined races as biological populations and reasserted a strong commitment to antiracism: "Available scientific knowledge provides no basis for believing that the groups of mankind differ in their innate capacity for intellectual and emotional development. There is no evidence that race mixture produces disadvantageous results from a biological point of view" (Montagu 1951, 146). Both of these claims were, however, phrased in the negative. The 1951 statement did not actually deny that race differences existed, it stated only that scientists did not as yet have convincing enough evidence to dismiss such differences definitively. They had no positive scientific evidence that the races were the same in mental capacity. "It is possible, though not proved, that some types of innate capacity for intellectual and emotional responses are commoner in one human group that in another," the statement read, "but it is certain that, within a single group, innate capacities vary as much as, if not more than, they do between different groups" (Montagu 1951, 144). Thus the second statement, while still strongly egalitarian and antiracist, contained a tentativeness in its wording that reflected scientists' deeper disagreements about race and heredity.

When the committee sent the second statement out to geneticists and physical anthropologists for comment before publication, the response of Hermann J. Muller was the most representative. Muller agreed with the basic message of the statement: that environmentally caused differences, whether between individuals, races, or nations, were more important than genetic ones. But, he continued, the averages or medians of the races do differ from one another in hereditary physical traits—the races look different—thus it would be odd if there were not also differences in hereditary mental traits between those racial averages. Individual differences, Muller conceded, even individual differences between people of the same race, might well be more important than any racial differences. But he still believed that hereditary mental differences between the races might exist, even though the solid scientific evidence for them was not yet forthcoming. Here Muller showed the same kind of tentativeness about racial difference that the authors of the second statement displayed. Muller's belief was clearly not the same as that expressed in the Geneticists' Manifesto, in which the signers were aligned openly behind a campaign for socialist eugenics. But the hereditarianism that inspired that earlier campaign was still very much alive in 1951.

Finally Muller addressed the problem raised by the UNESCO mandate for the statements. Just because one held the scientific belief that the races differed in hereditary mental capacities, one should not therefore abandon the egalitarian commitment to equal treatment and equal opportunity for all. A moral commitment to egalitarianism did not require a belief in the fallacious idea that the races are completely identical. Equality before the law should not depend on biological equality, and scientific facts must be kept separate from morality, values, and ethics. To address this point directly, both the first and second statements on race included a caveat that said, "We wish to emphasize that equality of opportunity and equality under the law in no way depend, as ethical principles, upon the assertion that human beings are in fact equal in endowment" (Montagu 1951, 145–146). But as debates in succeeding decades on the possible existence and meaning of race differences have shown, prying science apart from ethics is not always so easy.

In the postwar period, geneticists and anthropologists agreed that the correct moral position on race was one of equality. But behind this liberal consensus, there was still much disagreement on what race itself should actually mean. The commitment to egalitarianism was shared, as we have seen, by scientists across the board—a commitment maintained no longer by isolated individuals, but institutionalized in the policy that flowed from Gunnar Myrdal's work and in the public statements made by prominent scientific societies and organizations like UNESCO. In the scientific endorsement of human equality, we can see the complete reversal of the racial paradigm of typology and hierarchy that had been taken for granted only a century earlier. The revolution was now complete. The rejection of the concept of ineradicable essential racial differences was now wholesale. The new view of races not as static entities but as shifting populations was sustained by the synthesis of evolutionary theory and population genetics.

Yet in all the attempts at consensus discussed in this chapter—whether Myrdal's liberal orthodoxy or the UNESCO statements on race—the question was whether, and to what extent, difference really mattered. Myrdal and the assimilationists had implied that race was only skin deep and could be easily overcome. Montagu had basically agreed with them that race was a myth, and a dangerous one at that; it had no real meaning and should be ignored. In response, both the cultural pluralists who objected to Myrdal, and the geneticists who drafted the second UNESCO statement, contended that racial difference might run deeper than previously acknowledged. Race might matter—whether, as black nationalists maintained, from a cultural perspective, or as the geneticists believed, in hereditarian terms. Such divergent perspectives belied the notion that the orthodoxies of the 1950s had definitively settled the question of race.

Bibliographic Essay

Both the term and the concept of a "liberal orthodoxy" stemming from Gunnar Myrdal's *An American Dilemma* come from Walter Jackson's *Gunnar Myrdal and America's Conscience: Social Engineering and Racial Liberalism* (Chapel Hill: University of North Carolina Press, 1990). Jackson's book formed the basis for the discussion of Myrdal's work and of the post-Myrdal orthodoxy in this chapter. The impact of World War II on social science research, Myrdal's role, and the psychologizing of social scientific research on race in the 1950s are also treated by Ellen Herman in *The Romance of American Psychology: Political Culture in the Age of Experts* (Berkeley: University of California Press, 1995). John P. Jackson, Jr., discusses the impact of World War II on the scientific study of racial prejudice in *Social Scientists for Social Justice: Making the Case Against Segregation* (New York: New York University Press, 2001), and describes especially how such research prepared the ground for the damage argument used in *Brown v. Board of Education.*

In the "Experts in Prejudice" section, quotations are from: Resnis Likert, "Negroes and the War: A Study in Baltimore and Cincinnati," Special Report No.

16, Division of Surveys, Office of War Information, July 21, 1942, in Resnis Likert Papers, Box 9, folder 9–20, Bentley Historical Library, University of Michigan Archives, Ann Arbor; and from Alfred McClung Lee and Norman Humphrey, *Race Riot* (New York: Dryden Press, 1943). The quotation from the conclusion of the 1944 conference on anti-Semitism is from Ira M. Younker, "Scientific Research on Anti-Semitism in 1944," *The American Jewish Yearbook, 5706, 1945–46* (Philadelphia: Jewish Publication Society of America, 1945): 697.

In the section on Myrdal's book, all quotations are from Gunnar Myrdal, *An American Dilemma* (New York: Harper and Brothers, 1944).

In the discussion of the post-Myrdal orthodoxy, quotations are from *To Secure These Rights: The Report of the President's Committee on Civil Rights* (Washington, DC: Government Printing Office, 1947).

For an introduction to the scholarship on émigré scholars who fled Nazi Germany see the collected essays in Mitchell G. Ash and Alfons Söllner, eds., *Forced Migration and Scientific Change: Émigré German-Speaking Scientists and Scholars After 1933* (Cambridge: Cambridge University Press, 1996). Useful discussions of *The Authoritarian Personality* can be found in Martin Jay, *The Dialectical Imagination: A History of the Frankfurt School and the Institute for Social Research, 1923–1950* (Boston: Little Brown and Company, 1973); and Franz Samelson, "Authoritarianism From Berlin to Berkeley: On Social Psychology and History," *Journal of Social Issues* 42 (1986): 191–208. Quotations were taken from Theodor Adorno, Else Frenkel-Brunswik, Daniel J. Levinson, and R. Nevitt Sanford, *The Authoritarian Personality* (New York: Norton, 1969 [1950]).

Quotations in the section on the damage argument are from Abram Kardiner and Lionel Ovesey, *The Mark of Oppression: Explorations in the Personality of the American Negro* (Cleveland: World Publishing Co., 1951); and from Kenneth Clark and Mamie Clark, "Emotional Factors in Racial Identification and Preference in Negro Children," *Journal of Negro Education* 19 (1950): 341–350.

The discussion on the breakdown of the liberal orthodoxy quotes from Daniel Patrick Moynihan, *The Negro Family: The Case for National Action* (Washington, D.C.: Office of Policy Planning and Research, United States Department of Labor, March, 1965) and refers to "Liberalism and the Negro: A Roundtable Discussion," *Commentary* 37 (March 1964).

On the Geneticists' Manifesto, see Diane Paul, "Eugenics and the Left," *Journal of the History of Ideas* 45, Issue 4 (Oct–Dec 1984): 567–590. Quotations are from H. J. Muller, *Out of the Night: A Biologist's View of the Future* (New York: Vanguard Press, 1935); as well as from the Manifesto itself in "Social Biology and Population Improvement," *Nature* 144 (1939). In the section on wartime antiracism, quotations are from Ruth Benedict, *Race: Science and Politics* (New York: Viking Press, 1959), which includes Benedict and Weltfish, "The Races of

Mankind," from Ashley Montagu, *Man's Most Dangerous Myth: The Fallacy of Race* (5th Edition, New York: Oxford University Press, 1974); and from L. C. Dunn and Theodosius Dobzhansky, *Heredity, Race and Society* (New York: Mentor, 1959). On the UNESCO Statements, see William B. Provine, "Geneticists and Race," *American Zoologist* 26 (1986): 857–887 and Elazar Barkan, "The Politics of the Science of Race: Ashley Montagu and UNESCO's Anti-Racist Declarations," in *Race and Other Misadventures: Essays in Honor of Ashley Montagu in his Ninetieth Year*, eds. Larry T. Reynolds and Leonard Lieberman (New York: General Hall, 1996). The full text of the UNESCO Statements along with commentary appears in Ashley Montagu, *Statement on Race* (New York: Henry Schuman, 1951).

7

A Multicultural Science of Race, 1965 to the Present

hree seemingly contradictory trends are evident in the scientific study of race since 1965. First, race and racism took on a new importance in sociology and psychology as psychologists and sociologists intensified their claims that race and racism were central to society. Second, just as social scientists stressed the reality of race in the lives of individuals, geneticists and physical anthropologists firmly rejected race as a real biological category. Third, a small but vocal minority of scientists argued that the old view of the hierarchy of real biological races was correct after all; they claimed that the black race really was objectively inferior to the white race, especially in intelligence.

Movement Scholarship

In the wake of the *Brown v. Board of Education* decision in 1954, which declared segregation of public schools unconstitutional, African Americans began demanding their rights as guaranteed by the constitution. In the mid-1950s, African Americans in several southern American cities boycotted bus systems demanding nonsegregated seating. The most famous, the Montgomery bus boycott, began in 1955, lasted over a year and thrust a young Baptist minister, Martin Luther King, Jr., into the national spotlight, transforming him into the spokesman for the civil rights movement. But the civil rights movement went far beyond King. In 1957, in Little Rock, Arkansas, nine African American high school students braved mobs of angry whites and attended the previously all-white Central High School. President Eisenhower eventually dispatched federal troops to Arkansas to protect the "Little Rock Nine." In 1960, a group of college students in Greensboro, North Carolina, quietly sat at a lunch counter, protesting the fact that it was still segregated, setting off a wave of "sit-ins" at lunch counters all over the South. At the same time, black and white "Freedom Riders"

205

A bus carrying civil rights "Freedom Riders" is firebombed during a caravan to advocate black voting rights in 1961. (Library of Congress)

traveled on buses throughout the South where local authorities refused to protect them and in many cases encouraged local whites to attack them. In 1962, James Meredith, a black man, attempted to enroll at the University of Mississippi, sparking a riot that left three dead and hundreds injured. Many in the United States recoiled in horror at the television images of white southern police forces turning fire hoses and police dogs on peaceful marchers, many of them children, in places like Birmingham, Alabama.

If the nation was horrified by the southern reaction to black demands for civil rights, social scientists were mystified and more than a little embarrassed by their failure to see it coming. In his 1963 presidential address to the American Sociological Association, Everett C. Hughes asked, "Why did social scientists . . . not foresee the explosion of collective action of Negro Americans toward immediate full integration into American society?" (Hughes 1963, 879). The social scientists' failure to anticipate the civil rights movement underscored a growing dissatisfaction with the prevalent models for race relations and the assumptions on which they were based.

A key component of the change in social scientists' models for race relations was the change in the civil rights movement itself, which had started as a movement aimed at the Jim Crow system of segregation prevalent in the American South. In 1964 President Lyndon B. Johnson signed the Civil Rights Act ending legalized discrimination in the South. The following year, the Voting Rights Act of 1965 enfranchised southern African Americans for the first time since Reconstruction following the Civil War. Just as these victories came, however, large northern cities experienced a series of racial uprisings. African Americans in Los Angeles, Detroit, Newark, and other cities rose up, protesting racial inequalities. But these cities had never experienced the legalized segregation of the American South, and to explain the widespread violence required new thinking about race and race relations.

In the social sciences, scholars brought forth a number of new concepts in an attempt to recast the study of race relations. Many of these scholars were themselves products of the civil rights movement and the struggle for black rights. For these scholars, racism was not a problem with the attitudes of white people who did not adhere to the American Creed; rather the problem was with the American Creed itself. Racism was not an aberration in society, but was central to the very structure of society.

The Rejection of the Pathology of Black Culture

Central to Gunnar Myrdal's sociology, which had set the social scientific agenda for the two decades following its 1944 publication, was the idea that blacks wanted to become just like whites. For Myrdal there was nothing worth saving in black culture; it was a pathological culture because slavery and segregation had stripped blacks of their African culture and left only a poor reflection of white culture. The solution to this problem, Myrdal argued, was to remove the barriers that prevented blacks from fully entering the American mainstream. This view was forcefully articulated, not just by Myrdal, but also by many sociologists and psychologists including the African Americans E. Franklin Frazier and Kenneth B. Clark.

For that earlier generation of social scientists, the idea of the pathology of black culture was put forward in response to the scientific racism of writers like Madison Grant, Lothrop Stoddard, and others convinced of the biological and innate inferiority of black people. By arguing that black people were not naturally inferior, but rather were damaged by racial oppression, social scientists put forth the pathology of black culture as a liberating idea; blacks were just like whites, except damaged by racism. By the 1960s, however, many began seeing the pathology argument in a much different light.

No work exemplified the shift in racial thinking more than the "Moynihan Report." Daniel Patrick Moynihan would eventually become a U.S. senator but in

1973 he was a freshly minted Ph.D. in political science serving as an assistant secretary of labor. Moynihan was a new breed of civil servant, one who excelled at bringing the findings of social science to bear on social policy. As a believer in President Johnson's "War on Poverty," Moynihan prepared a report for the Department of Labor entitled, *The Negro Family: The Case for National Action*, popularly known as the "Moynihan Report."

Moynihan said nothing in his report that was not a staple of the liberal orthodoxy: the black family had suffered under slavery and segregation, as was evidenced by the prevalence of woman-headed households. Moynihan repeated the by now timeworn concept of blacks living in a culture of pathology and poverty. In the 1940s and 1950s, when contrasted with the racism of biological essentialism, these ideas were liberating. In the 1960s, the contrast was not to biological essentialism and Jim Crow but to a much different set of political questions and racial ideas.

By 1965, when Moynihan released his report, the formerly unified civil rights movement was splintering. Many black activists questioned integration as a goal of the movement in favor of self-determination and racial separatism. In 1966, for example, the Student Nonviolent Coordinating Committee voted to bar whites from membership. Part of the move toward racial separatism was the prevalence of "pathological" talk in the integrationist movement, as many blacks were increasingly distressed at the idea that they were somehow damaged and living in a diseased state. Black culture was no doubt different from white culture, but it was simply incorrect to assume that white culture was normal and black culture sick. In the founding volume of *The Journal of Black Studies*, Maurice Jackson argued that, "Black people have dreams, legends, myths, and other characteristics that give them gusto and joy in living as well as a tragic sense which they have gained from suffering . . . It is decidedly incorrect to characterize black people only in terms of pathology and morbidity: low self-esteem, personality disorganization, self-hate, family disorganization and so on" (Jackson 1970, 139). Many critics of the Moynihan Report argued that this talk of "pathology" was nothing more than racism in a subtler guise. Albert Murray argued that claims of damage to the black community "are all too obvious extensions of the process of degradation by other means, and have always functioned as an indispensable element in the vicious cycle that perpetuates white supremacy through the systematic exploitation of black people" (Murray 1972, 98). By the mid-1960s, then, many civil rights activists and social scientists influenced by them rejected the pathological view of their culture. It was summed up by a phrase that began in the movement and worked its way into scholarly discourse: Black Power.

Institutional Racism and Colonialism

Racial uprising was not isolated to the United States. In the post–World War II world, former colonial subjects rose against occupying powers. The colonial system that had begun with the "Age of Exploration" was becoming unraveled. In relatively short order, Europeans abandoned their colonies in the face of indigenous uprisings. Long, bloody conflicts led to the wholesale replacement of the colonial order within three decades of World War II.

One of the most eloquent writers for decolonialism was Frantz Fanon (1925–1961). Born into the colonial system in Martinique, Fanon took a degree in psychiatry at the University of Lyons. After fighting with the French army during World War II he joined the Algerian resistance movement in 1954, which eventually led to France abandoning its colony in the early 1960s. In two works, *Black Skin, White Masks* (1952) and particularly *The Wretched of the Earth* (1961), Fanon developed a psychiatric view of the colonial experience. He linked the colonial experience to psychiatric concepts of mental health. In *The Wretched of the Earth*, he used extensive psychiatric case studies to meticulously document the mental damage inflicted by the colonial power structure on both the oppressed and the oppressor. This was not told in the dispassionate tones of science, but in the voice of an armed warrior fighting a civil war. The colonizer did not go quietly, but needed to be forcibly evicted. The aims of decolonialization were literally to turn the power structure of the world upside down, which demanded violence: "The naked truth of decolonization," he wrote, "evokes for us the searing bullets and bloodstained knives which emanate from it" (Fanon 1966, 30).

Fanon's work had a deep impact on many activists in the United States, especially African American activists who began to question assimilation as a desirable goal for social action. The outspoken call for racial separatism by Malcolm X, especially in contrast to the integrationist ethos of Martin Luther King, Jr., underscored the shift in movement politics. In 1967, activist Stokely Carmichael brought "Black Power" out of the movement and into larger currency with a book of that title that he coauthored with political scientist Charles V. Hamilton. *Black Power* underscored many of the themes that would inform the sociology of race relations in the late 1960s and early 1970s and represented a radical shift in orientation from previous conceptualizations of race and racism. Central to the new view was the idea that racism was not, as Myrdal argued, a problem with attitudes, but a problem with social structures. Carmichael and Hamilton argued that there were two types of racism. The traditional form consisted "of overt acts by individuals," which should not be confused with "institutional racism . . . which originated in the operation of established and respected

Stokely Carmichael, speaking at the University of California (Library of Congress)

forces in society" (Carmichael and Hamilton 1967, 4). This institutional racism was more serious because it operated invisibly. Respectable whites could tell themselves they were not racists because they did not support Bull Connor's fire hoses in Birmingham while they "continue to support political officials and institutions that would and do perpetuate institutionally racist policies" (Carmichael and Hamilton 1967, 5).

Black Power looked for inspiration to Fanon's work and put forth a colonial metaphor that viewed African Americans' relationship with European Americans as the same relationship that Africans faced with occupying European powers. The first task, Carmichael and Hamilton argued, was to reject the notion that black culture was pathological: "Our basic need," they wrote, "is to reclaim our history and our identity from what must be called cultural terrorism" (Carmichael and Hamilton 1967, 34–35). Carmichael and Hamilton embraced the notion that black culture was not a warped version of white culture, but was based on African cultural characteristics and traits. The implication, they argued, was that assimilation was dangerous because it would wipe out black culture: "The fact is that integration, as traditionally articulated, would abolish the black community. The fact is that what must be abolished is not the black community, but the dependent colonial status that has been inflicted upon it" (Carmichael and Hamilton 1967, 55).

For Myrdal, the key problem was prejudice, an attitude that led to discriminatory barriers. Under the new view of racism, social scientists abandoned

Frantz Fanon (1925–1961)

Born on the island of Martinique, then a French possession, Frantz Fanon experienced racism at an early age. Raised in a middle-class family, Fanon nonetheless was discriminated against by the French whites who were the upper crust of Martinique. His early education was thoroughly French in design and assimilation into the French way of life was stressed throughout. In 1940, France fell to the Nazis and the French Vichy Administration declared its loyalty to the conquering Nazis. The

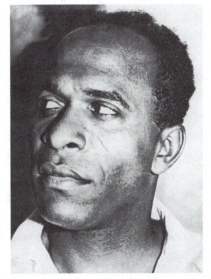

American fleet threw a blockade around the Caribbean island of Martinique to cut off the French fleet. French sailors came under the military control of the governor of Martinique who allowed the white French sailors to dominate the black population of the island. For the young Fanon, as well as for many other black Martinicans, their home was transformed into a totalitarian, racist state almost overnight. Fanon enrolled in the "free French" Army to oppose the Vichy regime and fought for France in North Africa during World War II, despite the blatant racism he experienced in the French army.

In 1947 Fanon went to France to pursue his education. After a brief stint in dentistry school, he enrolled at the University of

(Algerian Ministry of Information)

Lyon to study psychiatric medicine. In 1951, he received his medical degree and subsequently published papers on psychiatric medicine in Algeria and Tunisia when in residency under Professor Francois Tosquelles. In 1952, he published *Black Skin, White Masks* where he argued that the colonial order imposed false values on its subjects by demanding that they assimilate to the social thinking of the oppressor.

In 1953, Fanon passed his medical boards and took a position in Algiers, Algeria, then a colony of France. Algeria was beginning to experience rebel uprising against the governing power and Fanon became politically involved with the Front de Liberation Nationale. This led him to be treating the French torturers as a hospital employee during the day and their victims at night as a rebel sympathizer. In 1957, Fanon was expelled from Algeria for his rebel sympathies. He took up residence in Tunisia, becoming a full-time revolutionary, while teaching and working in a psychiatric hospital in Manouba. He achieved recognition as an important revolutionary writer within the burgeoning anticolonial movements in Africa. His most famous work, *The Wretched of the Earth*, was written as Fanon was dying of leukemia in 1960–1961. When it was published, with an introduction by Fanon's intellectual colleague, Jean-Paul Sartre, it was instantly recognized as one of the most powerful exposes of racism of the twentieth century.

the emphasis on prejudice. Robert Blauner, an American Jew, grew up sensitive to being an outsider to mainstream American culture. A sociologist at the University of California, Berkeley, Blauner was at one of the centers of 1960s student activism and provided one of the most extensive presentations of the new thinking in his 1972 book, *Racial Oppression in America*. Racism in the United States, Blauner argued, was primarily institutional. "These institutions," he wrote, "either exclude or restrict the participation of racial groups by procedures that have become conventional, part of the bureaucratic system of rules and regulations. Thus, there is little need for prejudice as a motivating force" (Blauner 1972, 10).

Blauner also argued for the internal colonial metaphor to replace the previous metaphor, the "immigration metaphor." Robert Park and the Chicago school of sociology had developed the model of the race relations cycle through a study of immigrant groups that came to the United States in the early part of the twentieth century. For Park, minority groups would inevitably be assimilated; blacks just as surely as Poles or Italians. Blauner argued that the immigration metaphor did not recognize the fundamental distinction between immigrants and colonized peoples: "immigrant groups enter a new territory or society voluntarily . . . Colonized groups become part of a new society through force or violence; they are conquered, enslaved, or pressured into movement" (Blauner 1972, 52). Blauner outlined four characteristics of the colonial system that apply to the relationship between white and black Americans: first, the mode of entry into the dominant society is forced, not voluntary; second, the dominant power enacts policies that serve to destroy traditional cultures; third, legal and regulatory processes ensure that the dominant group holds power over the subordinate group; and fourth, the dominant group singles out the subordinate group with racial markers that ensure their inferior status.

Blauner argued that the internal colonial metaphor explained the racial unrest of the 1960s better than the prevailing sociological models. The traditional colonial order was based on an inequitable distribution of power and wealth. The colony existed only to provide resources for the mother country whether in the form of natural resources, agricultural products, or cheap labor. The colonized people did not own these resources, even their own labor, and the wealth generated by this deliberate underdevelopment of the "third world" flowed to the "first world." This model, Blauner argued, applied to the ghettos of US cities. Living in tenements owned by absentee landlords, shopping at stores owned by whites who did not live in their communities, attending schools that were run by city governments that denied basic services to their neighborhoods, blacks were not "rioting, but rather undertaking a preliminary . . . form of mass rebellion against colonial status. . . . The guiding impulse . . . has not been integration with American society, but an attempt to stake out a sphere of control by moving against that society and destroying the symbols of its oppression" (Blauner 1972, 89).

The implications of this view are profound. No longer was racism an ideological concept with the belief that biological groups that can be ranked in a hierarchy. Rather racism was a matter of institutions perpetuating racist power relationships in society, often without the conscious knowledge of majority group members. This view meant that racism was built into the structure of American society rather than a byproduct of the mistaken beliefs of a few misguided Southerners. The former colonial societies in Africa embraced the term "self-determination" in the face of their colonial oppressors, and African American activists similarly embraced self-determination for their own schools and neighborhoods.

To favor self-determination meant favoring racial separatism and abandoning assimilation and integration. The racial group became socially real, abandoning the integrationist view that race was no more than "skin deep." Scholar/activist Harold Cruse, in a critique of sociological theories of assimilation, argued that group identities were central to society and that African Americans should abandon the individualist creed as a delusion. For Cruse, the United States was "in reality, a nation dominated by the social power of groups, classes, in-groups and cliques—both ethnic and religious" (Cruse 1967, 7). Just how this social reality was to be translated into social policy was not clear, however, and Cruse was just as ambivalent about the separatist wing of the movement, which, he argued, "might know what it wants generally, but does not know how to achieve it specifically" (Cruse 1967, 420). For some, the call for black separatism meant the abandonment of the rampant individualism and materialism, which were the hallmarks of American culture. Sociologists Joanna Zangrando and Robert Zangrando claimed, "A growing number of black people stand determined to achieve their own liberation from [the American Dream's] waking delusion" (Zangrando and Zangrando 1970, 154).

Movement scholarship brought a wave of new studies that examined racial discrimination in a new light. Racism was far more prevalent than the previous generation of scholars imagined. Race, as a *social* category, was real because being racially marked had real social consequences. The rise of the reality of race in the social realm was matched, ironically, by the decline of the reality of race in the biological realm.

Genetics, New Physical Anthropology, and the Abandonment of Race

As sociologists and psychologists emphasized the social reality of race, other disciplines began seriously challenging the biological reality of race. New developments in genetics, new techniques for detecting and measuring human variation, a new emphasis on process rather than type in physical anthropology and the sheer growth of anthropology as a discipline all combined to finally lead to the demise of the typological view of race.

Boas and his followers had led the scientific community to reject racial hierarchy and to cast significant doubt on the link between biological race and cultural attributes. However, many anthropologists remained agnostic, rather than atheistic, about Ashley Montagu's myth of race. Those trained in physical anthropology under Earnest Hooton at Harvard, most vocally Carleton S. Coon, were particularly resistant to eliminating race as an object of study.

The subsequent abandonment of the older race concept by physical anthropologists in the 1960s and 1970s owes to earlier developments in genetics. In the 1930s, genetics and evolutionary biology were merged into a coherent framework. This "evolutionary synthesis" merged two different groups of scientists: geneticists, who often worked in laboratories, and evolutionary biologists, who focused on fieldwork rather than laboratory experimentation. These two groups had viewed each other with suspicion, seldom sharing methods or objects of study. The heart of the conceptual disagreement was squaring Darwinism's emphasis on small, continuous variations with Mendelian emphasis on discontinuous variations. A key component to the synthesis was the work of mathematical population geneticists whose mathematical models showed that both groups were studying different aspects of the same system.

With the merging of evolutionary biology and genetics, views about the biological sciences also changed. The new concepts brought with them ideas that science should study the processes by which organisms took the forms they did, rather than assuming, as racial typography did, that organic forms were somehow static. A key factor in racial science after Darwin, after all, was the focus on "non-adaptive" traits that were immune to environmental influences. With the new sciences, physical anthropologists, geneticists, and evolutionary biologists turned away from a focus on these static features and to the process of change.

The geneticists brought another concept with them into evolutionary biology: population. A population, in genetics, was an isolated group of organisms characterized by breeding only within the group and by a shared pattern of genes. There were two implications of population thinking for the study of race. The first implication was that a population, however defined, was not a discrete entity because in the natural world some breeding outside the group always occurs. The geneticists and evolutionary biologists began to prefer discussing species as clines, a geographic gradation of a species. In 1950 William Boyd, one of the first scientists to work out the implications of population thinking for human races, described a cline as a situation wherein "the frequencies of some genes . . . change gradually in various geographical directions, so that the differences between populations are proportional to the distances between the localities which they inhabit" (Boyd 1950, 204). So a species may consist of different variations, but these variations fade into one another and there are no sharp lines distinguishing them.

This notion of cline leads to the second implication of the population concept for racial thought. If species are best thought of as clines, how does a geneticist determine the population within the species that shares genes? The answer, Boyd argued, had nothing to do with a real division within nature but with the needs of the scientist and what the scientist wished to discover: "Whether or not the systematist decides to break up the population into two or more sections and designate them as races is quite arbitrary. *This decision will be based upon consideration of expediency and nothing else*" (Boyd 1950, 204; emphasis in original).

The synthesis of genetics and Darwinism undercut the biological basis of racial thinking because racial ideology depended on the existence of subgroups of human populations that were distinct from one other. Under synthesis thinking, to the extent that there were no real divisions between human groupings in nature, the scientist was free to impose a division. But different scientists, investigating different questions, would produce different groupings of humans because the scientists *created* groups rather than *discovered* them in nature. Boyd concluded that one scientist might group people one way, although another scientist might find quite another way to group people. Additionally, some groupings, for example those that relied on blood groups, might join populations in Greenland and Australia into one population, though such a grouping made no sense in terms of traditional racial categories. He concluded "Most contemporary physical anthropologists will probably accept this as a necessary and not illogical conclusion" (Boyd 1950, 205–206).

Boyd's prediction in 1950 regarding physical anthropologists was prescient, although the acceptance of these findings took a decade or so. The key figure in bringing the new biological thinking into anthropology was Sherwood Washburn (1911–2000). Washburn trained in the strict tradition of typological anthropology under Earnest Hooton at Harvard, receiving his Ph.D. in physical anthropology in 1940. His first job was at Columbia University Medical School, where he became acquainted with Theodosius Dobzhansky, one of the architects of the evolutionary synthesis. In 1950 Washburn and Dobzhansky organized a conference to bring the new evolutionary thinking into anthropology. At the biological station on Charles Davenport's old stomping grounds, Cold Spring Harbor, Washburn put forth the call for what he called the new physical anthropology that would unite the fieldwork of physical anthropology with laboratory experimen-

Sherwood Washburn (1911–2000)

Physical anthropologist Sherwood Washburn received his Ph.D. at Harvard University in 1940 under Earnest A. Hooton, then the dean of American physical anthropologists. Hooton trained Washburn in a typological anthropology in which the scientist sought to show the reality of racial differences through measurement of bones and other bodily features. Washburn soon threw off Hooton's teachings regarding the reality of racial differences and the value of typological thinking. His

(Ted Streshinsky/Corbis)

first academic job was as an anatomist at Columbia University Medical School where he became acquainted with Theodosius Dobzhansky, a geneticist who was one of the architects of the evolutionary synthesis of evolutionary theory and genetics. At Columbia, Washburn studied the growth of rat skulls under a variety of laboratory conditions; however, the anthropology of the 1940s was still firmly associated with museums and collections of skulls and other bones. Washburn's laboratory methods were not seen as true anthropology by many.

In 1947, Washburn moved to the University of Chicago and in 1948 he visited Africa to study primate behavior. In 1950, Washburn and Dobzhansky organized a meeting at the Cold Spring Harbor Biological Laboratory. Here, Washburn declared his program of "new physical anthropology" wherein traditional typologies would be abandoned in favor of an evolutionary perspective based on population genetics rather than a static typology. Washburn's program marked his final intellectual break with his mentor, Hooton.

In 1957, Washburn moved from Chicago to the University of California, Berkeley, where he continued to advocate for a more biological anthropology. He organized two major conferences on human evolution in the early 1960s that promoted his vision of a new physical anthropology. In 1962, as a president of the American Anthropological Association, he argued quite forcefully that the new physical anthropology meant that the older concept of race should be abandoned as unscientific. Because of his success in promoting his version of a biological anthropology, the American Association of Physical Anthropologists presented the first Charles Darwin Lifetime Achievement Award to him in the 1980s.

tation. His goal was to eliminate the very kind of anthropology in which he was trained. The focus of anthropology was not to be on essentialist conceptions of race, but on dynamic conceptions of the new term, "population."

Physical anthropologists took up Washburn's call to action as laboratory methods and a focus on genetics began to overtake the older typological approach of measuring skulls and bodies. Anthropologists increasingly turned away from what in 1959 Edward Hunt called "remote racial history" and focused instead on "the adaptive value of racial features in different environments" (Hunt 1959, 82). A decade after Washburn's call for a new physical anthropology, Stanley Garn, who also trained at Harvard, declared the death of the old way. "Anthropometry is virtually gone," he declared in the pages of *The American Anthropologist*. "Typology is gone. Craniology with its indexes and skull types is gone too" (Garn 1962, 917).

The embrace of the new physical anthropology did not immediately mean that the term "race" was dispensed with, however. Stanley Garn, for instance, admitted that the older, typological view of the three primordial races—white, black, and yellow—was a myth, but that did not mean anthropologists should abandon the word "race." A race was a population, according to Garn, whose members "share a common history and a common locale. They have been exposed to common dangers, and they are the product of a common environment. For these reasons . . . members of a race have a common genetic heritage" (Garn 1961, 6). Though many physical anthropologists continued to use the term "race," very few were holding to the reality of folk categories for race. The black/white distinction was not a racial division, and the old Nordic/Alpine/Mediterranean division was almost unthinkable. By the 1970s, most introductory physical anthropology textbooks adopted the position advocated by Ashley Montagu in 1942; race was a myth and the use of the term caused more confusion than enlightenment.

Part of the explanation for the shift in anthropological thinking lies in the changing demographics of the profession. Before 1960 there were only twenty Ph.D.-granting departments of anthropology in the entire country. The world of anthropology was close-knit and revolved around a few elite institutions: Columbia, Harvard, Yale, Chicago, and a few others. By 1975 there were eighty Ph.D.-granting departments and many other departments that catered to undergraduates. The world of anthropology was no longer dominated by a few elite places but was part of the standard undergraduate curriculum. This meant that anthropology was no longer taught by, or consumed by, a privileged few but by a mass audience that was more sensitive to racial prejudice and discrimination. Just as the scientific racism of Madison Grant can be partly explained by his patrician background, just as the retreat of scientific racism lead by Boas can be partly explained by his Jewishness and the fact that many of his students were female, the decline of the race concept in the 1970s in the anthropology curriculum can be explained by who was producing and consuming anthropological knowledge.

While physical anthropologists were abandoning the race concept, geneticists used the population concept to further undercut the typological definition of race. In 1972, Harvard geneticist Richard Lewontin published a study that compared the traditional typological division of the races with a genetic population division of the races to answer the question, "How much of human diversity between populations is accounted for by more or less conventional racial classification?" (Lewontin 1972, 386). He answered the question by identifying genetic markers that a geneticist would use to identify a breeding population. These genetic markers were not based on physical, morphological characteristics but on hemoglobins and other nonvisual physiological attributes. In the final analysis there was much more variation within a traditional race than between those races. In other words, if you were to take two random people from the same racial group, as race was traditionally defined, the chances were greater that they would be as genetically different as would be two random individuals from two different racial groups. The visual markers of skin color or the historical or linguistic markers used in traditional racial taxonomies did not match modern genetics. Lewontin concluded, "It is clear that our perception of relatively large differences between human races and subgroups, as compared to the variation within these groups, is indeed a biased perception and that, based on randomly chosen genetic differences, human races and populations are remarkably similar to each other" (Lewontin 1972, 397).

Further work by population geneticists indicated that using genetic markers to trace the evolutionary histories of different populations did not necessarily map onto the traditional typological categories. This was in part because the questions scientists asked had changed, reflecting the new emphasis on discovering the process of evolution rather than discovering evidence for obvious racial categories. The new technology that made genetic study available also undercut the focus on external differences in skin color, head shape, or other morphological characteristics. Masotoshi Nei and Arun K. Roychoudhury argued that "the extent of genetic differentiation between human races is not always correlated with the degree of morphological differentiation" (Nei and Roychoudhury 1982, 44). In a project that ran over four decades, Stanford geneticist Luigi Luca Cavalli-Sforza traced human lineages based on blood groups and created an evolutionary tree that did not look like the traditional one created by trying to find similar physical characteristics among groups of people. He argued that the genetic tree gave a more accurate picture of our evolutionary history because "external body features, such as skin color, and body size and shape, are highly subject to the influence of natural selection due to climate . . . In reality, it is risky to use these features to study genetic history, because they reveal much about the geography of climates in which populations lived in the last millennia, and little about the history of fissions of a population" (Cavalli-Sforza and Cavalli-Sforza 1995, 115). Those features that have historically been the most striking for racial classification—skin color, body size, and head shape—truly were only skin deep according to Cavalli-Sforza: *"It is because they are external that these racial differences strike us so forcibly, and we automatically assume that differences of similar magnitude exist below the surface . . . This is simply not so; the remainder of our genetic makeup hardly differs at all"* (Cavalli-Sforza and Cavalli-Sforza 1995, 124, emphasis in original). These studies found no ground for the old racial divisions and certainly none for a racial hierarchy. However, the old racial divisions and hierarchy proved remarkably tenacious and would return with a vengeance before the end of the 1960s.

Forward to the Past: The Psychometrician Case for Race Differences

One hundred years after Francis Galton published *Hereditary Genius*, the research program he outlined there would be continued by University of California, Berkeley, psychologist Arthur Jensen. His 1969 article in the *Harvard Educational Review* entitled "How Much Can We Boost IQ and Scholastic Achievement" became one of the most cited papers in the history of twentieth-century psychology. In the controversy that followed Jensen's argument, a small group of experts in psychological tests and measurement, psychometricians, consistently put forward the position that the races differed in innate capacity for learning. Against them were other psychometricians and many other psychologists as well as geneticists, anthropologists, and sociologists.

Jensen's thesis was simple: IQ tests accurately measured intelligence, intelligence was fixed by the time a person was eight years old, there was a persistent gap in IQ and therefore intelligence between blacks and whites that could not be ameliorated by environmental influences. Therefore, educational opportunities should acknowledge the difference in genetic endowment and capacity for learning. None of his arguments were particularly novel. Galton laid out the basic premises a century before Jensen's article; indeed, Jensen looked to Galton as the founder of the enterprise he was undertaking.

In the postwar United States, however, the basic ideas were only really put forth by a very small group of psychologists who identified with the white South's struggle to preserve segregation. Henry E. Garrett, who had been the head of the psychology department at Columbia University until 1956 when he retired and moved back to his home state of Virginia, was the best known and most outspoken psychologist to hold these views in the midcentury United States. Garrett argued that the IQ gap between white and black students was grounds for continuing racial segregation in southern schools; he was an active participant in southern politics dedicated to fighting the civil rights movement.

Psychologist Arthur Jensen lecturing at the University of California at Berkeley (Time Life Pictures/Getty Images)

In the larger scientific community, few took Garrett seriously. His advocacy of the segregationist cause tainted him in most psychologists' eyes. Moreover, Otto Klineberg's work in the 1930s remained authoritative in undercutting the case for innate racial differences in IQ.

Jensen's article opened the case for innate racial differences in IQ once again for three reasons. First, he distanced himself from the crude racism of others of his time who put forth his views. Jensen refused to join Garrett in the segregationist cause and he firmly and forcefully proclaimed that his article had nothing to do with racial segregation, insisting he believed that individuals should be treated as individuals rather than as members of a racial group. Second, Jensen was a sophisticated analyst of the statistical methods that were at the heart of the psychometrician's enterprise. Third, Jensen's prose was strictly scientific. Garrett and his followers often allowed themselves to be carried away by the cause of racial purity at the expense of any appearance of scientific objectivity.

Jensen's 123-page article presented the case for racial differences in IQ. Its infamous first line declared, "Compensatory education has been tried and it apparently has failed" (Jensen 1972, 69). His targets were the programs of Johnson's War on Poverty that offered special educational benefits to poor schools to bring them educational equality with rich schools. These programs, Jensen argued, were based on the notion that poor children had the same capacity to learn as richer children; he believed that this was not so. Poor children were marked by low IQ and simply could not learn as much as their more gifted counterparts in richer schools. Moreover, IQ tests had consistently shown that black Americans scored, on average, 15 points below white Americans. This gap in scores persisted, according to Jensen, even in "culture free" tests and even where socioeconomic status was controlled for. Hence, he concluded, the fact was that blacks simply were not as smart, on average, as whites.

Immediately upon publication, Jensen's argument became more famous than nearly any other psychological paper of the twentieth century. In the racially divisive 1960s, the mass media picked up the story and many outlets reported that the latest science proved that blacks were not as smart as whites. The scientific community reacted quickly too. A 1972 book by Jensen listed 117 articles published on his article in the three years after its publication and the number has only grown since.

The case for racial differences in IQ was trotted out again 25 years after Jensen's article. Unlike Jensen's article, which appeared in a previously obscure academic journal, *The Bell Curve* was the work of Harvard psychologist Richard Herrnstein and political scientist Charles Murray and was published by a trade press and announced with a flourish at a press conference. The authors claimed they had an important new work with profound implications for social policy. In fact, the book was simply yet another retelling of Galton's *Hereditary Genius*. *The Bell Curve* was a massive book, 845 pages long, in which Herrnstein and Murray focused on class. But a large section of the book involved race and took Jensen's position regarding racial differences in IQ. Indeed, twenty-three of Jensen's works were in Herrnstein and Murray's bibliography. Herrnstein and Murray argued that low IQ, not racism, was responsible for the social status of ethnic minorities, particularly blacks, and urged that scholars avoid focusing on discrimination when discussing the social position of these minorities. "The evidence presented here," they wrote, "should give everyone who writes and talks about ethnic inequalities reason to avoid flamboyant rhetoric about ethnic oppression" (Herrnstein and Murray 1994, 340).

Most reviewers found the claims made in Jensen's 1969 article and *The Bell Curve* overstated and unproven. The public furor that arose around the aggressively promoted *Bell Curve* in the mid-1990s led the American Psychological Association to form a committee to draft and issue an authoritative report on the state of knowledge on issues surrounding IQ testing and group differences. Referring specifically to Jensen's work, the APA committee report concluded, "It is sometimes suggested that the Black/White differential in psychometric intelligence is partly due to genetic differences ... There is not much direct evidence on this point, but what there is fails to support the genetic hypothesis" (Neisser et. al. 1996, 95). There are a number of reasons why the genetic argument for race differences in intelligence has not won many adherents in the scientific community. First, even taken on its own terms, the case made by Jensen and his followers did not hold up to scrutiny. Second, the rise of population genetics undercut the claims for a genetic cause of intelligence. Third, the new understanding of institutional racism offered a better explanation for the existence of differences in IQ scores between the races.

Psychometrics, Intelligence, and Heritability

There was really only one thing that the pyschometricians and their critics agreed on: whites averaged 15 points higher than blacks on IQ tests. Disagreement followed immediately, however: What did IQ tests really measure? What was the cause of this gap? One problem with the psychometric case for innate differences in intelligence is that there is no consensus on what is meant by "intelligence." Jensen insisted that there was widespread agreement that intelligence was a single unitary factor, often referred to in the technical literature by the letter g for general intelligence, and that g was accurately measured by intelligence tests. Twenty-five years later, Herrnstein and Murray acknowledged that there were competing definitions of "intelligence" within the psychometric community and declared their allegiance to the "classical tradition," which held that "modern IQ test[s] . . . do a reasonably good job of measuring g. When properly administered, the tests are not measurably biased against socioeconomic, ethnic, or racial subgroups" (Herrnstein and Murray 1994, 15). In choosing their allegiance to this classical tradition, however, critics pointed out that Herrnstein and Murray ignored any findings from cross-cultural studies in anthropology, a field that had grown considerably in the 25 years since Jensen published his article. Michael Nunley argued that cross-cultural studies show that "human cognition is far too complex to be captured on a simple linear scale; that IQ measures only a very narrow band of all kinds of cognitive achievement; and that tests of cognitive achievement cannot avoid being culturally biased by the content, materials, and style of testing" (Nunley 1995). As an example Nunley pointed to research, ignored by *The Bell Curve*, that showed that white children were superior to Australian aboriginal children in arranging artificial objects such as scissors, safety pins, etc. on a grid. Aboriginal children, by contrast, were superior to white children when stones of different shapes were used for the same exercise. As with Otto Klineberg a generation earlier, culture pervaded all aspects of the testing experience according to cross-cultural studies of cognition.

A more serious problem for the psychometric case for innate differences in intelligence has to do with heritability, a technical term that often would be mis-used in the ensuing discussions of the psychometricians' work. Within any pop-ulation the distribution of a given trait, say height, is going to vary and within the population there will be a range of measured heights. That range is called "vari-ance." This variance can be expressed statistically as the 1.0, which signifies 100 percent of all the differences within the population. Variance can be further divided into "heritability" and "environmentability." Environmentability is the portion of the variance that owes to environmental factors, whereas heritability is the amount of variance that owes to heredity. Heritability, like environ-mentability, can be expressed statistically; for a trait that varies completely due to heredity, the heritability would be 1.0 (or 100 percent); for a trait that varies completely due to environmental factors, the heritability would be 0.0 (or 0 per-cent). Heritability and environmentability trade off against one another: if heri-tability is, for example, 0.4, then environmentability would be 0.6.

In his 1969 article, Jensen argued that the heritability for intelligence was 0.8, or 80 percent, which meant heritability for intelligence was fairly high. Because Jensen's estimate was based, in large part, on the research of Cyril Burt, which was later shown to be fraudulent, Herrnstein and Murray's estimate of the heritability of IQ was slightly lower, between 0.4 and 0.6.

The problem in the heritability argument, as critics quickly pointed out, was that, even if it were correct, it was irrelevant to establishing anything to do with Jensen's conclusions regarding the educability of black people. There were basic problems with the relationship between heritability as a statistical measure and psychometricians' claims about education. Heritability applies to a group, not to an individual. In everyday language, claims that the heritability of IQ is 80 percent may lead one to believe that 80 percent of an individual's IQ owes to heredity and 20 percent owes to environment. But that is not at all what Jensen was arguing. Because it is a measure of variance, then by definition heritability is a way to measure differences within a population. It is a meaningless figure for an individual. Jensen and Herrnstein were skilled psychometricians and made this clear in their writings; however, as their arguments moved into the public sphere, many commentators spoke as if they were making some claim about how much of an individual's IQ owed to genetics. Even Charles Murray, in his defenses of *The Bell Curve*, occasionally talked as if it did.

Heritability is not a fixed figure, as the psychometricians often treated it, but varies by population and environment. As the environment equalized, for example, heritability would increase; if the environment were much different, heritability would decrease, since they always trade off against one another. The psychometricians wrote as if heritability would somehow be unchangeable.

High heritability for a trait did not mean that trait was caused by genetics.

A trait with low heritability may be completely genetic. Humans have two eyes or two legs because of their genetic makeup. Any variance within the populations of humans for these traits, then, owes to environmental mishaps: as psychologist Graham Richards explained, the variance in number of eyes or legs "is almost entirely due to environmental (perhaps pre-natal) factors—thalidomide or stepping on a land mine" (Richards 1997, 266). So the heritability for the variance in the number of legs is nearly 0.0, but the trait itself is strictly genetic. Psychometricians, even when they discussed heritability correctly in a technical sense, often proceeded to conflate "heritable" with "inherited."

Heritability is a measure within a population. But Jensen and his followers used high heritability *within* a population (white IQ scores, for example) to argue that the *difference* between two different populations (whites and blacks) must be also be highly heritable. Jensen argued that a high heritability within a population increased the probability that the difference between the populations was also heritable. But, as geneticist Richard Lewontin argued, that was pure assertion on Jensen's part, as he had no plausible explanation for that probability. In fact, Lewontin concluded, it was possible for the difference to be genetic or environmental, both possibilities were observed in nature, and there was no reason that one was more probable than the other. Similarly the American Psychological Association committee concluded that "the high heritability of a trait within a given group has no necessary implication for the source of difference between groups" (Neisser 1996, 95).

For most scholars, the problems that the psychometricians had with heritability were so substantial that few thought the case was made for innate racial differences in IQ. But there were further problems with the psychometricians' case. It was no accident that one of Jensen's critics was Richard Lewontin, who like most geneticists found the case put forth by Jensen and Herrnstein and Murray to be nonsense.

Geneticists versus the Psychometricians

Like Galton, Jensen never spelled out the possible mechanism for the differential IQ scores between whites and blacks. Galton, of course, was writing when no one had a good explanation for how hereditary traits were passed from generation to generation. Jensen, and especially Herrnstein and Murray, however, wrote after DNA had been discovered and population genetics and molecular biology were unraveling more and more about the mechanisms of heredity. The new thinking of population genetics substantially undercut any basis for the old racial typologies. Yet, the psychometricians' program was firmly based on those typologies, which meant that for many geneticists the claims of Jensen and *The Bell Curve* were not just wrong, but genuinely unscientific. The key issue was how the psychometricians defined "race" when they made their claims about racial differences in intelligence.

Jensen wrote as if he were applying the new thinking about race by adopting the new language of population genetics. "Races are said to be 'breeding populations,'" he wrote, "which is to say that matings within the group have a much higher probability than matings outside the group" (Jensen 1972, 159). However, while adopting the language of population genetics, Jensen never actually embraced those methods. He did not define a group of people marked by shared frequency of genes; he accepted the social definition of race as someone possessing black or white skin. In no way could either population in the United States be thought of as breeding populations in the geneticists' sense. Moreover, Jensen's article was not based on any original research, but relied on other studies that reported racial differences in IQ. In order for Jensen to properly use population genetics, the participants in those studies would have had to be members of breeding populations, but they obviously were not—they were merely socially classified as black or white in the commonly understood way. In other words, even if Jensen were defining race as a population in the geneticists' sense, the authors of the studies on which he relied assuredly did not; indeed some studies he cited predated the population concept entirely.

Herrnstein and Murray avoided all pretense of basing their study on population genetics. They wrote, "The rule we follow here is to classify people according to the way they classify themselves" (Herrnstein and Murray 1994, 271). But, after admitting that they were using this social definition of race, they concluded that they would examine "cognitive differences among races as they might derive from genetic differences" without ever explaining how genetic differences might arise from socially defined groups (Herrnstein and Murray 1994, 272). C. Loring Brace, a physical anthropologist who had been a key participant in arguing for the use of population rather than race in his field, argued that Herrnstein and Murray "never once consider the possibility that human biological variation can be understood only when the concept of 'race' is abandoned and that the biologically adaptive dimensions in which people differ are best understood when each is handled separately in terms of its own clinal distribution . . . Their classification, then, is at best a kind of folk taxonomy without any validity from the perspective of evolutionary biology" (Brace 1996, S159).

A further problem for the psychometric case was that, even if they had a genetic cause for real races, they needed an evolutionary argument for the differential distribution of IQ among those races. Jensen attempted to shift the burden of proof on this issue, arguing only that "there is no reason to suppose that the brain should be exempt" from the forces of natural selection that also produced differences in skin color and other "racial" traits (Jensen 1972, 159–160). The problem for Jensen's claim is that skin color varies according to clinal geographical variation, gradually becoming lighter the further from the equator the population lives. The mechanism that produced light skin color for those in northern climates was well understood since the sun's rays produce vitamin D and lighter skin color allows for more absorption of that vitamin. In hot climates, by contrast, dark skin protects the skin from sunburn and skin cancer. Even so, skin cancer rates did not map simply onto skin color, as cultural practices that regulate exposure to the sun could greatly affect cancer rates.

In contrast to the geneticists' understanding of variations in skin color, Jensen never attempted to make an evolutionary case for differences in brain structure, nor did he attempt to explain the selection pressure that would lead to smart, white Europeans and dull, black Africans, perhaps because it would have linked him to discredited racial theories of Nordic supremacy. Herrnstein and Murray made no pretense, as Jensen did, of basing their work on population genetics or evolutionary biology, perhaps because the psychometric case had found no support from evolutionary biologists or geneticists. There was, according to evolutionary biologist Joseph Graves, "no established physiological link between the loci [on the gene] that determine skin pigmentation and those that determine any aspect of mental testing. Nor have the psychometricians been able to advance any credible evolutionary genetic mechanism to explain the origin of these consistent racial differences" (Graves 2001, 169). The psychometricians' case for genetic differences rested on inference: since they had a statistical regularity pointing to a near-constant gap in IQ scores between whites and blacks, they claimed to have discovered a relationship caused by heredity. Although such an argument might have been credible for Galton in 1869 when little was known about the nature of heredity, it was difficult to believe in 1969 when Jensen was writing, or 1994 when Herrnstein and Murray were writing, without some evidence from the established science of genetics. But it was not just the lack of evidence from genetics that was the problem for the psychometricians; the all-too-plausible evidence from psychology and sociology pointed to the continuing existence of institutionalized racism and discrimination.

The Psychometricians versus Scholars of Institutional Racism

The psychometricians made a series of causal arguments about how the genetics caused differences in IQ. They argued that the genetic factors that caused dark skin were the same genetic factors that caused low IQ. They further argued that poverty and low socioeconomic status were caused by low intelligence, because low intelligence was the cause of poor job performance, high crime, low self-control, increased drug use, and a host of other deleterious social consequences. In other words, the poverty of African Americans was genetic in origin and linked to their biological predisposition toward low IQ.

The problem, however, was that all the psychometricians had were a series of correlations. That is, low IQ and poverty existed together: where you found a population with low IQ you also found poverty. But a correlation of this sort does not indicate the direction of the causal connection, or indeed even the *existence* of a causal connection. For example, in the past twenty years, the use of personal computers and world population growth have both been growing steadily. As more people use computers there are more and more people on the planet. In other words, these two trends are perfectly correlated, but there is no evidence that the use of computers has in any way caused population growth. All the psychometricians had found was a correlation, which did not prove a causal connection.

The problem for the psychometricians was even more complicated, however. If poverty was correlated with low IQ, were people poor because of their low IQs or did they have low IQs because they were poor? For all their statistical sophistication, the psychometricians were limited to pointing to a correlation and not a cause, and certainly not to a causal direction between their two variables. Given that schooling, nutrition, health care, and motivation all contributed to academic performance, it was all too easy to reverse the causal arrow and argue that poverty was the cause of low IQ scores, not vice versa.

Those psychometricians who wanted to pinpoint race as the key causal variable faced additional problems: how to distinguish *direct* causation by genetics from *indirect* causation by genetics. In other words, skin color was a genetic trait inherited from parents. Suppose there was rampant discrimination against black people that caused systematic underfunding of schools for black people, which affected the IQ scores of students in those schools. If this were the case, then psychometricians would find exactly what Jensen found: the appearance of a genetic factor for intelligence. But the genetic factor was for skin color, and skin color was only relevant because of the social discrimination faced by black people in the United States. It was fundamentally impossible for Jensen to separate out direct from indirect genetic causation. It was discrimination that was the cause of low IQ scores, but the discrimination was targeted at a genetic trait: skin color. By refusing to acknowledge the intervening variable of discrimination, psychometricians made a fundamental mistake.

Jensen was writing at a time when psychologists and sociologists began a

Poor People's March at Lafayette Park and on Connecticut Avenue, Washington, D.C., 1968 (Library of Congress)

reexamination of racism and its effects on African Americans. Although Jensen talked of "culture-free" tests and "equal socio-economic circumstances," such talk looked increasingly naive amid sociological and psychological studies of institutional racism that were beginning at the same time Jensen published his article. Critics considered ridiculous Jensen's proclamation that the United States had tried compensatory education and it had failed, since the nation had made little effort to compensate blacks for the injustices inflicted on them. Black Americans, many argued, had suffered under slavery when it was illegal for blacks to go to school, and had then suffered under a legally segregated school system that was consistently underfunded and ignored by white school boards. In the North, blacks were relegated to the worst neighborhoods, the worst schools, and, in the terms of the time, lived under thumb of internal colonialism. Even if they made the same amount of money, the critics argued, whites and blacks lived in two separate worlds.

Because blacks had been and were subjected to discrimination, Jensen's work could not distinguish between a genetic component to intelligence and a genetic component for skin color. In other words, skin color was genetically determined, but affected the environment in which an individual lived. Black skin color in the United States led to deleterious consequences for diet, health care, living conditions, schooling, employment, and a host of other social factors, all of which could affect IQ scores. Jensen could not logically separate out a direct genetic cause for intelligence (that is, bad genes equal low IQ scores) from an indirect genetic cause (that is, genes for black skin equal poor treatment in society, which, in turn, equals low IQ scores).

The argument for indirect causation for low IQ scores in black Americans made more sense, given the other racial research of the time. Sociologists and psychologists increasingly pointed to the reality of race as a social construct. It was not that race was real in a biological sense for these writers; it was that race was treated as real by society and therefore had real social consequences. But, just as race was being recognized as socially real, it was being denied as biologically real.

The problem of distinguishing a direct from an indirect cause was even more severe for *The Bell Curve* because of a growing body of comparative work that indicated that discrimination could be a powerful factor in scholastic achievement. It was not just socioeconomic status (for which Herrnstein and Murray claimed to have controlled). As the American Psychological Association committee reported, "To imagine that any simple income- and education-based index can adequately describe the situation of African Americans is to ignore important categories of experience" (Neisser 1996, 94). The work of Nigerian anthropologist John Ogbu illustrated some of those categories of experience referred to by the committee. In reaction to Jensen's work, Ogbu set out to develop the critique of the immigration model that had started in the 1960s. In his 1978 book, *Minority Education and Caste: The American System in Cross-Cultural Perspective*, Ogbu argued that racial stratification functioned differently than class stratification. Ogbu stressed the involuntary nature of those forced into a "caste" and how it differed from ethnic minorities that entered into the dominant society, clearly following on the distinctions drawn earlier by theories of internal colonialism. What was new with Ogbu's work was the comparative perspective: he compared the experience of African Americans to other "involuntary minorities" in other societies. African American scholastic achievement was depressed, argued Ogbu, and their experiences were just like West Indians in Britain, lower castes in India, Buraku in Japan, and East-Asian Jews in Israel.

Ogbu's argument was particularly devastating for the genetic hypothesis because the castes in these other countries were the same people that Herrnstein and Murray argued were genetically superior in IQ. Asians have even higher IQ scores than whites, and Herrnstein and Murray pointed to genetic causes for this, but Ogbu clearly pointed to the poor academic performance of Koreans in Japan, where they are a subordinate minority. It was the Japanese belief in Korean inferiority that caused their poor performance, not any genetic inferiority of Koreans. American Indians were in a similar situation: according to genetic data they were genetically similar to high-scoring Asians, but their low IQ scores were similar to African Americans. Given that they shared the status of "involuntary minority" with African Americans but shared little genetic material with them, institutional racism was a more plausible explanation than genetics.

Critics of the psychometric case for genetic differences in IQ used the causal argument by arguing that the psychometricians had confused how scientists usually identify causes in nature. In order to isolate a cause in science, the most common method is to take two situations in which all variables are the same except one. So, to identify if cigarette smoke causes lung cancer a scientist would take two groups of mice, feed them the same diet, keep them in identical conditions in every way except expose one group to cigarette smoke and not the other. If the group exposed to cigarette smoke develops lung cancer and the other group does not, the scientist has a reasonable conjecture that the smoke was the cause of the lung cancer.

Obviously in human genetics, such tight control on other causal variables was not possible. Humans cannot be ethically experimented on in this way. However, the critics of the psychometricians' position argued that the other causal variables that could possibly depress IQ scores were in no way equalized in the United States. If the psychometricians were serious about finding the causes for the race/IQ gap, the logical thing to do was to work for a society where race had no social meaning. Once all vestiges of institutional racism were eliminated, critics argued, the psychometricians could begin investigating genetic differences in IQ scores. However, this recommendation cut against the policy recommendations offered by psychometricians who argued for racial differences in IQ.

Psychometric Case for Policy

Jensen, writing in the turbulent late 1960s and early 1970s, became the target of harassment by student radicals, and their outspokenness allowed him to assume the role of the persecuted scientist. Jensen portrayed himself as the dispassionate scientist whose work was silenced by radical politics. However, in strictly scientific terms, Jensen's work was anachronistic in 1969. Its assumptions, methods, and conclusions had been debated in the 1920s and rejected by most in the scientific community. He had a political agenda: indeed it was announced in the first line of his article with its condemnation of compensatory education. Beyond that simple declaration, however, Jensen's position became incoherent. Anxious to distance himself from the segregationist cause, Jensen loudly and repeatedly proclaimed that he was "opposed to according differential treatment to persons on the basis of their race, color, national origin, or social-class background"

(Jensen 1972, 329). If that was the case, why did he research racial differences at all? Jensen claimed that his research had important implications for educational policy, but what would those implications be unless educational policy were to be somehow based on race? It was this basic contradiction in Jensen's position that led many to question his claims to be a dispassionate scientist.

Herrnstein and Murray had even less of a basis for claiming to be disinterested in political affairs. In 1984, ten years before the publication of *The Bell Curve*, Charles Murray published *Losing Ground*, a book that argued for eliminating welfare benefits for the poor and returning to the laissez-faire policies of the nineteenth century. *Losing Ground* found an appreciative audience in Ronald Reagan's conservative revolution of the 1980s. However, when the same ideas were found in the policy recommendations of *The Bell Curve* many argued that the science in *The Bell Curve* was merely window dressing for the policies that Murray had long supported.

The relationship between the empirical findings in *The Bell Curve* and policy recommendations was not as clear as Herrnstein and Murray claimed. *The Bell Curve* argued that because IQ scores were not easily changed, the only solution for society was to return to a Spencerian social Darwinism, eliminating all government intervention aimed to lift the poor out of poverty and expand educational opportunities. Such efforts were wasted, according to *The Bell Curve*, because the poor were poor because they simply were not smart enough to help themselves and not because they lacked opportunities.

Many critics argued that if Herrnstein and Murray were right in their data about IQ scores, the logical policy recommendations were opposite from what was advocated in *The Bell Curve*. The logical policy, the critics argued, was more government intervention into education and welfare, not less. Philosopher Clark Glymour wrote, "Here is an alternative vision, one I claim is better warranted by the phenomena Herrnstein and Murray report: nationalized, serious, educational standards, tax-supported day and night care, minimal universal health care, a living minimum wage, capital invested in systems that enable almost anyone with reasonable training to do a job well" (Glymour 1998, 30).

The criticism of Jensen's and Herrnstein and Murray's policy recommendations was that they were committing a fallacy. To argue, as they did, that a trait was genetic did not mean that it was immutable. Take, for example, the problem of near-sightedness. Poor vision is often genetic in origin and yet a simple environmental fix, eyeglasses, eliminates its deleterious effects. A more telling example of a pure genetic disability was phenylketonuria (PKU). Phenylketonurics have a genetic defect that prevents them from metabolizing phenylalanine hydroxylase into tyrosine, which is necessary for proper brain development. Those who suffer from PKU are often mentally retarded as a result. However, starting in the early 1960s a prenatal screening method was developed for PKU. If a positive identification is made, then PKU can be treated by restricting the intake of foods with phenylalanine hydroxylase and supplementing the diet in other ways. The result is that individuals with PKU can develop nearly normally and not suffer from the debilitating effects of the disease. The message that psychometricians' critics took from the PKU case was that a disability that is a genetic ailment was nonetheless entirely remedied by an environmental fix. Even if the psychometricians were correct that intelligence was determined by genes, policy recommendation to restrict types of education to those with low IQs did not logically follow.

The PKU story, as a critique of genetic determinism, is not an unqualified success: the special diet is expensive and inconvenient and many phenylketonurics still experience some loss of IQ. But as a critique of the pyschometricians' position, that may make it more telling rather than detract from it. Amelioration of PKU was very difficult and to ameliorate racial disparities in IQ scores would take similar hard work. By the time Jensen published his article, sociologists and psychologists had substantially rethought the concept of racism, as we have seen. The differential distribution of power that resulted in a profound and inequitable distribution of resources in American society was seen as a permanent fixture rather than a temporary aberration. Yet even twenty-five years after Jensen's article, *The Bell Curve* barely mentioned such factors. Many critics wondered what to make of a book that purported to discuss race in the United States but did not contain index entries for the words "segregation," "discrimination," or "prejudice." "Racism" was only indexed six times and each mention of it was to question if it really existed and to discount it as a possible cause for low IQ scores. By contrast, the American Psychological Association committee's report argued that "only a single generation has passed since the Civil Rights movement opened doors for African Americans, and many forms of discrimination are still all too familiar in their experience today. Hard enough to bear in its own right, discrimination is also a sharp reminder of a still more intolerable past. It would be rash indeed to assume that those experiences, and that historical legacy, have no impact on intellectual development" (Neisser 1996, 95).

At the dawn of the twenty-first century, science has put forth two propositions: the traditional typology of race has no meaning in the biological sciences. Race, as Ashley Montagu argued six decades earlier, is a myth in this sense. However, in the social forces of society, race is all too real. People are racially marked in ways that have little to do with biology and a lot to do with how social power is arranged. Racism is still a social problem that has real social consequences. Just as race existed as a social category before it was a scientific category, it has outlasted its scientific standing but remains a social problem that demands our attention. In 1968, a few months before his assassination, Martin Luther King, Jr., gave an invited address to the American Psychological Association. There he proclaimed, "And so I can still sing, although many have stopped singing it, 'We shall overcome.' We shall overcome because the arch of the moral universe is long, but it bends toward justice. We shall overcome because Carlyle is right, 'No lie can live forever'" (King 1968, 476).

Bibliographic Essay

On the growth of movement scholarship in sociology see Stephen Steinberg, *Turning Back: The Retreat from Racial Justice in American Thought and Policy* (Boston: Beacon Press, 1995). For movement scholarship in psychology see Daryl Michael Scott, *Contempt and Pity: Social Policy and the Image of the Damaged Black Psyche, 1880–1996* (Chapel Hill: University of North Carolina Press, 1997). Everett C. Hughes's 1963 Presidential address to the American Sociological Association was printed as "Race Relations and the Sociological Imagination," *American Sociological Review* 28 (1963): 879–890.

On the general shift in ideology away from integration to separatism see Gary Peller, "Race-Consciousness," in Kimberle Crenshaw, Neil Gotanda, Gary Peller, and Kendall Thomas, eds., *Critical Race Theory: The Key Writings that Formed the Movement* (New York: The New Press, 1995); and John T. McCartney, *Black Power Ideologies: An Essay in African American Political Thought* (Philadelphia: Temple University Press, 1992). Key primary works are Stokely Carmichael and Charles V. Hamilton, *Black Power: The Politics of Liberation in America* (New York: Random House, 1967); and Harold Cruse, *The Crisis of the Negro Intellectual: From Its Origins to the Present* (New York: Morrow, 1967).

For the origin and reception of the Moynihan Report see Ellen Herman, *The Romance of American Psychology: Political Culture in the Age of Experts* (Berkeley: University of California Press, 1995); and Alice O'Connor, *Poverty Knowledge: Social Science, Social Policy, and the Poor in Twentieth Century U.S. History* (Princeton: Princeton University Press, 2001).

Steinberg, *Turning Back*, and Scott, *Contempt and Pity*, both contain good treatments on the rejection of the pathology of black culture. Primary sources include Maurice Jackson, "Toward a Sociology of Black Studies," *Journal of Black Studies* 1 (1970): 131–140; and Albert Murray, "White Norms, Black Deviance," in *The Death of White Sociology*, ed. Joyce A. Ladner (New York: Vintage, 1973).

Frantz Fanon is discussed in Steinberg, *Turning Back*, and Scott, *Contempt and Pity*, as well as in Graham Richards *"Race," Racism and Psychology:*

Toward a Reflexive History (London: Routledge, 1997); and Paul Nursey-Bray, "Race and Nation: Ideology in the Thought of Frantz Fanon," *Journal of Modern African Studies* 18 (1980): 135–142. Also see Frantz Fanon, *The Wretched of the Earth*, trans. Constance Farrington (New York: Grove Press, 1966).

On the internal colonialism metaphor see Steinberg, *Turning Back*, and Robert J. Hind, "The Internal Colonial Concept," *Comparative Studies in Society and History* 26 (1984): 543–568; and Joe Feagin, "Slavery Unwilling to Die: The Background of Black Oppression in the 1980s," *Journal of Black Studies* 17 (1986): 173–200. Robert Blauner recalls his own involvement with the concept in "'But Things are Much Worse for the Negro People': Race and Radicalism in my Life and Work," in John H. Stanfield II ed., *A History of Race Relations Research: First-Generation Recollections* (Newberry Park: Sage, 1993). For his work of the time see Robert Blauner, *Racial Oppression in America* (New York: Harper and Row, 1972).

The rise of the "new physical anthropology" is described in Donna J. Haraway, "Remodelling the Human Way of Life: Sherwood Washburn and the New Physical Anthropology, 1950–1980," in *Bones, Bodies, Behavior: Essays on Biological Anthropology*, George W. Stocking, Jr., ed. (Madison: University of Wisconsin Press, 1988). The influence of population genetics on racial concepts is described in Audrey Smedley, *Race in North America: Origin and Evolution of a Worldview*, 2d Edition (Boulder CO: Westview Press, 1999). On the gradual replacement of folk ideas of race in physical anthropology and the influence of the growth of the field see Alice Littlefield, Leonard Lieberman, and Larry T. Reynolds, "Redefining Race: The Potential Demise of a Concept in Physical Anthropology," *Current Anthropology* 23 (1982): 641–655. The primary works quoted in this chapter on the new physical anthropology are William C. Boyd, *Genetics and the Races of Man: An Introduction to Modern Physical Anthropology* (Boston: Little, Brown and Company, 1950); Edward E. Hunt, "Anthropometry, Genetics, and Racial History," *American Anthropologist* 61 (1959): 64–87; Stanley M. Garn, "The Newer Physical Anthropology," *American Anthropologist* 64 (1962): 917–918.

The primary source documents on population genetics redefining race are Richard C. Lewontin, "The Apportionment of Human Diversity," *Evolutionary Biology* 6 (1972): 381–398 and Masatoshi Nei and Arun K. Roychoudhury, "Genetic Relationship and Evolution of Human Races" *Evolutionary Biology* 14 (1982): 1–59; Luigi Luca Cavalli-Sforza and Francesco Cavalli-Sforza, *The Great Human Diasporas: The History of Diversity and Evolution* (Cambridge, MA: Perseus Books, 1995). A more authoritative (and technical) presentation is Luigi Luca Cavalli-Sforza, Paolo Menozzi, and Alberto Piazza, *History and Geography of Human Genes* (Princeton: Princeton University Press, 1994).

Three works by biological scientists that summarize current thinking about human diversity, comment on the history of their fields and the race concept, and offer stinging critiques of the psychometricians' argument for racial differences in IQ are Stephen J. Gould, *The Mismeasure of Man* (New York: Norton, 1981); Joseph L. Graves, Jr., *The Emperor's New Clothes: Biological Theories of Race at the Millennium* (New Brunswick: Rutgers University Press, 2001); and Jonathan Marks, *Human Biodiversity: Genes, Race, and History* (New York: Aldine De Gruyter, 1995).

The best description of the work of Arthur Jensen and the controversy over his work is William H. Tucker, *The Science and Politics of Racial Research* (Urbana: University of Illinois Press, 1994). Tucker also discusses Henry Garrett and the work of psychologists to preserve racial segregation. A work that places the controversy, and that of *The Bell Curve*, in their historical context and outlines the scientific objections to their program is Graham Richards, *"Race," Racism, and Psychology.*

Jensen's essay was originally published as "How Much Can We Boost IQ and Scholastic Achievement?" *Harvard Educational Review* 39 (1969): 1–123. This chapter quotes from the reprinted version in Arthur R. Jensen, *Genetics and Education* (New York: Harper and Row, 1972), which also includes a bibliography of articles about Jensen's work. A work that includes various critiques of Jensen's article, including an essay by Richard Lewontin, is N. J. Block and Gerald Dworkin, eds., *The IQ Controversy* (New York: Pantheon Books, 1976).

The return of the psychometricians' case for genetic differences in IQ was announced in Richard J. Herrnstein and Charles Murray, *The Bell Curve: Intelligence and Class Structure in American Life* (New York: The Free Press, 1994). An entire issue of the journal *American Behavioral Scientist* was devoted to articles taking issue with *The Bell Curve*, including Michael Nunley, *"The Bell Curve:* Too Smooth to be True," *American Behavioral Scientist* 39 (1995): 74–84. Additionally, an entire supplementary issue of *Current Anthropology* was devoted to critiques of *The Bell Curve*, which included C. Loring Brace "The Eternal Triangle: Race, Class, and IQ," *Current Anthropology* 37 (1996): S143-S181. Two other critiques quoted in this chapter were Clark Glymour, "What Went Wrong? Reflections on Science by Observation and *The Bell Curve*," *Philosophy of Science* 65 (1998): 1–32; and report of the American Psychological Association's Task Force, Ulric Neisser, et al., "Intelligence: Knowns and Unknowns," *American Psychologist* 51 (1996): 77–101.

In addition to these works, three edited volumes give a wealth of valuable historical, political, and scientific information on Jensen and *The Bell Curve*: Steven Fraser, ed., *The Bell Curve Wars: Race, Intelligence, and the Future of America* (New York: Basic Books, 1995); Russell Jacoby and Naomi Glauberman, eds., *The Bell Curve Debate: History, Documents, Opinions* (New York: Times Books, 1995); and Joe L. Kincheloe, Shirley R. Steinberg, and Aaron D. Gresson III, eds., *Measured Lies: The Bell Curve Examined* (New York: St. Martin's Press, 1996). Additional works that treat *The Bell Curve* in its historical context were published in a special symposium in the *Journal of the History of the Behavioral Sciences:* Franz Samelson, "On the Uses of History: The Case of *The Bell Curve*," *Journal of the History of the Behavioral Sciences* 33 (1997): 129–133; Leila Zenderland, "*The Bell Curve* and the Shape of History," *Journal of the History of the Behavioral Sciences* 33 (1997): 135–139; and Nadine Weidman, "Heredity, Intelligence, and Neuropsychology: Or Why *The Bell Curve* Is Good Science," *Journal of the History of the Behavioral Sciences* 33 (1997): 141–144.

Chronology

711	Muslims inhabit the Iberian Peninsula.
1441	African slaves first appear in Portugal.
1492	Columbus lands in the New World.
	Muslims expelled from Europe.
1550	Bartolomé de Las Casas and Ginés de Sepúlveda debate.
1619	First enslaved Africans arrive in North America.
1684	Francois Bernier publishes *The New Division of the Earth.*
1735	Carolus Linnaeus publishes *Systema Naturae.*
1749	Comte de Buffon publishes *Histoire Naturelle.*
1774	Henry H. Kames publishes *Sketches of the History of Man.*
1775	Johann Blumenbach publishes *On the Natural Varieties of Mankind.*
1776	The Declaration of Independence is adopted.
1787	Thomas Jefferson publishes *Notes on the State of Virginia.*
1789	United States adopts the U.S. Constitution.
	French Revolution begins.
1798	Thomas Robert Malthus publishes *An Essay on Human Population.*
1808	United States ends its slave trade.
1813	James Cowles Prichard publishes *Researches into the Physical History of Mankind.*
1815	Napoleon outlaws the French slave trade.
1817	American Colonialization Society founded.

1833   Slaves emancipated throughout the British Empire.

1839   Samuel Morton publishes *Crania Americana.*

1840   Anders Retzius introduces the cephalic index.

1844   Samuel Morton publishes *Crania Aegyptiaca.*

1845   Josiah Nott publishes *Natural History of the Caucasian and Negro Races.*

1850   Robert Knox publishes *The Races of Men.*

1853   Comte Arthur de Gobineau publishes *Essay on the Inequality of the Races.*

1854   Josiah Nott and George Gliddon publish *Types of Mankind.*

1856   Paul Broca publishes *Human Hybridity.*

1859   Charles Darwin publishes *On the Origin of Species.*

1861   U.S. Civil War begins.

1862   Herbert Spencer publishes *First Principles.*

1863   James Hunt founds the London Anthropological Society.

1864   Alfred Russel Wallace publishes "The Origin of Human Races and the Antiquity of Man Deduced from the Theory of 'Natural Selection,'" which is the first paper to apply natural selection to human races.

1865   U.S. Civil War ends. Slavery abolished in the United States.

John Lubbock publishes *Prehistoric Times, As Illustrated by Ancient Remains and the Manners and Customs of Modern Savages.*

1868   Ernst Haeckel publishes *History of Creation.*

1869   Francis Galton publishes *Hereditary Genius.*

1871   Charles Darwin publishes *On the Descent of Man.*

The Ethnological Society and the Anthropological Society merge to form the Anthropological Institute of Great Britain and Ireland.

1874   Richard L. Dugdale publishes *The Jukes: A Study in Crime, Pauperism, Disease, and Heredity.*

1882   Karl Pearson publishes *The Grammar of Science.*

The United States passes the Chinese Exclusion Act.

1883   Ludwig Gumplowicz publishes *Racial Struggle*.

1888   American Folklore Society founded.

1891   Wilhelm Schallmayer publishes *Concerning the Threatening Physical Degeneration of Civilized Humanity*.

1895   Alfred Ploetz publishes *The Fitness of Our Race and the Protection of the Weak*.

1896   Vacher de Lapouge publishes *Social Selection*.

U.S. Supreme Court declares segregated "separate but equal" facilities constitutional in *Plessy v. Ferguson*.

W. E. B. Du Bois publishes *The Philadelphia Negro*.

1899   Houston Stewart Chamberlain publishes *Foundations of the Nineteenth Century*.

Vacher de Lapouge publishes *The Aryan and His Social Role*.

William Z. Ripley publishes *The Races of Europe*.

1905   Society for Racial Hygiene founded in Germany.

Boasians take control of the American Anthropological Association.

1906   American Breeder's Association formed.

1910   Eugenics Records Office formed at the Station for the Study of Experimental Evolution at Cold Spring Harbor, New York.

1911   Franz Boas publishes *The Mind of Primitive Man*.

1912   Henry H. Goddard publishes *The Kallikak Family: A Study in the Heredity of Feeblemindedness*.

1913   American Breeder's Association reformed as the American Eugenics Association.

1914   World War I begins.

1916   Madison Grant publishes *The Passing of the Great Race*.

Arthur Estabrook publishes *The Jukes in 1915*.

1918   World War I ends.

1919   Red Summer—a series of brutal race riots throughout the United States.

1922   Lothrop Stoddard publishes *The Rising Tide of Color*.

Hans F. K. Günther publishes *Racial Studies of the German People*.

Harry Laughlin publishes *Eugenic Sterilization in the United States*.

Carl Brigham publishes *A Study of American Intelligence*.

1924   United States passes the Immigration Restriction Act.

1925   Alain Locke edits and publishes *The New Negro*.

1927   U.S. Supreme Court rules that involuntary sterilization is constitutional in *Buck v. Bell*.

Kaiser Wilhelm Institute for Anthropology, Human Genetics, and Eugenics founded in Germany.

1929   Charles Davenport and Morris Steggerda publish *Race Crossing in Jamaica*.

1931   Arthur Fauset publishes *Folklore from Nova Scotia*.

1933   Adolph Hitler named chancellor of Germany.

Hitler signs Law for the Reconstitution of the Professional Civil Service, which dismissed all non-Aryans from the civil service.

1935   Hitler signs the Nuremberg Laws, stripping Jews of German citizenship.

Julian Huxley and A. C. Haddon publish *We Europeans*.

Otto Klineberg publishes *Race Differences*.

Zora Neale Hurston publishes *Mules and Men*.

1937   Otmar von Verschuer publishes *Rassenbiologie der Juden*.

Allison Davis and John Dollard publish *Caste and Class in a Southern Town*.

1939   Hitler signs a law allowing physicians to grant "mercy killing" of the unfit.

Geneticists' Manifesto condemning Nazi racism is issued.

Hitler invades Poland, launching World War II.

E. Franklin Frazier publishes *The Negro Family in the United States.*

1941   Melville Herskovits publishes *The Myth of the Negro Past.*

1942   Ashley Montagu publishes *Man's Most Dangerous Myth.*

1943   Detroit, Los Angeles, and New York experience racial rioting.

Ruth Benedict and Gene Weltfish publish "The Races of Mankind."

1944   Gunnar Myrdal publishes *An American Dilemma.*

1945   World War II ends.

1946   L. C. Dunn and Theodosius Dobzhansky publish *Heredity, Race, and Society.*

1947   U. S. Government issues *To Secure These Rights*, arguing for extending civil rights to all Americans regardless of race.

1950   William Boyd publishes *Genetics and the Races of Man.*

Theodor Adorno, Else Frenkel-Brunswik, Daniel J. Levinson, and R. Nevitt Stanford publish *The Authoritarian Personality.*

UNESCO issues a Statement on Race.

Sherwood Washburn announces "The New Physical Anthropology" at Cold Spring Harbor.

1951   UNESCO issues the second Statement on Race.

Abram Kardiner and Lionel Ovesey publish *Mark of Oppression: Explorations in the Personality of the American Negro.*

1952   Frantz Fanon publishes *Black Skin, White Masks.*

1954   *Brown v. Board of Education* decision declares segregation unconstitutional in the United States, citing social scientific evidence.

Gordon W. Allport publishes *The Nature of Prejudice.*

1955   Montgomery bus boycott.

1957   Central High School in Little Rock, Arkansas, desegregated.

1960   Sit-in movement by African American students protesting segregated restaurants takes place in Greensboro, North Carolina.

1961   Frantz Fanon publishes *The Wretched of the Earth.*

1962   Frank Livingstone publishes "On the Nonexistence of Races."

1964   Civil Rights Act passes in the United States.

1965   Daniel Patrick Moynihan publishes *The Negro Family: The Case for National Action.*

1967   Stokely Carmichael and Charles Hamilton publish *Black Power.*

Gary Marx publishes *Protest and Prejudice.*

1968   Martin Luther King, Jr., addresses the American Psychological Association.

1969   Arthur Jensen publishes "How Much Can We Boost IQ and Scholastic Achievement?"

1970   *Journal of Black Studies* founded.

1972   Robert Blauner publishes *Racial Oppression in America.*

Richard Lewontin publishes "The Apportionment of Human Diversity."

1973   Joyce Ladner publishes *The Death of White Sociology.*

1978   John Ogbu publishes *Minority Education and Caste: The American System in Cross-Cultural Perspective.*

1984   Charles Murray publishes *Losing Ground.*

1994   Richard Herrnstein and Charles Murray publish *The Bell Curve.*

1996   American Psychological Association publishes "Intelligence: Knowns and Unknowns."

Glossary

abolitionism   the belief that slavery is wrong and that slaves should be freed; the practice of trying to end slavery.

Age of Exploration   the period of history from the fifteenth to the eighteenth century marked by the European discovery and settlement of colonies in the Americas.

allele   one of the two possible forms of a gene, either dominant or recessive.

American Creed   Gunnar Myrdal's term for the guarantee of life, liberty, and the pursuit of happiness to all people and their equality before the law, ideals that underlie democracy in the United States, and in which Myrdal thought all Americans believed.

anthropogenesis   the origin and evolution of human beings.

anthropometry   the practice of measuring human bodies and heads to determine racial classification.

anthroposociology   Georges Vacher de Lapouge's racial science, including beliefs in the dominance of civilized societies by dolichocephalics, a eugenic breeding program, and strict hereditarianism.

Anti-Semitism   prejudice against and hatred of Jews.

area of characterization   Ruth Benedict's term, developed as an alternative to "race," indicating a group of people that inbreed for a while, temporarily forming a set of stable, hereditary characteristics, which migration and interbreeding later undermine.

armchair anthropology   the nineteenth-century practice of describing foreign cultures, usually those considered primitive, without actually ever visiting them, but rather by collecting information about them from tales of travelers and explorers.

Aryan   a Caucasian of non-Jewish descent, usually referring to the Germanic peoples, from Germany and Scandinavia, who settled in Britain and the United States; often used synonymously with Anglo-Saxon.

Aryanism   the belief that the white or Caucasian race is superior to the others and the only one capable of civilization; synonymous with Teutonicism and Nordicism.

assimilation   complete acculturation of a minority group to the dominant group.

Atlantic system   the practice in which Europeans took Africans as slaves to the Americas to serve as a labor supply to generate wealth for Europe.

biogenetic law   Ernst Haeckel's term for the rule that ontogeny recapitulates phylogeny; that the individual organism, as it develops, passes through all the evolutionary stages of its ancestors.

biometrics   the statistical analysis of the variation of traits in a population.

Black Power   a phrase used by African American political leaders Stokely Carmichael and Malcolm X to encourage black self-determination, ethnic pride, and separatism.

blending inheritance   non-Mendelian theory of heredity according to which the traits of the parents mix in the offspring, and therefore an outlying or unusual trait can be swamped.

brachycephalic   short-headed (opposite of dolichocephalic).

calipers   a tool consisting of two movable, curved legs, used by nineteenth-century anthropologists to measure human bodies and heads for the purpose of racial classification.

caste   an exclusive and restrictive class or group; a rigid class distinction around which society is organized.

catastrophism   a geological theory according to which huge floods, earthquakes, volcanoes, and other catastrophes were active during the earth's history and were responsible for its present-day appearance.

Caucasian   a nineteenth-century racial classification distinguished by white skin and straight or wavy hair (named after the Caucasus Mountain region of eastern Europe, between the Black and Caspian seas).

cephalic index   the ratio of length to breadth of skull, a measure of size and shape of head developed by Anders Retzius to determine racial classification.

civil rights movement   the series of nonviolent protests against segregation led by Martin Luther King, Jr., and resulting legislation that desegregated public venues, gave black Americans the right to vote, and declared their equality before the law.

cline   distribution of a species over a geographic area.

colonialism   the practice of establishing European settlements in Africa, Asia, and the Americas designed to govern the indigenous people, disenfranchise them, and extract wealth from the land for the mother country; when a network of colonies is extended and developed into an empire, colonialism becomes imperialism. *See* **imperialism.**

comparative psychology   the science of the mind and behavior of animals and, in the nineteenth century, of members of the lower races.

contact hypothesis   the theory held by some twentieth-century social scientists that interracial interaction decreases racial prejudice.

continuity of the germ plasm   August Weismann's theory that the germ plasm, the cells that produce the gametes (sperm and egg), are unaffected by any change to the body or somatic cells and are transmitted unaltered from generation to generation.

cultural pluralism   the belief that every culture is unique and that all are equally worthy of respect.

cytology   the study of cells.

damage argument   the belief associated with some twentieth-century American sociologists that the personalities and family structures of black people are negatively affected, or damaged, by being the victims of racial discrimination. *See* **social pathology**.

Darwinism   the theory of evolution by natural selection, as developed by Darwin and presented in 1859 in *The Origin of Species*. According to natural selection, those organisms that possess favorable traits, given the environmental conditions under which they live, will survive and produce more offspring than those without such favorable traits. Adaptation to the prevailing conditions, and ultimately evolution of new species, will be the result.

deformation   a term used by the anatomist Robert Knox to indicate the potentialities of the embryo developing in a different direction from their ordinary course.

degenerationism   a late-nineteenth-century religious view holding that humankind had deteriorated from an original perfect state.

diffusionism   the view associated with monogenesis that the human species has migrated all over the earth from a single point of origin. Also used to mean the spreading of civilized culture from its origins in Asia to western Europe.

discrimination   differential and inequitable treatment of the members of races deemed inferior.

dolichocephalic   long-headed (opposite of brachycephalic).

dominant   one of a pair of alleles, or genes, that, when paired with a recessive allele, masks it and is therefore expressed in the organism.

dysgenic/dysgenesic   a mating that produces poor or defective offspring, believed by anthropologist and neurologist Paul Broca to occur when the members of widely different races are crossed.

Enlightenment   the period of the eighteenth century in Europe marked by beliefs in democratic government, equal rights for all, progress in society, and the attainment of knowledge by reason.

environmentalism   the belief that traits, particularly mental traits, are caused largely by education, experience, and social and cultural circumstances rather than by genes.

equilibration   the harmonious interaction of organism and environment that Herbert Spencer believed was the end point of evolution.

essence   the immutable, unchanging truth or ideal behind everyday appearances, usually considered more real than actual material or physical things.

essentialism   the belief that all the members of any given group share a common, core set of characteristics, an essence, that unites them and sets them apart from the members of other groups.

ethnicity   the classification of people according to culture, customs, language, or common history, as opposed to physical appearance.

ethnocentrism   the belief that one's own culture is superior to others.

ethnography   the study and description of the culture of a given people, usually achieved by fieldwork, in which an anthropologist lives in and observes that culture.

ethnology   the comparative study of different cultures.

eugenesic   a mating that produces healthy, strong, beautiful offspring.

eugenics   the term coined by Francis Galton in 1883 to mean the science of producing better human offspring by controlling who may reproduce. In positive eugenics, the fittest (wealthiest, most intelligent, most beautiful) are encouraged to breed, while in negative eugenics the unfit are prevented from breeding.

Eurocentrism   the belief that European culture is superior to others.

evolutionary synthesis   the integration of Darwinian evolutionary theory with Gregor Mendel's laws of genetics. Key tenets of the synthesis are that natural selection is the main motor of evolutionary change; that populations are groups of interbreeding organisms no two of which are exactly alike; and that the immense number of slight variations that exist in a population can be interpreted mathematically in terms of genes that assort and recombine to produce the ratios that Mendel had first described.

facial angle   a measure developed by Pieter Camper to assist in racial classification. A line drawn vertically from forehead to chin and a line drawn horizontally from bottom of ear to bottom of nose formed the angle. The closer to 90 degrees the angle was, Camper believed, the more advanced the race.

feeblemindedness   the quality Charles Davenport ascribed to any individual he considered defective and unfit to breed; a catch-all term that could mean not only stupidity or immorality but could also include various kinds of physical weakness or disease.

frustration-aggression hypothesis   theory developed by John Dollard and social science colleagues in the 1930s that the tendency for violent behavior is caused by an unfulfilled need, hope, or desire.

gene pool   the total of all the genes of a species.

genetics   the branch of biology that deals with heredity and variation.

genotype   the genetic makeup of an organism, as opposed to its outward appearance.

Great Chain of Being   the belief that everything in the universe, particularly all life-forms, can be arranged in a hierarchy from simplest to most complex.

hard heredity   theory of inheritance according to which there is a strict separation between the body or somatic cells and the germ plasm that produces the gametes, such that changes to the body in the course of its life are not reflected in or taken up by the gametes (the sperm and egg). *See* **continuity of the germ plasm.**

hereditarian   one who believes that genetic makeup is the key factor in determining traits, especially mental traits.

heritability   amount of variance of a trait in a population owing to genetics, not environment.

heterozygous   a trait determined by one dominant and one recessive allele.

homozygous   a trait determined by two dominant or two recessive alleles.

Immigration Restriction Act   the 1924 law prohibiting large numbers of southern and eastern Europeans from entering the United States in favor of immigrants from northern and western Europe. Quotas of immigrants under this law were set to the population ratios existing in the United States based on the 1880 census.

imperialism   the practice by western European nations of conquering, subduing, and ruling the countries of Africa, Asia, and the Americas; a practice driven by the belief that white Europeans were destined or divinely intended to so rule.

induction   method of generating scientific hypotheses in which a general rule is drawn from specific instances or observations.

innatism   the view that the mental, social, and cultural differences between peoples are inborn and therefore stable and permanent.

institutional racism   the belief that the inequitable treatment of racial minorities resides in the institutions—the systems of government and the economic and social structures—of a society and that such inequitable treatment therefore transcends the attitudes of individuals.

intercultural education movement   a series of programs designed in the 1940s and 1950s by civic and religious institutions and private foundations to teach the American public through radio programs, public school programs, and interethnic luncheons to tolerate ethnic diversity.

internal colonialism   Frantz Fanon's phrase to describe the situation of African Americans and other "involuntary minorities," such as Native Americans, in U. S. society. Brought by force to the United States, unlike European immigrants who came of their own will, these minorities existed in an exploitative relation to the dominant society that was much like the relationship of colonized to colonizer.

IQ   intelligence quotient; the ratio of mental age, as determined by a test, to chronological age.

Jim Crow   the system of segregation that existed in the U.S. South from the Civil War to the mid-1960s.

laissez-faire   the economic doctrine of free competition without any governmental interference or regulation (from the French, literally, let the people do as they please).

Lamarckism   the theory of inheritance developed by evolutionist Jean-Baptiste de Monet de Lamarck, holding that use strengthens and improves an organ, while disuse weakens it, and that such characteristics acquired during an organism's lifetime would be inherited by its offspring.

Lysenkoism   a theory of Lamarckian inheritance officially sanctioned by the Soviet government and named for its main proponent, biologist Trofim Lysenko.

Manifest Destiny   white people's expansion into and capture of Indian lands in the American West; the belief driving such expansion, that white Americans were destined or divinely intended to settle the land all the way to the Pacific Coast.

materialism   the belief that all life can be explained by matter in motion, according to natural laws, and without any reference to the supernatural (God, spirit, or soul). Synonymous with "naturalism."

Mendelism   the theory of heredity formulated by Austrian botanist Gregor Mendel. Mendel's laws are the independence of unit characters (each trait is inherited separately and independently of others); segregation (traits are determined by a pair of alleles; the pairs split up during reproduction and the germ cells or gametes take up one member of each pair); dominance (alleles can be dominant or recessive and combine in stable and predictable ratios); and independent assortment (pairs of alleles are inherited independently of other pairs).

mesmerism   the practice of eliciting trancelike states in a human subject by placing one's hands, or certain metals, on or near the subject's body.

miscegenation   pejorative term for interracial sex and marriage.

Monist League   an early-twentieth-century society founded by Ernst Haeckel and composed mainly of German biologists and social scientists, united by their beliefs in Aryan racial purity and a religion of nature.

monogenism/monogenesis   the theory that all peoples have sprung from a single, common origin, and that they therefore belong to one and the same species.

mulatto hypothesis   the belief associated with some twentieth-century race biologists that light-skinned blacks do better on IQ tests because they possess "white blood."

mutation   a sudden, spontaneously occurring hereditary change in an organism's genetic makeup.

natural history   the practice of close observation of the natural world, plants, animals, and insects, usually including the collection and classification of specimens.

natural philosophy   the practice of seeking to understand the laws of nature through observation, experiment, and reasoning; the predecessor to modern science.

natural selection   *See* **Darwinism.**

natural theology   the belief held by many early-nineteenth-century British naturalists that the perfect structures and complex adaptations observable in plants and animals provided evidence that an omniscient and omnipotent God created them and that the study of nature was therefore complementary to studying the revealed theology of the Bible.

naturalism   *See* **materialism.**

nature versus nurture   a shorthand way of referring to the debate over whether heredity or environment is more important in shaping mental and physical traits.

orthognathous   possessing a straight or upright jaw (opposite of prognathous).

pangenesis   Darwin's speculative hypothesis of blending inheritance, according to which tiny particles called gemmules are thrown off by the body's cells, gathered in the gametes, and passed on to the offspring. Pangenesis allowed for the inheritance of acquired characters, since any change to the body's cells undergone in its lifetime would be picked up by the gametes and passed on to the next generation.

phenotype   the outward appearance of an organism, as distinct from its genetic makeup.

phrenology   a nineteenth-century popular scientific practice of determining one's character, abilities, and propensities by "reading," that is, feeling the bumps on one's skull, which were supposedly correlated with underlying brain organs. The size of the bump and its underlying organ indicated the strength of its associated mental faculty.

physiognomy   the study of the shape of the face.

polygenism/polygenesis   the theory that the different human races originated in separate creations, each in its own geographical location, and that therefore each race represents its own distinct type. Some polygenists believed that the races were different species.

population   a group of organisms that have inbred for a period of time and that therefore share a set of genes.

population genetics   the method of mathematically calculating the gene frequencies in an inbreeding group, or population. Associated with the belief that populations can be defined only by shared genes, not by a common essence that all its members possess.

prejudice   an irrational, negative attitude or bias; in the context of this book, indicates hatred of a particular group of people.

prognathous   possessing a jaw that juts forward (opposite of orthognathous).

Progressive Era   the period from 1900 to about 1914 in the United States during which reformers emphasized government control and regulation of capitalism and scientific expertise to solve social problems.

psychologizing   the practice in twentieth-century social science of attributing problems in society to defects in individuals' personalities rather than to political, economic, or institutional structures.

psychometrics   psychological testing and measurement, particularly the statistical analysis and testing of intelligence.

race   a group of people distinguished by various physical features such as skin color, eye shape, or hair color or texture. In classical nineteenth-century race theory, each race also possessed its own set of different mental levels and moral attributes, which were inherited along with its physical traits.

racial hygiene   the practice of "purifying" or cleansing a given racial group, particularly the white or Nordic race, by preventing interbreeding and getting rid of those judged defective.

racial typology   the belief that the different races are biologically and immutably distinct from one another and that they represent different types or kinds.

racial zone   according to the polygenist Louis Agassiz, the separate geographical location in which each race was created and to which each properly belonged.

racism   the doctrine that one race is superior to another that seeks to maintain the purity of the races and that is put into practice by segregation and discrimination.

rapporteur   term for the official author of the UNESCO Statements on Race.

recessive   one of a pair of alleles, or genes, that, when paired with a dominant allele, is not expressed because it is masked by its dominant partner.

relativism   the belief that every culture must be understood on its own terms and according to its own standards rather than judged by a universal or absolute standard.

scientific racism   belief in the superiority of northern European peoples based on biological theories of the superiority of their blood or genetic endowment.

seasoning   the practice of allowing a person from one climate to live in and get used to another.

segregation   the practice of forcing members of different races, usually blacks and whites, to live separately in different neighborhoods, to use separate facilities in public venues like parks, theaters, and restaurants, and to attend different schools.

selective migration thesis   the theory held by some early-twentieth-century American psychologists that smarter blacks tend to migrate to the northern United States, leaving their less intelligent counterparts in the South. Opposed by the idea that better educational conditions in the North foster better performance on tests of intelligence.

self-determination   the belief that blacks should live in their own communities and by their own cultural standards; opposed to ideals of integration and assimilation.

social Darwinism   the belief often associated with Herbert Spencer that laissez-faire economic policy allows the "fittest" (smartest and most able) members of society to achieve wealth and power, while the "unfit," those unable to compete, die out. "Survival of the fittest" was Spencer's phrase summing up this doctrine.

social engineering   the belief that society can be managed, planned, and directed by the expertise of social scientists.

social pathology   a term used by sociologists to refer to the social and psychological damage produced in victims of racism and in their families and communities. *See* **damage argument.**

social selection   the process defined by Herbert Spencer by which the fittest members in society would garner wealth and power and would pass on their positive traits to their offspring, thereby ensuring that each generation would be an improvement on the preceding one.

sociocultural evolutionism   the late-nineteenth-century theory that cultural development passes through well-defined and strictly hierarchical stages from savagery, to barbarism, and finally to civilization.

soft heredity   the belief that both genetic traits and those due to environment may be passed on to the next generation.

spiritualism   the belief that the dead can communicate with the living with the help of an interpreter, or medium.

sports of nature   sudden, spontaneously occurring hereditary traits, usually widely different from the normal traits in a population.

stereotype   a fixed notion or conception about a particular group or race that invests all its members with the same set of characteristics, usually negative ones, and that does not recognize any variation among individuals.

survival of the fittest   *See* **social Darwinism.**

survivals   doctrine introduced by the anthropologist Edward Tylor according to which anthropologists looked for forms or relics of the past that have persisted into the present day and used them to reconstruct the general course of human development.

taxonomy   the science of classification of living organisms.

transcendental anatomy   the pre-Darwinian science that sought to discover the few basic essential forms, the "'ideal types," underlying the immense variety of animals.

uniformitarianism   the geological theory developed by geologist Charles Lyell that slow, gradual change over long stretches of time, caused by everyday processes now observable (wind, rain, erosion, etc.), is responsible for the present-day appearance of the earth. Opposed to the idea that catastrophes, giant earthquakes or floods, account for the earth's appearance.

variance   range of distribution of a given trait in a population.

Documents

*Like many scientists of the eighteenth century, Johann Friedrich
Blumenbach was concerned with the taxonomy of the natural world.
Three hallmarks of eighteenth century science are evident in this
selection from* On the Natural Varieties of Mankind. *First, Blumenbach
clearly sees human beings as part of the natural order, just like other
living things. Second, Blumenbach attempts to rely only on what he sees
as reliable source material rather than on secondhand accounts or other
less trustworthy sources. Finally, he tries to address the great confusion
about the number of races and the issue of whether or not the races were
fixed or could change according to climate.*

On the Natural Varieties of Mankind

JOHANN FRIEDRICH BLUMENBACH

For although there seems to be so great a difference between widely separate
nations, that you might easily take the inhabitants of the Cape of Good Hope, the
Greenlanders, and the Circassians for so many different species of man, yet
when the matter is thoroughly considered, you see that all do so run into one
another, and that one variety of mankind does so sensibly pass into the other,
that you cannot mark out the limits between them.

Very arbitrary indeed both in number and definition have been the varieties
of mankind accepted by eminent men. Linnæus[1] allotted four classes of inhabitants to the four quarters of the globe respectively. Oliver Goldsmith[2] reckons six.
I have followed Linnæus in the number, but have defined my varieties by other
boundaries. The first and most important to us (which is also the primitive one)
is that of Europe, Asia this side of the Ganges, and all the country situated to the
north of the Amoor, together with that part of North America, which is nearest
both in position[3] and character of the inhabitants. Though the men of these countries seem to differ very much amongst each other in form and colour, still when
they are looked at as a whole they seem to agree in many things with ourselves.
The second includes that part of Asia beyond the Ganges, and below the river
Amoor, which looks towards the south, together with the islands, and the greater
part of those countries which are now called Australian. Men of dark colour, snub
noses, with winking eye-lids drawn outwards at the corners, scanty, and stiff hair.
Africa makes up the third. There remains finally, for the fourth, the rest of America, except so much of the North as was included in the first variety[4].

It will easily appear from the progress of this dissertation in which of the
four varieties most discrepancies are still to be found, and on the contrary, that
many in other varieties have some points in common, or in some anomalous way
differ from the rest of their neighbours. Still it will be found serviceable to the
memory to have constituted certain classes into which the men of our planet

may be divided; and this I hope I have not altogether failed in doing, since for the reason I have given before I have tried this and that, but found them less satisfactory. Now I mean to go over one by one the points in which man seems to differ from man by the natural conformation of his body and in appearance, and I will investigate as far as I can the causes which tend to produce that variety.

First of all I shall speak of the whole bodily constitution, stature, and colour, and then I shall go on to the particular structure and proportion of individual parts. It will then be necessary carefully to distinguish those points which are due to art alone, and finally, though with reluctance, I shall touch upon nosology and practical medicine, both which chapters recent authors have tried to obtrude into natural history, but which I shall endeavour to vindicate for and restore to pathology.

The first three things I mean to discuss, the whole bodily constitution, the stature, and the colour, are owing almost entirely to climate alone. I must be brief on the first of these points, since I have had no opportunity of exercising my personal observation on the matter, and but few and scanty traces are to be gathered from authors. That in hot countries bodies become drier and heavier; in cold and wet ones softer, more full of juice and spongy, is easily noticed. It has long since been noticed by W. Cavendish, Marquis of Newcastle, that the bones of the wild horse have very small cavities, and those of the Frisian horses much larger ones[5], &c. This was confirmed by the elegant experiments of Kersting, a physician of Cassel, and a most skilled in the treatment of animals. He observed[6], amongst other things, that the bones of an Arab horse, of six years old, when subjected to the same degree of heat, were dissolved with much more difficulty in the machine of Papinus than those of a Frisian of the same age. It is very likely that similar differences would be observed in the bones of men born in different countries, although observations are wanting, and conclusions drawn from a few facts are unsatisfactory. Here and there indeed we find bones of Ethiopians[7] which are thick, compact, and hard; but I should be unwilling to attribute these properties to every skeleton coming from hot countries, since other instances occur of skulls of Ethiopians, about which the same remark has not been made[8]. The differences moroever are very great between the skulls of Europeans of the same country and the same age, which seem to depend, amongst other things, principally upon the mode of life[9]. Perhaps the same is the case as to the sutures, which Arrian says the heads of the Ethiopians are without, and Herodotus[10] says the same of the Persian skulls after the battle of Platæa. The observation about the whole habit of the body, that the northern[11] nations are more sinewy and square, and the southern more elegant, seems more reliable.

I go on to the human stature. It is an old opinion, that in very ancient times men were much larger and taller, and that they degenerate and diminish in size even now, that children are now born smaller than their parents, and all the things of this kind which the old poets[12] and philosophers[13] have said to discredit their own times.

But although this may be going too far, still we must allow something to climate, so far as that itself is altered by the lapse of time. The soil itself becomes milder, so that it may at last make its men less gigantic and less fierce. We have already spoken of an example of this change in our own Germany. But the idea that these differences of bodies in ancient and modern times have been enormous, is refuted by the mummies of Egypt, the fossil human skeletons[14], the sarcophagi, and a thousand other proofs.

Nor do a few skulls conspicuous for their age and size[15], scattered about here and there, prove anything more than those solid ones destitute of sutures, about which I was lately speaking. Some, it is clear, are diseased[16]. But as to the bones which credulous antiquity showed as those of giants, they have long since been restored to elephants and whales[17]. The investigation of the causes which in our days make the men of one country tall and another short is more subtle. The principal one seems to be the degree of cold or heat. The latter obstructs the increase of organic bodies, whilst the former adds to them and promotes their growth. It would be tedious even to touch upon a thing so well known and so much confirmed in both kingdoms, were it not that in our time men have come forward, and with the greatest confidence have presumed to think otherwise[18]. Experience teaches that both plants and animals are smaller in northern countries than in southern; why should not the same law hold good as to mankind? Linnæus long ago remarked in his *Flora Lapponica*[19], that alpine plants commonly reached twice as great an altitude out of the Alps. And the same thing may be observed frequently in those plants, some specimens of which are kept in a conservatory, while others stand out in a garden, of which the former come out much larger and taller than the others.

I have before me the most splendid specimens in a collection of plants from Labrador and Greenland, chosen by Brasen[20], which I owe to the liberality of my great friend, J. Sam. Lieberkühn, in which the common ones are almost all smaller than those which are obtained in Germany; and in some, as the *Rhodiola rosea*, which are common to both those regions of America, although their native soil is so near, yet the same difference is observed that the specimens from Labrador are somewhat larger than those from Greenland.

The same is the case with animals. The Greenland foxes are smaller than those of the temperate zone[21]. The Swedish and Scotch horses are low and small, and in the coldest part of North Wales so little as scarcely to exceed dogs in size[22]. It is however useless to bring a long string of examples about a thing so evident, when the difference of a few degrees in so many countries exhibits clearly the same difference. Thus, Henry Ellis[23] observed in Hudson's Strait, on its southern coasts, trees and men of fair size; at 61° shrubs only, and that the men became smaller by little and little, and at last at 67° that not a vestige of either was to be seen. And likewise Murray, within the limits of a few degrees, and in Gotha alone, declared he could observe so well, that whilst he was travelling, although he took no notice of the mile-stones, yet he could easily distinguish the different provinces by the difference of the inhabitants and of the animals. In Scania[24] the men are tall of stature and bony, the horses and cattle large, &c.: in Smaland they become sensibly smaller, and the cattle are active but little, which at last in Ostrogothia strikes the eye more and more.

The same thing may be observed in the opposite part of the world, almost under the same degrees, towards the antarctic circle. One example will suffice, taken from the most southern part of America, and compared with those European nations we have just been speaking of. The bodies of the notorious Patagonians answer to the lofty stature of the Scandinavians. A credulous antiquity indeed invented fabulous stories of their enormous size[25]. But in the progress of time, after Patagonia had often been visited by Europeans, the inhabitants, like that famous dog of Gellert, became sensibly smaller, until at last in our own days they retained indeed a sufficiently large stature, but were happily deprived of their gigantic form. If you go down from them towards the south, you will find much smaller men in the cold land of Terra del Fuego[26], who must be compared to the Smalands and the Ostrogoths, and by that example you will again see how nature is always like itself even in the most widely separated regions.

But besides the climate, there are other causes which exercise influence upon stature. Already, at first, I alluded to the mode of life[27], and it would be easy to bring here copious examples taken from the vegetable and animal kingdoms, in which the difference of nutrition may be detected by the greater or smaller stature. But these things are too well known already, and so many experiments of the kind have been made on Swiss cows, Frisian horses, &c., that I may easily pass over any proofs of this point. I omit also the causes of smaller importance which change the stature of organic bodies, which have been already most diligently handled by Haller[28], and I hasten to the last of those things which must be considered in the variety of mankind, that is, colour.

There seems to be so great a difference between the Ethiopian, the white, and the red American, that it is not wonderful, if men even of great reputation have considered them as forming different species of mankind. But although the discussion of this subject seems particularly to belong to our business, still so many important things have been said about the seat and the causes of this diversity of colour, by eminent men, that a good-sized volume would scarcely contain them; so that it is necessary for me to be brief in this matter, and only to mention those things which the industry of learned men has placed beyond all doubt. The skin of man and of most animals consists of three parts; the external epidermis, or cuticle; the *reticulum mucosum*, called from its discoverer the Malphigian; and lastly, the inner, or *corium*. The middle of these, which very much resembles the external, so that by many it is considered as another scale of it, is evidently more spongy, thick, and black in the Ethiopians; and in them, as in the rest of men, is the primary seat of the diversity of colour. For in all the *corium* is white, excepting where, here and there, it is slightly coloured by the adhering reticulum; but the epidermis seems to shade off into the same colour as the reticulum, yet still so, that being diaphanous[29] like a plate of horn, it appears even in black men, if properly separated, to be scarcely grey; and therefore can have little if any influence on the diversity of the colour of men.

The seat of colour is pretty clear, but for a very long time back there have been many and great disputes about the causes of it, especially in the Ethiopians. Some think it to be a sign of the curse of Cain[30] or Cham[31], and their posterity; others[32] have brongh forward other hypotheses, amongst which the bile played the most prominent part, and this was particularly advocated by Peter Barrere[33], following D. Santorini[34]. Although this view has been opposed by many[35], I do not think it ought altogether to be neglected. The instances of persons affected with jaundice, or chlorosis, of the fish mullet[36], and moreover the black bile[37] of the Ethiopians, are all the less open to doubt, since more recent authors[38] have observed the blood to be black, and the brain and the spinal marrow to be of an ashy colour; and the phlegm of the northern nations and other things of this kind seem to add weight to this opinion. But amongst all other causes of their blackness, climate, and the influence of the soil, and the temperature, together with the mode of life, have the greatest influence. This is the old opinion of Aristotle, Alexander, Strabo, and others[39], and one which we will try and confirm by instances and arguments brought forward separately.

In the first place, then, there is an almost insensible and indefinable transition from the pure white skin of the German lady through the yellow, the red, and the dark nations, to the Ethiopian of the very deepest black, and we may observe this, as we said just now in the case of stature, in the space of a few degrees of latitude. Spain offers some trite examples; it is well known that the Biscayan women are a shining white, the inhabitants of Granada on the contrary dark, to such an extent that in this region the pictures of the Blessed Virgin and other saints are painted of the same colour[40]. Those who live upon the northern bank of the river Senegal are of ashy colour and small body; but those beyond are black, of tall stature and robust, as if in that part of the world one district was green, and the other burnt up[41]. And the same thing was observed by some learned Frenchmen on the Cordilleras, that those who live immediately under the mountains towards the west, and exposed to the Pacific Ocean, seem almost as white as Europeans, whereas on the contrary, the inhabitants of the opposite side, who are exposed to constant burning winds, are like the rest of the Americans, copper-coloured[42].

It is an old observation of Vitruvius[43] and Pliny[44] that the northern nations are white, and this is clearly enough shown by many instances of other animals and plants. For partly the flowers[45] of plants, like the animals of the northern regions, are white, though they produce other colours in more southern latitudes; and partly in the more temperate zones animals only become white in winter, and in spring put on again their own natural colour. Of the former we have instances in the wolves[46], dogs[47], hares[48], cattle[49], crows[50], the chaffinch[51], &c., of the latter in the ermines[52], the squirrels[53], hares[54], the ptarmigan[55], the Corsican dog[56]. All of us are born nearly red, and at last in progress of time the skin of the Ethiopian infants turns to black[57], and ours to white, whereas in the American the primitive red colour remains, excepting so far as that by change of climate and the effects of their mode of life those colours sensibly change, and as it were degenerate.

It is scarce worth while to notice the well-known difference which occurs in the inhabitants of one and the same country, whose skin varies wonderfully in colour, according to the kind of life that they lead. The face of the working man or the artizan, exposed to the force of the sun and the weather, differs as much from the cheeks of a delicate female, as the man himself does from the dark American, and he again from the Ethiopian. Anatomists not unfrequently fall in with the corpses of the lowest sort of men, whose reticulum comes much nearer to the blackness of the Ethiopians than to the brilliancy of the higher class of European. Such an European, blacker than an Ethiop, was dissected by Chr. Gottl. Ludwig[58]; a very dark reticulum has been observed by Günz[59], and very frequently by many others[60]; and I recollect that I myself dissected at Jena a man's corpse of this kind, whose whole skin was brown, and in some parts, as in the scrotum, almost black; for it is well known that some parts of the human body become more black than others, as, for example, the genitals of either sex, the tips of the breasts, and other parts which easily verge towards a dark colour. Haller observed in the groin of a woman the reticulum so black[61] that it did not seem to differ much from that of an Ethiopian; one as dark in the groin of a man was in the possession of B. S. Albinus; and it is so common an occurrence in a woman's breast, that I cannot be enough astonished that eminent men have been found to reckon the dark teats of the Samoyeds as prodigies[62], and therefore to consider that nation as a particular species of man[63].

Such a diversity of the reticulum is seen in other animals also, and especially in the face of the *Papio mandril,* a part of which I have therefore had engraved, (Pl. II. fig. 3.) There is a region of the upper part of the eyelids, of the root of the nose, and of the eye-brows, in which you may observe almost every variety of reticulum; the nose is plainly black, and also the part where the eye-brows are inserted; but that part which is lower and more on the outside is sensibly brown, and at length towards the outer corners of the eyes becomes pale. Not indeed that I have found this blackness of the nose equally intense in all the specimens of this ape which I have seen, since in apes, as in man and in other animals, the greatest variety of colour occurs in the reticulum. In two specimens of the *Simia cynomolgus* the tint of the face was not very different from that of an Ethiopian or a dark European; and this difference is so well known and so common throughout the animal kingdom, especially in the domestic quadrupeds, but above all in the vegetable[64] kingdom, that I can scarcely take notice of it, but prefer to return at once to man.

We see white men in a lower class rendered brown by a hard life; and it is equally certain that men of southern regions become whiter when they are less exposed to the effects of the weather and the sun. We have the most copious accounts by travellers of the inhabitants of Guzerat[65], of the Malabar coast[66], of the Caffres[67], of the Canadians[68], and the Otaheitans[69]. But besides their mode of life, old age and the change of country have an influence in making the Ethiopians more white. For when the Ethiopians begin to approach their seventieth year, the reticulum sensibly loses its dark colour, so that at last the bulbs come out yellow[70], and the hair and beard are grey like other nations; and if the young Ethiopian infants are brought into colder climates, it is certain that they lose a sensible quantity of their blackness[71], and their colour begins to verge more and more towards brown.

On the other hand, it is apparent that when white men reside a considerable time in the torrid zones they become brown, and sensibly verge towards black with much greater facility. The Spaniards who dwell under the equator in the new world have so much degenerated towards the native colour of the soil, that it has seemed very probable to eminent men[72], that had they not taken care to preserve their paternal constitution by intermarrying with Europeans, but had chosen to follow the same kind of life as the American nations, in a short time they would have fallen into almost the same coloration, which we see in the natives of South America. An Englishman who had spent only three years with the Virginians, became exactly like them in colour, and Smith[73], his countryman, could only recognize him by his language. A colony of Portuguese, who were carried to Africa[74] in the fifteenth century, can scarcely now be distinguished from the aborigines. The French, whether they emigrate to Africa or America, are invariably tinged with the brown colour of those countries[75]. I do not adduce here the numerous examples of Europeans who have become unnaturally black in their own country[76], or have brought forth black children[77], nor of Ethiopians who have been, at all events in some parts of their bodies, suddenly turned white[78], since all these cases seem to include something diseased or morbid.

As by the climate so also by the mode of life the colours of the body are seen to be changed. And this appears most clearly in the unions of people of different tints, in which cases the most distinct and contrary colours so degenerate, that white men may sensibly pass and be changed into black, and the contrary. The hybrid offspring (if we may use that word) are distinguished by particular names; in using which, however, the authors of travels vary so much, that it seemed to me worth while to collect as many of these synonyms as I could, to reduce them into grades of descending affinity, and exhibit them in a synoptic form.

1. The offspring of a black man and a white woman, or the reverse, is called *Mulatto*[79], *Mollaka*[80], *Melatta;* by the Italians, *Bertin, Creole* and *Criole*[81]; by the inhabitans of Malabar, *Mestiço*[82]. The offspring of an American man and an European woman, *Mameluck*[83], and *Metif*[84].

2. The offspring of an European male with a Mulatto female is called *Terceron*[85], *Castiço*[86]. The son of an European female from a *Metif* is called a *Quarteroon*[87]. The offspring of two Mulattoes is called *Casque*[88]; and of blacks and Mulattoes, *Griffs*[89].

3. A Terceron female and an European produce *quaterons*[90], *postiços*[91]. But the American quarteroon (who is of the same degree as the black Terceron) produces from an European *octavoons*[92].

4. The offspring of a quateroon male and a white female, a *quinteroon*[93]; the child of an European woman with an American octavoon is called by the Spaniards *Puchuela*[94].

It is plain therefore that the traces of blackness are propagated to great-grandchildren; but they do not keep completely the degrees we have just noticed, for twins sometimes are born of different colours; such as Fermin[95] says came from an Ethiopian woman, of which the male was a mulatto, but the female, like the mother, an intense black. And from all these cases, this is clearly proved, which I have been endeavouring by what has been said to demonstrate, that colour, whatever be its cause, be it bile, or the influence of the sun, the air, or the climate, is, at all events, an adventitious and easily changeable thing, and can never constitute a diversity of species.

A great deal of weight has attached to this opinion in consequence of the well-known examples of those men, whose reticulum has been conspicuously variegated and spotted with different colours. Lamothe[96] has described very carefully a boy of this kind from the Antilles. Labat[97] saw the wife of a Grifole like this, a native of Cayenne, and in other respects handsome. Chr. D. Schreber[98] has collected many examples; and I myself had lately an opportunity of seeing an instance of this sort of variegated skin. One of my friends, a physician, has a reticulum of almost a purple colour, and distinctly marked with very white spots, of different sizes, but equal in other respects, and similar to the most shining skin. And on the back of his right hand there were five white spots of the same kind, of which each was almost equal to a thumb's breadth in diameter, interspersed with numerous smaller ones. This phenomenon very seldom occurs in men; but is very common in animals, especially in the reticulum of quadrupeds. The throats of rams, for example, are frequently so variegated, that you may observe in them the greatest similarity, both to the black skin of the Ethiop and the white skin of the European. I have examined many flocks of sheep in their pastures with this object, and I think I have observed, that the greater or smaller number of black spots in the jaws answer to the greater or smaller quantity of black wool on the animals themselves.

Notes

1   1 Syst. Nat. p. 29.

2   Hist. of the Earth, Vol. II. p. 211.

3   Comp. besides the English terraqueous globes, which by the liberality of our queen the university library possesses; and the Swedish ones of Akerman, a copy of which is due to the kindness of J. Andr. Murray, the maps of D'Anville, Stahlin, and Engel, and the more recent labours of de Vaugondy, Sur les pays de l'Asie et de l'Amérique situés au Nord de la mer du Sud. Par. 1774, 4to.

4   [33. Mankind divided into five varieties. Formerly in the first edition of this work I divided all mankind into four varieties; but after I had more accurately investigated the different nations of Eastern Asia and America, and, so to speak, looked at them more closely, I was compelled to give up that division, and to place in its stead the following five varieties, as more consonant to nature.

The first of these and the largest, which is also the primeval one, embraces the whole of Europe, including the Lapps, whom I cannot in any way separate from the rest of the Europeans, when their appearance and their language bear such testimony to their Finnish origin; and that western part of Asia which lies towards us, this side of the Obi, the Caspian sea, mount Taurus and the Ganges; also northern Africa, and lastly, in America, the Greenlanders and the Esquimaux, for I see in these people a wonderful difference from the other inhabitants of America; and, unless I am altogether deceived, I think they must be derived from the Finns. All these nations regarded as a whole are white in colour, and, if compared with the rest, beautiful in form.

The second variety comprises that of the rest of Asia, which lies beyond the Ganges, and the part lying beyond the Caspian Sea and the river Obi towards Nova Zembla. The inhabitants of this country are distinguished by being of brownish colour, more or less verging to the olive, straight face, narrow eye-lids, and scanty hair. This whole variety may be sub-divided into two races, northern and southern; of which one may embrace China, the Corea, the kingdoms of Tonkin, Pegu, Siam, and Ava, using rather monosyllabic languages, and distinguished for depravity and perfidiousness of spirit and of manners; and the other the nations of northern Asia, the Ostiaks, and the other Siberians, the Tunguses, the Mantohoos, the Tartars, the Calmucks, and the Japanese.

The third variety comprises what remains of Africa, besides that northern part which I have already mentioned. Black men, muscular, with prominent upper jaws, swelling lips, turned up nose, very black curly hair.

The fourth comprises the rest of America, whose inhabitants are distinguished by their copper colour, their thin habit of body, and scanty hair.

Finally, the new southern world makes up the fifth, with which, unless I am mistaken, the Sunda, the Molucca, and the Philippine Islands should be reckoned; the men throughout being of a very deep brown colour, with broad nose, and thick hair. Those who inhabit the Pacific Archipelago are divided again by John Reinh. Forster1 into two tribes. One made up of the Otaheitans, the New Zealanders, and the inhabitants of the Friendly Isles, the Society, Easter Island, and the Marquesas, &c., men of elegant appearance and mild disposition; whereas the others who inhabit New Caledonia, Tanna, and the New Hebrides, &c., are blacker, more curly, and in disposition more distrustful and ferocious. Edit. 1781, pp. 51, 52.-This is the first sketch of the still famous division of mankind by Blumenbach: the well-known terms Caucasian, &c. will be found in the third ed. below.-ED.]

5   Gen. Syst. of Horsemanship. [The passage alluded to stands thus in the edition of 1743, Vol. I. p. 21. "I have experienced this difference between the bone of the leg of a Barbary horse, and one from Flanders, that the cavity of the bone in the one shall hardly admit of a straw whilst you may thrust your finger into that of the other."-ED.]

6   Horses' bones are much more easily dissolved than those of mules, and asses' with still greater difficulty.

7   B. S. Albini, Supellex Rav. n. XXIX. P. Paaw, Prim. Anat. p. 29.

8   In the Leg. Rav. n. XIII. and n. XXI, it is said that the bones of the Malabar women are very thin. See also J. Beni. de Fischer, De modo quo ossa se vicin. accomm. part., L.B. 1743, Tab. III.

9   J. B. Com. a Covolo, De met. duor. oss. ped. in quad. aliquot, Bonon. 1765, p. 7.

10   Cæl. Rhodig. Lect. Ant. XIII. 28. p. 501. ed. Froben.

11   For the Lapps and Finns, Leem, Lules, Högström, Calmucks, Pallas, Greenlanders, Crantz, &c.

12   Homer says repeatedly that Tydides, Hector, Ajax, Telamon, &c. (whose gigantic knee-cap Pausanias describes as being shown long afterwards) were much more strong and large than the men of his day, olol vûv ßporol elsl. And he has been imitated in this by Virgil, who represents Turnus as equally large, not to be compared with "Such human forms as earth produces now."

13   Plin. VII. c. 16. Solin. v. Comp. more upon this point J. S. Elsholtz, Anthropom. p. 31, ed. 1663.

14   There is in the Museum of our University a fossil skull tolerably complete, of the greatest antiquity, the bones of the head very thick, but neither in magnitude nor form differing from a common skull.

15   Fabricius Hildan. Fürtreffl. nutz und nothw. d. anat. Bern. 1624, p. 209. Head of March. Dietzmann killed at Leipzig, 1307. Glafey, Saechss. Kernhist. Head of Henry of Austria in the famous burying-place of K nigsfeld. Faesi, Erdb. der eidgen. I.

16   Fossil head of Rheims. Dargenville, Oryct. T. 17, f. 3, two osseous heads Leg. rav. in Albin. p. 4.

17   J. Wallis, Antiq. of Northumberland. Dom. Gagliardi, An. Oss. p. 103. Even Felix

Plater, who was the best lecturer of his day in all Europe, suffered himself to be led into error by the bones dug up at Lucerne in 1577, and after careful comparison gave them out as those of a human giant, Obs. Med. l. III. Wagner, Hist. Nat. Helv. p. 149: but they have lately been proved to be elephant's bones. Erkl. der Gemäld auf die Kapellbr. zu Lucern. This is also the case with the ribs of the Hun in the church of Göttingen.

18 As Henr. Home, loc. cit. p. 12. It is in vain to ascribe to the climate the low stature of the Esquimaux, &c.

19 Prolegom. XVI. 8. Comp. Arwid Ehrenmalm, Asehle, p. 386.

20 The same observation has been made by Haller, Hist. Stirp. Helv. II. p. 317.

21 Cranz, Hist. v. Gr. p. 97.

22 Th. Birch, Hist. of the Royal Soc. III. p. 171.

23 Voy. to Hudson's Bay, p. 256.

24 Comp. Linn. Fauna Suecica, p. 1.

25 Comp. de Brosses, I. p. 193; II. beg. &c. De Pauw, l. c. l. p. 281, and Hist. gén. de l'As. Afr. et Améri. par M. L. A. R. Vol. XIII. Par. 1755, p. 50. Thos. Falkner, Descr. of Patagonia, p. 126, "The Patagonians, or Puelches, are a large-bodied people; but I never heard of that gigantic race, which others have mentioned, though I have seen persons of all the different tribes of southern Indians."

26 Sydney Parkinson, p. 7, Pl. 1. 11. "None of them seemed above five feet ten inches high."

27 p. 73.

28 Physiol. l. XXX. s. 1, § 16.

29 If the epidermis were less thin and not so transparent, perhaps it would seem just as dark as the reticulum; Jo. Fanton, Diss. VII. Anat. pr. renov. Taurini, 1741, 8vo. p. 27.

30 A recent supporter of this opinion is the learned Sam. Engel in Ess. sur cette question quand et comm. l'Amér. a. t. clle été peuplée, T. IV. p. 96.

31 Mem. de Trevoux, T. LXXIV. p. 1155.

32 B. S. Albinus has collected many in De sede et causa color. ˌth. et cet. hom. L. B. 1737, with the beautifully coloured plates of that capital artist, J. Ladmiral.

33 Diss. sur la cause phys. de la couleur des nègres. Paris, 1741, 12mo. Comp. Dict. Encycl. by De Felice, T. XXX. p. 199.

34 Obs. Anat. p. 1.

35 Le Cat, De la coul. de la peau hum. p. 72.

36 Santorini, l. c.

37 Barrere, l. c.

38 Meckel, Mém. de Berl. 1753, 1757. The lice of the negroes are black, Long. II. p. 352.

39 Cæl. Rhodig. Lect. Ant. IX. 15, p. 439, ed. Ald. Comp. Macrob. in Somn. Scip. p. 128, ed. H. Steph.

40 Comp. a scale of colour in Mém. de Trev. l. c. p. 1190.

41 Hier. Cardanus, De subtilit. L. XI. T. III. Oper. p. 555.

42 Bouguer, Voyage à Perou. Mém. de l'Acad. des Sc. de Paris, 1744, p. 274.

43 In the north are to be found nations of white colour, p. 104, ed. De Laert.

44 On the opposite and icy side of the world are nations of white skin, T. I. p. 111, ed. Hard.

45 Comp. Murray, Prodr. Stirp. Goett. p. 18, who instances the Campanula decurrens, the common primrose, &c.

46 Cranz, Groenl. p. 97.

47 Ib. p. 100.

48 Ib. p. 95.

49 Ehrenmalm, l. c. p. 342, "The further you go towards the north, the more frequently do animals of that kind occur."

50 Jo. Nich. Pechlin, De habitu et colore Æthiopum. Kilon. 1677, 8vo. p. 141.

51 Frisch, Gesch. der Vogel. Faso. 1.

52 Wagner, *Hist. nat. Helv.* p. 180. Linn, *Faun. suec.* p. 7. I myself have seen specimans in our own neighborhood.

53 Linn. l. c. p. 13. I have known too some caught near Jena.

54 Ib. p. 10. Jetze, Monogr. Lüb. 1749, 8vo.

55 Cranz, l. c. p. 101.

56 Linn. Syst. Nat. Append.

57 Albinus, l. c. p. 12. Comp. Camper, Dem. Anat. Path. I. p. 1.

58 Ep. ad Haller. Script. Vol. I. p. 393.

59 On Hippoc. De humor. p. 140.

60 Franc. de Riet, De tact. org. in coll. Haller, T. IV. p. 10. See Haller, Physiol. T. V. p. 18.

61 l. c. Abr. Kaav. Boerh. Perspir. Hipp. p. 21; so dark in the pudenda, that you would not believe the skin to be that of an European.

62 Mém. sur les Samojedes et les Lappons, 1762, 8vo. p. 44.

63 Lord Kames, l. c.

64 Two hundred years ago it was only the yellow tulip which was known in Europe; but what a variety of different coloured ones horticulturists are now acquainted with! See Haller, on the subject of the varieties of man. Bibl. raisonnée, 1744.

65 J. Sohreyer, Oslind. reis. p. 121.

66 Tranquebar Miss. Ber. 22. Contin. p. 896. The more they dwell towards the north, and the more agreeable the race is, the more their black colour changes into brown, red, and yellow. The people of Barar are for the most part very black, and for the whole day long they work and are burnt up in sweat and dust by the rays of the sun. The better class of people do not go so much into the sun, and consequently they are not so black, &c. Comp. 30. Contin. p. 660.

67 Müller. Linn. Syst. Nat. I. p. 95.

68 Sir Franois Roberval in Hakluyt, Vol. III. p. 242. "The savages of Canada are very white, but they are all naked, and if they were apparelled as the French are they would be white and as fayre. But they paint themselves for feare of heat and sunne burning." "Those who are painted and who wear clothes, become so delicate in colour that they would be more readily taken for Spaniards than for Indians." La Houtan, I. ep. 16.

69 Hawkesworth, II. p. 187.

70 Wilh. J. Müller, Fetu, p. 279. Mich. Hemmersam, Westind. Reisen, p. 38.

71 The Colchians in the time of Herodotus were still black and had curly hair, p. 125, ed. Gronov. Leo Afric. P. I. s. 3. L. M. A. a most competent judge, says in his Instit. Physiolog. Patav. 1773, 8vo. p. 194: "A cobbler of this nation is still living at Venice, whose blackness after a long lapse of years (for he came a boy to this country) has so sensibly diminished that he looks as if suffering slightly from jaundice." And I myself have seen a mulatto woman born from an Ethiopian father and a white mother near Gotha, who in her very earliest infancy was sufficiently dark; but in progress of time has so degenerated from her native colour, that she now only retains a sort of cherry or yellow tint of skin.

72 Mitchell, Philos. Transact. n. 474.

73 Hist. Virgin. p. 116.

74 Rech. sur les Améric. I. p. 186.

75 Mém. de Trevoux, l. c. p. 1169.

76 Many instances are collected by Le Cat, Coul. de la peau, p. 130.

77 Cæl. Rhodig. l. c. p. 776. Froben, Le Cat, p. 109. A black princess was born to the queen of Louis XIV. Mém. de Trevoux, l. c. p. 1168. Abr. Kaav. Boerh. impet. fac. p. 354.
78 Le Cat, p. 100. Frank, Philos. Tr. Vol. LI. Part I. p. 176.
79 Hist. of Jamaica, II. p. 260. Aublet, Plantes de la Guiane Françoise, T. II. p. 122, App.
80 Hemmersam, l. c. p. 36.
81 Thomas Hyde on Abr. Perizol. Cosmograph. p. 99, ed. Oxon. 1691, 4to.
82 Christ. Langhan's Ostind. Reise. p. 216. Tranquebar Miss. Ber. Cont. 33, p. 919. Mestiço Lusitan. that is, of mixed race.
83 Hist. de l'Ac. des Sc. de Paris, 1724, p. 18.
84 Labat, Voy. aux Isles de l'Amér. II. p. 132. Recherch. sur les Amér. 1. p. 199. Newly-born metifs are distinguished by the colour of the genitals from true blacks, for it is well known that those parts are black even in the Ethiopian fœtus. Phil. Fermin, Sur l'oeconomie animale, Part 1. p. 180. This author calls the offspring of the black male and the Indian female Kahougle, and the offspring of these and the whites Mulattas, p. 179.
85 Hist. of Jamaica, l. c.
86 Langhan's Tranqu. Ber. l. c. Castiço, de boa casta, of a good stock.
87 De Pauw, l. c.
88 Comment. Paris. l. c.
89 Ib. p. 17. It is plain that the offspring of a Mestiço and a Malabar woman are black. Relat. Tranqueb. l. c. Those from a Mulatto are called Sambo in Hist. of Jamaica, l. c. p. 261, and the offspring of these and blacks become blacks again.
90 Hist. of Jam. l. c. p. 260.
91 Langhan's Rel. Tranq. l. c. Postiço means adopted: thus çabello postiço, false hair.
92 De Pauw, l. c. p. 200.
93 Hist. of Jam. l. c. The children of Postiços and whites are clearly white. Tranqu. Ber. l. c. According to the author of the Hist. of Jamaica the children of a quinteroon and a white man become white.
94 De Pauw, l. c.
95 l. c. p. 178.
96 Hamb. Mag. XIX. p. 400.
97 Voy. en Esp. et en Ital. I. p. 176.
98 Saeugthiere, p. 15. I shall speak below about the spotting of the skin from disease, which must be clearly distinguished from the instances in the text.

European writers often viewed the New World as a degenerate place,
where civilization could never flower to the extent it had in Europe. Few
writers were more vehement in their defense of the New World than
Thomas Jefferson, one of the great political leaders of the American
Revolution. In this selection, Jefferson is defending American Indians
against charges that they were racial savages. Yet, he cannot completely
escape judging them as a "barbarous" people. Thus, Jefferson illustrates
both the Enlightenment optimism that civilization could bloom in the
New World, while simultaneously embracing the notion that it had not
done so among the primitive natives of the region.

Notes on the State of Virginia, Chapter 6

THOMAS JEFFERSON

Of the Indian of South America I know nothing; for I would not honor with the appellation of knowledge, what I derive from the fables published of them. These I believe to be just as true as the fables of Aesop. This belief is founded on what I have seen of man, white, red, and black, and what has been written of him by authors, enlightened themselves, and writing amidst an enlightened people. The Indian of North America being more within our reach, I can speak of him somewhat from my own knowledge, but more from the information of others better acquainted with him, and on whose truth and judgment I can rely. From these sources I am able to say, in contradiction to this representation, that he is neither more defective in ardor, nor more impotent with his female, than the white reduced to the same diet and exercise: that he is brave, when an enterprize depends on bravery; education with him making the point of honor consist in the destruction of an enemy by stratagem, and in the preservation of his own person free from injury; or perhaps this is nature; while it is education which teaches us to[1] honor force more than finesse: that he will defend himself against an host of enemies, always chusing to be killed, rather than to[2] surrender, though it be to the whites, who he knows will treat him well: that in other situations also he meets death with more deliberation, and endures tortures with a firmness unknown almost to religious enthusiasm with us: that he is affectionate to his children, careful of them, and indulgent in the extreme: that his affections comprehend his other connections, weakening, as with us, from circle to circle, as they recede from the center: that his friendships are strong and faithful to the uttermost[3] extremity: that his sensibility is keen, even the warriors weeping most bitterly on the loss of their children, though in general they endeavour to appear superior to human events: that his vivacity and activity of mind is equal to ours in the same situation; hence his eagerness for hunting, and for games of chance. The women are submitted to unjust drudgery. This I believe is the case with every barbarous people. With such, force is law. The stronger sex therefore imposes on the weaker. It is civilization alone which replaces women in the enjoyment of their natural equality. That first teaches us to subdue the selfish passions, and to respect those rights in others which we value in ourselves. Were we in equal barbarism, our females would be equal drudges. The man with them is less strong than with us, but their woman stronger than ours; and both for the same obvious reason; because our man and their woman is habituated to labour, and formed by it. With both races the sex which is indulged with ease is least athletic. An Indian man is small in the hand and wrist for the same reason for which a sailor is large and strong in the arms and shoulders, and a porter in the legs and thighs.—They raise fewer children than we do. The causes of this are to be found, not in a difference of nature, but of circumstance. The women very frequently attending the men in their parties of war and of hunting, child-bearing becomes extremely inconvenient to them. It is said, therefore, that they have learnt the practice of procuring abortion by the use of some vegetable; and that it even extends to prevent conception for a considerable time after. During these parties they are exposed to numerous hazards, to excessive exertions, to the greatest extremities of hunger. Even at their homes the nation depends for food, through a certain part of every year, on the gleanings of the forest: that is, they experience a famine once in every year. With all animals, if the female be badly fed, or not fed at all, her young perish: and if both male and female be reduced to like want, generation becomes less active, less productive. To the obstacles then of want and hazard, which nature has opposed to the multiplication of wild animals, for the purpose of restraining their numbers within certain bounds, those of labour and of voluntary abortion are added with the Indian. No wonder then if they multiply less than we do. Where food is regularly supplied, a single farm will shew more of cattle, than a whole country of forests can of buffaloes. The same Indian women, when married to white traders, who feed them and their children plentifully and regularly, who exempt them from excessive drudgery, who keep them stationary and unexposed to accident, produce and raise as many children as the white women. Instances are known, under these circumstances, of their rearing a dozen children. An inhuman practice once prevailed in this country of making slaves of the Indians. It is a fact well known with us, that the Indian women so enslaved produced and raised as numerous families as either the whites or blacks among whom they lived.—It has been said, that Indians have less hair than the whites, except on the head. But this is a fact of which fair proof can scarcely be had. With them it is disgraceful to be hairy on the body. They say it likens them to hogs. They therefore pluck the hair as fast as it appears. But the traders who marry their women, and prevail on them to discontinue this practice, say, that nature is the same with them as with the whites. Nor, if the fact be true, is the consequence necessary which has been drawn from it. Negroes have notoriously less hair than the whites; yet they are more ardent. But if cold and moisture be the agents of nature for diminishing the races of animals, how comes she all at once to suspend their operation as to the physical man of the new world, whom the Count acknowledges to be 'a peu pres de meme stature que l'homme de notre monde,' and to let loose their influence on his moral faculties? How has this 'combination of the elements and other physical causes, so contrary to the enlargement of animal nature in this new world, these obstacles to the developement and formation of great germs,' been arrested and suspended, so as to permit the human body to acquire its just dimensions, and by what inconceivable process has their action been directed on his mind alone? To judge of the truth of this, to form a just estimate of their genius and mental powers, more facts are wanting, and great allowance to be made for those circumstances of their situation which call for a display of particular talents only. This done, we shall probably find that they are formed in mind as well as in body, on the same module with the[4] 'Homo sapiens Europaeus.' The principles of their society forbidding all compulsion, they are to be led to duty and to enterprize by personal influence and persuasion. Hence eloquence in council, bravery and address in war, become the foundations of all consequence with them. To these acquirements all their faculties are directed. Of their bravery and address in war we have multiplied proofs, because we have been the subjects on which they were exercised. Of their eminence in oratory we have fewer examples, because it is displayed chiefly in their own councils. Some, however, we have of very superior lustre. I may challenge the whole orations of Demosthenes and Cicero, and of any more eminent orator, if Europe has furnished more eminent, to produce a single passage, superior to the speech of Logan, a Mingo chief, to Lord Dunmore, when governor of this state. And, as a testimony of their talents in this line, I beg leave to introduce it, first stating the incidents necessary for understanding it. In the spring of the year 1774, a robbery and murder were committed on an inhabitant of the frontiers of Virginia, by two Indians of the Shawanee tribe. The neighbouring whites, according to their custom, undertook to punish this outrage in a summary way. Col. Cresap, a man infamous for the many murders he had committed on those much-injured people, collected a party, and proceeded down the Kanhaway in quest of vengeance. Unfortunately a canoe of women and children, with one man only, was seen coming from the opposite shore, unarmed, and unsuspecting an hostile attack from the whites. Cresap and his party concealed themselves on the bank of the river, and the moment the canoe reached the shore, singled out their objects, and, at one fire, killed every person in it. This happened to be the family of Logan, who had long been distinguished as a friend of the whites. This unworthy return provoked his vengeance. He accordingly signalized himself in the war which ensued. In the autumn of the same year, a decisive battle was fought at the mouth of the Great Kanhaway, between the collected forces of the Shawanees, Mingoes, and Delawares, and a detachment of the Virginia militia. The Indians were defeated, and sued for peace. Logan however disdained to be seen among the suppliants. But, lest the sincerity of a treaty should be distrusted, from which so distinguished a chief absented himself, he sent by a messenger the following speech to be delivered to Lord Dunmore.

'I appeal to any white man to say, if ever he entered Logan's cabin hungry, and he gave him not meat; if ever he came cold and naked, and he clothed him not. During the course of the last long and bloody war, Logan remained idle in his cabin, an advocate for peace. Such was my love for the whites, that my countrymen pointed as they passed, and said, 'Logan is the friend of white men.' I had even thought to have lived with you, but for the injuries of one man. Col. Cresap, the last spring, in cold blood, and unprovoked, murdered all the relations of Logan, not sparing even my women and children. There runs not a drop of my blood in the veins of any living creature. This called on me for revenge. I have sought it: I have killed many: I have fully glutted my vengeance. For my country, I rejoice at the beams of peace. But do not harbour a thought that mine is the joy of fear. Logan never felt fear. He will not turn on his heel to save his life. Who is there to mourn for Logan?—Not one.'

Before we condemn the Indians of this continent as wanting genius, we must consider that letters have not yet been introduced among them. Were we to compare them in their present state with the Europeans North of the Alps, when the Roman arms and arts first crossed those mountains, the comparison would be unequal, because, at that time, those parts of Europe were swarming with numbers; because numbers produce emulation, and multiply the chances of improvement, and one improvement begets another. Yet I may safely ask, How many good poets, how many able mathematicians, how many great inventors in arts or sciences, had Europe North of the Alps then produced? And it was sixteen centuries after this before a Newton could be formed. I do not mean to deny, that there are varieties in the race of man, distinguished by their powers both of body and mind. I believe there are, as I see to be the case in the races of other animals. I only mean to suggest a doubt, whether the bulk and faculties of animals depend on the side of the Atlantic on which their food happens to grow, or which furnishes the elements of which they are compounded? Whether nature has enlisted herself as a Cis or Trans-Atlantic partisan? I am induced to suspect, there has been more eloquence than sound reasoning displayed in support of this theory; that it is one of those cases where the judgment has been seduced by a

glowing pen: and whilst I render every tribute of honor and esteem to the celebrated Zoologist, who has added, and is still adding, so many precious things to
the treasures of science, I must doubt whether in this instance he has not cher-
ished error also, by lending her for a moment his vivid imagination and bewitch-
ing language.

So far the Count de Buffon has carried this new theory of the tendency of
nature to belittle her productions on this side the Atlantic. Its application to the
race of whites, transplanted from Europe, remained for the Abbe Raynal. 'On
doit etre etonne (he says) que l'Amerique n'ait pas encore produit un bon poete,
un habile mathematicien, un homme de genie dans un seul art, ou une seule science.' 7. Hist. Philos. p. 92. ed. Maestricht. 1774. 'America has not yet produced
one good poet.' When we shall have existed as a people as long as the Greeks did
before they produced a Homer, the Romans a Virgil, the French a Racine and
Voltaire, the English a Shakespeare and Milton, should this reproach be still true,
we will enquire from what unfriendly causes it has proceeded, that the other
countries of Europe and quarters of the earth shall not have inscribed any name
in the roll of poets[5]. But neither has America produced 'one able mathematician,
one man of genius in a single art or a single science.' In war we have produced a
Washington, whose memory will be adored while liberty shall have votaries,
whose name will triumph over time, and will in future ages assume its just station among the most celebrated worthies of the world, when that wretched philosophy shall be forgotten which would have arranged him among the degen-
eracies of nature. In physics we have produced a Franklin, than whom no one of
the present age has made more important discoveries, nor has enriched philosophy with more, or more ingenious solutions of the phaenomena of nature. We
have supposed Mr. Rittenhouse second to no astronomer living: that in genius he
must be the first, because he is self-taught. As an artist he has exhibited as great
a proof of mechanical genius as the world has ever produced. He has not indeed
made a world; but he has by imitation approached nearer its Maker than any man
who has lived from the creation to this day[6]. As in philosophy and war, so in government, in oratory, in painting, in the plastic art, we might shew that America,
though but a child of yesterday, has already given hopeful proofs of genius, as
well of the nobler kinds, which arouse the best feelings of man, which call him
into action, which substantiate his freedom, and conduct him to happiness, as of
the subordinate, which serve to amuse him only. We therefore suppose, that this
reproach is as unjust as it is unkind; and that, of the geniuses which adorn the
present age, America contributes its full share. For comparing it with those countries, where genius is most cultivated, where are the most excellent models for
art, and scaffoldings for the attainment of science, as France and England for
instance, we calculate thus. The United States contain three millions of inhabi-

tants; France twenty millions; and the British islands ten. We produce a Washington, a Franklin, a Rittenhouse. France then should have half a dozen in each of these lines, and Great-Britain half that number, equally eminent. It may be true, that France has: we are but just becoming acquainted with her, and our acquaintance so far gives us high ideas of the genius of her inhabitants. It would be injuring too many of them to name particularly a Voltaire, a Buffon, the constellation of Encyclopedists, the Abbe Raynal himself, &c. &c. We therefore have reason to believe she can produce her full quota of genius. The present war having so long cut off all communication with Great-Britain, we are not able to make a fair estimate of the state of science in that country. The spirit in which she wages war is the only sample before our eyes, and that does not seem the legitimate offspring either of science or of civilization. The sun of her glory is fast descending to the horizon. Her philosophy has crossed the Channel, her freedom the Atlantic, and herself seems passing to that awful dissolution, whose issue is not given human foresight to scan[7].

Notes

1   Sol Rodomonte sprezza di venire
Se non, dove la via meno e sicura.
Ariosto. 14. 117.

2   In so judicious an author as Don Ulloa, and one to whom we are indebted for the most precise information we have of South America, I did not expect to find such assertions as the following. 'Los Indios vencidos son los mas cobardes y pusilanimes que se peuden ver:-se hacen inocentes, se humillan hasta el desprecio, disculpan su inconsiderado arrojo, y con las suplicas y los ruegos dan seguras pruebas de su pusilanimidad.-o lo que resieren las historias de la Conquista, sobre sus grandes acciones, es en un sentido figurado, o el caracter de estas gentes no es ahora segun era entonces; pero lo que no tiene duda es, que las Naciones de la parte Septentrional subsisten en la misma libertad que siempre han tenido, sin haber sido sojuzgados por algun Principe extrano, y que viven segun su regimen y costumbres de toda la vida, sin que haya habido motivo para que muden de caracter; y en estos se ve lo mismo, que sucede en los del Peru, y de toda la America Meridional, reducidos, y que nunca lo han estado.' Noticias Americanas. Entretenimiento XVIII. 1. Don Ulloa here admits, that the authors who have described the Indians of South America, before they were enslaved, had represented them as a brave people, and therefore seems to have suspected that the cowardice which he had observed in those of the present race might be the effect of subjugation. But, supposing the Indians of North America to be cowards also, he concludes the ancestors of those of South America to have been so too, and therefore that those authors have given fictions for truths. He was probably not acquainted himself with the Indians of North America, and had formed his opinion of them from hear-say. Great numbers of French, of English, and of Americans, are perfectly acquainted with these people. Had he had an opportunity of enquiring of any of these, they would have told him, that there never was an instance known of an Indian begging his life when in the power of his enemies: on the contrary, that he courts death by every possible insult and provocation. His reasoning then would have been reversed thus. 'Since the present Indian of North America is brave, and authors tell us, that the ancestors of those of

South America were brave also; it must follow, that the cowardice of their descendants is the effect of subjugation and ill treatment.' For he observes, ib. (symbol omitted). 27. that 'los obrages los aniquilan por la inhumanidad con que se les trata.'

3   A remarkable instance of this appeared in the case of the late Col. Byrd, who was sent to the Cherokee nation to transact some business with them. It happened that some of our disorderly people had just killed one or two of that nation. It was therefore proposed in the council of the Cherokees that Col. Byrd should be put to death, in revenge for the loss of their countrymen. Among them was a chief called Silouee, who, on some former occasion, had contracted an acquaintance and friendship with Col. Byrd. He came to him every night in his tent, and told him not to be afraid, they should not kill him. After many days deliberation, however, the determination was, contrary to Silouee's expectation, that Byrd should be put to death, and some warriors were dispatched as executioners. Silouee attended them, and when they entered the tent, he threw himself between them and Byrd, and said to the warriors, 'this man is my friend: before you get at him, you must kill me.' On which they returned, and the council respected the principle so much as to recede from their determination.

4   Linn. Syst. Definition of a Man.

5   Has the world as yet produced more than two poets, acknowledged to be such by all nations? An Englishman, only, reads Milton with delight, an Italian Tasso, a Frenchman the Henriade, a Portuguese Camouens: but Homer and Virgil have been the rapture of every age and nation: they are read with enthusiasm in their originals by those who can read the originals, and in translations by those who cannot.

6   There are various ways of keeping truth out of sight. Mr. Rittenhouse's model of the planetary system has the plagiary appellation of an Orrery; and the quadrant invented by Godfrey, an American also, and with the aid of which the European nations traverse the globe, is called Hadley's quadrant.

7   In a later edition of the Abbe Raynal's work, he has withdrawn his censure from that part of the new world inhabited by the Federo-Americans; but has left it still on the other parts. North America has always been more accessible to strangers than South. If he was mistaken then as to the former, he may be so as to the latter. The glimmerings which reach us from South America enable us only to see that its inhabitants are held under the accumulated pressure of slavery, superstition, and ignorance. Whenever they shall be able to rise under this weight, and to shew themselves to the rest of the world, they will probably shew they are like the rest of the world. We have not yet sufficient evidence that there are more lakes and fogs in South America than in other parts of the earth. As little do we know what would be their operation on the mind of man. That country has been visited by Spaniards and Portugueze chiefly, and almost exclusively. These, going from a country of the old world remarkably dry in its soil and climate, fancied there were more lakes and fogs in South America than in Europe. An inhabitant of Ireland, Sweden, or Finland, would have formed the contrary opinion. Had South America then been discovered and seated by a people from a fenny country, it would probably have been represented as much drier than the old world. A patient pursuit of facts, and cautious combination and comparison of them, is the drudgery to which man is subjected by his Maker, if he wishes to attain sure knowledge.

Robert Knox was outspoken in his belief that science offered firm proof of white supremacy. However, the political implication he drew from this central idea was not what we might expect. Rather than arguing that Great Britain should extend her empire in order to dominate and civilize the inferior races, Knox was a staunch anti-imperialist who argued that the science of race had proven that each race should remain in its homeland. In this selection, Knox argues for the withdrawal of Europe from the tropics because the racial composition of Europeans necessitated it.

The Races of Man

Robert Knox

SECTION II. *Can a race of men permanently change their locality—say Continental, or rather Terrestrial Zone? Can a Saxon become an American? or an African? Can an Asiatic become a European? Can any race live and thrive in all climates?*

The earth was made for man, and man was made for the earth. The one proposition is quite as intelligible as the other. That it was not always so we now know, thanks to anatomical research and true science. The necessary conditions of his existence were not always present; his tenancy of the globe, according to the most orthodox and best received doctrines, has been but of short duration. This is not my opinion; but I promised to consider first, in as far as I could, man as he is now, tracing him back into the unknown past as far as truth and science enable us to go.

Can any race of men live and thrive in any climate? Need I discuss this question seriously? Will any one venture to affirm it of man? Travel to the Antilles, and see the European struggling with existence, a prey to fever and dysentery, unequal to all labour, wasted and wan, finally perishing, and becoming rapidly extinct as a race, but for the constant influx of fresh European blood. European inhabitants of Jamaica, of Cuba, of Hispaniola, and of the Windward and Leeward Isles, what progress have you made since your first establishment there? Can you say you are established? Cease importing fresh European blood, and watch the results. Labour you cannot, hence the necessity for a black population; your pale, wan, and sickly offspring would in half a century be non-productive; face to face with the energetic negro race, your colour must alter—first brown, then black; look at Hayti: with a deepening colour vanishes civilization, the arts of peace, science, literature, abstract justice; Christianity becomes a mere name, or puts on a fetichian robe—why not? The Roman robe was, and is, Pagan; the Byzantine, misnamed Greek, has an outrageous oriental look; the Protestant is a calculating, sober, drab-coloured cloak; why may not the fetiche be attached to the cloak as well as the mitre and the incense-box? Is the one superior to the other? The European, then, cannot colonize a tropical country; he cannot identify himself with it; hold it he may, with the sword, as we hold India, and as Spain once held Central America, but inhabitants of it, in the strict sense of the term, they cannot become. It never can absolutely become theirs; nature gave it not to them as an inheritance; they seized it by fraud and violence, holding it by deeds of blood and infamy, as we hold India; still it may be for a short tenure, nay, it may even be at any time measured. Withdraw from a tropical country the annual fresh influx of European blood, and in a century its European inhabitants cease to exist.

Mr. Canning made his celebrated boast in the English Parliament, that if he had lost the influence and support of Old Spain, he had created the South American Republics—free states, whose traffic (it is always traffic with an English statesman)—whose traffic with England would amply supply the loss of that influence! But where are these free states now? Mr. Canning was too high a statesman to take into calculation the element of race. When the boast was made, I put this plain question to myself and others—Who are the Mexicans? the Peruvians? the Chilians? the Argentines? the Brazilians? Whence do they spring, and what are the vital forces supplying their population? Applying the physiological laws, which seemed to me sufficiently well ascertained, I had little difficulty in arriving at the following results: Man has found it difficult to destroy a race of man, nor do I think that he has yet succeeded even in this; still it is a possible event apparently, but he has not yet succeeded in effecting it. To *create* a race of men or animals is entirely beyond his power. A Mexican nation may be formed by a protocol, a treaty, a victory; an illustrious robber may found a nation; an iron despot may chain together the free Saxon and the slavish Pruss; another may yoke in common chains the Slavonian and the German, the Italian and the Hun; but will such things have a permanence? Consult history, and you will find that it cannot be. Still less can any power create a Mexican or Peruvian people, or race. Look at the elements of Mr. Canning's free states; analyze them; try them by any of the physiological laws I have spoken of, and observe the result. A Celt-Iberian and Lusitanian population make a descent on America; Old Spain and Portugal send forth their emigrants—men of a race already decaying, men of a province of Rome, an off-set of Carthage—a combination of races themselves in decay, and tottering to their fall. These, under some bold leaders, seize on Southern and Central America, consolidate their power as masters, and enter on absolute possession of the soil; one-half a vast continent becomes thus a mere province of two paltry European states. During this period of 300 years, all things were favourable for an absolute consolidation with Spain and Portugal—undisturbed possession, peace, continual emigration, wealth. Where are they now? When the act of separation from the so-called mother country took place, the population of Mexico and Peru consisted of—1, pure Spaniards, whether European or Creole it matters not; 2, pure Indians, that is, the original and only true American—the native; 3, a motley crew, composed of a mixture of these, more or less tinged; 4, a sprinkling of Negro blood, pure, or mixed with the Indian and the European. By the act of disunion, the influx of European blood, by which alone the pure race could be maintained against climate, and against the continual aggression of the other more numerous races, was suddenly withdrawn; even now it rapidly disappears, and in a century it will have become extinct, for in these climates a European race cannot labour, cannot appropriate the soil to themselves, cannot multiply their offspring. But, secondly, with the cessation of the supply of European blood, the mulatto of all shades must also cease; he cannot extend his race, for he is of no race; there is no place for him in nature. So soon as he has no longer the pure blood of some other race to intermingle with, he ceases to be, receding towards the black, or advancing to the white, as the case may be; thus the population I speak of lost by Mr. Canning's act, or will lose in time, the main-spring of their population, falling back on the *native*, that is, the American Indian—the race implanted there by nature—the race in unison with the forest and the climate, the soil, the air, the place—the race of whose origin man knows nothing, any more than he does of the lama and the tapir, the cavia and the condor—the vegetable and animal world of that continent on which Columbus gazed with such delight. All these he found distinct from the rest of the world; and so was the American man from his fellow man, as different as is the nandu from the ostrich, the lama from the camel.

But this last element of population, on which the Mexican and Peruvian and Chilian no doubt were thus thrown back, had already mysteriously run its course; they were on the decline when Cortes landed; they had passed through their determined eras and civilization; on the curved line indicating their course they seemed to have passed the zenith; their population then, as it is now, was on the wane—was gradually becoming extinct. This the motley group called Mexicans and Peruvians now feel—they are instinctively conscious that the period approaches when all again must become desert or Indian—a moral or a physical desert; absence of life or absence of mind. But for the Saxon invasion from the north, it might have happened in Mexico and Peru, and in Chili, that the desolation of these countries—say a hundred years hence—would have burst on Europe as an astounding and inexplicable fact. The man of the United States, who as yet delights in no name, might have walked into the land without any interruption or hindrance from any race. Penetrating to the centre of the so-called Empire, he might have once more seen the sacrificial fires kindled on the pyramids of Cholula. A native population of nearly pure Indian would once more have regained its ascendency, to perish ultimately—to return to that nothing out of which they came.

But now the Saxon, grasping at more wealth, more land, comes in as a new element upon the already effete creations of Canning. Will he fare better? Will he be able to extinguish a race—the Indian of South America—and put himself in its place? I believe not, in that climate at least. Will he succeed even in North America? Is the boasted Union to be permanent? The pettifogging politicians of the day say, seriously and gravely, that in their opinions it must come to a monarchy at last! Profound politicians! A half dozen monarchies at last—a king of New York, a Leopold installed in Kentucky, an Otho in Michigan, a liberal despotism under a prince of the noble house of Brunswick or Brandenburg. But you forget that these people are Saxons—democrats by their nature. Look at the Dutch Saxon at the Cape, a handful of Boors—yes, a mere handful of Boors—bearding your best cavalry officer at the head of six regiments. You have yet to discover the true nature of the *Saxon*; you will not yet understand it, and yet you received a sharp lesson at Boston and at New Orleans, losing the mightiest colony ever founded by any race or nation. Australia comes next; then South Africa; your Norman government cannot profit by experience. But to return.

As the Southern States of America become depopulated by the operation of the physiological laws laid down, that vast land will fall an easy prey to the Saxon and Celtic races now occupying the northern States. That they will ultimately seize on them there cannot be a doubt, driving before them the expiring remains of native and Lusitanian, Celt-Iberian and Mulatto—a worthless race—effete, exhausted, before even Hannibal and a handful of Carthaginians held the country from which they sprung as a mere appendage of Carthage. A single Roman legion was enough for Old Spain; it could hold it yet. The United States men, the descendents of Anglo-Saxon, the Fleming and Celt, with a sprinkling of South and Middle German, are now in possession of North America—it seems to be absolutely theirs: they form a union—they begin to talk of natives and foreigners—they have forgotten who they are, and fancy themselves *Americans* because they choose to call themselves so; just as our West India planters might have assumed the name and title of native true-born Caribs. The "United States man" believes himself to be independent of Europe, by which, if he means anything, he must mean independent of the *race* or races from which he sprung.

Now, before I apply this great question to the present United States men, trace back with me the narrative, the chronicle of events called history. If history be philosophy (which I doubt) teaching by examples, it should enlighten us somewhat on such questions as these—the extinction of one race by another, and the substitution of one race for another. The world, with man on it, is said to be not old; and yet the end of the world we are told approaches; the millennium is at hand; the Jews are becoming Christians; the Celtic Irish abandoning pagan Rome, and adopting the Saxon ritual, as by law established! Do not believe those who tell you so. Nature alters, no doubt; but *physical* changes must precede the *moral*, and I see no symptoms of such.

The chronicles called histories tell us that the Roman empire extended from the Clyde and Forth to the Tigris and Euphrates. Northern, extra-tropical Africa was said to be thoroughly Roman; Italy, of course, was Roman to the core. Where are the Romans now? What races have they destroyed? What races have they supplanted? For fourteen centuries they lorded it over the semi-civilized world; and now they are of no more note than the ancient Scythians or Mongols, Copts or Tartars. They established themselves nowhere as Romans. Perhaps they never were a race at all. But be this as it may, they destroyed no other race, supplanted no other race: and now look over the map of their empire, and tell me where you find a physical vestige of the race; on the Thames or Danube, Rhine or Guadalquivir, Rhone or Nile. Italy itself seems all but clear of them. Southern Italy was Græcia Magna before they invaded it; and Sicily is even now more Greek than Italian. Byzantium was a Roman city, and so was York. And so it is with other conquering races. Northern Africa never was Phænician, properly speaking, any more than Algiers is Celtic now, or India English. Even in Corsica the Celtic race of France have failed to establish themselves, though, from its proximity to France and presumed analogy of climate, and, as has been erroneously asserted, of races, there seems no reason why Corsica should not become Celtic or French. But it is not so. The Corsicans are not Celts, they are not Frenchmen; nor are the Sardinians Italians, properly speaking. It is not merely the empires of Rome and Carthage which have become extinct in Northern Africa; it is the races which founded these empires that are no longer to be found there. It may perhaps be urged, that Northern Africa never really was either Carthaginian or Roman; but this does not affect the question, which is, Can one race supplant another on a soil foreign to their nature; foreign to their origin?

The Greeks, who, under Alexander, marched victorious to the Indus, supplanted no other race. Rome and Carthage failed. Attila and his Huns also failed; and so did the Mongol. The remnant of Huns in Hungary now struggle for existence; they are interlopers seemingly amongst the Slavonian race, and will probably perish. But neither have the Slavonians succeeded in supplanting the Italian, though masters, under the name of Austrian and Germans, of Italy for nearly ten centuries. For at least two thousand years have the Scandinavian and South Germans made war on the Celtic race in the west, and made head against the Sarmatian and Slavonian races in the east, without advancing a single step, in so far as I can discover. These races hold the same position to each other which they did in the remotest period of authentic history.

The whole force of the so-called German Empire, headed by Austria, could not dislodge the Slavonian from Bohemia; the Norman, though he met in South

England a kindred race, could not destroy the *Saxon race* of North England. To this day the country seems to be divided between them, notwithstanding the centralizing influence of Flemish London. The Celts still hold the western limits of Britain and Ireland, just as they did before the period of authentic history.

But it may be said, England is a colony from Scandinavia, from Holstein, and Jutland; Ireland seemingly of Spain; the Celtic colony has not been prosperous; nevertheless, numerically it has thriven; the Saxon colony has succeeded to admiration. The parent country of the Anglo-Saxon, ancient Scandinavia, has withered in presence of the blighting influence of the abhorred Sarmatian (Russ and Pruss) and Slavonian (Hapsburg—Gotho-Austrian) governments. Why may not, then, the Celt prosper in Africa—the Saxon in Australia, in Southern Africa, in Northern America? Do we not see how the Saxon thrives in these countries? Look at the population of the States! Mark its progress; and then admit the fact that man was made to thrive everywhere. Should this argument fail, the Utopian falls back on a final cause: "Vast regions are deserted; why not occupy them? Is it not clear that they were intended to be occupied by man?" Lastly, they go back on the humanities, and claim for a suffering, over-stocked population, the sad privilege designed them by a wise Providence, to quit the land of their birth, and seize on the soil of any other race who promise the richest spoils with the least resistance. This is the Utopian, the man of final causes, of necessities, humanities, and expediencies. What has science to do with such notions?

Charles Darwin's great book On the Origin of Species *changed the way many naturalists viewed the natural world; but Darwin did not apply his theory of natural selection to human beings until twelve years after the book's publication. As this selection makes clear, by the time Darwin took up the question of humans and natural selection, he was joining an ongoing spirited debate among other naturalists regarding the applicability of his theory of organic change to the racial question. This selection highlights the gradualism that pervaded all of Darwin's thought, as he argued that firm lines could not be drawn between races, or, indeed, between species.*

The Descent of Man, and Selection in Relation to Sex

CHARLES DARWIN

The question whether mankind consists of one or several species has of late years been much agitated by anthropologists, who are divided into the two schools of monogenists and polygenists. Those who do not admit the principle of evolution, must look at species either as separate creations or in some manner distinct entities; and they must decide what forms to rank as species by the analogy of other organic beings which are commonly thus received. But it is a hopeless endeavour to decide this point on sound grounds, until some definition of the term "species" is generally accepted; and the definition must not include an element which cannot possibly be ascertained, such as an act of creation. We might as well attempt without any definition to decide whether a certain number of houses should be called a village, or town, or city. We have a practical illustration of the difficulty in the never-ending doubts whether many closely-allied mammals, birds, insects, and plants, which represent each other in North America and Europe, should be ranked species or geographical races; and so it is with the productions of many islands situated at some little distance from the nearest continent.

Those naturalists, on the other hand, who admit the principle of evolution, and this is now admitted by the greater number of rising men, will feel no doubt that all the races of man are descended from a single primitive stock; whether or not they think fit to designate them as distinct species, for the sake of expressing their amount of difference[1]. With our domestic animals the question whether the various races have arisen from one or more species is different. Although all such races, as well as all the natural species within the same genus, have undoubtedly sprung from the same primitive stock, yet it is a fit subject for discussion, whether, for instance, all the domestic races of the dog have acquired their present differences since some one species was first domesticated and bred by man; or whether they owe some of their characters to inheritance from distinct species, which had already been modified in a state of nature. With mankind no such question can arise, for he cannot be said to have been domesticated at any particular period.

When the races of man diverged at an extremely remote epoch from their common progenitor, they will have differed but little from each other, and been few in number; consequently they will then, as far as their distinguishing characters are concerned, have had less claim to rank as distinct species, than the existing so-called races. Nevertheless such early races would perhaps have been ranked by some naturalists as distinct species, so arbitrary is the term, if their differences, although extremely slight, had been more constant than at present, and had not graduated into each other.

It is, however, possible, though far from probable, that the early progenitors of man might at first have diverged much in character, until they became more unlike each other than are any existing races; but that subsequently, as suggested by Vogt[2], they converged in character. When man selects for the same object the offspring of two distinct species, he sometimes induces, as far as general appearance is concerned, a considerable amount of convergence. This is the case, as shewn by Von Nathusius[3], with the improved breeds of the pig, which are descended from two distinct species; and in a less well-marked manner with the improved breeds of cattle. A great anatomist, Gratiolet, maintains that the anthropomorphous apes do not form a natural sub-group; but that the orang is a highly developed gibbon or semnopithecus; the chimpanzee a highly developed macacus; and the gorilla a highly developed mandrill. If this conclusion, which rests almost exclusively on brain-characters, be admitted, we should have a case of convergence at least in external characters, for the anthropomorphous apes are certainly more like each other in many points than they are to other apes. All analogical resemblances, as of a whale to a fish, may indeed be said to be cases of convergence; but this term has never been applied to superficial and adaptive resemblances. It would be extremely rash in most cases to attribute to convergence close similarity in many points of structure in beings which had once been widely different. The form of a crystal is determined solely by the molecular forces, and it is not surprising that dissimilar substances should sometimes assume the same form; but with organic beings we should bear in mind that the form of each depends on an infinitude of complex relations, namely on variations which have arisen, these being due to causes far too intricate to be followed,—on the nature of the variations which have been preserved, and this depends on the surrounding physical conditions, and in a still higher degree on the surrounding organisms with which each has come into competition,—and lastly, on inheritance (in itself a fluctuating element) from innumerable progenitors, all of which have had their forms determined through equally complex relations. It appears utterly incredible that two organisms, if differing in a marked manner, should ever afterwards converge so closely as to lead to a near approach to identity throughout their whole organisation. In the case of the convergent pigs above referred to, evidence of their descent from two primitive stocks is still plainly retained, according to Von Nathusius, in certain bones of their skulls. If the races of man were descended, as supposed by some naturalists, from two or more distinct species, which had differed as much, or nearly as much, from each other, as the orang differs from the gorilla, it can hardly be doubted that marked differences in the structure of certain bones would still have been discoverable in man as he now exists.

Although the existing races of man differ in many respects, as in colour, hair, shape of skull, proportions of the body, &c., yet if their whole organisation be taken into consideration they are found to resemble each other closely in a multitude of points. Many of these points are of so unimportant or of so singular a nature, that it is extremely improbable that they should have been independently acquired by aboriginally distinct species or races. The same remark holds good with equal or greater force with respect to the numerous points of mental similarity between the most distinct races of man. The American aborigines, Negroes and Europeans differ as much from each other in mind as any three races that can be named; yet I was incessantly struck, whilst living with the Feugians on board the "Beagle," with the many little traits of character, shewing how similar their minds were to ours; and so it was with a full-blooded negro with whom I happened once to be intimate.

He who will carefully read Mr. Tylor's and Sir J. Lubbock's interesting works[4] can hardly fail to be deeply impressed with the close similarity between the men of all races in tastes, dispositions and habits. This is shewn by the pleasure which they all take in dancing, rude music, acting, painting, tattooing, and otherwise decorating themselves,—in their mutual comprehension of gesture-language—and, as I shall be able to shew in a future essay, by the same expression in their features, and by the same inarticulate cries, when excited by various emotions. This similarity, or rather identity, is striking, when contrasted with the different expressions which may be observed in distinct species of monkeys. There is good evidence that the art of shooting with bows and arrows has not been handed down from any common progenitor of mankind, yet the stone arrow-heads, brought from the most distant parts of the world and manufactured at the most remote periods, are, as Nilsson has shewn[5], almost identical; and this fact can only be accounted for by the various races having similar inventive or mental powers. The same observation has been made by archaeologists[6] with respect to certain widely-prevalent ornaments, such as zigzags, &c.; and with respect to various simple beliefs and customs, such as the burying of the dead under megalithic structures. I remember observing in South America[7], that there, as in so many other parts of the world, man has generally chosen the summits of lofty hills, on which to throw up piles of stones, either for the sake of recording some remarkable event, or for burying his dead.

Now when naturalists observe a close agreement in numerous small details of habits, tastes and dispositions between two or more domestic races, or between nearly-allied natural forms, they use this fact as an argument that all are descended from a common progenitor who was thus endowed; and consequently that all should be classed under the same species. The same argument may be applied with much force to the races of man.

As it is improbable that the numerous and unimportant points of resemblance between the several races of man in bodily structure and mental faculties (I do not here refer to similar customs) should all have been independently acquired, they must have been inherited from progenitors who were thus characterised. We thus gain some insight into the early state of man, before he had spread step by step over the face of the earth. The spreading of man to regions widely separated by the sea, no doubt, preceded any considerable amount of divergence of character in the several races; for otherwise we should sometimes meet with the same race in distinct continents; and this is never the case. Sir J. Lubbock, after comparing the arts now practised by savages in all parts of the world, specifies those which man could not have known, when he first wandered from his original birth-place; for if once learnt they would never have been for-gotten[8]. He thus shews that "the spear, which is but a development of the knife-point, and the club, which is but a long hammer, are the only things left." He admits, however, that the art of making fire probably had been already discov-ered, for it is common to all the races now existing, and was known to the ancient cave-inhabitants of Europe. Perhaps the art of making rude canoes or rafts was likewise known; but as man existed at a remote epoch, when the land in many places stood at a very different level, he would have been able, without the aid of canoes, to have spread widely. Sir J. Lubbock further remarks how improbable it is that our earliest ancestors could have "counted as high as ten, considering that so many races now in existence cannot get beyond four." Nevertheless, at this early period, the intellectual and social faculties of man could hardly have been inferior in any extreme degree to those now possessed by the lowest savages; oth-erwise primeval man could not have been so eminently successful in the struggle for life, as proved by his early and wide diffusion.

From the fundamental differences between certain languages, some philol-ogists have inferred that when man first became widely diffused he was not a speaking animal; but it may be suspected that languages, far less perfect than any now spoken, aided by gestures, might have been used, and yet have left no traces on subsequent and more highly-developed tongues. Without the use of some lan-guage, however imperfect, it appears doubtful whether man's intellect could have risen to the standard implied by his dominant position at an early period.

Whether primeval man, when he possessed very few arts of the rudest kind, and when his power of language was extremely imperfect, would have deserved to be called man, must depend on the definition which we employ. In a series of forms graduating insensibly from some ape-like creature to man as he now exists, it would be impossible to fix on any definite point when the term "man" ought to be used. But this is a matter of very little importance. So again, it is almost a matter of indifference whether the so-called races of man are thus des-ignated, or are ranked as species or sub-species; but the latter term appears the most appropriate. Finally, we may conclude that when the principles of evolution are generally accepted, as they surely will be before long, the dispute between the monogenists and the polygenists will die a silent and unobserved death.

One other question ought not to be passed over without notice, namely, whether, as is sometimes assumed, each sub-species or race of man has sprung from a single pair of progenitors. With our domestic animals a new race can readily be formed from a single pair possessing some new character, or even from a single individual thus characterised, by carefully matching the varying offspring; but most of our races have been formed, not intentionally from a selected pair, but unconsciously by the preservation of many individuals which have varied, however slightly, in some useful or desired manner. If in one country stronger and heavier horses, and in another country lighter and fleeter horses, were habitually preferred, we may feel sure that two distinct sub-breeds would, in the course of time, be produced, without any particular pairs or individuals having been separated and bred from in either country. Many races have been thus formed, and their manner of formation is closely analogous with that of natural species. We know, also, that the horses which have been brought to the Falkland Islands have become, during successive generations, smaller and weaker, whilst those which have run wild on the Pampas have acquired larger and coarser heads; and such changes are manifestly due, not to any one pair, but to all the individuals having been subjected to the same conditions, aided, perhaps, by the principle of reversion. The new sub-breeds in none of these cases are descended from any single pair, but from many individuals which have varied in different degrees, but in the same general manner; and we may conclude that the races of man have been similarly produced, the modifications being either the direct result of exposure to different conditions, or the indirect result of some form of selection. But to this latter subject we shall presently return.

Notes

1   See Prof. Huxley to this effect in the Fortnightly Review 1865, p. 275.

2   "Lecture on Man." Eng. Translat. 1864, p. 468.

3   "Die Racen des Schweines." 1860, s. 46. "Vorsteudien für Geschichte, &c., Schweineschädel." 1864, s. 104. With respect to cattle, see M. de Quatrefages, "Unité de l'Espèce Humaine." 1861, p. 119.

4   Tylor's "Early History of Mankind," 1865; for the evidence with respect to gesture-language, see p. 54. Lubbock's "Prehistoric Times," 2nd edit. 1869.

5   "The Primitive Inhabitatns of Scandinavia," Eng. Translat. Edited by Sir J. Lubbock, 1868, p. 104.

6   Hodder M. Westropp, on Cromlechs, &c., "Journal of Wthnological Soc." As given in Scientific Opinion, June 2nd, 1869, p. 3.

7   "Journal of Researches: Voyage of the 'Beagle,'" p. 46.

8   "Prehistoric Times," 1869, p. 574.

If one reads this selection from William Z. Ripley in conjunction with
the selection from Johann Friedrich Blumenbach one is struck by how
little progress taxonomists made in the 125 years that separated the two
writers. Like Blumenbach, Ripley notes the confusion among
anthropologists regarding the number of races and how to properly
identify a race. He clearly outlines the difficulties that any given racial
trait is going to be evident in any number of racial groups and that
there will be great overlap in the distribution of racial traits.
Nonetheless, Ripley persists and finally concludes that the failure of
science to identify a perfect racial type should be no bar to the scientific
study of race.

The Races of Europe: A Sociological Study

WILLIAM Z. RIPLEY

It may smack of heresy to assert, in face of the teaching of all our text-books on geography and history, that there is no single European or white race of men; and yet that is the plain truth of the matter. Science has advanced since Linnæus' single type of *Homo Europæus albus* was made one of the four great races of mankind[1]. No continental group of human beings with greater diversities or extremes of physical type exists. That fact accounts in itself for much of our advance in culture. We have already shown in the preceding chapters that entire communities of the tallest and shortest of men as well as the longest and broadest headed ones, are here to be found within the confines of Europe. Even in respect of the colour of the skin, hair, and eyes, responsible more than all else for the misnomer "white race," the greatest variations occur[2]. To be sure, the several types are to-day all more or less blended together by the unifying influences of civilization; there are few sharp contrasts in Europe such as those between the Eskimo and the American Indian, or the Malay and the Papuan in other parts of the world. We have been deceived by this in the past. It is high time for us to correct our ideas on the subject, especially in our school and college teaching.

Instead of a single European type there is indubitable evidence of at least three distinct races, each possessed of a history of its own, and each contributing something to the common product, population, as we see it to-day. If this be established it does away at one fell swoop with most of the current mouthings about Aryans and pre-Aryans; and especially with such appellations as the "Caucasian" or the "Indo-Germanic" race. Supposing for present peace that it be allowed that the ancestors of some peoples of Europe may once have been within sight of either the Caspian Sea or the Himalayas, we have still left two thirds of our European races and population out of account. As yet it is too early to discuss the events in the history of these races; that will claim our attention at a later time. The present task before us is to establish first of all that three such racial types exist in Europe.

The sceptic is already prepared perhaps to admit that what we have said about the several physical characteristics, such as the shape of the head, stature, and the like, may all be true. But he will continue to doubt that these offer evidence of distinct races because ordinary observation may detect such gross inconsistencies on every hand. Even in the most secluded hamlet of the Alps, where population has remained undisturbed for thousands of years, he will be able to point out blond-haired children whose parents were dark, short sons of tall fathers, and the like. Diversities confront us on every hand even in the most retired corner of Europe. What may we not anticipate in more favoured places, especially in the large cities?

Traits in themselves are all right, our objector will maintain: but you must show that they are hereditary, persistent. More than that, you must prove not alone the transmissibility of a single trait by itself, you must also show that combinations of traits are so handed down from father to son. Three stages in the development of our proof must be noted: first, the distribution of separate *traits;* secondly, their association into *types;* and, lastly, the hereditary character of these types which alone justifies the term *races.* We have already taken the first step: we are now essaying the second. It is highly important that we should keep these distinct. Even among professed anthropologists there is still much confusion of thought upon the subject—so much so, in fact, that some have, it seems to us without warrant, abandoned the task in despair. Let us beware the example of the monkey in the fable. Seeking to withdraw a huge handful of racial nuts from the jar of fact, we may find the neck of scientific possibility all too small. We may fail because we have grasped too much at once. Let us examine.

There are two ways in which we may seek to assemble our separate physical traits into types—that is, to combine characteristics into living personalities. The one is purely anthropological, the other inferential and geographical in its nature. The first of these is simple. Answer is sought to a direct question. In a given population, are the blonds more often tall than the brunets, or the reverse? Is the greater proportion of the tall men at the same time distinctly longer-headed or otherwise? and the like. If the answers to these questions be constant and consistent, our work is accomplished. Unfortunately, they are not always so, hence our necessary recourse to the geographical proof: but they at least indicate a slight trend, which we may follow up by the other means.

Let it be boldly confessed at the outset that in the greater number of cases no invariable association of traits in this way occurs. This is especially true among the people of the central part of Europe. The population of Switzerland, for example, is persistently aberrant in this respect; it is everything anthropologically that it ought not to be. This should not surprise us. In the first place, mountainous areas always contain the "ethnological sweepings of the plains," as Canon Taylor puts it. Especially is this true when the mountains lie in the very heart of the continent, at a focus of racial immigration. Moreover, the environment is competent to upset all probabilities, as we hope to have shown. Suppose a brunet type from the south should come to Andermatt and settle. If altitude, indeed, exerts an influence upon pigmentation, as we have sought to prove; or if its concomitant poverty in the ante-tourist era should depress the stature; racial equilibrium is as good as vanished in two or three generations. It is therefore only where the environment is simple; and especially on the outskirts of the continent, where migration and intermixture are more infrequent; that any constant and normal association of traits may be anticipated. Take a single example from many. We have always been taught, since the days of Tacitus, to regard the Teutonic peoples—the Goths, Lombards, and Saxons—as tawny-haired, "large-limbed giants." History is filled with observations to that effect from the earliest times[3]. Our maps have already led us to infer as much. Nevertheless, direct observations show that tall stature and blondness are by no means constant companions in the same person. In Scandinavia, Dr. Arbo asserts, I think, that the tallest men are at the same time inclined to be blond. In Italy, on the other edge of the continent, the same combination is certainly prevalent[4]. Over in Russia, once more on the outskirts of Europe[5], the tall men are again said to be lighter complexioned as a rule. In the British Isles[6], in Holstein[7], in parts of Brittany[8] and southern France[9], in Savoy[10], and in Würtemberg[11] it is more often true than otherwise. But if we turn to other parts of Europe we are completely foiled. The association in the same individual of stature and blondness fails or is reversed in Bavaria[12], in Baden[13], along the Adriatic[14], in Poland[15], and in upper Austria and Salzburg[16], as well as among the European recruits observed in America during our civil war[17]. It seems to be significant, however, that when the association fails, as in the highlands of Austria; where the environment is eliminated, as in lower Austria, the tall men again become characteristically more blond than the short ones. In this last case environment is to blame; in others, racial intermixture, or it may be merely chance variation, is the cause[18].

In order to avoid disappointment, let us bear in mind that in no other part of the world save modern America is such an amalgamation of various peoples to be found as in Europe. History, and archæology long before history, show us a continual picture of tribes appearing and disappearing, crossing and recrossing in their migrations, assimilating, dividing, colonizing, conquering, or being absorbed. It follows from this, that, even if the environment were uniform, our pure types must be exceedingly rare. Experience proves that the vast majority of the population of this continent shows evidence of crossing, so that in general

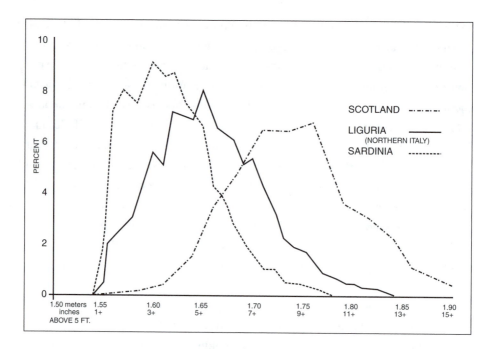

we can not expect that more than one third of the people will be marked by the simplest combination of traits. We need not be surprised, therefore, that if we next seek to add a third characteristic, say the shape of the head, to a normal combination of hair and eyes, we find the proportion of pure types combining all three traits in a fixed measure to be very small indeed. Imagine a fourth trait, stature, or a fifth, nose, to be added, and our proportion of pure types becomes almost infinitesimal. We are thus reduced to the extremity in which my friend Dr. Ammon, of Baden, found himself, when I wrote asking for photographs of a pure Alpine type from the Black Forest. He has measured thousands of heads, and yet he answered that he really had not been able to find a perfect specimen in all details. All his round-headed men were either blond, or tall, or narrow-nosed, or something else that they ought not to be.

Confronted by this situation, the tyro is here tempted to turn back in despair. There is no justification for it. It is not essential to our position, that we should actually be able to isolate any considerable number, nor even a single one, of our *perfect* racial types in the life. It matters not to us that never more than a small majority of any given population possesses even two physical characteristics in their proper association; that relatively few of these are able to add a third to the combination; and that almost no individuals show a perfect union of all traits under one head, so to speak, while contradictions and mixed types are everywhere present. Such a condition of affairs need not disturb us if we understand ourselves aright. We should indeed be perplexed were it otherwise.

Consider how complex the problem really is! We say the people of Scotland are on the average among the tallest in Europe. True! But that does not exclude a considerable number of medium and undersized persons from among them. We may illustrate the actual condition best by means of the accompanying diagram[19]. Three curves are plotted therein for the stature of large groups of men chosen at random from each of three typical parts of Europe. The one at the right is for the tall Scotch, the middle one for the medium-sized northern Italians, and the one at the left for Sardinians, the people of this island being among the shortest in all Europe. The height of each curve at any given point indicates the percentage within each group of men, which possessed the stature marked at the base of that vertical line. Thus eight per cent of the Ligurian men were five feet five inches tall (1.65 metres), while nine per cent of the Sardinians were fully two inches shorter (1.60 metres). In either case these several heights were the most common, although in no instance is the proportion considerable at a given stature. There is, however, for each country or group of men, some point about which the physical trait clusters. Thus the largest percentage of a given stature among the Scotch occurs at about five feet nine inches and a half. Yet a very large number of them, about five per cent, fall within the group of five feet seven inches (1.70 metres)—that is to say, no taller than an equal percentage of the Ligurians—and even in Sardinia there is an appreciable number of that stature. We must understand, therefore, when we say that the Scotch are a tall people or a long-headed or blond one; that we mean thereby, not that all the people are peculiar in this respect even to a slight degree, but merely that in this region there are more specimens of these special types than elsewhere. Still it remains that the great mass of the people are merely neutral. This is a more serious obstacle to overcome than direct contradictions. They merely whet the appetite. Our most difficult problem is to separate the typical wheat from the non-committal straw; to distinguish our racial types from the general mean or average which everywhere constitutes the overwhelming majority of the population.

We have now seen how limited are the racial results attainable by the first of our two means of identification—that is, the purely somatological one. It has appeared that only in the most simple conditions are the several traits constant and faithful to one another in their association in the same persons. Nor are we justified in asking for more. Our three racial types are not radically distinct seeds which, once planted in the several parts of Europe, have there taken root; and, each preserving its peculiarities intact, have spread from those centres outward until they have suddenly run up against one another along a racial frontier. Such was the old-fashioned view of races, in the days before the theory of evolution had remodelled our ways of thinking—when human races were held to be distinct creations of a Divine will. We conceive of it all quite differently. These types for us are all necessarily offshoots from the same trunk. The problem is far more complex to us for this reason. It is doubly dynamic. Up-building and demolition are taking place at the same time. By our constitution of racial types we seek to simplify the matter—for a moment to lose sight of all the destructive forces, and from obscure tendencies to derive ideal results. We picture an anthropological goal which might have been attained had the life conditions only been less complicated.

Are we in this more presumptuous than other natural scientists? Is the geologist more certain of his deductions, in his restoration of an ideal mountain chain from the denuded roots which alone bear witness to the fact to-day? In this case all the superstructure has long since disappeared. The restoration is no less scientific. It represents more clearly than aught else, the rise and disappearance, the results and future tendencies of great geological movements. We take no more liberties with our racial types than the geologist with his mountains; nor do we mean more by our restorations. The parallel is instructive. The geologist is well aware that the uplifted folds as he depicts them never existed in completeness at any given time. He knows full well that erosion took place even as lateral pressure raised the contorted strata; that one may even have been the cause of the other. If indeed denudation could have been postponed until all the elevation of the strata had been accomplished, then the restoration of the mountain chain would stand for a once real but now vanished thing. This, the geologist is well aware, was not thus and so. In precisely the same sense do we conceive of our races. Far be it from us to assume that these three races of ours ever, in the history of mankind, existed in absolute purity or isolation from one another. As soon might the branch grow separate and apart from the parent oak. No sooner have environmental influences, peculiar habits of life, and artificial selection commenced to generate distinct varieties of men from the common clay; no sooner has heredity set itself to perpetuating these; than chance variation, migration, intermixture, and changing environments, with a host of minor dispersive factors, begin to efface this constructive work. Racial upbuilding and demolition, as we have said, have ever proceeded side by side. Never is the perfect type in view, while yet it is always possible. "Race," says Topinard ([79]), "in the present state of things is an abstract conception, a notion of continuity in discontinuity, of unity in diversity. It is the rehabilitation of a real but directly unattainable thing." In this sense alone do we maintain that there are three ideal racial types in Europe to be distinguished from one another. They have often dissolved in the common population; each particular trait has gone its own way; so that at the present time rarely, if indeed ever, do we discover a single individual corresponding to our racial type in every detail. It exists for us nevertheless.

Notes

1   The progress of classification, chronologically, is indicated in our supplementary Bibliography, under the index title of Races. It is significant of the slow infiltration of scientific knowledge into secondary literature that the latest and perhaps best geographical text-book in America still teaches the unity of the European or "Aryan" race. Zoölogical authorities also in English seem to be unaware of the present state of our information. Thus Flower and Lyddeker in their great work on the mammals make absolutely no craniological distinctions. They have not advanced a whit beyond the theory of the "oval head" of a half century ago.

On the latest and most elaborate classification, that by Deniker, consult our Appendix D.

2   Huxley's (1870) celebrated classification into Melanochroi and Xanthochroi is based on this entirely.

3   Hervé, 1897, gives many texts. Cf. also references in Taylor, 1890, p. 108.

4   Livi, 1896 a, pp. 74, 76, 143.

5   Zograf, 1892 a, p. 173; though denied by Anutchin, 1893, p. 285, and Eichholz, 1896, p. 40.

6   Beddoe, 1867-'69 a, reprint, p. 171; also Rolleston, 1884, i, p. 279. Not true so often in Scotland.

7   Meisner, 1889, p. 118; but contradictory, p. 111; also 1891, p. 323,

8   Collignon, 1890 a, reprint, p. 15.

9   Lapouge, 1894 a, p. 498; 1897-'98, p. 314.

10 Carret, 1883, p. 106.

11 Von Hölder, 1876, p. 6; Ecker, 1876, p. 259, agrees.

12 Ranke. Beiträge zur Anth. und Urg. Bayerns, v, 1883, pp. 195 seq.; and 1886-'87, ii, p. 124.

13 Ammon, 1890, p. 14; 1899, pp. 175-184.

14 Weisbach, 1884, p. 26.

15 Elkind, 1896.

16 Weisbach, 1895 b, p. 70.

17 Baxter, 1875, i, pp. 23 and 38; with exception of the Germans, however.

18 In Appendix E, the association of the other primary physical traits in individuals is discussed.

19 The curve for the Scotch, taken from the Report of the Anthropometric Committee of the British Association for the Advancement of Science for 1883, has been arbitrarily corrected to correspond to the metric system employed by Dr. Livi in the other curves. A centimetre is roughly equal to 0.4 of an inch. It is assumed that in consequence only 0.4 as many individuals will fall within each centimetre class as in the groups of stature differing by inches. The ordinates in the Scotch diagram have therefore been reduced to 0.4 of their height in the original curve.

The best technical discussion of such curves among anthropologists will be found in Goldstein, 1883; Stieda, 1883; Ammon, 1893 and 1896 c; Livi, 1895 and 1896 a, pp. 22 et seq.; and in the works of Bowditch, Galton, etc. Emme, 1887, gives a pointed criticism of the possible fallacy in mere averages. Dr. Boas has contributed excellent material, based upon the American Indians for the most part.

*Georges Vacher de Lapouge was an enormously influential scholar
among European racial writers of the late nineteenth and early
twentieth centuries and laid some of the cornerstones for Nazi racial
ideology. Several important aspects of his thought are illustrated by
this selection. First, that racial type could be identified by skull shape,
with the dolichocephalic (long-headed) Aryans superior to the
brachycephalic (round-headed) races. Second, that Aryans could be
found everywhere there had been civilization, with the clear
implication that the Aryans were therefore responsible for the
development of that civilization. Finally, the political implication,
here blithely asserted as scientific fact, that the "dolicho-blond" Aryans
were the master class of ancient civilizations who created culture with
no input from inferior racial types.*

Old and New Aspects of the Aryan Question

Georges Vacher de Lapouge

Dominant Race among the Primitive Aryan Peoples

We take up now a subject of more direct interest, and one which does not appear
to have been as yet anywhere satisfactorily treated. It will, therefore, be necessary to enter more into detail, since there exists no literature to which I can refer
the reader.

First it is necessary clearly to understand the question. Formerly, when the
Aryan peoples were regarded as descended from a single family, it was permis-
sible to ask what was the anthropological type of that family. This manner of
view can no longer be tolerated when it is realized that the Aryan peoples proceeded from the evolution of earlier peoples. The unity of type possible within a
single family is no longer found throughout a tribe. Probably no tribe in the world
can be found entirely homogeneous, and this appears to be equally true of tribes
in the past, as far as we can study them in the light of prehistoric anthropology.

In order to solve question as formerly framed, "What was the type of he
primitive Aryan?", it would be necessary that prehistoric anthropology should
show us a homogeneous population in the region and epoch of the formation of
the first Aryan civilization. The region was that to the north of the Seine, the
Alps, the Balkans, and the western part of the Black Sea; the epoch was that of
the middle and end of the period of polished stone. Now, instead of a homogeneous population, there existed a considerable number of human types, among
which it is necessary to choose. The question ought, therefore, to be framed thus:
*Of the races present among the Aryan peoples, which race was socially pre-
dominant, to which ought the civilization to be attributed?*

It is necessary to exclude the races represented only by the servile element, or only by savage tribes existing more or less separately from the Aryan peoples, like the Indians in the United States, or only by strangers, who may have been slaves brought from a distance, or travelers or adventurers. Among every people, in fact, and especially among peoples like the early Aryans or the Indo-Chinese of the present day, it is necessary to distinguish between the element which counts and that which does not count, between that which is influential and that which simply exists within the society without playing any active roll.

This less simple aspect of the problem is more in conformity with the real conditions, but it cannot be said that the problem in this form becomes easy of solution.

Five or six thousand years before our era, at the earliest possible epoch of the beginnings of the Aryan civilization, there existed already in central Europe and the British-Scandinavian region a confused mixture of types. Later in this work we shall study them more in detail; at this point I will simply enumerate them:

1. *Homo Europœus.*—He existed everywhere from the British Isles and the north of France to Moscow and Ladoga Lake.

2. *H. spelœus.*—The so-called race of Cro-Magnon, which appears to have come from the southwest of Europe, and which from this epoch begins to be less common in a pure state, is found in the region with which we are concerned only as an accidental element, but the neolithic burial places furnish subjects who are more or less closely related to this type. It is mentioned here mainly for the sake of completeness.

3. *H. meridionalis.*—The Mediterranean race, represented by subjects sometimes pure, sometimes mixed with the two preceding races, abounds in the Long-Barrows of Great Britain. It appears to have played a smaller rôle in central Europe, but is found in some degree in the various regions.

4. *H. contractus.*—This race, which I first distinguished in the ossuaries of the Cévennes of the copper age, is found as an important element in various parts of France. It appears to have come from the northeast, and by further study its presence would probably be recognized in the neolithic series of central Europe.

5. *Pygmy races.*—The excavations of the Schweizersbild have furnished examples of dolichocephalic pygmies with long narrow faces, who differ from *H. contractus*, and who may be regarded as a distinct race.

6. *H. hyperboreus.*—This, the characteristic race of the Laps, has been found in the dolmens and other neolithic sepultures in Denmark, Sweden, and

the north of Russia. Its presence in Belgium appears to be established by one of the skulls of Sclaigneaux and by other remains.

7. *Race of Borreby*—Another brachycephalic race, but of tall stature and with a broad high face, has been found in several localities, notably in Denmark and the British Isles. This race appears only at the very end of the neolithic epoch. It is probably the result of a cross between *H. Europœus* and some brachycephalic race of tall stature analogous to *H. Dinaricus.* Some remains in central Europe may be assigned to this last race. These tall brachycephalics have been wrongly associated with certain mixed Mongolian races. There is nothing in common between them except the characteristics resulting from the presence of *Acrogonus* among the common ancestors of these races.

8. *Race of Furfooz.*—This race, also a mixed one, played a rôle of some importance in the western part of central Europe toward the end of the polished-stone period. It has been wrongly associated with the Finns, who appear to be mixed races of recent formation, for the different Finnic types of the present day do not appear in the sepultures before the Middle Ages. No trace of them is found in the neolithic or protohistoric tombs of Russia.

9. *H. Alpinus.*—I cite this form of half-breed of *Acrogonus* mainly for the sake of completeness, for I am not sure that it is allowable to assign it to the various neolithic skulls hitherto regarded as "Celto-Slav."

10. *Acrogonus.*—I cite also for the sake of completeness this type, whose existence is proved by the existence of mixed races which sprang therefrom, and necessarily, too, in various localities, for they inherit a part of their characteristics from the local races of each region from Galacia to Tibet.

I do not deem it necessary to include in this enumeration *H. Asiaticus*, the Chinese type, which, originating in Kashgaria, appears to have moved constantly toward the east, nor the cross between it and *Acrogonus*, the Mongol in the proper sense, so unhappily designated by Bory as *H. Scythicus*[1].

Of all these races only one is found everywhere in the neolithic sepultures—the dolichocephalic-blond, *Homo Europœus.* In certain regions this type is found alone, in forms varying somewhat, but often identical with those of the present population of the same locality. In other sections it is represented by individuals of practically pure race, and also by cross-breeds, in which the type is, however, clearly recognizable. In most localities, however, this race is found represented by only a part, perhaps one-half, of the remains in the sepultures. Among the other elements the brachycephalics become more and more numerous toward the end of the polished-stone period, and they are represented by very diverse types, the greater part of which do not correspond to any fixed race existing at the present day.

The remains that are found in the sepultures of the polished-stone period probably do not represent accurately the relative proportion of the different races in the population of the time. A careful study of the sepultures leads to the conclusion that the skulls and other bones belong almost exclusively to the chiefs or to families above the masses of the people, and these remains belong almost uniformly to *H. Europæus* or to crosses between this race and other races occupying apparently a lower position in the social scale. On the other hand, it is only rarely that these sepultures contain individuals distinctly typical of races other than the dolichocephalic-blond. The subjects who do not belong to this race appear to be women taken from the inferior classes or from savage races living in juxtaposition to the Aryan civilization, half-breeds resulting from chance unions, and sometimes simply slaves put to death to accompany their masters in the other world. Apart from such cases of joint interment, the representatives, probably more numerous than is often supposed, of the slaves of foreign race, and of savages living on the confines of the relative civilization of the Aryans, do not appear to have practiced modes of burial capable of transmitting their bones to us. I may cite, as a typical example, *H. contractus*, the rigorously pure examples of which are all feminine.

We reach, then, the conclusion that the dominant class among the primitive Aryans was dolicho-blond. Whether that predominance was at once social and numerical, or merely social, matters little. The civilization of a people is the creation of the master class, even if with the language it is shared by the slaves, the serfs, and the foreign element. Our solution of the Aryan question is, then, the identification, in the sense and in the degree indicated above, of the Aryan with *H. Europæus*.

Notes
1   No one has maintained seriously the Asiatic origin of the dolichocephalic-brown race, although their affinities with the most ancient populations of the Orient are incontestable. It is the same for the dolichocephalic-blond race; those writers who regard it as originating in the south of Russia have not connected it by any genealogical tie with the yellow races. It is different, however, in the case of the brachycephalics who have been for a long time regarded as directly related to H. Scythicus, the brachycephalic Tartar of central Asia. This idea is connected at once with the theory of the Asiatic origin of the Aryans, these being regarded by certain writers as brachycephalic, and with the theory of Pruner-Bey, which associated all the primitive inhabitants of Europe, even the dolichocephalics, with the yellow races. This last theory is not wholly incorrect. H. priscus was certainly very closely related to the Esquimaux, and the latter have several characteristics in common with the yellow races, especially the

color of the skin, to which so much importance was attached in the rudimentary stage of anthropology. The false part of Pruner-Bey's theory is the attempt to establish a tie of blood-relationship between the brachycephalics of Europe and those of Asia.

The Mongolian characteristics occasionally appearing among western people may be adequately explained by occasional crossing with isolated individuals of the Mongolian or the Chinese type who came in connection with the incursions of the Middle Ages or under various circumstances. These characteristics are of extreme tenacity, and may reappear through atavism after an interval of many generations. Often, also, the supposed resemblances are due simply to individual variation, the possible range of which is greater than often supposed.

Our ultra-brachycephalics of the regions of the Cévennes and of the eastern Alps far excel any of the Mongols in the degree of their brachycephaly. This brachycephaly is, moreover, the sole characteristic which they have in common with the latter, and even in this point the analogy in cephalic index is not accompanied by an analogous form of skull.

Tappeiner, who is the authority on the ultra-brachycephalics of the eastern Alps, has made a special study of this question. The conclusions of his work are categorical (Der europäische Mensch und die Tiroler, Meran, 1896): "Ich habe bei der anthropologischen Untersuchung der 3,400 lebenden hochbrachycephalen Tiroler keinen einzigen Mann gefunden, welcher die characteristichen Merkmale der mongolischen Rasse an sich gehabt hat (p. 42). So wird auch der weitere Schluss nicht bezweifelt werden können, dass alle europäischen brachycephalen Schädel wesentlich verschieden von den mongolischen Schädeln sind, dass also die europäischen Brachycephalen keine Nachkommen der Mongolen sein können, und dass daher eine prähistorische Einwanderung von Mongolen aus Asien ein anthropologischer Irrthum ist" (p. 48; cf. also p. 53).

To this testimony of Tappeiner, based on his study of 3,400 living subjects and 927 skulls, I may add my own, which rests on about equally extensive studies in the Cévennes. I have not found a single subject of the Mongolian type. The reader may be referred for details to my Matériaux pour l'Anthropologie de l'Aveyron and Recherches sur 127 ultra-brachycephales de 95 à 100 et plus. I may say, further, that I have been unable to find any Mongolian types among ancient skulls of brachycephalic Europeans preserved in the museums.

The question has, moreover, of late taken a new turn. The anthropological researches in Russia, in the Caucasus, in eastern Siberia, and in Turkestan have not yet furnished a single Mongolian skull anterior to the Huns, the Turks, and the Tartars. The arrival of the yellow brachycephalics in central Asia does not appear to have antedated our era. It is to be added that migrations by a route north of the Caspian Sea were not exactly easy until an epoch tolerably near the historic period.

On the other hand, our brachycephalics are, in part, very closely related to those of Asia Minor, of Armenia, and of neighboring regions, as far as north Persia and the Pamir. These last, studied by Ujfalvy, are, moreover, according to their own traditions, colonists brought to Bactria by the Macedonians. These are the Galtchas in whom Topinard saw Savoyards retarded in their migration toward the west!

It is well to take this occasion to finish with another myth connected with the one we have been discussing. It is currently assumed that the yellow race is brachycephalic. This is an error which I have several times exposed, as has also my friend Ujfalvy, but it appears to have a tenacious hold upon life. The true H. Asiaticus, of small or medium stature, yellow skin, black hair, black oblique eyes, is dolichocephalic. It is the cross between this race and some form of Acrognus that is brachycephalic. In fact, of the seven hundred millions of the yellow races not one-quarter are brachycephalic. Yellow populations whose index is as high as the average of the brachycephalics of Europe are not numerous, and those with indices above 84 are comparatively rare. They consist of only a few tribes (Manchus, 84; Usbeks, 84; Kirghiz, 85; Kalmuks, 86). Their total number is not over three million. The yellow peoples of Siberia are usually below 80 or only slightly above it. The Ladikis of Pamir measured by Ujfalvy gave an average index of 77 for thirty-six individuals. Risley found an average of 80.7 for 388 mountaineers of Darjeeling. The people of Tibet are more dolichocephalic. Hagen found averages between 80 and 86.9 for numerous series of Malays, but the Malays are in part of another race. For 15,582 Chinese he found an average index of 81.7—lower than those of France, Germany, Austria, Russia, Italy, and the Balkan peninsula.

There are, then, in China, and among the yellow race generally, relatively fewer brachycephalics than in Europe, and there, as here, the brachycephalics represent a foreign or intruding element.

Unlike William Z. Ripley, who cautiously asserted science's ability to identify certain racial types, Madison Grant wrote with a blustering authority. Grant clearly lays out what he sees as absolute differences among the races, especially with regard to their capacities for civilization. Grant has a clear political agenda that he puts forth as scientific fact: the United States is in danger because it is allowing degenerate racial types to outbreed the superior Nordics who founded the country. Grant was a tremendously influential writer both in the United States and in Europe, especially Germany.

The Passing of the Great Race, or the Racial Basis of European History

MADISON GRANT

The Competition of Races

Where two races occupy a country side by side, it is not correct to speak of one type as changing into the other. Even if present in equal numbers one of the two contrasted types will have some small advantage or capacity which the other lacks toward a perfect adjustment to surroundings. Those possessing these favorable variations will flourish at the expense of their rivals, and their offspring will not only be more numerous, but will also tend to inherit such variations. In this way one type gradually breeds the other out. In this sense, and in this sense only, do races change.

Man continuously undergoes selection through the operation of the forces of social environment. Among native Americans of the Colonial period a large family was an asset, and social pressure and economic advantage counselled early marriage and numerous children. Two hundred years of continuous political expansion and material prosperity changed these conditions and children, instead of being an asset to till the fields and guard the cattle, became an expensive liability. They now require support, education, and endowment from their parents, and a large family is regarded by some as a serious handicap in the social struggle.

These conditions do not obtain at first among immigrants, and large families among the newly arrived population are still the rule, precisely as they were in Colonial America, and are to-day in French Canada, where backwoods conditions still prevail.

The result is that one class or type in a population expands more rapidly than another, and ultimately replaces it. This process of replacement of one type by another does not mean that the race changes, or is transformed into another. It is a replacement pure and simple and not a transformation.

The lowering of the birth rate among the most valuable classes, while the birth rate of the lower classes remains unaffected, is a frequent phenomenon of prosperity. Such a change becomes extremely injurious to the race if unchecked, unless nature is allowed to maintain by her own cruel devices the relative numbers of the different classes in their due proportions. To attack race suicide by encouraging indiscriminate reproduction is not only futile, but is dangerous if it leads to an increase in the undesirable elements. What is needed in the community most of all, is an increase in the desirable classes, which are of superior type physically, intellectually and morally, and not merely an increase in the absolute numbers of the population.

The value and efficiency of a population are not numbered by what the newspapers call souls, but by the proportion of men of physical and intellectual vigor. The small Colonial population of America was, man for man, far superior to the present inhabitants, although the latter are twenty-five times more numerous. The ideal in eugenics toward which statesmanship should be directed is, of course, improvement in quality rather than quantity. This, however, is at present a counsel of perfection, and we must face conditions as they are.

The small birth rate in the upper classes is, to some extent, offset by the care received by such children as are born, and the better chance they have to become adult and breed in their turn. The large birth rate of the lower classes is, under normal conditions, offset by a heavy infant mortality, which eliminates the weaker children.

Where altruism, philanthropy, or sentimentalism intervene with the noblest purpose, and forbid nature to penalize the unfortunate victims of reckless breeding, the multiplication of inferior types is encouraged and fostered. Efforts to indiscriminately preserve babies among the lower classes often result in serious injury to the race.

Mistaken regard for what are believed to be divine laws and a sentimental belief in the sanctity of human life, tend to prevent both the elimination of defective infants and the sterilization of such adults as are themselves of no value to the community. The laws of nature require the obliteration of the unfit, and human life is valuable only when it is of use to the community or race.

It is highly unjust that a minute minority should be called upon to supply brains for the unthinking mass of the community, but it is even worse to burden the responsible and larger, but still overworked, elements in the community with an ever increasing number of moral perverts, mental defectives and hereditary cripples.

The church assumes a serious responsibility toward the future of the race whenever it steps in and preserves a defective strain. The marriage of deaf mutes was hailed a generation ago as a triumph of humanity. Now it is recognized as an absolute crime against the race. A great injury is done to the community by the perpetuation of worthless types. These strains are apt to be meek and lowly, and as such make a strong appeal to the sympathies of the successful. Before eugenics were understood much could be said from a Christian and humane viewpoint in favor of indiscriminate charity for the benefit of the individual. The societies for charity, altruism, or extension of rights, should have, however, in these days, in their management some small modicum of brains, otherwise they may continue to do, as they have sometimes done in the past, more injury to the race than black death or smallpox.

As long as such charitable organizations confine themselves to the relief of suffering individuals, no matter how criminal or diseased they may be, no harm is done except to our own generation, and if modern society recognizes a duty to the humblest malefactors or imbeciles, that duty can be harmlessly performed in full, provided they be deprived of the capacity to procreate their defective strain.

Those who read these pages will feel that there is little hope for humanity, but the remedy has been found, and can be quickly and mercifully applied. A rigid system of selection through the elimination of those who are weak or unfit—in other words, social failures—would solve the whole question in one hundred years, as well as enable us to get rid of the undesirables who crowd our jails, hospitals, and insane asylums. The individual himself can be nourished, educated, and protected by the community during his lifetime, but the state through sterilization must see to it that his line stops with him, or else future generations will be cursed with an ever increasing load of victims of misguided sentimentalism. This is a practical, merciful, and inevitable solution of the whole problem, and can be applied to an ever widening circle of social discards, beginning always with the criminal, the diseased, and the insane, and extending gradually to types which may be called weaklings rather than defectives, and perhaps ultimately to worthless race types.

Efforts to increase the birth rate of the genius producing classes of the community, while most desirable, encounter great difficulties. In such efforts we encounter social conditions over which we have as yet no control. It was tried two thousand years ago by Augustus, and his efforts to avert race suicide and the extinction of the old Roman breed were singularly prophetic of what some far seeing men are attempting in order to preserve the race of native Americans of Colonial descent.

Man has the choice of two methods of race improvement. He can breed from the best, or he can eliminate the worst by segregation or sterilization. The first method was adopted by the Spartans, who had for their national ideals, military efficiency and the virtues of self-control, and along these lines the results were completely successful. Under modern social conditions it would be extremely difficult in the first instance to determine which were the most desirable types, except in the most general way, and even if a satisfactory selection were finally made, it would be, in a democracy, a virtual impossibility to limit by law the right to breed to a privileged and chosen few.

Experiments in limiting reproduction to the undesirable classes were unconsciously made in medieval Europe under the guidance of the church. After the fall of Rome, social conditions were such that all those who loved a studious and quiet life, were compelled to seek refuge from the violence of the times in monastic institutions, and upon such the church imposed the obligation of celibacy, and thus deprived the world of offspring from these desirable classes.

In the Middle Ages, through persecution resulting in actual death, life imprisonment, and banishment, the free thinking, progressive, and intellectual elements were persistently eliminated over large areas, leaving the perpetuation of the race to be carried on by the brutal, the servile, and the stupid. It is now impossible to say to what extent the Roman Church by these methods has impaired the brain capacity of Europe, but in Spain alone, for a period of over three centuries, from the years 1471 to 1781, the Inquisition condemned to the stake or imprisonment an average of 1,000 persons annually. During these three centuries no less than 32,000 were burned alive, and 291,000 were condemned to various terms of imprisonment and other penalties, and 7,000 persons were burned in effigy, representing men who had died in prison or had fled the country.

No better method of eliminating the genius producing strains of a nation could be devised, and if such were its purpose the result was eminently satisfactory, as is demonstrated by the superstitious and unintelligent Spaniard of to-day. A similar elimination of brains and ability took place in northern Italy and in France, and in the Low Countries, where hundreds of thousands of Huguenots were murdered or driven into exile.

Under existing conditions the most practical and hopeful method of race improvement is through the elimination of the least desirable elements in the nation by depriving them of the power to contribute to future generations. It is well known to stock breeders that the color of a herd of cattle can be modified by continuous destruction of worthless shades, and of course this is true of other characters. Black sheep, for instance, have been practically destroyed by cutting out generation after generation all animals that show this color phase, until in carefully maintained flocks a black individual only appears as a rare sport.

In mankind it would not be a matter of great difficulty to secure a general consensus of public opinion as to the least desirable, let us say ten per cent of the community. When this unemployed and unemployable human residuum has been eliminated, together with the great mass of crime, poverty, alcoholism, and feeblemindedness associated therewith, it would be easy to consider the advisability of further restricting the perpetuation of the then remaining least valuable types. By this method mankind might ultimately become sufficiently intelligent to choose deliberately the most vital and intellectual strains to carry on the race.

In addition to selection by climatic environment, man is now, and has been for ages, undergoing selection through disease. He has been decimated throughout the centuries by pestilences such as the black death and bubonic plague. In our fathers' days yellow fever and smallpox cursed humanity. These plagues are now under control, but similar diseases now regarded as mere nuisances to childhood, such as measles, mumps, and scarlatina, are terrible scourges to native populations without previous experience with them. Add to these smallpox and other white men's diseases, and one has the great empire builders of yesterday. It was not the swords in the hands of Columbus and his followers that decimated the American Indians, it was the germs that his men and their successors brought over, implanting the white man's maladies in the red man's world. Long before the arrival of the Puritans in New England, smallpox had flickered up and down the coast until the natives were but a broken remnant of their former numbers.

At the present time the Nordic race is undergoing selection through alcoholism, a peculiarly Nordic vice, and through consumption, and both these dread scourges unfortunately attack those members of the race that are otherwise most desirable, differing in this respect from filth diseases like typhus, typhoid, or smallpox. One has only to look among the more desirable classes for the victims of rum and tubercle to realize that death or mental and physical impairment through these two causes have cost the race many of its most brilliant and attractive members.

By the end of the nineteenth century, the cephalic index (which was a measure of head shape) was touted as the best measure of racial differences by many physical anthropologists. Because head shape had no adaptive significance, it was thought to be stable generation after generation. Anthropologist Franz Boas challenged the assumption that racial types were stable and argued, on the basis of a study he undertook for the U.S. Immigration Commission, that supposedly stable racial markers could change in as little as one generation. In this selection, Boas responds to his critics and defends his conclusion that there are no stable racial types.

New Evidence in Regard to the Instability of Human Types

FRANZ BOAS

A number of years ago I carried on, under the auspices of the United States Immigration Commission, an investigation on the physical types of immigrants and of their descendants. One of the results of this inquiry was the establishment of the fact that there is a difference in appearance between the immigrants and their descendants. So far as the bulk of the body is concerned, this information was not new. Analogous phenomena had been observed in 1877 by H. P. Bowditch in Boston, and by Peckham in Milwaukee. It was new, however, that there is also a change in such features as the cephalic index and the width of the face. It was found that on the average the heads of descendants of immigrants of East European types are more elongated, and those of the descendants of South Europeans more rounded, than those of their parents. The data were obtained partly by a generalizing method, partly by a comparison between parents and children.

The results of this inquiry have been attacked by many writers, on the basis that they decline to believe that such changes can occur. I have not found any actual criticism of my method and of the results, except by Corrado Gini, who doubts the inferences drawn in regard to the populations of Italian cities which also show a modification of the cephalic index.

I think the hesitation of many authors to accept the results is due largely to a misinterpretation of their significance. I may be allowed to state concisely here what I think has been proved, and what inferences seem justifiable.

The investigation has a direct bearing upon the question of the classification of human local types, more particularly of European types. Many attempts have been made to give a satisfactory classification of the divergent types that occur in Europe. Pigmentation, stature, form of the head, and form of the face, show material differences in various parts of Europe, notwithstanding the fundamental sameness of the whole race. Authors like Deniker, and many others, have carried out on this basis an elaborate classification of European types in a number of 'races' and 'sub-races.'

In this classification the assumption is made that each race that we find at the present time in its particular environment is an hereditary type different from the others. In order to express this assumption, I should like to use the term that these races and sub-races represent, 'genetic' types—genetic in the sense that their characteristics are determined by heredity alone. The question, however, has not been answered, whether these types are really genetic types, or whether they are what I might call 'ecotypes,' in so far as their appearance is determined by environmental or ecological conditions. If we include in this term not only environmental conditions in a geographical and social sense, but also conditions that are determined by the organism itself, we might, perhaps, still better call them physiological types, in the same sense in which the biologist speaks of physiological races. My investigation then was directed to the question in how far a certain type of man may be considered a genetic type, in how far a physiological type. If there is any kind of environmental influence, it is obvious that we can never speak of a genetic type *per se*, but that every genetic type appears under certain environmental or physiological conditions, and that in this sense we are always dealing with the physiological form of a certain genetic type. The question, then, that demands an answer, is, in how far genetic types may be influenced by physiological changes.

I believe, that, on the basis of the material that I collected, we must maintain that the same genetic type may occur in various physiologically conditioned forms, and that so far as stature, head-form, and width of face are concerned, the differences between the physiological forms of the same genetic type are of the same order as the differences between the races and sub-races which have been distinguished in Europe. I must add, however, that these remarks do not refer to pigmentation, for, contrary to a widespread belief, we have no proof of environmental influences upon pigmentation. For this reason the classification of European races cannot be considered as proving genetic differentiation.

The whole investigation which I carried on, and certain comparable observations obtained from older literature, do not indicate in any way to what physiological conditions the observed changes may be due. The only physiological causes in regard to which evidence is available relate to the bulk of the body, and to a certain extent to the proportions of the limbs. The size of the body depends upon the conditions under which growth takes place. Growth depends upon nutrition, upon pathological conditions during childhood, and upon many other causes, all of which have an effect upon the bulk of the body of the adult. When these conditions are favorable, the physiological form of a certain genetic type will be large. If there is much retardation during early life, the physiological form of the same genetic type will be small. Retardation and acceleration of growth may also account for varying proportions of the limbs. On the other hand, we have no information whatever that would allow us to determine the cause of the physiological diminution in the size of the face that has been observed in America, nor for the change in the head-index that occurs among the descendants of immigrants.

Furthermore, there is nothing to indicate that these changes are in any sense genetic changes; that is to say, that they influence the hereditary constitution of the germ. It may very well be that the same people, if carried back to their old environment, would revert to their former physiological types.

In fact, it can be shown that certain features are strictly hereditary, and that, although the physiological form of a genetic type may vary, nevertheless the genetic type as such will exert its influence. Professor von Luschan has repeatedly called attention to this fact as revealed in the modern populations of Asia Minor, where, notwithstanding the mixture which has continued for at least four thousand years, the characteristic Armenian, Northwest European, and Mediterranean types survive in the mixed population. Similar examples may be observed in Italy. I have calculated the variability of the head-form that is found in different parts of Italy, based on the data collected by Ridolfo Livi. The head-form of the North Italians is excessively short. The head-form of the South Italians is decidedly elongated. In between we find intermediate forms. In the Apennines, we have, in addition to the mixture of these two Italian forms, a marked immigration from the Balkan Peninsula, which introduced another short-headed type. As a result of these long-continued mixtures, we observe low degrees of variability in northern and southern Italy, high degrees of variability in the central regions, particularly in the Abruzzi. These indicate permanence of the component types of the mixed population.

During the last few years some new data have been collected that confirm my previous observations. I have pointed out several times that changes of types have been observed in Europe wherever a careful comparison between city population and country population has been made. Generally the changes that occur there have been ascribed to selective influences; but the intensity of selection would have to be so great, that it does not seem plausible that they can be explained by this cause.

In conjunction with Miss Helene M. Boas, I have made a comparison

between the head-forms of the city populations of Italy and of the rural population in the areas surrounding the cities, and compared these data with the information given in the Italian census in regard to the immigration into cities. I found
throughout that the variability of head-form in each city is smaller than would be
found in a population in which all the constituent genetic types were present
without physiological modification. This result has been criticised by Corrado
Gini, on the basis that in former times migration was less than what it is now. I
grant this point; but nevertheless it is quite obvious, that, although no exact data
are available, the mixture of population in a city like Rome or like Florence must
be very great, since the political conditions for the conflux of Italians, and even
of individuals from outside of Italy, have been favorable for a very long period. If
this is true, we should expect a very high degree of variability in Rome, which,
however, is not found.

Turning to new data, I wish to mention the observation made by Dr.
Hrdlicka, who, in a paper read before the Pan-American Scientific Congress, has
stated that he found the width of face of Americans of the fourth generation—
that is to say, of descendants of Europeans who had no foreign-born ancestor
after the fourth generation back—was materially decreased as compared to the
width of face found among European types. This conforms strictly with what I
found among the descendants of immigrants of all nationalities.

A year ago I had the opportunity to make an anthropometric investigation
of a considerable number of natives of Porto Rico. This work was carried on in
connection with the Natural History Survey of Porto Rico organized by the New
York Academy of Sciences. The population of Porto Rico is derived from three
distinct sources—from people belonging to the Mediterranean type of Europe,
from West Indian aborigines, and from Negroes. The Mediterranean ancestry of
the Porto Ricans leads back to all parts of Spain; but among the more recent
immigrants, Catalans, people from the Balear Islands and from the Canary
Islands prevail. There are also a fair number of Corsicans. The Spanish immigration has been quite strong even up to the present time. Among the individuals
whom I measured, 14% had Spanish-born fathers, some even Spanish-born mothers. From all we know about the history of the people of Porto Rico, we must
consider them essentially as descendants of male immigrants who intermarried
with native women. It is evident that in early times this must have led to the
development of a Mestizo population, in which, however, the amount of Indian
blood must have decreased very rapidly owing to the continued influx of Spanish blood, and the elimination from the reproductive series of the male Mestizo
element. The Negro population is settled particularly on the outer coast of the
island; while the amount of Negro blood in the interior is apparently not very
great, except near the principal routes of travel.

According to European observations, the Spanish ancestors of this population, while living in Spain, are long-headed. The Negro element is of mixed provenience; from many different parts of Africa, but, on the whole, the Negro in Africa is also long-headed. The West Indian element, judging from the few prehistoric crania that have been recovered, represents a very short-headed type. The modern Porto Rican is short-headed to such a degree that even a heavy admixture of Indian blood could not account for the degree of short-headedness. If we apply the results of known instances of intermixture to our particular case, and assume stability of type, we find that, even if the population were one-half Indian and one-half Spanish and Negro, the head-index would be considerably lower than what we actually observe. There is therefore no source that would account for the present head-form as a genetic type; and we are compelled to assume that the form which we observe is due to a physiological modification that has occurred under the new environment. The head-form of those individuals whose fathers were born in Spain is noticeably more elongated than that of the individuals whose parents are both Porto Ricans. The head-index of the Mulatto population is intermediate between the index of the native Porto Ricans and that of those whose one parent is Spanish. The average index of the Porto Rican is 82.5. The average index of the Spaniard in Spain is less than 77. We find, therefore, an increase of five units here, which can in no way be accounted for by genetic considerations.

I may mention in this connection that the average stature of the Porto Ricans is apparently almost the same as that of the Sicilians in New York, and that throughout the period of growth the stature follows about the same curve as that represented by Sicilian children living in America. If anything, the stature is a little lower, and there is no indication of that acceleration of development which is so often claimed to be characteristic of a tropical environment. Undoubtedly poor nutrition, and probably also pathological causes, have a retarding influence here, which might easily be overcome by better hygienic conditions.

It is unfortunate that we have no accurate statistics of Porto Rican immigration and emigration, which would enable us to state with much greater definiteness what genetic type should be expected here. There is a popular belief in Porto Rico that in certain parts of the island, in the so-called 'Indiera,' Indian types have persisted to a greater extent than elsewhere. I have not been able to find any definite indication of a difference in type; but I have measured only a few individuals from these districts. The material that I have been able to study comes from all parts of the island, but principally from the western-central part. The phenomena here described occur with equal intensity in all parts of the island.

The question of the degree of instability of human types seems to my mind an exceedingly important one for a clear understanding of the problems of physical anthropology. It would be particularly desirable to study the problem among immigrants living in different rural communities of the United States, and it would be even more desirable to have information in regard to the types that develop among the East Europeans and South Europeans who return to Europe and settle in their old geographical environment.

Psychologists aided the U.S. Army in World War I by administering intelligence tests to recruits in order to ensure that the Army operated with maximum efficiency. After the war, psychologists had a massive amount of data on the intelligence of a large number of people. Carl C. Brigham broke his data down into racial results, finding that only the Nordic was truly intelligent, thus echoing the arguments of Madison Grant and Georges Vacher de Lapouge, but giving them the imprimatur of the new science of psychological testing. Despite the confident tone here, Brigham publicly recanted only eight years later, declaring in 1930 that there was no evidence of racial differences in intelligence.

A Study of American Intelligence

CARL C. BRIGHAM

Section VIII

The Race Hypothesis

The results of the examination of the nativity groups suggest immediately that the race factor may underlie the large differences found. If we do find the common factor of race underlying the differences between the various nativity groups, it will give our results much greater reliability, for the chance factors of sampling particularly inferior or superior groups in the small nativity samples would disappear in combination. Our figures are based on country of birth and no statistics are available for race. The race hypothesis must therefore be examined indirectly.

Writers on immigration, for the most part, divide the countries of Europe into two groups (1) Northern and Western, and (2) Eastern and Southern, and usually assume that the immigration from Northern and Western Europe has been mostly Nordic. This traditional method is open to two very serious objections. In the first place, the classification fails to differentiate the Alpine and

Mediterranean race groups. In the second place the assumption that the immigration from Northern and Western Europe was mostly of a pure Nordic type is unwarranted, for this classification includes Germany and Ireland, two countries that have contributed very largely to our immigration in the past. The following figures [in the table below] show the size of the Irish and German immigration:

Decade	Total Immigration	Per Cent. from Ireland	Per Cent. from Germany	Per Cent. from Ireland and Germany
1820–1830	143,439	35%	5%	40%
1831–1840	599,125	35%	25%	60%
1841–1850	1,171,251	46%	25%	71%
1851–1860	2,598,214	35%	37%	72%
1861–1870	2,314,824	19%	34%	53%
1871–1880	2,812,191	15%	26%	41%
1881–1890	5,246,613	12%	28%	40%
1891–1900	3,844,420	11%	14	25%
1901–1910	8,795,386	4%	4%	8%
1911–1920	5,735,811	2½%	2½%	5%

These figures show clearly the fallacy of assuming that the immigration from Northern and Western Europe has been predominately Nordic, for Ireland is largely Mediterranean and Germany largely Alpine.

If we wish to obtain even approximate estimates of the contributions of each of the three European races to our importations, it is necessary to abandon the Northern and Western, and Eastern and Southern classification and try another method. If it were possible to make even approximate estimates of the percentage of Nordic, Alpine and Mediterranean blood in each of the European nations sending immigrants to this country, such approximate estimates would be very much superior to the present method.

In collaboration with students of this subject, I have constructed Table 33 which contains tentative estimates of the present blood constitution of the countries sending immigrants to this country. This table is, of course, only an approximation to the truth, and many persons will disagree with the estimates. For this reason, I am re-publishing in Table 34, Table 68, page 100, of the *Statistical Abstract for the United States* for 1920, which shows the arrivals of alien passengers and immigrants by nationalities and by decades from 1820 to 1920. My own Tables 9 and 10 give the distribution of the intelligence scores on the combined scale for the nativity groups we are studying. Anybody who disagrees with the estimates given in Table 33 may take these tables and split them according to any other estimates he wishes to make. However, minor changes in the proportions given in Table 33 would make very little difference in the final results. The

TABLE NO. 33 Tentative estimates of the proportion of Nordic, Alpine and Mediterranean blood in each of the European countries.

	Per Cent. Nordic	Per Cent. Alpine	Per Cent. Mediterranean
Austria-Hungary	10	90	0
Belgium	60	40	0
Denmark	85	15	0
France	30	55	15
Germany	40	60	0
Greece	0	15	85
Italy	5	25	70
Netherlands	85	15	0
Norway	90	10	0
Sweden	100	0	0
Russia (including Poland)	5	95	0
Poland	10	90	0
Spain	10	5	85
Portugal	5	0	95
Roumania	0	100	0
Switzerland	35	65	0
Turkey (unclassified)	0	20	80
Turkey (in Europe)*	0	60	40
Turkey (in Asia)	0	10	90
England	80	0	20
Ireland	30	0	70
Scotland	85	0	15
Wales	40	0	60
British North America	60	40	0

* including Serbia, Montenegro and Bulgaria

figures which follow are merely estimates based on Table 33. I am not claiming that these figures are absolutely reliable, but merely that they represent very much closer approximations to the truth than would be obtained from the Northern and Western, and Southern and Eastern classification.

To obtain an estimate of the proportion of Nordic, Alpine, and Mediterranean blood in our immigration since 1840, the immigration figures by countries, given in Table 34, have been cut according to the proportions given in Table 33 and re-combined into percentage estimates which are given in Table 35. These estimates show in general an immigration prior to 1890 which ran 40% or 50% Nordic blood.

Since 1890, the proportion of Nordic blood has dropped to 20% or 25%, the Alpine stock now constituting about 50% of the total and the Mediterranean 20% or 25%.

The proportions given in Table 35 are shown graphically in Figure 41. The

TABLE NO. 34   No. 68. Arrivals of Alien Passengers and Immigrants,
1820 to 1920: By Nationalities and by Decades.

Country of Last Permanent Residence	Oct. 1, 1820, to Sept. 30, 1830	Oct. 1, 1830, to Dec. 31, 1840	Jan. 1, 1841, to Dec. 31, 1850	Jan. 1, 1851, to Dec. 31, 1860
Austria-Hungary				
Belgium	27	22	5,074	4,738
Denmark	169	1,063	539	3,749
France	8,497	45,575	77,262	76,358
Germany	6,761	152,454	434,626	951,667
Greece[1]				
Italy	408	2,253	1,870	9,231
Netherlands	1,078	1,412	8,251	10,789
Norway				
Sweden	91	1,201	13,903	20,931
Russia, including Russian Poland[2]	91	646	656	1,621
Spain[3]				
Portugal[4]	2,622	2,954	2,759	10,353
Rumania[1]				
Switzerland	3,226	4,821	4,644	25,011
Turkey in Europe[5]				
United Kingdom:				
England	22,167	73,143	263,332	385,643
Scotland	2,912	2,667	3,712	38,331
Ireland	50,724	207,381	780,719	914,119
Wales[6]				
Total United Kingdom	75,803	283,191	1,047,763	1,338,093
Europe, not specified	43	96	155	116
Total Europe	98,816	495,688	1,597,502	2,452,657
British North America[7]	2,277	13,624	41,723	59,309
Mexico[7]	4,817	6,599	3,271	3,078
Central America	105	44	368	449
West Indies: Bermuda and Miquelon	3,834	12,301	13,528	10,660
South America	531	856	3,579	1,224
Total America[7]	11,564	33,424	62,469	74,720
Islands of the Atlantic	352	103	337	3,090
China	2	8	35	41,397
India[8]				
Japan[8]				
Turkey in Asia[8]				
Other Asia	8	40	47	61
Total Asia	10	48	82	41,458
Total Oceania	2	9	29	158
Total Africa	16	52	55	210
All other countries	32,679	69,801	52,777	25,921
GRAND TOTAL	**143,439**	**599,125**	**1,713,251**	**2,598,214**

Sources: Records of the Bureau of Statistics prior to 1896; subsequently, reports of the Commissioner General of Immigration,Department of Labor. The figures represent "alien passengers" from Oct. 1, 1820, to Dec. 31, 1867; "immigrants" from Jan. 1, 1868, to date.

1 Included in "Europe, not specified," prior to 1891-1900.
2 Includes also Finland after 1872.
3 Includes Canary and Balearic Islands after 1900.
4 Figures include the Azores and Cape Verde Islands after 1879, they being classed with Portugal so far as that country is separately shown.
5 Includes Serbia, Bulgaria, and Montenegro prior to 1920; included in "Europe, not specified," prior to 1891–1900; also, after 1919, Czechoslovakia, Poland, and the Kingdom of the Serbs, Croats, and Slovenes.
6 Not separately stated prior to 1891–1900.
7 Immigrants from British North America and Mexico were not reported from 1886 to 1895, inclusive.
8 Not separately enumerated prior to 1899.

| | Years Ended June 30 | | | | |
Jan. 1, 1861, to June 30, 1870	1871 to 1880	1881 to 1890	1891 to 1900	1901 to 1910	1911 to 1920
7,800	72,969	353,719	597,047	2,145,266	896,342
6,734	7,221	20,177	20,062	41,635	33,746
17,094	31,771	88,132	52,670	65,285	41,983
35,984	72,206	50,464	36,006	73,379	61,897
787,468	718,182	1,452,970	543,922	341,498	143,945
			15,996	167,519	184,201
11,728	55,759	307,309	655,694	2,045,877	1,109,524
9,102	16,541	53,701	31,816	48,262	43,718
			95,265	190,505	66,395
109,298	211,245	568,362	230,679	249,534	95,074
4,536	52,254	265,088	593,703	1,597,306	921,957
			6,723	27,935	68,611
8,493	9,893	6,535	23,010	69,149	89,732
			14,559	53,008	13,311
23,286	28,293	81,988	33,149	34,922	23,091
			2,562	118,202	77,098
568,128	460,479	657,488	271,094	388,017	249,944
38,768	87,564	149,869	60,053	120,469	78,601
435,778	436,871	655,482	403,496	339,065	145,937
			11,186	17,464	13,107
1,042,674	984,914	1,462,839	745,829	865,015	487,589
210	656	10,318	4,370	1,719	18,350
2,064,407	2,261,904	4,721,602	3,703,061	8,136,016	4,376,564
153,871	383,269	392,802	2,631	179,226	742,185
2,191	5,362	1,913	746	49,642	219,004
96	210	462	1,183	8,112	17,159
9,043	13,957	29,042	35,040	107,548	123,424
1,396	928	2,304	3,059	17,280	41,899
166,597	403,726	426,523	42,659	361,808	1,143,671
3,446	10,056	15,798			
64,301	123,201	61,711	23,166	20,605	21,278
			26	4,713	2,082
			26,855	129,797	83,837
			8,398	77,393	79,389
308	622	6,669	28,370	11,059	5,973
64,609	123,823	68,380	86,815	243,567	192,559
221	10,913	12,574	8,793	12,973	13,427
312	229	437	1,343	7,368	8,443
15,232	1,540	1,299	1,749	33,654	1,147
2,314,824	**2,812,191**	**5,246,613**	**3,844,420**	**8,795,386**	**5,735,811**

percentage estimates, given in Figure 35 and shown graphically in Figure 41, should be considered in connection with the total volume of immigration for each decade given in Table 34 and shown graphically in Figure 42.

TABLE NO. 35　**Estimate of the amount of Nordic, Alpine and Mediterranean blood coming to this country from Europe in each decade since 1840.**

Decade	Total Immigration	Per Cent. Nordic Blood	Per Cent. Alpine Blood	Per Cent. Mediterranean Blood	Per Cent. Others and Unclassified
1841–1850	1,713,251	40.5	19.0	36.2	4.3
1851–1860	2,598,214	42.3	25.5	28.9	3.3
1861–1870	2,314,824	50.6	26.0	19.2	4.2
1871–1880	2,812,191	48.8	28.5	16.7	6.0
1881–1890	5,246,613	46.1	35.2	16.0	2.7
1891–1900	3,844,420	30.2	43.8	22.5	3.5
1901–1910	8,795,386	19.8	51.3	24.3	4.6
1911–1920	5,735,811	22.6	44.0	23.7	9.7

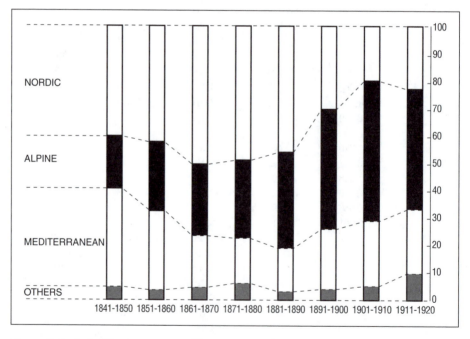

Figure 41. Analysis of immigration to the United Sates according to the estimated amount of Nordic, Mediterranean and Alpine blood. Each bar represents 100%. The Figure was drawn from the percentages given in Table 35. Our estimates show that the Nordic immigration has fallen from about 50% to 20% or 25%, while the Alpine immigration has risen steadily from 20% or 25% to 50%. The initial decrease in the proportion of the Mediterranean immigration is due to the gradual falling off of the Irish immigration, while its subsequent recovery is due to the large numbers coming from Italy, Turkey and Greece.

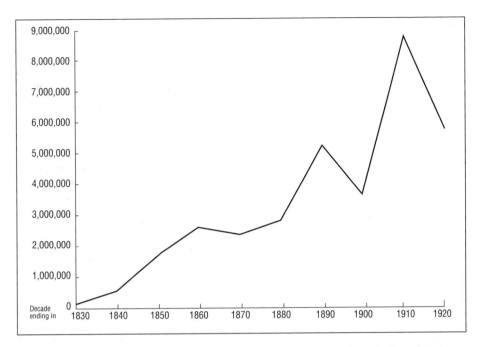

Figure 42. Volume of immigration by decades. The percentage analysis, shown in Figure 41, should be considered in connection with the total volume of immigration shown in Tables 34 and 35 and indicated graphically above. The immigration in the decade of 1820 to 1830 was less than 150,000, in the decade 1830 to 1840, less than 600,000. Between 1901 and 1910, over 8 3/4 millions came to this country. In this period (1901 to 1910), Austria-Hungary, Russia and Italy, send over 5 3/4 millions.

In order to obtain an estimate of the intelligence of the three European races in this country, the distributions of the intelligence scores on the combined scale given in Table 9 were cut according to the proportions given in Table 33, and re-combined into Nordic, Alpine, and Mediterranean groups. The final distributions are, of course, neither purely Nordic, Alpine, nor Mediterranean, but the sample of individuals we have thus selected as Nordic is undoubtedly more typical of the Nordic race type than it is of the Alpine and Mediterranean types. In the same way, the Alpine and Mediterranean groups are more typical of each of these race types than they are of either of the other two. With thus much of apology for the method, I will, in the following pages, simply for brevity of expression, call these groups Nordic, Alpine, and Mediterranean. The reader must bear in mind that the distributions are only approximate samplings.

The actual distributions on the combined scale of the three race groups so selected are given in Table 36, together with the proportions in each thousand. The distribution curves of the three groups are shown in Figure 43, in which the horizontal direction represents scores on the combined scale, and the vertical direction proportions in each thousand making each intelligence score.

The differences found are very marked. The difference between the Nordic and Alpine group is 1.61 ± 0.042, a difference which is 38.3 times the probable error of the difference. The difference between the Nordic and Mediterranean group is 1.85 ± 0.042, a difference which is 44 times the probable error of the difference. The Alpine and Mediterranean groups are, on the other hand, very much closer together, the difference being 0.24 ± 0.04, a difference which is 6 times the probable error of the difference.

TABLE NO. 36 **Analysis of the foreign born white draft by races. Distributions of the intelligence scores of the Nordic, Alpine and Mediterranean groups.**

Combined Scale Intervals	Actual Distribution			Proportion in Each Thousand		
	Nordic	Alpine	Mediterranean	Nordic	Alpine	Mediterranean
24.0–24.9						
23.0–23.9						
22.0–22.9	3	1	1	1		
21.0–21.9	8	5	2	2	1	
20.0–20.9	19	11	5	5	2	2
19.0–19.9	37	22	11	11	5	3
18.0–18.9	71	47	26	21	10	6
17.0–17.9	135	90	55	39	19	13
16.0–16.9	238	155	103	69	32	24
15.0–15.9	357	246	180	103	51	43
14.0–14.9	469	372	296	136	78	71
13.0–13.9	566	544	468	164	114	111
12.0–12.9	528	650	591	153	136	141
11.0–11.9	371	628	590	107	132	140
10.0–10.9	260	595	569	75	125	136
9.0–9.9	184	546	523	53	115	125
8.0–8.9	112	403	376	32	85	90
7.0–7.9	59	248	223	17	52	53
6.0–6.9	26	124	108	8	26	26
5.0–5.9	9	52	47	3	11	11
4.0–4.9	3	19	16	1	4	4
3.0–3.9	1	6	5		2	1
2.0–2.9		2	1			
1.0–1.9						
No. of cases	3456	4766	4196			
Average	13.28	11.67	11.43			
S. D.	2.70	2.87	2.70			

The easiest and most obvious objection that can be made to these findings is that the superiority of the Nordic group is due to the fact that it contains so many English speaking persons, and that lack of facility in the use of English is a handicap to the non-English speaking foreign born in the army tests. We have

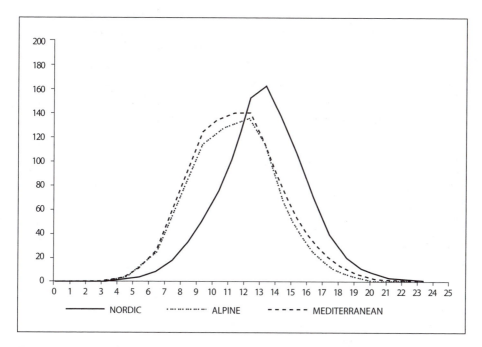

Figure 43. The distributions of the intelligence scores of the Nordic, Mediterranean and Alpine groups. This chart indicates clearly the superiority of the Nordic group. 73.9% of the Nordic group are above the average Alpine, and 76.5% of the Nordic group are above the average Mediterranean. The Mediterranean and Alpine groups are very similar, 52.3% of the Alpines exceeding the average Mediterranean.

previously examined this hypothesis in connection with the argument establishing the fact that each succeeding five year period since 1902 shows a gradual deterioration in the intelligence of the immigrants examined in the army, and have definitely shown that the language factor does not distort the scores of the years of residence groups. There is, however, a considerable amount of wishful thinking on the subject of race, and it is well to make assurance doubly sure by testing the hypothesis that the superiority of the Nordic group is caused by the presence in the group of English speaking populations.

It is possible to split the Nordic distribution in such a way that one group will contain representatives from countries which are predominantly English speaking (England, Scotland, Ireland and Canada), while the other group will contain representatives from countries which are predominantly non-English speaking (Holland, Denmark, Germany, Sweden, Norway, Belgium, Austria, Russia, Italy and Poland). This we have done, and the results are given in Table 37, the two distributions being shown in Figure 44.

The distributions of the English speaking Nordic group and the non-English speaking Nordic group show a difference of 0.87 ± 0.065, a difference which is 13.4 times the probable error of the difference. There are, of course, cogent

TABLE No. 37   **Analysis of the total Nordic sample into an English speaking Nordic group and a non-English speaking Nordic group.**

Combined Scale Intervals	Actual Distribution		Proportion in Each Thousand	
	English Speaking Nordic	Non-English Speaking Nordic	English Speaking Nordic	Non-English Speaking Nordic
24.0-24.9				
23.0-23.9	1			
22.0-22.9	2		2	
21.0-21.9	7	2	6	1
20.0-20.9	12	6	10	3
19.0-19.9	21	16	17	7
18.0-18.9	39	32	32	14
17.0-17.9	67	67	54	30
16.0-16.9	108	131	87	59
15.0-15.9	143	214	116	96
14.0-14.9	176	293	143	132
13.0-13.9	201	365	163	164
12.0-12.9	172	356	139	160
11.0-11.9	109	262	88	118
10.0-10.9	70	189	57	85
9.0- 9.9	49	135	40	61
8.0- 8.9	31	82	25	37
7.0- 7.9	16	43	13	19
6.0- 6.9	7	19	6	9
5.0- 5.9	2	7	2	3
4.0- 4.9	1	2		2
3.0- 3.9		1		
2.0- 2.9				
1.0- 1.9				
No. of cases	1234	2222		
Average	13.84	12.97		
S. D.	2.79	2.60		

historical and sociological reasons accounting for the inferiority of the non-English speaking Nordic group. On the other hand, if one wishes to deny, in the teeth of the facts, the superiority of the Nordic race on the ground that the language factor mysteriously aids this group when tested, he may cut out of the Nordic distribution the English speaking Nordics, and still find a marked superiority of the non-English speaking Nordics over the Alpine and Mediterranean groups. The difference between the non-English speaking Nordic group and the Alpine group is 1.30 ± 0.047, a difference which is 27.6 times the probable error of the difference. The difference between the non-English speaking Nordic group and the Mediterranean group is 1.54 ± 0.047, a difference which is 31.3 times the probable error of the difference. The distributions are shown graphically in Figure 45.

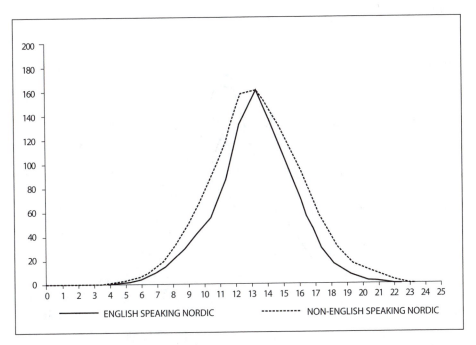

Figure 44. The distributions of the intelligence scores of the English speaking Nordic group and the non-English speaking Nordic group. These distributions were obtained by splitting the total Nordic group into two parts. The difference shown here is significant (63.4 % of the English speaking Nordic group exceeding the average of the non-English speaking Nordic group), but not as large as the difference between the non-English speaking Nordic group and the Mediterranean and Alpine groups shown in Figure 45.

Discarding the English speaking Nordics entirely, we still find tremendous differences between the non-English speaking Nordic group and the Alpine and Mediterranean groups, a fact which clearly indicates that the underlying cause of the nativity differences we have shown is race, and not language.

It may be convenient for some to interpret the differences found between the representatives of the three European races in this country in terms of the standards having popular significance which were used in Section VI. The criteria of the per cent. A and B, and the per cent. D, D—and E give the . . . results [in the table below]:

	Per Cent. A and B	*Per Cent. D,D — and E*
English speaking Nordic	12.3	19.9
Total Nordic	8.1	25.8
Non-English speaking Nordic	5.7	29.1
Alpine	3.8	50.3
Mediterranean	2.5	53.6

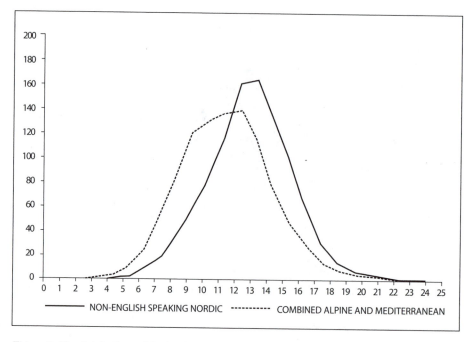

Figure 45. The distributions of the intelligence scores of the non-English speaking Nordic group and the combined Alpine and Mediterranean groups. The differences are very significant. 70.5% of the non-English speaking Nordic group exceed the average Alpine, and 73.3% exceed the average Mediterranean. If one is inclined to believe that the language factor will account for the superiority of the total Nordic group, he may disregard the English speaking Nordic group entirely, and still find the non-English speaking Nordic group superior to the Alpine and Mediterranean groups, proving that the race differences are due to intelligence and not to facility in the use of English.

The criteria of the per cent. at or above the average white officer, and at or below the average of the negro draft give the . . . results [in the table below]:

	Per Cent. at or Above Average White Officer	*Per Cent. at or Below Average of the Negro Draft*
English speaking Nordic	4.0	10.9
Total Nordic	2.3	14.5
Non-English speaking Nordic	1.3	16.5
Alpine	1.0	34.5
Mediterranean	0.5	36.5

The criterion of the per cent. below an approximate "mental age" of eight gives the . . . results [in the table below]:

Per Cent. Below "Mental Age" 8	
English speaking Nordic	0.8
Total Nordic	1.1
Non-English speaking Nordic	1.3
Alpine	4.2
Mediterranean	4.2

Section IX

Re-Examination of Previous Conclusions in the Light of the Race Hypothesis

It is now necessary to retrace our steps for a moment to examine some of our previous conclusions in the light of this new hypothesis. The hypothesis that the differences between the nativity groups found in the army tests are due to the race factor may be used to re-test our previous conclusions that each succeeding five year period of immigration since 1902 has given us an increasingly inferior selection of individuals (Section IV). The periods which we sample by means of the army data, and the average score on the combined scale of each sample are as follows:

Period	Number of Cases	Combined Scale Average
1887–1897	764	13.82
1898–1902	771	13.55
1903–1907	1897	12.47
1908–1912	4287	11.74
1913–1917	3576	11.41

Table 35, which gives our estimates of the per cent. of Nordic, Alpine and Mediterranean blood coming to this country, shows that the big change in immigration came between the decades 1881–1890 and 1891–1900, the percentage of Nordic blood which formerly ran from 40% to 50% having dropped to 30% in the decade 1891–1900, and to approximately 20% or 25% in the two subsequent decades. On the other hand, the big drop in the intelligence of immigrants arriving came after 1902. The change in character of the immigration would account for part of the decline in the average intelligence of succeeding periods of immigration, but not for all of it. The decline in intelligence is due to two factors, the change in the races migrating to this country, and to the additional factor of the sending of lower and lower representatives of each race.

The only tendency which would relieve this deplorable situation would be a current of emigration strong enough to counteract the current of immigration. Table 6 preceding shows the ratio between emigration and immigration for each of the nativity groups involved in this study, and we find in general between 1908 and 1917 a return current approximately one third of the arriving current.

Unfortunately, no emigration statistics are available prior to 1908, and the figures after 1912 are distorted by the Balkan and European wars. The only sample that we can take that is comparatively free from outside influences is the sample 1908–1912. Taking the figures of arrivals and departures for this period, and dividing them into Nordic, Alpine and Mediterranean groups according to the method previously outlined, we obtain the following percentage estimates:

	Alien Immigrants Admitted	*Alien Emigrants Departed*	*Net Immigration*
Per cent. of Nordic Blood	21.2	16.0	23.9
Per cent. of Alpine Blood	50.4	50.6	50.2
Per cent. of Mediterranean blood	23.2	28.6	20.5
Per cent. others and unclassified	5.2	4.8	5.4

The sample from this five year period shows a slight change (approximately 3%) in favor of the Nordic type and against the Mediterranean type, the Alpine immigration holding its own. There is therefore no relief from our receding curve of intelligence from emigration, if this five year period be taken as typical of the outward alien passenger movement in other years.

It will be remembered that the army authors tentatively offered the hypothesis that the more intelligent immigrants remained in this country, while the more stupid ones went home, as a possible method of accounting for the increase of intelligence scores with increasing years of residence. The gain of 3% in favor of the Nordic immigration would produce a very slight tendency in this direction, but not enough to account for the actual increase of intelligence scores found with increasing years of residence, 11.41 (1913–1917) to 13.82 (1887–1897).

It will also be remembered that the army writers offered the hypothesis of the better adaptation of the more thoroughly Americanized group to the situation of the examination to account for the increases shown. The factor of the adaptation to the situation of the examination cannot be dissected out of the total scores of the test. If such a factor were present, it would fall equally heavily on Nordic, Alpine and Mediterranean alike, unless the change in the character of immigration were so complete that the groups sampled at the two extremes of the residence groups (1887–1897 and 1913–1917) represented different race groups.

But the difference between these two years of residence groups (2.41 ± 0.0735) is so marked that it would be necessary to assume (if our Nordic group were the more thoroughly Americanized) that the 1887–1897 group was composed entirely of English speaking Nordics or their equivalent in intelligence, and that our 1913–1917 group was composed entirely of Mediterraneans or their equivalent in intelligence, assumptions quite unwarranted in view of the fact that in the two years of residence groups 1887–1897 and 1898-1902 we sampled 1545 individuals, while our Nordic group includes 3456 cases, and also in view of the fact that the Nordic immigration has dropped, in the period observed, at the outside from 45% to 20%. We may therefore conclude that the intangible factor of "the more thoroughly Americanized group" can not be used to explain the high test record of the Nordic group.

There is only one other possible escape from the conclusion that our test results indicate a genuine intellectual superiority of the Nordic group over the Alpine and Mediterranean groups, and that is the assumption that the situation of the examination involved a situation that was "typically Nordic." This assumption of course lands us in a perfect circle of reasoning. It would leave us with the conclusion that there was something mysteriously Nordic about alpha and beta that favored this race. We should have to assume that the Nordic, no matter where he may be, in the Canadian Northwest, in the Highlands of Scotland, or on the shores of the Baltic, is always ready for an intelligence test. Perhaps it would be easier to say that the Nordic is intelligent. A situation "typically Nordic" could not be used, however, to account for the slight but real difference between the English speaking Nordic and the non-English speaking Nordic groups. It is therefore best to abandon the attempt to account for the differences by the more or less feeble hypotheses that would make these differences an artifact of the method of examining, and recognize the fact that we are dealing with real differences in the intelligence of immigrants coming to our shores.

We have previously noted the fact that the foreign born in the army sampled as representative of the immigrants coming to this country between 1887 and 1897 were statistically identical with the native born white draft. The change in the character of our immigration came between 1890 and 1900. The real drop in the curve of intelligence, however, started about 1900. We, therefore, cannot account for the drop in the intelligence of the immigrants sampled as representatives of those coming to this country in each five year period since 1902 by the race hypothesis entirely.

No other scientist encapsulated the scientific, racial doctrines of Nazi Germany more than Hans F. K. Günther. In this selection, Günther outlines the widely shared view among racial writers of the time that the key to history was race. He warned that Germany was endangered by the "denordization" of its racial stock. Günther's debt to American writers, particularly Madison Grant and Lothrop Stoddard, is all too evident in this selection, which indicates the similarity between German and American Nordicists. Less obvious, but still present here, is the argument that individuals must be prepared to sacrifice for the racial good of the state. This view of the state of the organism wherein the parts must be subservient to the whole was one of the more subtle ways biological thought overlapped with social thought historically.

The Racial Elements of European History

HANS F. K. GÜNTHER

The Nordic Ideal—a Result of the Anthropological View of History

If degeneration (that is, a heavy increase in inferior hereditary tendencies) and denordization (that is, disappearance of the Nordic blood) have brought the Asiatic and south European peoples of Indo-European speech to their decay and fall, and if degeneration and denordization now, in turn, threaten the decay and fall of the peoples of Germanic speech, then the task is clearly to be seen which must be taken in hand, if there is still enough power of judgment left: the advancement of the peoples of Germanic speech will be brought about through an increase of the valuable and healthy hereditary tendencies, and an increase of the Nordic blood. The works on general eugenics show how the valuable hereditary tendencies can be increased. Here, therefore, we will only deal with the question of the renewal of the Nordic element.

    The French Count Arthur Gobineau (1816–82), was the first to point out in his work, *Essai sur l'inégalité des races humaines* (1853–5), the importance of the Nordic race for the life of the peoples. Count Gobineau, too, was the first to see that, through the mixture of the Nordic with other races, the way was being prepared for what to-day (with Spengler) is called the 'Fall of the West' (cp. P. 198). Gobineau's personality as investigator and poet ('all the conquering strength of this man') has been described by Schemann[1], and it is, thanks to Schemann, through his foundation in 1894 of the Gobineau Society (to further Gobineau's ideas), and through his translation of the *Essay on the Inequality of Human Races*, which appeared 1898–1901, that Gobineau's name and the foundations he traced for the Nordic ideal have not fallen into forgetfulness[2]. The very great importance of Gobineau's work in the history of the culture of our day is shown by Schemann in his book, *Gobineaus Rassenwerk* (1910).

It is evident that Gobineau's work on race, which was carried out before investigations into race had reached any tangible results, is in many of its details no longer tenable to-day. The basic thought of this work, however, stands secure. From the standpoint of racial science we may express ourselves as to Gobineau's work in somewhat the same way as Eugen Fischer, the anthropologist: 'The racial ideal must and will force its way, if not quite in the form given it by Gobineau, at any rate from the wider point of view quite in his sense; he was the great forerunner.'[3]

The turn of the century, when Schemann's translation appeared, may be said to be the time from which onwards a certain interest in racial questions was aroused. About the same time, too, in 1899, appeared the work which for the first time brought the racial ideal, and particularly the Nordic ideal, into the consciousness of a very wide circle through the enthusiasm, and also the opposition, which it aroused: this work was *The Foundations of the Nineteenth Century*, by H. S. Chamberlain (born 1855), at that time an Englishman, now a German. On this work from the standpoint of racial science we may pass a judgment somewhat like that of Eugen Fischer: 'Undeterred by the weak foundations of many details, and recklessly changing even well-established conceptions to serve his purpose, he raises a bold structure of thought, which thus naturally offers a thousand points for attack, so that the real core of the matter escapes attack—and it would stand against it.'[4]

Since the works of Gobineau and Chamberlain appeared, many investigators, in the realms of natural and social science, have devoted themselves eagerly to bringing light into racial questions, so that to-day not only the core of the theory both of Gobineau and of Chamberlain stands secure, but also much new territory has been won for an ideal of the Nordic race. A new standpoint in history, the 'racial historical standpoint,' is shaping itself.

The Nordic race ideal naturally meets with most attention among those peoples which to-day still have a strong strain of Nordic blood, of whom some are even still very predominantly Nordic—that is, among the peoples of Germanic speech in Europe and North America. It is unlikely that Gobineau's thought will find a home among the peoples of Romance speech, even though the first scientific work from the racial historical standpoint, *L'Aryen, son rôle social* (which likewise appeared in 1899), has a Frenchman, Georges Vacher de Lapouge, for its author. Denordization has probably already gone too far in France also. Any great attention towards race questions is unlikely, too, among peoples of Slav speech.

But the result was bound to be that in all those peoples who came to know

Gobineau's theory there were some persons who were deeply moved by them. Since the end of last century we can, as was said above, even speak of a growing interest in race questions, although we cannot yet speak of a spread of clear ideas. Following the terms used by Gobineau and Chamberlain, we come here and there upon more or less clear conceptions of the need for keeping the 'Germanic' blood pure, or (following Lapouge) of keeping the 'Aryan' blood pure.[5] In this way the door is always left wide open to the confusion of race and people or of racial and linguistic membership, and a clear definition of aims is impossible. What was (and still is) lacking is a knowledge of the conception of 'race' (cp. p. 3), and a knowledge of the races making up the Germanic peoples (that is, peoples speaking Germanic tongues) and the Indo-European peoples (that is, peoples speaking Indo-European tongues). There was (and still is) lacking a due consideration of the racial idiotype (hereditary formation) of the Nordic man, as the creator of the values which characterize the culture of the Indo-European ('Aryan') and the Germanic peoples. A racial anthropology of Europe could not be written in Gobineau's time. Many detailed investigations were still needed.[6]

But more was (and is still) wanting: Gobineau, like his contemporaries, had as yet no knowledge of the importance of selection for the life of peoples. The Nordic race may go under without having been mixed with other races, if it loses to other races in the competition of the birth-rate, if in the Nordic race the marriage rate is smaller, the marrying age higher, and the births fewer. Besides an insight into the 'unique importance of the Nordic race' (Lenz) there must be also a due knowledge of the laws of heredity and the phenomena of selection, and this knowledge is just beginning to have its deeper effect on some of the members of various nations.

Maupertius (1744, 1746) and Kant (1775, 1785, 1790) had been the first to point out the importance of selection for living beings. But the influence of the conception of selection only really begins to show itself after the foundations of modern biology were laid by Darwin's *Origin of Species* in 1859. The conception of selection was bound to have an effect on the view taken of the destiny of the peoples. Darwin's cousin, Francis Galton (1822–1911), the 'father of eugenics,' was the first to see this.[7] He was the first to show that it is not environment but heredity which is the decisive factor for all living beings, and therefore for man too, and drew the outlines of a theory of eugenics in the knowledge that the improvement of a people is only possible by a sensible increase of the higher hereditary qualities. But it took nearly forty years for Galton's importance to be rightly understood and for his work to bear fruit.

Galton's views had as yet no scientific theory of heredity on which to build. This was created in its main outlines by Johann Mendel (1822–84), an Augustinian father in Brünn (in religion he was known as Gregor), whose life-work, after its recovery in 1900, had so deep an effect that research after research was undertaken, and to-day a wide-embracing science of heredity stands secure.

Through researches such as these Gobineau's teachings received a deeper meaning, and found fresh support from all these sources, from the sciences of heredity, eugenics, and race: the Nordic movement was born. It had to come into being in those countries where there was still enough Nordic blood running in the peoples to make a Nordic new birth possible. Thus in Germany societies have been founded aiming at the propagation of the Nordic ideal; thus societies of the same kind have been founded in the United States; and such societies would seem sometimes to go beyond these countries.

If the Nordic ideal in Germany has been active longer than in other countries, it would seem, owing to the splitting up of its followers into small groups, not to have found the same diffusion which it has in North America. In the United States the books of Grant and Stoddard[8] have had a remarkable success; Grant's book through its racial theories, and its warning against the threatened dying out of the Nordic race, the 'Great Race'; Stoddard's books through their warning against the 'yellow' and 'black' peril (cp. p. 65) which threaten from without the peoples under Nordic leadership and through their warning against the degeneration which threatens these peoples from within owing to the heavy increase in inferior hereditary tendencies. The highly developed eugenic research, which in North America has become something like a patriotic preoccupation, gave Grant's and Stoddard's works a sure scientific foundation, and had already made the ground ready everywhere for the reception of racial and eugenic theories. Further, there has been the whole-hearted support of leading men, and of a section of the Press; while President Harding in a public speech (on 26th October 1921) pointed out the importance of Stoddard's book, *The Rising Tide of Color*, and Congress, accepting Grant's views, passed the Immigration Laws, which are to encourage the wished-for north-west European immigration, and to put a bar on the unwished-for immigration from south and east Europe. Immigration from Asia, and the immigration of undesirables in general, is forbidden. Grant himself has been chosen as vice-president of the Immigration Restriction League. It may be presumed that the Immigration Laws as now passed are only the first step to still more definite laws dealing with race and eugenics. In North America, especially, where there is the opportunity to examine the races and racial mixtures of Europe from the point of view of their civic worth, the importance of the Nordic race could not stay hidden. Leading statesmen have seen the importance of this race, and are proclaiming their knowledge.[9] In North America a significant change is taking place in our own day: Europe as an area of emigration is no longer looked at in the light of its states or peoples, but in the light of its races. How Germany (or the pick of German emigrants) in this regard strikes America, may be seen from the fact that Germany, as a land of emigrants, is the most highly favoured of all European countries.

The peril of denordization (*Finis Americae*, Grant) has been recognized by many Americans since Grant's book appeared. Associations have been formed among the Nordic and predominantly Nordic Americans of Anglo-Saxon descent, such as 'The Nordic Guard,' and among Americans of German descent ('The Nordic Aryan Federation,' and so on). Some of the Nordic-minded North Americans seem to have joined together in co-operative unions, so as to make themselves gradually economically independent of big capital in non-Nordic hands. It would seem as though the Nordic-minded sections of North America had begun with great forethought and efficiency to take steps for the maintenance and increase of Nordic blood. A better insight, however, is perhaps still needed into the importance of the birth-rate for all such aims.

When it is remembered that the Nordic ideal in Germany had taken root here and there as long ago as the end of last century, we do not get, on the whole, from the Nordic strivings of this country that picture of unity and purpose which is shown by North America. However, we must not overlook the economically very straitened circumstances in which the German followers of the Nordic ideal, who in greatest part belong to the middle classes, find themselves—circumstances which are always piling up hindrances to any forward striving. The hindrances, however, in the path of a Nordic movement lie partly in the German nature itself, in the splitting up into small exclusive groups each with its own 'standpoint,' which is found over and over again. This splitting up is the reason why the 'societies for the defence of the Nordic race' (Ploetz) in Germany can only be looked on as the beginning of an interest in race questions, and why we must agree with Ploetz when he speaks of[10] these 'defensive societies' as being 'considerably poorer in membership and influence than those of the Jews'; indeed, we cannot yet speak of any 'influence' of the Nordic ideal.

These endeavours along Nordic lines, however, are not to be undervalued as tokens of an awakening attention to race questions. Those among the youth who have been gripped by the Nordic ideal have already done much to spread their views, even under the crushing conditions of to-day in Germany, and in spite of the lack of money. The beginnings may be humble, but the deep change is full of importance; 'Individualism,' so highly prized in the nineteenth century, and still loudly proclaimed by yesterday's generation, is coming to an end. The stress laid on each man's individuality, which up till yesterday was proclaimed with the resounding shout of 'Be thyself,' has become a matter of doubt, even of contempt, to a newer generation. It set me pondering, when, during the writing of this book, the statement of the aims of a 'Young Nordic Association' reached me, in which I find the following sentence: 'We wish to keep the thought always before us that, if our race is not to perish, it is a question not only of choosing a Nordic mate, but over and above this, of helping our race through our marriage to a victorious birth-rate.'

Up to the other day such a view of life would not have met with any understanding, and to yesterday's generation it must still seem beyond comprehension. The present age, indeed, was brought up amidst the ideas of the 'natural equality of all men,' and of the distinct individuality of each one of us ('Individualism,' 'Cultivation of personality'). When we look back to-day, we are astonished to see how long the biologically untenable theories of the Age of Enlightenment and of Rousseau (1712–78) could hold the field, and how, even to-day, they determine the attitude towards life of great masses of men, although men like Fichte and Carlyle had already gone beyond such views.[11] Although really discredited, the ideas of equality and individualism still hold the field, since they satisfy the impulses of an age of advanced degeneration and denordization, or at least hold out hopes of doing so, and yield a good profit to those exploiting this age. If, without giving any heed to the definitions of current political theories, we investigate quite empirically what is the prevailing idea among the Western peoples of the essential nature of a nation, we shall find that by a nation no more is generally understood than the sum of the now living citizens of a given State. We shall find, further, that the purpose of the State is generally held to be no more than the satisfaction of the daily needs of this sum of individuals, or else only of the sum of individuals who are banded together to make up a majority. The greatest possible amount of 'happiness' for individuals is to be won by majority decisions.[12]

Racial and eugenic insight brings a different idea of the true nature of a people. A people is then looked upon as a fellowship with a common destiny of the past, the living, and the coming generations—a fellowship with one destiny, rooted in responsibility towards the nation's past, and looking towards its responsibility to the nation's future, to the coming generations. The generation living at any time within such a people is seen by the Nordic ideal as a fellowship of aims, which strives for an ever purer presentment of the Nordic nature in this people. It is thus only that the individual takes a directive share in the national life through his active responsibility. But in this fellowship of aims it is the predominantly Nordic men who have the heaviest duties: 'O, my brothers, I dedicate and appoint you to a new nobility: ye shall become my shapers and begetters, and sowers of the future' (Nietzsche, *Also sprach Zarathustra*).

The striving that can be seen among the youth for an 'organic' philosophy of life—that is, a philosophy sprung from the people and the native land, bound up with the laws of life, and opposed to all 'individualism'—must in the end bind this youth to the life of the homeland and of its people, just as the German felt himself bound in early times, to whom the clan tie was the very core of his life.

It could be shown that the old German view of life was so in harmony with the laws of life that it was bound to increase the racial and eugenic qualities of the Germans, and that, with the disappearance of this view of life in the Middle Ages, both the race and the inheritance of health were bound to be endangered. And a Nordic movement will always seek models for its spiritual guidance in the old Germanic world, which was an unsullied expression of the Nordic nature.[13]

In the nations of Germanic speech the Nordic ideal still links always with popular traditions handed down from Germanic forbears whose Nordic appearance and nature is still within the knowledge of many. Unexplained beliefs, unconscious racial insight, are always showing themselves; this is seen in the fact that in Germany a tall, fair, blue-eyed person is felt to be a 'true German,' and in the fact that the public adoption offices in Germany are asked by childless couples wishing to adopt children far oftener for fair, blue-eyed, than for dark ones. The Nordic ideal as the conception of an aim has no difficulty in taking root within the peoples of Germanic speech, for in these peoples the attributes of the healthy, capable, and high-minded, and of the handsome man, are more or less consciously still summed up in the Nordic figure. Thus the Nordic ideal becomes an ideal of unity: that which is common to all the divisions of the German people—although they may have strains of other races, and so differ from one another—is the Nordic strain. What is common to northern and to southern England—although the south may show a stronger Mediterranean strain—is the Nordic strain. It is to be particularly noted that in the parts of the German-speaking area which are on the whole predominantly Dinaric, and in Austria, too, the Nordic ideal has taken root, and unions of predominantly Nordic men have been formed.

Thus a hope opens out for some union among the peoples of Germanic speech; what is common to these peoples, although they may show strains of various races, is the Nordic strain. If the Nordic ideal takes root within them, it must necessarily come to be an ideal of harmony and peace. Nothing could be a better foundation and bulwark of peace among the leading peoples than the awakening of the racial consciousness of the peoples of Germanic speech. During the Great War Grant had written[14] that this was essentially a civil war, and had compared this war in its racially destructive effects to the Peloponnesian War between the two leading Hellenic tribes. The Nordic-minded men within the peoples of Germanic speech must strive after such an influence on the governments and public opinion, that a war which has so destroyed the stock of Nordic blood as the Great War has done (cp. pp. 247 ff., and 130) shall never again be possible, nor a war in the future into which the nations are dragged in the way described by Morhardt, the former president of the French League for the Rights of Man, in his book, *Les preuves* (Paris, 1925). The Nordic ideal must widen out into the All-Nordic ideal; and in its objects and nature the All-Nordic ideal would necessarily be at the same time the ideal of the sacredness of peace among the peoples of Germanic speech.

In the war of to-day, and still more in that of to-morrow, there can no longer be any thought of a 'prize of victory' which could outweigh the contra-selection necessarily bound up with any war. For any one who has come to see this, it seems very doubtful whether even the most favourable political result of a contest deserves to be called a 'victory,' if the fruits of this 'victory' fall to those elements of a nation who, as a result of their hereditary qualities, have slipped through the meshes of the modern war-sieve. The real victims in any future war between the Great Powers, whether in the losing or in the 'winning' nation, are the hereditary classes standing out by their capacity in war and spirit of sacrifice. It will be one of the tasks of the followers of the Nordic ideal to bring this home to their peoples and governments.

If this prospect of a political influence wielded by the Nordic ideal seems to-day a very bold forecast, yet the task of bringing about a Nordic revival seems to arise very obviously from the history of the (Indo-European) peoples under Nordic leadership, as the most natural ideal to set against the 'decline' which to-day is also threatening the peoples of Germanic speech. There is no objection against the Nordic ideal[15] which can be given any weight in the face of a situation which Eugen Fischer (in 1910) described as follows for the German people: 'To-day in Italy, Spain, and Portugal, the Germanic blood, the Nordic race, has already disappeared. Decline, in part insignificance, is the result. France is the next nation that will feel the truth of this; and then it will be our turn, without any doubt whatever, if things go on as they have gone and are going to-day.'[16] And since this utterance there has been the dreadful contra-selection of the Great War.

This being the situation, the problem is how to put a stop to denordization, and how to find means to bring about a Nordic revival. How are Nordics and those partly Nordic to attain to earlier marriages and larger families?—that is the question from the physical side of life. How is the spirit of responsibility, of efficiency, and of devotion to racial aims to be aroused in a world of selfishness, of degeneration, and of unbounded 'individualism'?—that is the question from the spiritual side of life.

Once this question is seen by thoughtful men in the peoples of Germanic speech to be the one vital question for these peoples, then they will have to strive to implant in the predominantly Nordic people of all classes a spirit of racial responsibility, and to summon their whole nation to a community of aims. An age of unlimited racial mixture has left the men of the present day physically and mentally rudderless, and thus powerless for any clear decision. There is no longer any ideal of physical beauty and spiritual strength to make that bracing call on the living energies which fell to the lot of earlier times. If selection within a people cannot be directed towards an ideal, unconsciously or consciously pursued, then its power to raise to a higher level grows weaker and weaker, and it ends by changing its direction, turning its action towards the less creative races, and the inferior hereditary tendencies. Every people has had assigned to it a particular direction of development, its own special path of selective advance. The selective advance in the peoples of Germanic speech can have as its goal only the physical and spiritual picture presented by the Nordic race. In this sense the Nordic race is (to use Kant's expression) not given as a gift but as a task; and in this sense it was that, in speaking of 'the Nordic ideal among the Germans,' we necessarily spoke of the Nordic man as the model for the working of selection in the German people, and showed that no less a task is laid on the Nordic movement than the revival of a whole culture.

The question is not so much whether we men now living are more or less Nordic; but the question put to us is whether we have courage enough to make ready for future generations a world cleansing itself racially and eugenically. When any people of Indo-European speech has been denordicized, the process has always gone on for centuries; the will of Nordic-minded men must boldly span the centuries. Where selection is in question, it is many generations that must be taken into the reckoning, and the Nordic-minded men of the present can only expect one reward in their lifetime for their striving: the consciousness of their courage. Race theory and investigations on heredity call forth and give strength to a New Nobility: the youth, that is, with lofty aims in all ranks which, urged on like Faust, seeks to set its will towards a goal which calls to it from far beyond the individual life.[17]

Since within such a movement profit and gain is not to be looked for, it will always be the movement of a minority. But the spirit of any age has always been formed by minorities only, and so, too, the spirit of that age of the masses in which we live. The Nordic movement in the end seeks to determine the spirit of the age, and more than this spirit, from out of itself. If it did not securely hold this confident hope, there would be no meaning or purpose in any longer thinking the thoughts of Gobineau.

Notes

1   Gobineau (vol. i., 1913; vol. ii., 1916). As many will probably not read Gobineau's *Essai* because of its length, Kleinecke's *Gobineaus Rassenlehre*, 1920, may here be mentioned. Gobineau's life and works are also shortly described in Hahne's *Gobineau* (Reclam 6517-18).

2   Although in France a statesman and historian like Alexis de Tocqueville and an anthropologist like Broca had been attracted by Gobineau's work on race; while men like Renan and Viollet-le-Duc had been influenced by him, and men like Albert Sorel and Le Bon had become his followers—it was not till late years that the importance of Gobineau was again recognized. But in Germany, too, where men such as A. von Hum-

boldt, I. H. Fichte (Fichte's son), A. von Keller, and, above all, Richard Wagner were his champions, and where Lotze came under his influence, Gobineau would probably have been forgotten without Schemann's efforts. In our day (1924) Gobineau is fashionable in France. His imaginative works are coming out in new editions; well-known reviews devote special numbers to Gobineau, the artist; indeed, we may speak of an over-valuation of this side of Gobineau's work, while the very small number of the followers of his race-theory is dwindling more and more in France.

3   Following Schemann, Neues aus d. Welt Gobineaus; reprinted from the Polit.-anthrop. Revue, 1912.

4   In Handwörterbuch d. Naturw., under 'Sozialanthropologie.'

5   Philology used formerly often give the name of Aryan to the Indo-European languages; nowadays the term 'Aryan' is mostly applied only to the Indo-Persian branch of these. Racial investigation in the beginning sometimes called the (non-existing) white or Caucasian race Aryan; later the peoples of Indo-European speech were occasionally called Aryan; and finally the Nordic race also was termed Aryan. To-day the term Aryan has gone out of scientific use, and its use is not advisable, especially since in lay circles the word Aryan is current in still other meanings, and mostly with a very confused application to the peoples who do not speak Semitic languages; the 'Semites' are then opposed to the 'Aryans.' The term 'Semites,' however, has been likewise given up in anthropology, since men and peoples of very various racial descent speak Semitic tongues (cp. on this the fourth chapter above).

6   Cp. the section, 'Einiges zur Geschichte der Rassenkunde,' etc., in my Rassenkunde des deutschen Volkes.

7   For an account of Galton, cp. K. Pearson's Francis Galton, 1922.

8   Grant, The Passing of the Great Race, 4th ed., 1921. Stoddard, The Rising Tide of Color, 1919; The Revolt against Civilization, 1924; and Racial Realities in Europe, 1925.

9   Thus, quite lately Davis, the Minister for Labour. The Oslo newspaper, Morgenbladet, of 1st July 1924, writes after his astonishingly frank utterances: 'It is, anyhow, an undisputed fact that it was the so-called Nordic race which, coming as immigrants into America, has taken on the heaviest burdens. They have driven the road, ploughed the land, built up industry, while the Italians and Greeks polish boots, sell fruit, and make bombs for "use at home," and the Jews lead an easy life in their Loan Banks and secondhand shops, and on friendly loans at 20 per cent. This is, of course, speaking in general terms, but it hits the nail on the head. If you travel towards the north-west, you understand what has been done by the Nordic race, and particularly the Scandinavians, for agriculture. Most of them began with two empty hands and an iron will. The result can be seen in the form of flourishing districts. If you go into the great towns and wander through the various "Little Italys" and "Little Greeces" and through the Jewish quarters, and then take a trip to where "our people" live, you will feel relief at once again breathing clean air.'

10 Op. cit.

11 L. F. Clauss has arrived at a statement of aims in accordance with the Nordic ideal by a philosophical investigation from the phenomenological standpoint; see his Die Nordische Seele, 1923, and Rasse und Seele, 1926.

12 Faguet shows (Le culte de l'incompétence, 1921) that the political theories of the nineteenth century and the present time have had the effect only of 'worshipping incapacity.' The historical causes of this worship are set out by Le Bon, Lois psychologiques de l'évolution des peuples, 17th ed., 1922.

13 Hence we will here refer the reader to Neckel, Die Altnordische Literatur, 1923, and Altgermanische Kultur, 1925. As the most profound description of the old Ger-

manic world may be mentioned the work in four volumes of V. Grönbech, Vor Folkeaet i Oldtiden, which appeared 1909-12. Of Grönbech it may be truly said that his investigation reaches the innermost being of the old Germanic soul.

14 Op. cit.

15 In Der Nordische Gedanke unter den Deutschen, 1925, I have tried to sift and refute many of the objections against the Nordic ideal.

16 Sozialanthropologie, etc., 1910.

17 'Neo-Aristocracy,' the spirit of a new nobility, is what Stoddard, too, seeks to rouse with the last section of his book, The Revolt against Civilization.

World War II and the racial atrocities of the Nazi regime resulted in a sea change in American scientific attitudes about race. After the war, many scientists believed they should use their scientific expertise to fight against race prejudice and discrimination. Some of them were active in the legal campaign led by the National Association for the Advancement of Colored People (NAACP) against racial segregation in public schools. These social scientists wrote this brief to be submitted to the U.S. Supreme Court in a case that eventually found that racial segregation was unconstitutional. The brief made three points that reflected the new scientific thinking about race. First, that there were no racial differences in intelligence or ability to learn. Second, that racial segregation was psychologically damaging to both majority and minority group children. Third, that desegregation could be accomplished smoothly, and that people of different races could live peacefully side by side. All three of these arguments were radical breaks with the racial thinking of just fifty years before.

The Effects of Segregation and the Consequences of Desegregation: A Social Science Statement

I

The problem of the segregation of racial and ethnic groups constitutes one of the major problems facing the American people today. It seems desirable, therefore, to summarize the contributions which contemporary social science can make toward its resolution. There are, of course, moral and legal issues involved with respect to which the signers of the present statement cannot speak with any special authority and which must be taken into account in the solution of the problem. There are, however, also factual issues involved with respect to which certain conclusions seem to be justified on the basis of the available scientific evidence. It is with these issues only that this paper is concerned. Some of the issues have to do with the consequences of segregation, some with the problems of changing from segregated to unsegregated practices. These two groups of issues will be dealt with in separate sections below. It is necessary, first, however, to define and delimit the problem to be discussed.

Definitions

For purposes of the present statement, *segregation* refers to that restriction of opportunities for different types of associations between the members of one racial, religious, national or geographic origin, or linguistic group and those of other groups, which results from or is supported by the action of any official body or agency representing some branch of government. We are not here concerned with such segregation as arises from the free movements of individuals which are neither enforced nor supported by official bodies, nor with the segregation of criminals or of individuals with communicable diseases which aims at protecting society from those who might harm it.

Where the action takes place in a social milieu in which the groups involved do not enjoy equal social status, the group that is of lesser social status will be referred to as the *segregated* group.

In dealing with the question of the effects of segregation, it must be recognized that these effects do not take place in a vacuum, but in a social context. The segregation of Negroes and of other groups in the United States takes place in a social milieu in which "race" prejudice and discrimination exist. It is questionable in the view of some students of the problem whether it is possible to have segregation without substantial discrimination. Myrdal[1] states: "Segregation ⋯ is financially possible and, indeed, a device of economy only as it is combined with substantial discrimination" (p. 629). The imbededness of segregation in such a context makes it difficult to disentangle the effects of segregation *per se* from the effects of the context. Similarly, it is difficult to disentangle the effects of segregation from the effects of a pattern of social disorganization commonly associated with it and reflected in high disease and mortality rates, crime and delinquency, poor housing, disrupted family life and general substandard living conditions. We shall, however, return to this problem after consideration of the observable effects of the total complex in which segregation is a major component.

II

At the recent Mid-century White House Conference on Children and Youth, a fact-finding report on the effects of prejudice, discrimination and segregation on the personality development of children was prepared as a basis for some of the deliberations.[2] This report brought together the available social science and psychological studies which were related to the problem of how racial and religious prejudices influenced the development of a healthy personality. It highlighted the fact that segregation, prejudices and discriminations, and their social concomitants potentially damage the personality of all children — the children of the majority group in a somewhat different way than the more obviously damaged children of the minority group.

The report indicates that as minority group children learn the inferior status to which they are assigned — as they observe the fact that they are almost always segregated and kept apart from others who are treated with more respect by the society as a whole — they often react with feelings of inferiority and a sense of personal humiliation. Many of them become confused about their own personal worth. On the one hand, like all other human beings they require a sense of personal dignity; on the other hand, almost nowhere in the larger society do they find their own dignity as human beings respected by others. Under these conditions, the minority group child is thrown into a conflict with regard to his feelings about himself and his group. He wonders whether his group and he himself are worthy of no more respect than they receive. This conflict and confusion leads to self-hatred and rejection of his own group.

The report goes on to point out that these children must find ways with which to cope with this conflict. Not every child, of course, reacts with the same patterns of behavior. The particular pattern depends upon many interrelated factors, among which are: the stability and quality of his family relations; the social and economic class to which he belongs; the cultural and educational background of his parents; the particular minority group to which he belongs; his personal characteristics, intelligence, special talents, and personality pattern.

Some children, usually of the lower socio-economic classes, may react by overt aggressions and hostility directed toward their own group or members of the dominant group.[3] Anti-social and delinquent behavior may often be interpreted as reactions to these racial frustrations. These reactions are self-destructive in that the larger society not only punishes those who commit them, but often interprets such aggressive and anti-social behavior as justification for continuing prejudice and segregation.

Middle class and upper class minority group children are likely to react to their racial frustrations and conflicts by withdrawal and submissive behavior. Or, they may react with compensatory and rigid conformity to the prevailing middle class values and standards and an aggressive determination to succeed in these terms in spite of the handicap of their minority status.

The report indicates that minority group children of all social and economic classes often react with a generally defeatist attitude and a lowering of personal ambitions. This, for example, is reflected in a lowering of pupil morale and a depression of the educational aspiration level among minority group children in segregated schools. In producing such effects, segregated schools impair the ability of the child to profit from the educational opportunities provided him.

Many minority group children of all classes also tend to be hypersensitive and anxious about their relations with the larger society. They tend to see hostility and rejection even in those areas where these might not actually exist.

The report concludes that while the range of individual differences among members of a rejected minority group is as wide as among other peoples, the evidence suggests that all of these children are unnecessarily encumbered in some ways by segregation and its concomitants.

With reference to the impact of segregation and its concomitants on children of the majority group, the report indicates that the effects are somewhat more obscure. Those children who learn the prejudices of our society are also being taught to gain personal status in an unrealistic and non-adaptive way. When comparing themselves to members of the minority group, they are not required to evaluate themselves in terms of the more basic standards of actual personal ability and achievement. The culture permits and at times, encourages them to direct their feelings of hostility and aggression against whole groups of people the members of which are perceived as weaker than themselves. They often develop patterns of guilt feelings, rationalizations and other mechanisms which they must use in an attempt to protect themselves from recognizing the essential injustice of their unrealistic fears and hatreds of minority groups.[4]

The report indicates further that confusion, conflict, moral cynicism, and disrespect for authority may arise in majority group children as a consequence of being taught the moral, religious and democratic principles of the brotherhood of man and the importance of justice and fair play by the same persons and institutions who, in their support of racial segregation and related practices, seem to be acting in a prejudiced and discriminatory manner. Some individuals may attempt to resolve this conflict by intensifying their hostility toward the minority group. Others may react by guilt feelings which are not necessarily reflected in more humane attitudes toward the minority group. Still others react by developing an unwholesome, rigid, and uncritical idealization of all authority figures — their parents, strong political and economic leaders. As described in *The Authoritarian Personality*,[5] they despise the weak, while they obsequiously and unquestioningly conform to the demands of the strong whom they also, paradoxically, subconsciously hate.

With respect to the setting in which these difficulties develop, the report emphasized the role of the home, the school, and other social institutions. Studies[6] have shown that from the earliest school years children are not only aware of the status differences among different groups in the society but begin to react with the patterns described above.

Conclusions similar to those reached by the Mid-century White House Conference Report have been stated by other social scientists who have concerned themselves with this problem. The following are some examples of these conclusions:

Segregation imposes upon individuals a distorted sense of social reality.[7]

Segregation leads to a blockage in the communications and interaction between the two groups. Such blockages tend to increase mutual suspicion, distrust and hostility.[8]

Segregation not only perpetuates rigid stereotypes and reinforces negative attitudes toward members of the other group, but also leads to the development of a social climate within which violent outbreaks of racial tensions are likely to occur.[9]

We return now to the question, deferred earlier, of what it is about the total society complex of which segregation is one feature that produces the effects described above — or, more precisely, to the question of whether we can justifiably conclude that, as only one feature of a complex social setting, segregation is in fact a significantly contributing factor to these effects.

To answer this question, it is necessary to bring to bear the general fund of psychological and sociological knowledge concerning the role of various environmental influences in producing feelings of inferiority, confusions in personal roles, various types of basic personality structures and the various forms of personal and social disorganization.

On the basis of this general fund of knowledge, it seems likely that feelings of inferiority and doubts about personal worth are attributable to living in an underprivileged environment only insofar as the latter is itself perceived as an indicator of low social status and as a symbol of inferiority. In other words, one of the important determinants in producing such feelings is the awareness of social status difference. While there are many other factors that serve as reminders of the differences in social status, there can be little doubt that the fact of enforced segregation is a major factor.[10]

This seems to be true for the following reasons among others: (1) because enforced segregation results from the decision of the majority group without the consent of the segregated and is commonly so perceived; and (2) because historically segregation patterns in the United States were developed on the assumption of the inferiority of the segregated.

In addition, enforced segregation gives official recognition and sanction to these other factors of the social complex, and thereby enhances the affects of the latter in creating the awareness of social status differences and feelings of inferiority.[11] The child who, for example, is compelled to attend a segregated school may be able to cope with ordinary expressions of prejudice by regarding the prejudiced person as evil or misguided; but he cannot readily cope with symbols of authority, the full force of the authority of the State — the school or the school board, in this instance — in the same manner. Given both the ordinary expression of prejudice and the school's policy of segregation, the former takes on greater force and seemingly becomes an official expression of the latter.

Not all of the psychological traits which are commonly observed in the social complex under discussion can be related so directly to the awareness of status differences — which in turn is, as we have already noted, materially contributed to by the practices of segregation. Thus, the low level of aspiration and defeatism so commonly observed in segregated groups is undoubtedly related to the level of self-evaluation; but it is also, in some measure, related among other things to one's expectations with regard to opportunities for achievement and, having achieved, to the opportunities for making use of these achievements. Similarly, the hypersensitivity and anxiety displayed by many minority group children about their relations with the larger society probably reflects their awareness of status differences; but it may also be influenced by the relative absence of opportunities for equal status contact which would provide correctives for prevailing unrealistic stereotypes.

The preceding view is consistent with the opinion stated by a large majority (90%) of social scientists who replied to a questionnaire concerning the probable effects of enforced segregation under conditions of equal facilities. This opinion was that, regardless of the facilities which are provided, enforced segregation is psychologically detrimental to the members of the segregated group.[12]

Similar considerations apply to the question of what features of the social complex of which segregation is a part contribute to the development of the traits which have been observed in majority group members. Some of these are probably quite closely related to the awareness of status differences, to which, as has already been pointed out, segregation makes a material contribution. Others have a more complicated relationship to the total social setting. Thus, the acquisition of an unrealistic basis for self-evaluation as a consequence of majority group membership probably reflects fairly closely the awareness of status differences. On the other hand, unrealistic fears and hatreds of minority groups, as in the case of the converse phenomenon among minority group members, are probably significantly influenced as well by the lack of opportunities for equal status contact.

With reference to the probable effects of segregation under conditions of equal facilities on majority group members, many of the social scientists who responded to the poll in the survey cited above felt that the evidence is less convincing than with regard to the probable effects of such segregation on minority group members, and the effects are possibly less widespread. Nonetheless, more than 80% stated it as their opinion that the effects of such segregation are psychologically detrimental to the majority group members.[13]

It may be noted that many of these social scientists supported their opinions on the effects of segregation on both majority and minority groups by reference to one or another or to several of the following four lines of published and unpublished evidence.[14] First, studies of children throw light on the relative priority of the awareness of status differentials and related factors as compared to the awareness of differences in facilities. On this basis, it is possible to infer some of the consequences of segregation as distinct from the influence of inequalities of facilities. Second, clinical studies and depth interviews throw light on the genetic sources and causal sequences of various patterns of psychological reaction; and, again, certain inferences are possible with respect to the effects of segregation *per se*. Third, there actually are some relevant but relatively rare instances of segregation with equal or even superior facilities, as in the cases of certain Indian reservations. Fourth, since there are inequalities of facilities in racially and ethnically homogeneous groups, it is possible to infer the kinds of effects attributable to such inequalities in the absence of effects of segregation and by a kind of subtraction to estimate the effects of segregation *per se* in situations where one finds both segregation and unequal facilities.

III

Segregation is at present a social reality. Questions may be raised, therefore, as to what are the likely consequences of desegregation.

One such question asks whether the inclusion of an intellectually inferior group may jeopardize the education of the more intelligent group by lowering educational standards or damage the less intelligent group by placing it in a situation where it is at a marked competitive disadvantage. Behind this question is the assumption, which is examined below, that the presently segregated groups actually are inferior intellectually.

The available scientific evidence indicates that much, perhaps all, of the observable differences among various racial and national groups may be adequately explained in terms of environmental differences.[15] It has been found, for instance, that the differences between the average intelligence test scores of Negro and white children decrease, and the overlap of the distributions increases, proportionately to the number of years that the Negro children have lived in the North.[16] Related studies have shown that this change cannot be explained by the hypothesis of selective migration.[17] It seems clear, therefore, that fears based on the assumption of innate racial differences in intelligence are not well founded.

It may also be noted in passing that the argument regarding the intellectual inferiority of one group as compared to another is, as applied to schools, essentially an argument for homogeneous groupings of children by intelligence rather than by race. Since even those who believe that there are innate differences between Negroes and whites in America in average intelligence grant that considerable overlap between the two groups exists, it would follow that it may be expedient to group together the superior whites and Negroes, the average whites and Negroes, and so on. Actually, many educators have come to doubt the wisdom of class groupings made homogeneous solely on the basis of intelligence.[18] Those who are opposed to such homogeneous grouping believe that this type of segregation, too, appears to create generalized feelings of inferiority in the child who attends a below average class, leads to undesirable emotional consequences in the education of the gifted child, and reduces learning opportunities which result from the interaction of individuals with varied gifts.

A second problem that comes up in an evaluation of the possible consequences of desegregation involves the question of whether segregation prevents or stimulates inter-racial tension and conflict and the corollary question of whether desegregation has one or the other effect.

The most direct evidence available on this problem comes from observations and systematic study of instances in which desegregation has occurred. Comprehensive reviews of such instances[19] clearly establish the fact that desegregation has been carried out successfully in a variety of situations although outbreaks of violence had been commonly predicted. Extensive desegregation has taken place without major incidents in the armed services in both Northern and Southern installations and involving officers and enlisted men from all parts of the country, including the South.[20] Similar changes have been noted in housing[21] and industry.[22] During the last war, many factories both in the North and South hired Negroes on a non-segregated, non-discriminatory basis. While a few strikes occurred, refusal by management and unions to yield quelled all strikes within a few days.[23]

Relevant to this general problem is a comprehensive study of urban race riots which found that race riots occurred in segregated neighborhoods, whereas there was no violence in sections of the city where the two races lived, worked and attended school together.[24]

Under certain circumstances desegregation not only proceeds without major difficulties, but has been observed to lead to the emergence of more favorable attitudes and friendlier relations between races. Relevant studies may be cited with respect to housing,[25] employment,[26] the armed services[27] and merchant marine,[28] recreation agency,[29] and general community life.[30]

Much depends, however, on the circumstances under which members of previously segregated groups first come in contact with others in unsegregated situations. Available evidence suggests, first, that there is less likelihood of unfriendly relations when the change is simultaneously introduced into all units of a social institution to which it is applicable — *e.g.*, all of the schools in a school system or all of the shops in a given factory.[31] When factories introduced Negroes in only some shops but not in others the prejudiced workers tended to classify the desegregated shops as inferior, "Negro work." Such objections were not raised when complete integration was introduced.

The available evidence also suggests the importance of consistent and firm enforcement of the new policy by those in authority.[32] It indicates also the importance of such factors as: the absence of competition for a limited number of facilities or benefits;[33] the possibility of contacts which permit individuals to learn about one another as individuals;[34] and the possibility of equivalence of positions and functions among all of the participants within the unsegregated situation.[35] These conditions can generally be satisfied in a number of situations, as in the armed services, public housing developments, and public schools.

IV

The problem with which we have here attempted to deal is admittedly on the frontiers of scientific knowledge. Inevitably, there must be some differences of opinion among us concerning the conclusiveness of certain items of evidence, and concerning the particular choice of words and placement of emphasis in the preceding statement. We are nonetheless in agreement that this statement is substantially correct and justified by the evidence, and the differences among us, if any, are of a relatively minor order and would not materially influence the preceding conclusions.

FLOYD H. ALLPORT, Syracuse, New York
GORDON W. ALLPORT, Cambridge, Mass.
CHARLOTTE BABCOCK, M.D., Chicago, Ill.
VIOLA W. BERNARD, M.D., N. Y., N. Y.
JEROME S. BRUNER, Cambridge, Mass.
HADLEY CANTRIL, Princeton, New Jersey
ISIDOR CHEIN, New York, New York
KENNETH B. CLARK, New York, N. Y.
MAMIE P. CLARK, New York, New York
STUART W. COOK, New York, New York
BINGHAM DAI, Durham, North Carolina
ALLISON DAVIS, Chicago, Illinois
ELSE FRENKEL-BRUNSWIK, Berkeley, Calif.
NOEL P. GIST, Columbia, Missouri

CHARLES S. JOHNSON, Nashville, Tennessee
DANIEL KATZ, Ann Arbor, Michigan
OTTO KLINEBERG, New York, New York
DAVID KRECH, Berkeley, California
ALFRED MCCLUNG LEE, Brooklyn, N. Y.
R. N. MACIVER, New York, New York
PAUL F. LAZARSFELD, New York, N. Y.
ROBERT K. MERTON, New York, N. Y.
GARDNER MURPHY, Topeka, Kans.
THEODORE M. NEWCOMB, Ann Arbor, Mich.
ROBERT REDFIELD, Chicago, Illinois
IRA DEA. REID, Haverford, Pennsylvania
ARNOLD M. ROSE, Minneapolis, Minn.
GERHART SAENGER, New York, New York
R. NEVITT SANFORD, Poughkeepsie, N. Y.
S. STANFIELD SARGENT, New York, N. Y.
M. BREWSTER SMITH, New York, N. Y.
SAMUEL A. STOUFFER, Cambridge, Mass.
WELLMAN WARNER, New York, N. Y.
GOODWIN WATSON, New York, New York
ROBIN M. WILLIAMS, Ithaca, New York
Dated: September 22, 1952.

References

Adorno, T. W.; Frenkel-Brunswik, E.; Levinson, D. J.; Sanford, R. N., *The Authoritarian Personality*, 1951.

Allport, G. W., and Kramer, B., Some Roots of Prejudice, *J. Psychol.*, 1946, 22, 9-39.

Bauer, C., Social Questions in Housing and Community Planning, *J. of Social Issues.* 1951, VII, 1-34.

Brameld, T., Educational Costs *Discrimination and National Welfare*, Ed. by MacIver, R. M., 1949.

Brenman, M., The Relationship Between Minority Group Identification in A Group of Urban Middle Class Negro Girls, *J. Soc. Psychol.*, 1940, 11, 171-197.

Brenman, M., Minority Group Membership and Religious, Psycho-sexual and Social Patterns In A Group of Middle-Class Negro Girls, *J. Soc. Psychol.*, 1940, 12, 179-196.

Brenman, M., Urban Lower-Class Negro Girls, *Psychiatry*, 1943, 6, 307-324.

Brooks, J. J., Interage Grouping on Trial, Continuous Learning, *Bulletin No. 87 of the Association for Childhood Education*, 1951.

Brophy, I. N., The Luxury of Anti-Negro Prejudice, *Public Opinion Quarterly*, 1946, 9, 456-466 (Integration in Merchant Marine).

Chein, I., What are the Psychological Effects of Segregation Under Conditions of Equal Facilities?, *International J. Opinion & Attitude Res.*, 1949, 2, 229-234.

Clark, K. B., Effect of Prejudice and Discrimination on Personality Development, *Fact Finding Report Mid-Century White House Conference on Children and Youth*, Children's Bureau-Federal Security Agency, 1950 (mimeographed).

Clark, K. B. and Clark, M. P., Emotional Factors in Racial Identification and Preference in Negro Children, *J. Negro Educ.*, 1950, 19, 341-350.

Clark, K. B. and Clark, M. P., Racial Identification and Preference in Negro Children, *Readings in Social Psychology*, Ed. by Newcomb & Hartley, 1947.

Conover, R. D., *Race Relations at Codornices Village, Berkeley-Albany, California: A Report of the Attempts to Break Down the Segregated Pattern On A Directly Managed Housing Project*, Housing and Home Finance Agency, Public Housing Administration, Region I, 1947 (mimeographed).

Davis, A., The Socialization of the American Negro Child and Adolescent, *J. Negro Educ.*, 1939, 8, 264-275.

Dean, J. P., *Situational Factors in Intergroup Relations: A Research Progress Report*, paper presented to American Sociological Society, Dec. 28, 1949 (mimeographed).

Delano, W., Grade School Segregation: The Latest Attack on Racial Discrimination, *Yale Law Journal*, 1952, 61, 730-744.

Deutscher, M. and Chein, I., The Psychological Effects of Enforced Segregation: A Survey of Social Science Opinion, *J. Psychol.*, 1948, 26, 259-287.

Deutsch, M. and Collins, M. E., *Interracial Housing, A Psychological Study of a Social Experiment*, 1951.

Feldman, H., The Technique of Introducing Negroes Into the Plant, *Personnel*, 1942, 19, 461-466.

Frazier, E., *The Negro In the United States*, 1949.

Harding, J. and Hogrefe, R., Attitudes of White Department Store Employees Toward Negro Co-Workers. *J. Social Issues*, 1952, 8, 19-28.

Irish, D. P., Reactions of Residents of Boulder, Colorado, to the Introduction of Japanese Into the Community, *J. Social Issues*, 1952, 8, 10-17.

Kenworthy, E. W., The Case Against Army Segregation, *Annals of the American Academy of Political and Social Science*, 1951, 275, 27-33.

Klineberg, O., *Characteristics of American Negro*, 1945.

Klineberg, O., *Negro Intelligence and Selective Migration*, 1935.

Klineberg, O., *Race Differences*, 1936.

Krech, D. & Crutchfield, R. S., *Theory and Problems of Social Psychology*, 1948.

Lane, R. H., *Teacher in Modern Elementary School*, 1941.

Lee, A. McClung and Humphrey, N. D., *Race Riot*, 1943.

Lee, A. McClung, Race Riots Aren't Necessary, *Public Affairs Pamph*let, 1945.

Merton, R. K.; West, P. S.; Jahoda, M., *Social Fictions and Social Facts: The Dynamics of Race Relations in Hilltown;* Bureau of Applied Social Research, Columbia University, 1949 (mimeographed).

Minard, R. D., The Pattern of Race Relationships in the Pocahontas Coal Field, *J. Social Issues*, 1952, 8, 29-44.

Myrdal, G., *An American Dilemma*, 1944.

Newcomb, T., *Social Psychology*, 1950.

Nelson, Lt. D. D., *The Integration of the Negro in the U. S. Navy*, 1951.

Rackow, F., Combatting Discrimination in Employment, *Bulletin No. 5, N. Y. State School of Industrial and Labor Relations*, Cornell Univ., 1951.

Radke, M.; Trager, H.; Davis, H., Social Preceptions and Attitudes of Children, *Genetic Psychol, Monog.*, 1949, 40, 327-447.

Radke, M., Trager, H., Children's Perceptions of the Social Role of Negroes and Whites, *J. Phsycol.*, 1950, 29, 3-33.

Reid, Ira, What Segregated Areas Mean, *Discrimination and National Welfare*, Ed. by MacIver, R. M., 1949.

Rose, A., The Influence of Legislation on Prejudice Chapter 53 in *Race Prejudice and Discrimination*, Ed. by Rose, A., 1951.

Rose, A., *Studies in Reduction of Prejudice*, Amer. Council on Race Relations, 1948.

Rutledge, E., *Integration of Racial Minorities in Public Housing Projects; A Guide for Local Housing Authorities on How to Do It*. Public Housing Administration, New York Field Office (mimeographed).

Saenger, G. and Gilbert, E., Customer Reactions to the Integration of Negro Sales Personnel, *International Journal of Attitude and Opinion Research*, 1950, 4, 57-76.

Saenger, G. & Gordon, N. S., The Influence of Discrimination on Minority Group Members in its Relation to Attempts to Combat Discrimination, *J.Soc. Psychol.*, 1950, 31.

Southall, S. E., *Industry's Unfinished Business*, 1951.

Stouffer, S., et al., *The American Soldier*, Vol. I, Chap. 19, A Note on Negro Troops in Combat, 1949.

Watson, G., *Action for Unity*, 1947.

Watson, J., Some Social and Psychological Situations Related to Change in Attitude, *Human Relations*, 1950, 3, 1.

Weaver, G. L-P., *Negro Labor, A National Problem*, 1941.

Williams, D. H., *The Effects of an Interracial Project Upon the Attitudes of Negro and White Girls Within the Young Women's Christian Association*, Unpublished M. A. thesis, Columbia University, 1934.

Williams, R., Jr., *The Reduction of Intergroup Tensions*, Social Science Research Council, 1947.

Wilner, D. M.; Walkley, R. P.; and Cook, S. W., Intergroup Contact and Ethnic Attitudes in Public Housing Projects, *J. Social Issues*, 1952, 8, 45-69.

Windner, A. E., *White Attitudes Towards Negro-White Interaction in in an Area of Changing Racial Composition*, Paper delivered at the Sixtieth Annual Meeting of The American Psychological Association, Washingtion, September 1952.

Opinions about Negro Infantry Platoons in White Companies in Several Divisions, *Information and Education Divisions, U. S. War Department, Report No. B-157*, 1945.

Educational Policies Commission of the National Education Association and the American Association of School Administration Report in *Education for All Americans*, published by the N.E.A., 1948.

Notes

1   Myrdal, G., An American Dilemma, 1944.

2   Clark, K. B., Effect of Prejudice and Discrimination on Personality Development, Fact Finding Report Mid-century White House Conference on Children and Youth, Children's Bureau, Federal Security Agency, 1950 (mimeographed).

3   Brenman, M., The Relationship Between Minority Group Identification in A Group of Urban Middle Class Negro Girls, J. Soc. Psychol., 1940, 11, 171-197; Brenman, M.,

Minority Group Membership and Religious, Psycho-sexual and Social Patterns in A Group of Middle-Class Negro Girls. J. Soc. Psychol., 1940, 12, 179-196; Brenman, M., Urban Lower-Class Negro Girls, Psychiatry, 1953, 6, 307-324; Davis, A., The Socialization of the American Negro Child and Adolescent, J. Negro Educ., 1939, 8, 264-275.

4   Adorno, T. W.; Frenkel-Brunswik, E.; Levinson, D. J.; Sanford, R. N., The Authoritarian Personality, 1951.

5   Adorno, T. W.; Frenkel-Brunswik, E.; Levinson, D. J.; Sanford, R. N., The Authoritarian Personality, 1951.

6   Clark, K. B. & Clark, M. P., Emotional Factors in Racial Identification and Preference in Negro Children, J. Negro Educ., 1950, 19, 341-350; Clark, K. B. & Clark, M. P., Racial Identification and Preference in Negro Children, Readings in Social psychology, Ed. by Newcomb & Hartley, 1947; Radke, M.; Trager, H.; Davis, H., Social Perceptions and Attitudes of Children, Genetic Psychol. Monog., 1949, 40, 327-447; Radke, M.; Trager, H.; Children's Perceptions of the Social Role of Negroes and Whites, J. Psychol., 1950, 29, 3-33.

7   Reid, Ira, What Segregated Areas Mean; Brameld, T., Educational Cost, Discrimination and National Welfare, Ed. by MacIver, R. M., 1949.

8   Frazier, E., The Negro in the United States, 1949; Krech, D. & Crutchfield, R. S., Theory and Problems of Social Psychology, 1948; Newcomb, T., Social Psychology, 1950.

9   Lee, A. Mclung and Humphrey, N. D., Race Riot, 1943.

10   Frazier, E., The Negro in the United States, 1949; Myrdal, G., An American Dilemma, 1944.

11   Reid, Ira, What Segregated Areas Mean. Discrimination and National Welfare, Ed. by MacIver, R. M., 1949.

12   Deutscher, M. and Chein, I., The Psychological Effects of Enforced Segregation: A Survey of Social Science Opinion, J. Psychol., 1948, 26, 259-287.

13   Deutscher, M. and Chein, I., The Psychological Effects of Enforced Segregation: A Survey of Social Science Opinion, J. Psychol., 1948, 26, 259-287.

14   Chein, I., What Are the Psychological Effects of Segregation Under Conditions of Equal Facilities?, International J. Opinion and Attitude Res., 1949, 2, 229-234.

15   Klineberg, O., Characteristics of American Negro, 1945; Klineberg, O., Race Differences, 1936.

16   Klineberg, O., Negro Intelligence and Selective Migration, 1935.

17   Klineberg, O., Negro Intelligence and Selective Migration, 1935.

18   Brooks, J. J., Interage Grouping on Trial-Continuous Learning, Bulletin No. 87, Association for Childhood Education, 1951; Lane, R. H., Teacher in Modern Elementary School, 1941; Educational Policies Commission of the National Education Association and the American Association of School Administration Report in Education For All Americans, published by the N. E. A., 1948.

19   Delano, W., Grade School Segregation: The Latest Attack on Racial Discrimination, Yale Law Journal, 1952, 61, 5, 730-744; Rose, A., The Influence of Legislation on Prejudice, Chapter 53 in Race Prejudice and Discrimination, Ed. by Rose, A., 1951; Rose, A., Studies in Reduction of Prejudice, Amer. Council on Race Relations, 1948.

20   Kenworthy, E. W., The Case Against Army Segregation, Annals of the American Academy of Political and Social Science, 1951, 275, 27-33; Nelson, Lt. D. D., The Integration of the Negro in the U. S. Navy, 1951; Opinions About Negro Infantry Platoons in White Companies in Several Divisions, Information and Education Division, U. S. War Department, Report No. B.157, 1945.

21   Conover, R. D., Race Relations at Codornices Village, Berkeley-Albany, California;

A Report of the Attempt to Break Down the Segregated Pattern on A Directly Managed Housing Project, Housing and Home Finance Agency, Public Housing Administration, Region I, December 1947 (mimeographed); Deutsch, M. and Collins, M. E., Interracial Housing, A Psychological Study of A Social Experiment, 1951; Rutledge, E., Integration of Racial Minorities in Public Housing Projects: A Guide for Local Housing Authorities on How to Do It, Public Housing Administration, New York Field Office (mimeographed).

22 Minard, R. D., The Pattern of Race Relationships in the Pocahontas Coal Field, J. Social Issues, 1952, 8, 29-44; Southall, S. E., Industry's Unfinished Business, 1951; Weaver, G. L-P, Negro Labor, A National Problem, 1941.

23 Southall, S. E., Industry's Unfinished Business, 1951; Weaver, G. L-P, Negro Labor, A National Problem, 1941.

24 Lee, A. McClung and Humphrey, N. D., Race Riot, 1943; Lee, A. McClung, Race Riots Aren't Necessary, Public Affairs Pamphlet, 1945.

25 Deutsch, M. and Collins, M. E., Interracial Housing, A Psychological Study of A Social Experiment, 1951; Merton, R. K.; West, P. S.; Jahoda, M., Social Fictions and Social Facts: The Dynamics of Race Relations in Hilltown, Bureau of Applied Social Research, Columbia Univ., 1949 (mimeographed); Rutledge, E., Integration of Racial Minorities in Public Housing Projects; A Guide for Local Housing Authorities on How To Do It, Public Housing Administration, New York Field Office (mimeographed); Wilner, D. M.; Walkley, R. P., and Cook, S. W., Intergroup Contact and Ethnic Attitudes in Public Housing Projects, J. Social Issues, 1952, 8, 45-69.

26 Harding, J. and Hogrefe, R., Attitudes of White Department Store Employees Toward Negro Co-workers, J. Social Issues, 1952, 8, 19-28; Southall, S. E., Industry's Unfinished Business, 1951; Weaver, G. L-P., Negro Labor, A National Problem, 1941.

27 Kenworthy, E. W., The Case Against Army Segregation, Annals of the American Academy of Political and Social Science, 1951, 275, 27-33; Nelson, Lt. D. D., The Integration of the Negro in the U. S. Navy, 1951; Stouffer, S., et al., The American Soldier, Vol. I, Chap. 19, A Note on Negro Troops in Combat, 1949; Watson, G., Action for Unity, 1947; Opinions About Negro Infantry Platoons in White Companies in Several Divisions, Information and Education Division, U. S. War Department, Report No. B-157, 1945.

28 Brophy, I. N., The Luxury of Anti-Negro Prejudice, Public Opinion Quarterly, 1946, 9, 456-466 (Integration in Merchant Marine); Watson, G., Action for Unity, 1947.

29 Williams, D. H., The Effects of an Interracial Project Upon the Attitudes of Negro and White Girls Within the Young Women's Christian Association, Unpublished M.A. thesis, Columbia University, 1934.

30 Dean, J. P., Situational Factors in Intergroup Relations: A Research Progress Report. Paper Presented to American Sociological Society, 12/28/49 (mimeographed); Irish, D. P., Reactions of Residents of Boulder, Colorado, to the Introduction of Japanese Into the Community, J. Social Issues, 1952, 8, 10-17.

31 Minard, R. D., The Pattern of Race Relationships in the Pocahontas Coal Field, J. Social Issues, 1952, 8, 29-44; Rutledge, E., Integration of Racial Minorities in Public Housing Projects; A Guide for Local Housing Authorities on How to Do It, Public Housing Administration, New York Field Office (mimeographed).

32 Deutsch, M. and Collins, M. E., Interracial Housing, A Psychological Study of A Social Experiment, 1951; Feldman, H., The Technique of Introducing Negroes Into the Plant, Personnel, 1942, 19, 461-466; Rutledge, E., Integration of Racial Minorities in Public Housing Projects; A Guide for Local Housing Authorities on How to Do It, Public Housing Administration, New York Field Office (mimeographed); Southall, S. E.,

Industry's Unfinished Business, 1951; Watson, G., Action for Unity, 1947.
33 Deutsch, M. and Collins, M. E., Interracial Housing, A Psychological Study of A Social Experiment, 1951; Feldman, H., The Technique of Introducing Negroes Into the Plant, Personnel, 1942, 19, 461-466; Rutledge, E., Integration of Racial Minorities in Public Housing Projects; A Guide for Local Housing Authorities on How to Do It, Public Housing Administration, New York Field Office (mimeographed); Southall, S. E., Industry's Unfinished Business, 1951; Watson, G., Action for Unity, 1947.
34 Wilner, D. M.; Walkley, R. P.; and Cook, S. W., Intergroup Contact and Ethnic Attitudes in Public Housing Projects, J. Social Issues, 1952, 8, 45-69.
35 Allport, G. W., and Kramer, B., Some Roots of Prejudice, J. Psychol., 1946, 22, 9-39; Watson, J., Some Social and Psychological Situations Related to Change in Attitude, Human Relations, 1950, 3, 1.

Physical anthropology, which had taken the identification of racial types as its central mission for at least a century, turned its back on that focus in the 1950s. Sherwood Washburn's presidential address to American Anthropological Association (AAA) in 1962 laid out the new scientific thinking clearly by outlining how new methods in genetics had shown that the older, typological thinking about race was completely erroneous. Although it is not obvious in the text, Washburn's address was designed to serve as an authoritative scientific statement from the discipline of anthropology regarding race. In the heated racial politics of the American civil rights movement, anthropological science was under attack from southern segregationists who claimed that liberal politics had corrupted the science of Madison Grant and Lothrop Stoddard. Washburn was asked by the AAA to clearly lay out the scientific case against the older racial concept that was being embraced in the American South.

The Study of Race

S. L. WASHBURN

Delivered as the presidential address at the annual meeting of the American Anthropological Association, November 16, 1962, in Chicago.

The Executive Board has asked me to give my address on the subject of race, and, reluctantly and diffidently, I have agreed to do so. I am not a specialist on this subject. I have never done research on race, but I have taught it for a number of years.

Discussion of the races of man seems to generate endless emotion and confusion. I am under no illusion that this paper can do much to dispel the confusion; it may add to the emotion. The latest information available supports the traditional findings of anthropologists and other social scientists—that there is no scientific basis of any kind for racial discrimination. I think that the way this conclusion has been reached needs to be restated. The continuation of antiquated biological notions in anthropology and the oversimplification of facts weakens the anthropological position. We must realize that great changes have taken place in the study of race over the last 20 years and it is up to us to bring our profession into the forefront of the newer understandings, so that our statements will be authoritative and useful.

This paper will be concerned with three topics—the modern concept of race, the interpretation of racial differences, and the social significances of race. And, again, I have no illusion that these things can be treated briefly; I shall merely say a few things which are on my mind and which you may amplify by turning to the literature, and especially to Dobzhansky's book, *Mankind Evolving*. This book states the relations between culture and genetics in a way which is useful to social scientists. In my opinion it is a great book which puts the interrelations of biology and culture in proper perspective and avoids the oversimplifications which come from overemphasis on either one alone.

The races of man are the result of human evolution, of the evolution of our species. The races are open parts of the species, and the species is a closed system. If we look, then, upon long-term human evolution, our first problem must be the species and the things which have caused the evolution of all mankind, not the races, which are the results of local forces and which are minor in terms of the evolution of the whole species.

The evolution of races is due, according to modern genetics, to mutation, selection, migration, and genetic drift. It is easy to shift from this statement of genetic theory to complications of hemoglobin, blood groups or other technical information. But the point I want to stress is that the primary implication of genetics for anthropology is that it affirms the relation of culture and biology in a far firmer and more important way than ever in our history before. Selection is for reproductive success, and in man reproductive success is primarily determined by the social system and by culture. Effective behavior is the question, not something else.

Drift depends on the size of population, and population size, again, is dependent upon culture, not upon genetic factors as such. Obviously, migration depends on clothes, transportation, economy, and warfare and is reflected in the archeological record. Even mutation rates are now affected by technology.

Genetic theory forces the consideration of culture as the major factor in the evolution of man. It thus reaffirms the fundamental belief of anthropologists that we must study man both as a biological and as a social organism. This is no longer a question of something that might be desirable; it must be done if genetic theory is correct.

We have, then, on the one hand the history of genetic systems, and on the other hand the history of cultural systems, and, finally, the interrelation between these two. There is no evolution in the traditional anthropological sense. What Boas referred to as evolution was orthogenesis—which receives no support from modern genetic theory. What the geneticist sees as evolution is far closer to what Boas called history than to what he called evolution, and some anthropologists are still fighting a nineteenth-century battle in their presentation of evolution. We have, then, the history of cultural systems, which you may call history; and the history of genetic systems, which you may call evolution if you want to, but if you use this word remember that it means selection, migration, drift—it is real history that you are talking about and not some mystic force which constrains mankind to evolve according to some orthogenetic principle.

There is, then, no possibility of studying human raciation, the process of race formation, without studying human culture. Archeology is as important in the study of the origin of races as is genetics; all we can do is reconstruct as best we can the long-term past, and this is going to be very difficult.

Now let me contrast this point of view with the one which has been common in much of anthropology. In the first place, anthropology's main subject, the subject of race, disregarded to an amazing degree the evolution of the human species. Anthropologists were so concerned with the subdivisions within our species and with minor detailed differences between small parts of the species that the physical anthropologists largely forgot that mankind is a species and that the important thing is the evolution of this whole group, not the minor differences between its parts.

If we look back to the time when I was educated, races were regarded as types. We were taught to go to a population and divide it into a series of types and to re-create history out of this artificial arrangement. Those of you who have read *Current Anthropology* will realize that this kind of anthropology is still alive, amazingly, and in full force in some countries; relics of it are still alive in our teaching today.

Genetics shows us that typology must be completely removed from our thinking if we are to progress. For example, let us take the case of the Bushmen. The Bushmen have been described as the result of a mixture between Negro and Mongoloid. Such a statement could only be put in the literature without any possible consideration of migration routes, of numbers of people, of cultures, of any way that such a mixing could actually take place. The fact is that the Bushmen had a substantial record in South Africa and in East Africa and there is no evidence that they ever were anywhere else except in these areas. In other words, they are a race which belongs exactly where they are.

If we are concerned with history let us consider, on the one hand, the ancestors of these Bushmen 15,000 years ago and the area available to them, to their way of life, and, on the other hand, the ancestors of Europeans at the same time in the area available to them, with their way of life. We will find that the area available to the Bushmen was at least twice that available to the Europeans. The Bushmen were living in a land of optimum game; the Europeans were living close to an ice sheet. There were perhaps from three to five times as many Bushmen ancestors as there were European ancestors only 15,000 years ago.

If one were to name a major race, or a primary race, the Bushmen have a far better claim in terms of the archeological record than the Europeans. During the time of glacial advance more than half of the Old World available to man for life was in Africa. The numbers and distributions that we think of as normal and the races whose last results we see today are relics of an earlier and far different time in human history.

There are no three primary races, no three major groups. The idea of three primary races stems from nineteenth-century typology; it is totally misleading to put the black-skinned people of the world together—to put the Australian in the same grouping with the inhabitants of Africa. And there are certainly at least three independent origins of the small, dark people, the Pygmies, and probably more than that. There is no single Pygmy race.

If we look to real history we will always find more than three races, because there are more than three major areas in which the raciation of our species was taking place.

If we attempt to preserve the notion of three races, we make pseudotypological problems. Take for example, again, the problem of the aboriginal Australian. If we have only three races, either they must be put with the people of Africa, with which they have nothing in common, or they must be accounted for by mixture, and in books appearing even as late as 1950, a part of the aboriginal Australian population is described as European, and listed with the Europeans, and the residue is listed with the Africans and left there.

The concept of race is fundamentally changed if we actually look for selection, migration, and study people as they are (who they are, where they are, how many they are); and the majority of anthropological textbooks need substantial revision along these lines.

Since races are open systems which are intergrading, the number of races will depend on the purpose of the classification. This is, I think, a tremendously important point. It is significant that as I was reviewing classifications in preparing this lecture, I found that almost none of them mentioned any purpose for which people were being classified. Race isn't very important biologically. If we are classifying races in order to understand human history, there aren't many human races, and there is very substantial agreement as to what they are. There are from six to nine races, and this difference in number is very largely a matter of definition. These races occupied the major separate geographical areas in the Old World.

If one has no purpose for classification, the number of races can be multiplied almost indefinitely, and it seems to me that the erratically varying number of races is a source of confusion to student, to layman, and to specialist. I think we should require people who propose a classification of races to state in the first place why they wish to divide the human species and to give in detail the important reasons for subdividing our whole species. If important reasons for such classification are given, I think you will find that the number of races is always exceedingly small.

If we consider these six or nine geographical races and the factors which produced them, I think the first thing we want to stress is migration.

All through human history, where we have any evidence of that history, people have migrated. In a recent *Anthropologist* there is a suggestion that it took 400,000 years for a gene that mutated in China to reach Europe. We know, historically, that Alexander the Great went from Greece into Northern India. We know that Mongol tribes migrated from Asia into Europe. Only a person seeking to believe that the races are very separate could possibly believe such a figure as that cited.

Migration has always been important in human history and there is no such thing as human populations which are completely separated from other human populations. And migration necessarily brings in new genes, necessarily reduces the differences between the races. For raciation to take place, then, there must be other factors operating which create difference. Under certain circumstances, in very small populations, differences may be created by genetic drift, or because the founders are for chance reasons very different from other members of the species.

However, the primary factor in the creation of racial differences in the long term is selection. This means that the origin of races must depend on adaptation and that the differences between the races which we see must in times past have been adaptive. I stress the question of time here, because it is perfectly logical to maintain that in time past a shovel-shaped incisor, for example, was more efficient than an incisor of other forms and that selection would have been for this, and at the same time to assert that today this dental difference is of absolutely no social importance. It is important to make this point because people generally take the view that something is always adaptive or never adaptive, and this is a fundamental oversimplification of the facts.

Adaptation is always within a given situation. There is no such thing as a gene which has a particular adaptive value; it has this value only under set circumstances. For example, the sickle-cell gene, if Allison and others are right, protects against malaria. This is adaptive if there is malaria, but if there is not malaria it is not adaptive. The adaptive value of the gene, then, is dependent on the state of medicine and has no absolute value. The same is true of the other characteristics associated with race.

The American civil rights movement fragmented in the mid-1960s. Some activists rejected the integrationist ideal in favor of various forms of Black Nationalism that called for racial separatism. Some scholars called for a new science of race and race relations that took notice of the separate social realities faced by black Americans. Joseph Scott outlined the new approach toward racial science in a variety of areas. Scholars like Scott argued not for a rejection of the scientific method, but for a reformulation of science that acknowledged the inherent racism of the older scientific approaches that were based almost entirely on white experiences and assumed that those experiences applied with equal validity to blacks.

Black Science and Nation-Building

JOSEPH SCOTT

What is the relevance of the scientific method for Black research conducted on the Black experience? In what specific ways can science be applied in sociology, psychology, political science and economics? What have been the limitations of the application of the scientific method in the past when applied to Blacks? In the following essay, the author attempts to answer these questions by analyzing several popular "white experience" models, showing their irrelevance to Blacks and proposing alternative models based on the Black experience.

Science has been defined both as a set of methods and techniques, and as a body of facts, theories and models.[1] In methodological terms, science is one of the ways man can know about the real world and can change the conditions of the real world if he finds them unsatisfactory. What makes scientific knowledge different from intuitive knowledge is that the values of science require that scientific knowledge be verifiable and empirical—experiential. This causes scientists to use sampling designs, experimentation and classification. The knowledge derived by these methods consists of verifiable observations and generalizations, which we call facts and theories respectively.

The use of science is mandatory for Black people if they are to get and keep control over the physical and social forces that determine their life-chances.

Nation-building requires that they be able to control not only a national territory but also the natural resources, natural forces, economic forces, social forces, political forces, and psychological forces that make life possible or impossible. One of the first prerequisites of nation-building is knowledge. Black people will not be able to develop themselves as a people and develop their land (once they get it) into a productive, harmonious place to live and work without specialized knowledge.

Today as Blacks apply the existing theories and models in an attempt to make life more predictable and to get control over the external and internal forces that shape their lives, they are finding that the theories and models which were developed on whites do not apply well to Blacks. Scientific knowledge in the social sciences in this country is mostly a body of facts and generalizations about white experience. More specifically, it is about the white middle-class experience. In the behavioral sciences, for example, the attitude tests have been "validated" on white people. The intelligence tests have been "standardized" on white people. The statistical curves "represent" the response patterns of white people. The theories of society, of government, of economy, of education and of personality are descriptive of white people.

These observations should tell us something: either present practices are invalid, or it is scientifically valid to focus exclusively on one societal group and to generalize from this for all other societal groups. Scientific knowledge claims not to be culture-bound or race-bound, but the assertion of universality does not make it empirically so. Black social scientists must be extremely skeptical of any research, theories or models that come out of exclusively white experience. They must not be misled into believing that there is no difference between white experience and Black experience, for in America whites have not been slaves or peons for three hundred and fifty years as Blacks have been; whites have never been disenfranchised as Blacks have been; whites have never been chattels or property as Blacks have been; whites have never been subject to systematic exploitation by means of legislative and legal decrees. Thus the theories, models and generalizations about government, economy, education and personality cannot possibly be the same for white people as for Black people. The scientific concepts and categories may come close, but they can hardly be a "good fit." Some types of white experience may coincide with some patterns of the Black experience, and some psychological illnesses may be the same as those found in the Black communities, but they can hardly be derived from the same type of racial oppression.

To continue to equate white experience with Black experience is fraudulent behavior. Black social scientists of the future who have had these errors brought to their attention will not be able to claim that they are not being deceptive when they start trying to predict and to explain Black life by white-experience models and theories. They will simply be identified as unwilling or unable to use a Black perspective. Applicable theories and models must be those derived from the experiences of Blacks as perceived and reacted to by Blacks. For example, regardless of how much whites see the Vietnam war as a struggle to make the world "safe for democracy," for Blacks, the war is a nightmare, a struggle to make "democracy safe for the world," an imperialistic threat to the world.

Virtually everything that maximizes the benefits and profits of whites means more exploitation of Black peoples. So in observing the operation of social, economic, political and psychological forces in the empirical world, the vantage point must be that of Black peoples. The way to acquire the Black perspective is to see the impact these forces have on their lives.

As researches are conducted and interpreted from the viewpoint of Black experience, almost every contemporary theory in the behavioral sciences will require modification. Several Black scholars have already begun the call for a new orientation.

Robert Chrisman, editor of *The Black Scholar*, and professor of English, has suggested that "the vanguard of black intellectuals, artists and behavioral scientists"[2] address themselves to the development of revolutionary values and resources latent among Black Americans. The intellectuals, artists, and scientists must, he feels, develop standards for the fine arts, and develop techniques of behavioral science that fit the Black experience. He believes that the present cultural schemes, concepts, and theories (like functionalism) of the Anglo-American cannot answer the needs of Afro-Americans, for contemporary culture is largely the culture of oppressors, and its contents relate mostly to how to oppress others, not how to liberate others. The Anglo-American culture was in large part developed to enslave and subjugate Blacks, so what the intellectuals, artists and behavioral scientists must do, according to Chrisman, is to "analyze, in truth and depth, Black class structure, Black economic conditions, the psychology of Blackness, and translate that analysis into practical formulas for revolutionary action."[3] Further, we must develop a Black propaganda system, a revolutionary esthetic and the mechanism for mutual criticism between the vanguard and the Black community.

James M. Jones, a Black social psychologist, discussing the Black perspective in the study of Black political behavior, writes: "Black politics is the art and science of moving black people from a present, objective reality which is oppressive to a new reality, which is the liberation from that oppression."[4] The "moving" of Black people requires knowledge of the oppressor and his conditions of oppression. Jones has concluded correctly that "knowledge is relevant because knowledge is control, and control is what we need, what we must have."[5]

Black political scientists, he adds, must be about the business of "Black culture, Black ideology, Black revolution." In a sense there is only one objective to Black politics—Black liberation. And Black political scientists should lead the way. Jones suggests that Black political scientists must be oriented toward "the liberation of Black people from the political control of an alien power."[6] They must help to "wrest control from the hands of the alien powers, and to control our own behavior and value systems."[7]

Joseph White,[8] a Black psychologist, writes: "Black psychologists are still operating with a lot of assumptions and machinery that have been developed by white psychologists primarily for white people." As an alternative, he suggests that Black psychologists start legitimizing Black experience and building psychological models based on that experience. The behavior of Black children, he adds, must be viewed as positive responses to a "complicated and hostile environment" and evaluated from the point of view of "mental toughness," "survival skills," "cleverness and originality," rather than as pathological or deviant behavior. White concludes that Black psychologists "must begin to develop a model of Black psychology which is free from the built-in assumptions and values of the dominant culture."

Robert C. Vowels,[9] a Black economist, has charged that "In the real world where the political economy of American racism holds indisputable sway, nonblack decision-making within nonblack organizations poses a formidable barrier to black higher status employment opportunities and aspiration."[10] He adds that contemporary economics "tend to deemphasize racial economic discrimination as a factor in the economic problems of minority groups."[11] Yet all sorts of white agencies, corporations and organizations making economic decisions are using race as a factor in their decision-making, and the market result is that Blacks pay more for goods and services and receive less. Perhaps even more important, schools, housing, food and other goods and services are denied Blacks altogether, whether they can pay the unfair prices or not. Vowels sums it up nicely: "When everyone is poor, black people are even poorer. And when everyone is prosperous, black people are still poor."[12]

What Black economists must do, he feels, is to include the factor of racial discrimination in their economic analyses and models. If the dynamics of racial discrimination are included in the theories and models, a new economics might emerge with different types of supply-and-demand relationships. Since racial discrimination is such an important market force in the lives of Blacks, and since it is left out of all major economic theories and models, it is logical to conclude that these present theories and models do not apply to Blacks. Black economists thus have a major goal, according to Henry Coleman, "to find a solution to the color problem that you know exists."[13]

Examples of Inapplicable White Experience Models and Theories: An Assimilation Theory

Robert Park,[14] a white sociologist, believed that he had accurately represented the Black experience when he applied his white-derived model to Afro-Americans. He characterized U.S. race relations as a process of evolving through five stages, with assimilation the final stage. The processual model was:

> Contact—> Competition—> Conflict—> Accommodation—> Assimilation.
> (Presumably assimilation refers to full integration into the organizations, agencies, corporations, and institutions of "the mainstream.")

This model, however, which is derived from white experience, reflects neither the range nor the quality nor the subtleties of the Black experience.

A Black experience model would be quite different from Park's and definitely different from the experience models of the Irish, the Germans, the Scandinavians and other white ethnic groups. A Black model would "tell it like it has been and like it is now." For example, it would reflect the fact that Afro-Americans have been a captive people who are still under a colonialistic system of domination and exploitation. It would reflect the despotic power still entrenched in the grasp of the white power elite, and it would reflect the struggle for liberation by Black people. From my study of cultural, legal and economic history, a processual model based on Afro-American experience would be as [in the table below]:

	White Strategies	*Black Strategies*
Epoch 1	Despotism[1]—>	<—[2]Abolitionism
Epoch 2	Jim Crowism[3]—>	<—[4]Neo-Abolitionism
Epoch 3	Integrationism[5]—>	<—[6]Communal Separatism
Epoch 4	Containmentism[7]—>	<—[8]National Separatism

In short, from the beginning of time, the relationship has been one of overt and covert conflict. There is no period not dominated by conflict.

The Consumer Sovereignty Theory

A second white experience model is found in economics. One basic theory in economics is the Consumer Sovereignty Theory.[15] This theory posits first that the consumer can make highly rational distinctions between products and prices in the marketplace, and second that the producer-sellers have no individual control over consumer choices, product pricing and aggregate demand. The postulated process is that the consumer stimulates the producer-seller into producing saleable products, which are priced in terms of the costs of production and other competitors in the market, who are all supposed to be operating independently in such a way as to keep the prices of the products close to the costs of making the products. In sum, the transaction begins with the consumers suggesting products to the producer-sellers and determining the prices mostly by what they, the consumers, are supposedly willing to pay. Thus the consumer is the sovereign figure in the producer-seller-consumer exchange.

A model based on Black experience would suggest that the producer-sellers are sovereign. It would reflect the fact that the Black consumer is manipulated by the various participants[16] in the marketplace—peddlers, retailers, advertisers, bankers, financiers and salesmen; that the producer-sellers do not wait to be stimulated by the Black consumer but produce products at their own initiative which they "market" or "sell" by various mechanisms—"buy-now-pay-later arrangements," "revolving charge accounts" and so on. Finally, the model would reflect the fact that Black consumers are designated "high risk" creditors and are denied the usual low-interest credit and the usual high-quality products, which are accessible only through the regular retail outlets that accept only low-risk creditors. Forced into a dilemma, Black consumers must either do without what they need or pay exorbitantly high interest rates and service charges to retailers of questionable repute who sell low-quality goods at high-quality prices and use various mechanisms to induce perpetual indebtedness.

The Deferred Gratification Theory

White social psychologists have made much ado about the deferred-gratification pattern of middle-class white children, arguing that Black children have not usually developed this trait and are thus more impulsive and non-rational in their behavior. They claim that white children are taught to delay immediate gratification for greater future rewards; to be future-oriented rather than present-oriented, inhibited rather than hedonistic, but that Blacks (and other lower-class children), who have not been taught by their parents to delay immediate gratification, do not make the long-range plans required for socioeconomic advancement.

High aspirations and achievements supposedly require a future orientation, the ability to defer gratification. Nondeferred gratification is said to lead to impulsive behavior, which is often antisocial, nonutilitarian and nonproductive. Thus Black children show higher rates of detected deviance and low achievement than white children.

It is evident to anyone acquainted with the Black experience in America that lower racial status is tantamount to a life of forced menial labor and a scarcity of food, clothing, shelter and police protection. In short, a deferred gratification pattern as a perpetual way of life is not a matter of personal preference. Young Black children, because of the societal rationing of those things making up "the good life," learn to live with deprivation much better than white children. Black children learn to defer immediate gratification as a regular fact of life; to expect very little future reward for persistent hard work and self-denial. White children can reasonably expect a future reward from immediate investments in inhibition, but Blacks cannot. The only ways out for Blacks are to sanctify the impoverished life or to profane it. The profane behavior of Black children is often the *result* of an imposed deferred gratification pattern, rather than the result of a lack of experience with it. The Deferred Gratification Theory is obviously a white experience theory, based on the reasonable expectations inherent in middle-class white life, rather than on the reasonable expectations of future reward inherent in Black lower-status life. Thus it is inapplicable to Black children.

The Multidisciplinary Approach to the Black Experience

The Black experience itself in the United States is in essence a multifaceted experience, neither primarily economic, nor primarily political, nor primarily psychological, nor primarily sociological. It is all of these and more; it is also historical. The white oppressor (and that is what he has been, with no racism implied) not only erected economic barriers to Black advancement and productivity, but erected social, political and psychological barriers as well.

To use a metaphor, the institutional barriers are like rows and rows of intertwined barbed-wire fences surrounding a Black population which is in the main young, eager, talented, idealistic and energetic. The first fence could be thought of as the judicial and legislative barriers; the second fence, as the economic barriers to commerce and labor; the third fence, as the psychological barriers, specifically educational barriers which keep Blacks from acquiring the knowledge and skill to be creative, self-sustaining and productive; the fourth fence, as racial barriers which deny equal access to public accommodations and to purely social areas. Finally, these various rows of barriers, which keep Blacks disabled, disadvantaged and dispossessed in the competition for life, liberty and property, are themselves interlaced and reenforced by wires of racism which tie them together in a mutually supportive way. Under these conditions, one barrier cannot be removed without severing all the racist ties as well. Together, these barriers create a very difficult set of conditions to break through, especially when there are supporting troops to repair any breaches that Blacks might make from time to time.

Given the multiplicity of barriers to Black progress, the approach to overcoming these conditions must obviously be manifold. Malcolm X came to realize this and advocated "all means necessary" to overturn the situation. Malcolm was hearing voices of the past, the voices of Garnet, Holly, Hall, Turner, Delaney, Trotter, Du Bois, Garvey, Douglass, Washington, Randolph, King, Young, and he came to the conclusion that there are layers of barriers superimposed on one another, tied together by racism. Contrary to what many Blacks think, the barriers are not like a circular stockade of tree trunks, with each trunk representing a different barrier—economic, political, social, psychological, etc.—so that all Blacks have to do is knock over one trunk to break out. A more appropriate model, as we have said, is a series of barbed-wire fences intertwined one behind the other and tied together by reenforcing wires of racism. This means that litigation, legislation, emigration, demonstration, rebellion, destruction, assimilation, separation, education, commercialization and coalition, among other strategies, are all essential ways of breaking through the barriers that constrain and thwart Black people. All types of means were necessary in the past, and they are still necessary today.

The contemporary Black assault troops are manifold in their approach: The Black Panthers, The National Urban League, The National Association for the Advancement of Colored People, The Black Muslims, The Afro-American Repatriation Society, The Congress of Racial Equality, and The United Negro College Fund. Considering them all together, we have almost all the means that we need; judicial, legislative, economic, political and psychological movements operating to liberate Blacks.

Given the fact that there are a variety of liberation movements afoot among Blacks today—and that their various strategies have been refined over the past three hundred years—Black behavioral scientists must become multidisciplinary in their approach. They must be able to contribute analyses that include the interactional effects of the imposed economic, political, social and psychological barriers facing Black people. Their Black experience models must reflect the manifold reality. Their theories must focus on the interrelated strategies for overcoming all the barriers simultaneously, not just one barrier at a time.

From the Sociological Perspective

According to some recent studies, Afro-Americans are more residentially segregated now in major cities than they were a decade ago. The 1970 *Current Population Reports, Series P-23, No. 38*, indicate that three of every five Blacks in the United States live in a central city of a major metropolitan area, and the rate at which Blacks have been herded into the central cities has been increasing; the percentage has increased from 59 percent in 1950 to 74 percent in 1970.

From the *Bureau of Labor Statistics Bulletin 1699* of 1971 we learn:

"Urban Blacks have been segregated, residentially, and indications are that their segregation has been increasing through the mid-1960's.[17] Residential segregation has many consequences. One of these is school segregation; Blacks have, since 1950, become increasingly segregated in schools, and it is now public knowledge that many Northern schools are more segregated than some schools in the South.

An incredible result of forced school segregation is subeducation. Black schools get less support, in terms of facilities and trained faculties, than white schools. The white-controlled school administrations have been known to manipulate the hiring of teachers and to concentrate the lowest-quality white teachers in schools for Black children. Rejected white teachers from white schools are commonly assigned to schools where there is a predominance of Black children. The better teachers are dissuaded from asking for assignments in schools that are predominantly Black. The net result is inferior instruction for Black children. The longer Black children remain in such schools, the less well prepared they become and the less well they perform on national achievement tests (which are in any case biased toward middle-class standards). The U.S. government found in its study that "The gap in achievement levels between Negro and white students widened between the sixth and twelfth grades."[18] According to national tests, at the end of the twelve years Blacks have received an average of only nine years of education.

White employers use the results of educational achievement tests to discriminate against Blacks in salaries. Often this discrimination goes beyond merely adjusting wages proportionate to the degree that their education does not measure up; Blacks may be offered a lower amount of money than whites with the same degree of education simply because they are powerless to negotiate for a higher salary. The difference has been estimated at about a thousand dollars per male. The Council of Economic Advisers reported in 1965: "If Negroes received the same average pay as whites having the same education, the personal income of Negroes and of the Nation would be $12.8 billion higher."[19] The final result is that "At each educational level, Black men have less income than white men. The disparity is greatest at the college level."[20]

From the Psychological Perspective

Behind racial discrimination are both a private set of attitudes and a tacit public consensus among whites that Blacks are to be kept unequal. Even nonprejudiced officials discriminate racially in attempts to satisfy the tacit agreement among whites to keep Blacks out of certain residential, occupational and educational spheres.

Social psychologists have recently studied the attitudes of white citizens on a national scale.[21] They have found that whites have no great inclination to bring Blacks home to dinner, to share the same residential areas with them, to inter-marry or to extend any other private sectors of their lives to include Blacks. The whites in the South favor discrimination more than those in the North, and their attitudes against full participation by Blacks in all areas of society are stronger. The authors of the study conclude: "Certainly there is no evidence that the majority of American whites eagerly look forward to integration. Most are more comfortable in a segregated society, and they would prefer that the demonstra-tors slow down or go away while things are worked out more gradually."[22]

On an eight-point scale measuring pro-integration sentiment, the average score for white Americans was around 4.3. Full integration into the institutional life of the society in the minds of many Blacks means liberation. In the minds of many whites, too, full integration means the liberation of Blacks from social, political and economic shackles. The social-psychological data on the attitudes of whites clearly indicate that they are not enthusiastic about this. This negative attitude governs the making and implementing of political and economic deci-sions resulting in residential, occupational and educational subordination in American society.

From the Political Perspective

From political scientists we learn that the subordination of Blacks in the United States has been forced and financed by the officials of the federal and state gov-ernments. For example, in the area of residential segregation, the Federal Hous-ing Administration has practiced a policy of guaranteeing mortgages only in racially segregated areas. An FHA manual stated: "If a neighborhood is to retain stability, it is necessary that properties shall continue to be occupied by the same society and race group." During the 1950s millions of homes built mostly in the suburban areas were, by mortgage denials, closed to Blacks. The federal gov-ernment in effect financed the white exodus from the central cities and forced the containment of Blacks there. The containment practice is still in effect, as sociologists have discovered.

Segregated education is a second example of government facilitation of racial discrimination. As previously stated, Black children are more segregated in schools today than they were a decade ago; this is because the government implementers of the School Desegregation Decision of 1954 have permitted the forces of segregation to continue to operate almost unhindered. Government agencies like HEW have adhered to a doctrine of gradualism. Officials of the judi-cial and executive branches of the government have implemented the decision in such a way that token integration could satisfy the requirements of the law. They have not required "racial balance," nor have they required "representative proportions" in school desegregation plans.

Support of segregation by the federal government has not stopped with the public education system; it has been practiced throughout the public manpower training programs as well. Herbert Hill of the NAACP has found that "Negroes, with some few exceptions, are being limited to programs that simply perpetuate the traditional concentration of Negroes in menial and unskilled jobs."[23] Hill also found: "The Department of Health, Education, and Welfare each year distributes fifty-five millions of dollars of federal funds for education under the Smith-Hughes Act; a very large part of this is given to vocational training programs in which Negroes are totally excluded or limited to unequal segregated facilities."[24] Instance after instance of governmental policy and implementation of policy resulting in the subeducation of Black Americans can be presented.

Finally, there is federal government facilitation of employment discrimination. Even though the federal government has had a fair-employment practices policy for decades, it has not stopped employers' discrimination practices. Employers have been able to conduct "business as usual." Gradualism has been the doctrine followed by the government in its attempt to force compliance with the nondiscrimination provisions of the various codes and contracts, and the result is that little change in Black employment patterns has occurred. Even the Equal Employment Opportunities Commission has not produced any significant changes. A key reason for this, we learn from the *Wall Street Journal* of July 22, 1969, is that the EEOC has decided against public hearings to question employers about their discriminatory hiring practices. The net result is that billions of dollars in government contracts have been awarded to corporations and universities that do not comply with fair employment practices standards. The government provision outlawing discrimination in employment by corporations and universities holding U.S. government contracts has not been enforced. It should not be surprising, therefore, that despite the laws, codes, executive orders and policies, Blacks are still by and large concentrated in the same sectors, paid the same low wages, as they were at the time of the Emancipation Proclamation.

From the Economic Perspective

As we have seen, segregation has a psychological, sociological and political side. Let us now look at the economic side. Economic researchers have found that "the incidence of substandard units is higher, at every income category, for owners as well as renter Negro families,"[25] and that "the poor condition of Negro housing arises from discriminatory treatment in the housing market, so that the purchasing power of the dollar spent by nonwhites is less than that of the dollar spent by whites."[26] The data from several studies indicate that Blacks at all rental levels "show a higher proportion of substandard units than do whites."[27] Blacks not only receive less quality for the money they pay, they also "obtain smaller units than whites." One economist, after one such extensive study, has concluded that "the Negro who achieves middle-class status is rewarded in the housing market by an increasing burden of price and locational discrimination."[28] The pricing and supplying mechanisms for housing and residential areas clearly operate to deny the Black American his "just dues."

In the area of education, certain economic mechanisms operate to keep Blacks subeducated. Investing less money in the development of a Black child than one invests in the development of a white is one such mechanism. Investments in human development in the form of education and training are essential for any society to maintain itself over time. Nevertheless economists have found that "the value of the stock of human capital embodied in the average male adult Negro is on the order of $10,000 smaller than the human capital embodied in the average white male."[29]

The Council of Economic Advisers has corroborated this finding in its own study, which concluded: "If Negroes also had the same educational attainments as white workers, and earned the same pay and experienced the same unemployment as whites, their personal income—and that of the nation—would be $20.6 billion higher."[30]

Some employment discrimination, too, is based on economic mechanisms. Because of the powerlessness of Blacks, whites have used them for capital accumulation. The fruits of Black labor have been siphoned off through various wage-price devices. By underpaying Blacks for over three hundred years, whites have drained Blacks to the point of near-bankruptcy.

A second mechanism is job allocation processes. The industrial managers of the economy have, over the past hundred years, successfully pushed Blacks from the central position as the main source of skilled labor, relegating them to the marginal parts of the economy. William Tabb, an economist, writes: "The economy provides work for the Black underclass, but not the chance for advancement. The labor market, in fact, functions to maintain Blacks in the role of exploited undifferentiated labor. Most Blacks are allowed only a marginal attachment to the labor force."[31]

The Department of Labor confirms this: Black families earn only about 62 percent of what white families earn, and they are unemployed and underemployed two to three times more often.

The industrial executives, who "manage" the labor market in the United States, discriminate racially in the process of economic decision making. "In a slack labor market, employers can pick and choose, both in recruiting and in promoting. They exaggerate the skill, education, and experience requirements of their jobs. They use diplomas, or color, or personal histories as convenient screening devices. In a tight market, they are forced to be realistic, to tailor job specifications to the available supply, and to give on-the-job training."[32]

Economic decisions can be—and are—skewed racially by tacit collusion and informal agreement.

Conclusion

Based on what has been said, we may conclude that the methodological aims of Black researchers should be: First, to perceive, record and theorize about the external world from the viewpoint of Black people; second, to apply to Black people explanatory models and theories which are derived solely from Black rather than white experience; third, to reevaluate and expose the inapplicabilities of all white experience theories and models as they have been applied to Black behavior; fourth, to be ideologically nonconformist and technically innovative in setting about the tasks of problem selection, data gathering and concept building; fifth, to be Black value-oriented instead of value-free in the interpretation of data and in conclusions; sixth, to approach data interpretation from the standpoint of how the data contribute to Black liberation and Black nation-building.

Notes
1   William J. Goode and Paul K. Hatt, Methods in Social Research (New York: McGraw-Hill, 1952).
2   Robert Chrisman, "The Formation of a Revolutionary Black Culture," The Black Scholar, 8 (June 1970), pp. 2-9.
3   Ibid., p. 8.
4   James M. Jones, "The Political Dimensions of Black Liberation," The Black Scholar, 1 (September 1971), pp. 67-75.
5   Ibid., p. 73.
6   Ibid., p. 67.
7   Ibid., p. 69.
8   See "Guidelines for Black Psychologists," this volume.
9   Robert C. Vowels, "The Political Economy of American Racism—Nonblack Decision-Making and Black Economic Status," The Review of Black Political Economy, 4 (Summer 1971), pp. 3-42.
10 Ibid., p. 28.
11 Ibid., p. 4.
12 Ibid., p. 24.
13 Henry A. Coleman, "Student Symposium—Economics, With or Without Color?" The Review of Black Political Economy, 4 (Summer 1971), p. 142.
14 Robert E. Park, Race and Culture (New York: Free Press, 1950).
15 John Kenneth Galbraith, The New Industrial State (New York: The New American

Library, Inc., 1967).

16 David Caplovitz, The Poor Pay More (New York: Free Press, 1967).

17 Ibid., p. 14.

18 Ibid., p. 86.

19 Council of Economic Advisers, "The Economic Cost of Discrimination," in John F. Kain, Race and Poverty: The Economics of Discrimination (Englewood Cliffs, N.J.: Prentice-Hall), p. 58.

20 Ibid., p. 82.

21 Paul B. Sheatsley, "White Attitudes Toward the Negro," pp. 128-38.

22 Ibid., p. 138.

23 Herbert Hill, "Racial Inequality in Employment: The Patterns of Discrimination," in John F. Kain, op. cit., p. 82.

24 Ibid., p. 83.

25 Chester Rapkin, "Price Discrimination Against Negroes in the Rental Housing Market," in John F. Kain, op. cit., p. 113.

26 Ibid., p. 113.

27 Ibid., p. 114.

28 Ibid., p. 121.

29 Barbara R. Bergmann, "Investment in the Human Resources of Negroes," in John F. Kain, op. cit., p. 52.

30 Council of Economic Advisers, in John F. Kain, op. cit., p. 59.

31 William K. Tabb, The Political Economy of the Black Ghetto (New York: W. W. Norton & Co., 1971), p. 106.

32 James Tobin, "Improving the Economic Status of the Negro," in The Negro American, Talcott Parsons and Kenneth B. Clark, eds. (Boston: Houghton-Mifflin Co., 1966), p. 456.

At the end of the twentieth century, the typological view of race had lost any scientific standing in mainstream anthropological thought. The clinal view, that there are no large groupings of races but rather small geographical variations that fade into one another, is now dominant. It is interesting that a scientific organization such as the American Anthropological Association turns to the history of science in order to explain the persistence of racial thinking.

American Anthropological Association Statement on "Race"

(MAY 17, 1998)

The following statement was adopted by the Executive Board of the American Anthropological Association, acting on a draft prepared by a committee of representative American anthropologists. It does not reflect a consensus of all members of the AAA, as individuals vary in their approaches to the study of "race."

We believe that it represents generally the contemporary thinking and scholarly positions of a majority of anthropologists.

In the United States both scholars and the general public have been conditioned to viewing human races as natural and separate divisions within the human species based on visible physical differences. With the vast expansion of scientific knowledge in this century, however, it has become clear that human populations are not unambiguous, clearly demarcated, biologically distinct groups. Evidence from the analysis of genetics (e.g., DNA) indicates that most physical variation, about 94%, lies *within* so-called racial groups. Conventional geographic "racial" groupings differ from one another only in about 6% of their genes. This means that there is greater variation within "racial" groups than between them. In neighboring populations there is much overlapping of genes and their phenotypic (physical) expressions. Throughout history whenever different groups have come into contact, they have interbred. The continued sharing of genetic materials has maintained all of humankind as a single species.

Physical variations in any given trait tend to occur gradually rather than abruptly over geographic areas. And because physical traits are inherited independently of one another, knowing the range of one trait does not predict the presence of others. For example, skin color varies largely from light in the temperate areas in the north to dark in the tropical areas in the south; its intensity is not related to nose shape or hair texture. Dark skin may be associated with frizzy or kinky hair or curly or wavy or straight hair, all of which are found among different indigenous peoples in tropical regions. These facts render any attempt to establish lines of division among biological populations both arbitrary and subjective.

Historical research has shown that the idea of "race" has always carried more meanings than mere physical differences; indeed, physical variations in the human species have no meaning except the social ones that humans put on them. Today scholars in many fields argue that "race" as it is understood in the United States of America was a social mechanism invented during the 18th century to refer to those populations brought together in colonial America: the English and other European settlers, the conquered Indian peoples, and those peoples of Africa brought in to provide slave labor.

From its inception, this modern concept of "race" was modeled after an ancient theorem of the Great Chain of Being, which posited natural categories on a hierarchy established by God or nature. Thus "race" was a mode of classification linked specifically to peoples in the colonial situation. It subsumed a growing ideology of inequality devised to rationalize European attitudes and treatment of the conquered and enslaved peoples. Proponents of slavery in particular during the 19th century used "race" to justify the retention of slavery. The ideology magnified the differences among Europeans, Africans, and Indians, established a rigid hierarchy of socially exclusive categories, underscored and bolstered unequal rank and status differences, and provided the rationalization that the inequality was natural or God-given. The different physical traits of African-Americans and Indians became markers or symbols of their status differences.

As they were constructing US society, leaders among European-Americans fabricated the cultural/behavioral characteristics associated with each "race," linking superior traits with Europeans and negative and inferior ones to blacks and Indians. Numerous arbitrary and fictitious beliefs about the different peoples were institutionalized and deeply embedded in American thought.

Early in the 19th century the growing fields of science began to reflect the public consciousness about human differences. Differences among the "racial" categories were projected to their greatest extreme when the argument was posed that Africans, Indians, and Europeans were separate species, with Africans the least human and closer taxonomically to apes.

Ultimately "race" as an ideology about human differences was subsequently spread to other areas of the world. It became a strategy for dividing, ranking, and controlling colonized people used by colonial powers everywhere. But it was not limited to the colonial situation. In the latter part of the 19th century it was employed by Europeans to rank one another and to justify social, economic, and political inequalities among their peoples. During World War II, the Nazis under Adolf Hitler enjoined the expanded ideology of "race" and "racial" differences and took them to a logical end: the extermination of 11 million people of "inferior races" (e.g., Jews, Gypsies, Africans, homosexuals, and so forth) and other unspeakable brutalities of the Holocaust.

"Race" thus evolved as a worldview, a body of prejudgments that distorts our ideas about human differences and group behavior. Racial beliefs constitute myths about the diversity in the human species and about the abilities and behavior of people homogenized into "racial" categories. The myths fused behavior and physical features together in the public mind, impeding our comprehension of both biological variations and cultural behavior, implying that both are genetically determined. Racial myths bear no relationship to the reality of human capabilities or behavior. Scientists today find that reliance on such folk beliefs about human differences in research has led to countless errors.

At the end of the 20th century, we now understand that human cultural behavior is learned, conditioned into infants beginning at birth, and always subject to modification. No human is born with a built-in culture or language. Our temperaments, dispositions, and personalities, regardless of genetic propensities, are developed within sets of meanings and values that we call "culture."

Studies of infant and early childhood learning and behavior attest to the reality of our cultures in forming who we are.

It is a basic tenet of anthropological knowledge that all normal human beings have the capacity to learn any cultural behavior. The American experience with immigrants from hundreds of different language and cultural backgrounds who have acquired some version of American culture traits and behavior is the clearest evidence of this fact. Moreover, people of all physical variations have learned different cultural behaviors and continue to do so as modern transportation moves millions of immigrants around the world.

How people have been accepted and treated within the context of a given society or culture has a direct impact on how they perform in that society. The "racial" worldview was invented to assign some groups to perpetual low status, while others were permitted access to privilege, power, and wealth. The tragedy in the United States has been that the policies and practices stemming from this worldview succeeded all too well in constructing unequal populations among Europeans, Native Americans, and peoples of African descent. Given what we know about the capacity of normal humans to achieve and function within any culture, we conclude that present-day inequalities between so-called "racial" groups are not consequences of their biological inheritance but products of historical and contemporary social, economic, educational, and political circumstances.

Note: For further information on human biological variations, see the statement prepared and issued by the American Association of Physical Anthropologists, 1996 (AJPA 101:569–570).

AAA Position Paper on "Race": Comments?

As a result of public confusion about the meaning of "race," claims as to major biological differences among "races" continue to be advanced. Stemming from past AAA actions designed to address public misconceptions on race and intelligence, the need was apparent for a clear AAA statement on the biology and politics of race that would be educational and informational. Rather than wait for each spurious claim to be raised, the AAA Executive Board determined that the Association should prepare a statement for approval by the Association and elicit member input.

Commissioned by the Executive Board of the American Anthropological Association, a position paper on race was authored by Audrey Smedley (*Race in North America: Origin and Evolution of a Worldview*, 1993) and thrice reviewed by a working group of prominent anthropologists: George Armelagos, Michael Blakey, C. Loring Brace, Alan Goodman, Faye Harrison, Jonathan Marks, Yolanda Moses, and Carol Mukhopadhyay. A draft of the current paper was published in the September 1997 *Anthropology Newsletter* and posted on the AAA website http://www.aaanet.org for a number of months, and member comments were requested. While Smedley assumed authorship of the final draft, she received comments not only from the working group but also from the AAA membership and other interested readers. The paper above was adopted by the AAA Executive Board on May 17, 1998, as an official statement of AAA's position on "race."

As the paper is considered a *living statement*, AAA members', other anthropologists', and public comments are invited. Your comments may be sent via mail or e-mail to Peggy Overbey, Director of Government Relations, American Anthropological Association, 4350 N. Fairfax Dr., Suite 640, Arlington, VA 22201.

Bibliography

Primary Sources

Adorno, Theodor, Else Frenkel-Brunswik, Daniel J. Levinson, and R. Nevitt Sanford. 1969 [1950]. *The Authoritarian Personality.* New York: Norton.

Agassiz, Louis. 1850. "The Diversity and Origin of the Human Races." *Christian Examiner* 58: 110–145.

Benedict, Ruth. 1959. *Race: Science and Politics.* New York: Viking Press.

Blauner, Robert. 1972. *Racial Oppression in America.* New York: Harper and Row.

———. 1993. "'But Things Are Much Worse for the Negro People': Race and Radicalism in My Life and Work." in *A History of Race Relations Research: First-Generation Recollections.* John H. Stanfield II, ed. 1–36. Newberry Park, CA: Sage.

Block, N. J., and Gerald Dworkin, eds. 1976. *The IQ Controversy.* New York: Pantheon.

Boas, Franz. 1940. *Race, Language, and Culture.* New York: The Free Press.

Boyd, William C. 1950. *Genetics and the Races of Man: An Introduction to Modern Physical Anthropology.* Boston: Little, Brown.

Buck v. Bell 247 U.S. 200 (1927).

Caldwell, Charles. 1830. *Thoughts on the Original Unity of the Human Races.* New York: E. Bliss.

Carmichael, Stokely, and Charles V. Hamilton. 1967. *Black Power: The Politics of Liberation in America.* New York: Random House.

Cavalli-Sforza, Luigi Luca, and Francesco Cavalli-Sforza. 1995. *The Great Human Diasporas: The History of Diversity and Evolution.* Cambridge, MA: Perseus Books.

Cavalli-Sforza, Luigi Luca, Paolo Menozzi, and Alberto Piazza. 1994. *History and Geography of Human Genes*. Princeton: Princeton University Press.

Clark, Kenneth B., and Mamie P. Clark. 1950. "Emotional Factors in Racial Identification and Preferences in Negro Children." *Journal of Negro Education* 19: 341–350.

Cruse, Harold. 1967. *The Crisis of the Negro Intellectual: From Its Origins to the Present*. New York: Morrow.

Darwin, Charles.1964 [1859]. *On the Origin of Species*. Cambridge: Harvard University Press.

———. 1981 [1879]. *The Descent of Man and Selection in Relation to Sex*. Princeton: Princeton University Press.

———. 1989 [1839]. *Voyage of the Beagle*. New York: Penguin Books.

Du Bois, W. E. B. 1939. *Black Folk Then and Now*. New York: Henry Holt.

———. 1941. "A Chronicle of Race Relations." *Phylon* 2: 172–190.

Dunn, L. C., and Theodosius Dobzhansky. 1959. *Heredity, Race, and Society*. New York: Mentor.

Eden, Richard. 1885. *The First Three English Books on America*. Edward Arber, ed. Birmingham, UK: Turnbull and Spears.

Fanon, Frantz. 1966. *The Wretched of the Earth*. New York: Grove Press.

Frazier, E. Franklin. 1939. *The Negro Family in the United States*. Chicago: University of Chicago Press.

———. 1940. *Negro Youth at the Crossways: Their Personality Development in the Middle States*. Washington, DC: American Council on Education.

———. 1949. *The Negro in the United States*. New York: Macmillan.

———. 1957. *Black Bourgeosie*. Glencoe IL: Free Press.

Galton, Francis. 1952 [1869]. *Hereditary Genius: An Inquiry into Its Laws and Consequences*. New York: Horizon Press.

Garn, Stanley M. 1962. "The Newer Physical Anthropology." *American Anthropologist* 64: 917–918.

Glymour, Clark. 1998. "What Went Wrong? Reflections on Science by Observation and *The Bell Curve*." *Philosophy of Science* 65: 1–32.

Grant, Madison. 1916. *The Passing of the Great Race or the Racial Basis of European History*. New York: Scribner's.

———. 1933. *The Conquest of a Continent or the Expansion of Races in America.* New York: Scribner's.

Herrnstein, Richard J., and Charles Murray. 1994. *The Bell Curve: Intelligence and Class Structure in American Life.* New York: The Free Press.

Herskovits, Melville J. 1941. *The Myth of the Negro Past.* New York: Harper and Row.

Hughes, Everett C. 1963. "Race Relations and the Sociological Imagination." *American Sociological Review* 28: 879–890.

Hunt, Edward E. 1959. "Anthropometry, Genetics, and Racial History." *American Anthropologist* 61: 64–87.

Hunt, James. 1854. *The Negro's Place in Nature.* New York: Van Evrie, Horton and Co.

Jackson, Maurice. 1970. "Toward a Sociology of Black Studies." *Journal of Black Studies* 1: 131–140.

Jenkin, Fleeming. 1867. "Review of *Origin of Species.*" *North British Review* 46: 277–318.

Jensen, Arthur R. 1969. "How Much Can We Boost IQ and Scholastic Achievement?" *Harvard Educational Review* 39: 1–123.

———. 1972. *Genetics and Education.* New York: Harper and Row.

Johnson, Charles S. 1967. *Growing Up in the Black Belt: Negro Youth in the Rural South.* New York: Schocken.

Kames, Henry Home. 1774. *Sketches of the History of Man.* Edinburgh: W. Creech.

Kardiner, Abram, and Lionel Ovesey. 1951. *The Mark of Oppression: Explorations in the Personality of the American Negro.* Cleveland: World Publishing.

Knox, Robert. 1850. *Races of Men: A Fragment.* Philadelphia: Lea and Blanchard.

Laughlin, Harry H. 1922. "Analysis of America's Melting Pot." Report prepared for the House Committee on Immigration and Naturalization, House of Representatives, 67th Congress, 3d Session.

Lawrence, William. 1822. *Lectures on Physiology, Zoology, and the Natural History of Man.* London: Benbow.

Lee, Alfred McClung, and Norman Humphrey. 1943. *Race Riot.* New York: Dryden.

Lewontin, Richard C. 1972. "The Apportionment of Human Diversity." *Evolutionary Biology* 6: 381–398.

Linschoten, Jan Heygenvan. 1885. *The Voyage of John Huyghen Van Linschoten to the East Indies: From the Old English Translation of 1598*. Arthur Coke Burnell and P. A. Tiele, eds. London: Haklyut Society.

Lubbock, John. 1978. *Origin of Civilization and the Primitive Condition of Man*. Peter Riviere, ed. Chicago: University of Chicago Press.

Montagu, Ashley. 1951. *Statement on Race*. New York: Henry Schuman.

———. 1974 [1942]. *Man's Most Dangerous Myth: The Fallacy of Race*. New York: Oxford University Press.

Morton, Samuel George. 1839. *Crania America: or, a Comparative View of the Skulls of Various Aboriginal Nations of North and South America*. Philadelphia: J. Dobson.

———. 1844. *Crania Aegyptiaca: or, Observations on Egyptian Ethnography, Derived From Anatomy, History, and the Monuments*. Philadelphia: J. Pennington.

Moynihan, Patrick. 1965. *The Negro Family: The Case for National Action*. Washington, DC: Office of Planning and Research, United States Department of Labor.

Muller, Herbert J. 1935. *Out of the Night: A Biologist's View of the Future*. New York: Vanguard Press.

Murray, Albert. 1973. "White Norms, Black Deviance." In *The Death of White Sociology*, Joyce A. Ladner, ed. 96–113. New York: Vintage.

Myrdal, Gunnar. 1944. *An American Dilemma*. New York: Harper and Brothers.

Nei, Masatoshi, and Arun K. Roychoudhury. 1982. "Genetic Relationship and the Evolution of Human Races." *Evolutionary Biology* 14: 1–59.

Neisser, Ulric, Gwyneth Boodoo, Thomas J. Bouchard Jr., Wade A. Boykin, Nathan Brody, Stephen Ceci, Diane F. Halpern, John C. Loehlin, Robert Perloff, Robert J. Sternberg, and Susana Urbina. 1996. "Intelligence: Knowns and Unknowns." *American Psychologist* 51: 77–101.

Nott, Josiah. 1843. "The Mulatto a Hybrid: Probable Extermination of the Two Races If Whites and Blacks Are Allowed to Marry." *American Journal of the Medical Sciences* 6: 252–256.

Nott, Josiah, and George R. Gliddon. 1854. *Types of Mankind*. Philadelphia: Lippincott, Grambo.

Prichard, James Cowles. 1843. *The Natural History of Man: Comprising Inquiries into the Modifying Influence of Physical and Moral Agencies on the Different Tribes of the Human Families*. London: H. Baillaire.

————. 1973. *Researches into the Physical History of Mankind.* George W. Stocking, Jr., ed. Chicago: University of Chicago Press.

"Social Biology and Population Improvement." 1939. *Nature* 144: 521.

Spencer, Herbert. 1851. *Social Statics; or, The Conditions Essential to Human Happiness Specified, and the First of Them Developed.* London: J. Chapman.

————. 1979. "The Comparative Psychology of Man." In *Images of Race.* Michael Biddiss, ed. 189–204. New York: Holmes and Meier.

Stoddard, Lothrop. 1921. *The Rising Tide of Color against White World-Supremacy.* New York: Scribner's.

United States President's Committee on Civil Rights. 1947. *To Secure These Rights: The Report of the President's Committee on Civil Rights.* Washington, DC: Government Printing Office.

Wallace, Alfred Russel, 1864. "The Origin of Human Races and the Antiquity of Man Deduced from the Theory of 'Natural Selection.'" *Journal of the Anthropological Society of London* 2: clviii-clxx.

White, Charles. 1799. *An Account of the Regular Gradation in Man, and in Different Animals and Vegetables, and From the Former to the Latter.* London: C. Dilly.

Younker, Ira. 1945. "Scientific Research on Anti-Semitism in 1944." *The American Jewish Yearbook, 5706, 1945–46.* Philadelphia: Jewish Publication Society of America.

Secondary Sources

Allen, Garland E. 1986. "The Eugenics Record Office at Cold Spring Harbor, 1910–1940: An Essay in Institutional History." *Osiris* 2: 225–264.

————. 2001. "The Biological Basis of Crime: An Historical and Methodological Study." *Historical Studies in the Physical and Biological Sciences* 31: 183–222.

Allen, John S. 1989. "Franz Boas's Physical Anthropology: The Critique of Racial Formalism Revisited." *Current Anthropology* 30: 79–84.

Ash, Mitchell G., and Alfons Söllner, eds. 1996. *Forced Migration and Scientific Change: Émigré German-Speaking Scientists and Scholars After 1933.* Cambridge: Cambridge University Press.

Augstein, Hannah Franziska. 1999. *James Cowles Prichard's Anthropology: Remaking the Science of Man in Early Nineteenth-Century Britain.* Amsterdam: Rodopi.

Baker, Lee D. 1998. *From Savage to Negro: Anthropology and the Construction of Race, 1896–1954*. Berkeley: University of California Press.

Bank, Andrew. 1996. "Of 'Native Skulls' and 'Noble Caucasians': Phrenology in Colonial South Africa." *Journal of Southern African Studies* 22: 387–403.

Bannister, Robert C. 1970. "'The Survival of the Fittest Is Our Doctrine': History or Histrionics?" *Journal of the History of Ideas* 31: 377–398.

Banton, Michael. 1987. *Racial Theories*. New York: Cambridge University Press.

Barkan, Elazar. 1992. *The Retreat of Scientific Racism: Changing Concepts of Race in Britain and the United States between the World Wars*. Cambridge: Cambridge University Press.

———. 1996. "The Politics of the Science of Race: Ashley Montagu and UNESCO's Anti-Racist Declarations." In *Race and Other Misadventures: Essays in Honor of Ashley Montagu in His Ninetieth Year*. Larry T. Reynolds and Leonard Lieberman, eds. 96–105. Dix Hills, NJ: General Hall.

Bellomy, Donald C. 1984. "'Social Darwinism' Revisited." *Perspectives in American History, New Series* 1: 1–129.

Berlin, Ira. 1998. *Many Thousands Gone: The First Two Centuries of Slavery in North America*. Cambridge: Harvard University Press.

Blackburn, Robin. 1997. *The Making of New World Slavery: From the Baroque to the Modern, 1492–1800*. London: Verso.

Blanckaert, Claude. 1988. "On the Origins of French Ethnology: William Edwards and the Doctrine of Race." In *Bones, Bodies, and Behavior*. George Stocking, ed. 18–55. Madison: University of Wisconsin Press.

Boulton, Alexander O. 1995. "American Paradox: Jeffersonian Equality and Racial Science." *American Quarterly* 47: 467–492.

Bowler, Peter J. 1984. *Evolution: The History of an Idea*. Berkeley: University of California Press.

Brace, C. Loring. 1996. "The Eternal Triangle: Race, Class and IQ." *Current Anthropology* 37: S143–S181.

Braude, Benjamin. 1997. "The Sons of Noah and the Construction of Ethnic and Geographical Identities in the Medieval and Early Modern Periods." *William and Mary Quarterly* 54: 103–142.

Browne, Janet. 1995. *Charles Darwin: Voyaging*. New York: Knopf.

———. 2002. *Charles Darwin: The Power of Place*. New York: Knopf.

Carneiro, Robert L., and Robert G. Perrin. 2002. "Herbert Spencer's Principles of Sociology: A Centennial Retrospective and Appraisal." *Annals of Science* 59: 221–261.

Cerroni-Long, E. L. 1987. "Benign Neglect?: Anthropology and the Study of Blacks in the United States." *Journal of Black Studies* 17: 438–459.

Chaplin, Joyce E. 1997. "Natural Philosophy and an Early Racial Idiom in North America: Comparing English and Indian Bodies." *William and Mary Quarterly* 54: 229–252.

Churchill, Frederick B. 1987. "From Heredity Theory to Vererbung: The Transmission Problem, 1850–1915." *Isis* 78: 337–364.

Claeys, Gregory. 2001. "The 'Survival of the Fittest' and the Origins of Social Darwinism." *Journal of the History of Ideas* 61: 223–240.

Cooke, Kathy J. 1998. "The Limits of Heredity: Nature and Nurture in American Eugenics Before 1915." *Journal of the History of Biology* 31: 263–278.

Cowan, Ruth Schwartz. 1972. "Francis Galton's Statistical Ideas: The Influence of Eugenics." *Isis* 63, no. 219: 509–528.

Curtin, Philip. 1969. *The Atlantic Slave Trade: A Census*. Madison: University of Wisconsin Press.

Davis, David Brion. 1966. *The Problem of Slavery in Western Culture*. Ithaca, NY: Cornell University Press.

———. 1999. "The Culmination of Racial Polarities and Prejudice." *Journal of the Early Republic* 19: 757–775.

Desmond, Adrian, and James Moore. 1991. *Darwin: The Life of a Tormented Evolutionist*. New York: Warner Books.

Diggins, John P. 1976. "Slavery, Race, and Equality: Jefferson and the Pathos of the Enlightenment." *American Quarterly* 28: 206–228.

Dikötter, Frank. 1998. "Race Culture: Recent Perspectives on the History of Eugenics." *American Historical Review* 103: 467–478.

Drescher, Seymour. 1990. "The Ending of the Slave Trade and the Evolution of European Scientific Racism." *Social Science History* 14: 415–450.

Dubow, Saul. 1995. *Scientific Racism in Modern South Africa*. New York: Cambridge University Press.

Eltis, David. 1993. "Europeans and Rise and Fall of African Slavery in the Americas: An Interpretation." *American Historical Review* 98: 1399–1423.

Esguerra, Jorge Canizares.1999. "New World, New Stars: Patriotic Astrology and the Invention of Indian and Creole Bodies In Colonial Spanish America, 1500–1650." *American Historical Review* 104: 33–68.

Farber, Paul L. 1972. "Buffon and the Concept of Species." *Journal of the History of Biology* 5: 259–284.

———. 2000. *Finding Order in Nature: The Naturalist Tradition From Linnaeus to E. O. Wilson.* Baltimore: Johns Hopkins University Press.

Feagin, Joe. 1986. "Slavery Unwilling to Die: The Background of Black Oppression in the 1980s." *Journal of Black Studies* 17: 173–200.

Field, Geoffrey G. 1977. "Nordic Racism." *Journal of the History of Ideas* 38: 523–540.

———. 1981. *Evangelist of Race: The Germanic Vision of Houston Stewart Chamberlain.* New York: Columbia University Press.

Fields, Barbara J. 1982. "Race and Ideology in American History." in *Region, Race, and Reconstruction: Essays in Honor of C. Vann Woodward.* J. Morgan Kousser and James M. McPherson, eds. 143–177. New York: Oxford University Press.

Francis, Mark. 1978. "Herbert Spencer and the Myth of Laissez-Faire." *Journal of the History of Ideas* 39: 317–328.

Fraser, Steven, ed. 1995. *The Bell Curve Wars: Race, Intelligence, and the Future of America.* New York: Basic Books.

Fredrickson, George M. 2002. *Racism: A Short History.* Princeton: Princeton University Press.

Gasman, Daniel. 1971. *The Scientific Origins of National Socialism: Social Darwinism in Ernst Haeckel and the German Monist League.* New York: American Elsevier.

Gillham, Nicholas W. 2001. *A Life of Francis Galton: From African Exploration to the Birth of Eugenics.* New York: Oxford University Press.

Glass, Bentley. 1986. "Geneticists Embattled: Their Stand against Rampant Eugenics and Racism in America during the 1920s and 1930s." *Proceedings of the American Philosophical Society* 130: 130–154.

Gökyigit, Emil Aileen. 1994. "The Reception of Francis Galton's *Hereditary Genius* in the Victorian Periodical Press." *Journal of the History of Biology* 27: 215–240.

Gossett, Thomas F. 1963. *Race: The History of an Idea in America.* Dallas: Southern Methodist University Press.

Gould, Stephen J. 1981. *The Mismeasure of Man.* New York: Norton.

Graves , Joseph L., Jr. 2001. *The Emperor's New Clothes: Biological Theories of Race at the Millennium.* New Brunswick: Rutgers University Press.

Greene, John C. 1977. "Darwin as a Social Evolutionist." *Journal of the History of Biology* 10: 1–27.

Haller, John S. 1971. *Outcasts from Evolution: Scientific Attitudes of Racial Inferiority 1859–1900.* Urbana: University of Illinois Press.

Halliday, R. J. 1971. "Social Darwinism: A Definition." *Victorian Studies* 14: 389–405.

Handler, Richard. 1990. "Boasian Anthropology and the Critique of American Culture." *American Quarterly* 42: 252–273.

Hannaford, Ivan. 1996. *Race: The History of an Idea in the West.* Baltimore: Johns Hopkins University Press.

Haraway, Donna J. 1988. "Remodelling the Human Way of Life: Sherwood Washburn and the New Physical Anthropology, 1950–1980." in *Bones, Bodies, Behavior: Essays on Biological Anthropology.* George W. Stocking Jr., ed. Madison: University of Wisconsin Press.

Harmer, Harry. 2001. *The Longman Companion to Slavery, Emancipation, and Civil Rights.* New York: Pearson Education.

Harrison, Mark. 1996. "'Tender Frame of Man': Disease, Climate, and Racial Difference in India and the West Indies, 1760–1860." *Bulletin of the History of Medicine* 70: 68–93.

Haskell, Thomas L. 1985. "Capitalism and the Origins of the Humanitarian Sensibility, Part I." *American Historical Review* 90: 339–361.

———. 1985. "Capitalism and the Origins of the Humanitarian Sensibility, Part II." *American Historical Review* 90: 547–566.

Hawkins, Mike. 1997. *Social Darwinism in European and American Thought, 1860-1945.* Cambridge: Cambridge University Press.

Hecht, Jennifer Michael. 1999. "The Solvency of Metaphysics: The Debate over Racial Science and Moral Philosophy in France, 1890–1919." *Isis* 90: 1–24.

———. 2000. "Vacher De Lapouge and the Rise of Nazi Science." *Journal of the History of Ideas* 61: 285–304.

Helbring, Mark. 1994. "Feeling Universality and Thinking Particularistically: Alain Locke, Franz Boas, Melville Herskovits, and the Harlem Renaissance." *Prospects* 19: 289–314.

Herman, Ellen. 1995. *The Romance of American Psychology: Political Culture in the Age of Experts.* Berkeley: University of California Press.

Hind, Robert J. 1984. "The Internal Colonial Concept." *Comparative Studies in Society and History* 26: 543–568.

Hofstadter, Richard. 1955. *Social Darwinism in American Thought.* Boston: Beacon Press.

Hoover, Dwight W. 1981. "A Paradigm Shift: The Concept of Race in the 1920s and 1930s." *Conspectus of History* 1: 82–100.

Horsman, Reginald. 1987. *Josiah Nott of Mobile: Southerner, Physician, and Racial Theorist.* Baton Rouge: University of Louisiana Press.

Hudson, Nicholas. 1996. "From 'Nation' to 'Race': The Origin of Racial Classification in Eighteenth-Century Thought." *Eighteenth-Century Studies* 29: 247–264.

Jackson, John P., Jr. 2001. *Social Scientists for Social Justice: Making the Case against Segregation.* New York: New York University Press.

Jackson, Walter A. 1986. "Melville Herskovits and the Search for Afro-American Culture." In *Malinowski, Rivers, Benedict, and Others: Essays on Culture and Personality*, George W. Stocking, ed. 95–186. Madison: University of Wisconsin Press.

———. 1990. *Gunnar Myrdal and America's Conscience: Social Engineering and Racial Liberalism, 1938-1987.* Chapel Hill: University of North Carolina Press.

Jacoby, Russell, and Naomi Glauberman, eds. 1995. *The Bell Curve Debate: History, Documents, Opinions.* New York: Times Books.

Jacques, T. Carlos. 1997. "From Savages and Barbarians to Primitives: Africa, Social Typologies, and History in Eighteenth Century French Philosophy." *History and Theory* 36: 190–215.

Jay, Martin. 1973. *The Dialectical Imagination: A History of the Frankfurt School and the Institute for Social Research, 1923–1950.* Boston: Little Brown.

Jones, Greta. 1980. *Social Darwinism and English Thought: The Interaction between Biological and Social Theory.* Atlantic Highland, NJ: Humanities Press.

Kevles, Daniel J. 1985. *In the Name of Eugenics: Genetics and the Uses of Human Heredity.* New York: Knopf.

Kincheloe, Joe L., Shirley R. Stenberg, and Aaron D. Gresson, eds. 1996. *Measured Lies: The Bell Curve Examined.* New York: St. Martin's Press.

Kottler, Malcolm Jay. 1974. "Alfred Russel Wallace, the Origin of Man, and Spiritualism." *Isis* 65, no. 227: 145–192.

Kühl, Stefan. 1994. *The Nazi Connection: Eugenics, American Racism, and German National Socialism.* New York: Oxford University Press.

Littlefield, Alice, Leonard Lieberman, and Larry T. Reynolds. 1982. "Redefining Race: The Potential Demise of a Concept in Physical Anthropology." *Current Anthropology* 23: 641–655.

Littlefield, Daniel C. 1991. *Rice and Slaves: Ethnicity and the Slave Trade in Colonial South Carolina.* Urbana: University of Illinois Press.

Lombardo, Paul A. 1985. "Three Generations, No Imbeciles: New Light on *Buck v. Bell.*" *New York University Law Review* 60: 30–62.

Marks, Jonathan. 2000. "Human Biodiversity As a Central Theme of Biological Anthropology: Then and Now." *Kroeber Anthropological Society Papers* 84: 1–10.

McCartney, John T. 1992. *Black Power Ideologies: An Essay in African American Political Thought.* Philadelphia: Temple University Press.

Michael, John S. 1988. "A New Look at Morton's Craniological Research." *Current Anthropology* 29: 349–354.

Moore, James. 1986. "Socializing Darwinism: Historiography and the Fortunes of a Phrase." In *Science as Politics.* Les Levidow, ed. 38–80. London: Free Association Books.

Mosse, George L. 1985. *Toward the Final Solution: A History of European Racism.* New York: Howard Fertig.

Müller-Hill, Benno. 1988. *Murderous Science: Elimination by Scientific Selection of Jews, Gypsies, and Others, Germany 1933–1945.* New York: Oxford University Press.

———. 1999. "The Blood of Auschwitz and the Silence of the Scholars." *History and Philosophy of the Life Sciences* 21: 331–365.

Nunley, Michael. 1995. "*The Bell Curve:* Too Smooth to Be True." *American Behavioral Scientist* 39: 74–84.

Nursey-Bray, Paul. 1980. "Race and Nation: Ideology in the Thought of Frantz Fanon." *Journal of Modern African Studies* 18: 135–142.

O'Connor, Alice. 2001. *Poverty Knowledge: Social Science, Social Policy, and the Poor in Twentieth-Century U.S. History.* Princeton: Princeton University Press.

Pascoe, Peggy. 1996. "Miscegenation Law, Court Cases, and Ideologies of 'Race' in Twentieth-Century America." *Journal of American History* 83: 44–69.

Paul, Diane B. 1984. "Eugenics and the Left." *Journal of the History of Ideas* 45: 567–590.

———. 1995. *Controlling Human Heredity: 1865 to the Present*. Atlantic Highlands, NJ: Humanities University Press International.

Pellar, Gary. "Race-Consciousness." 1995. In *Critical Race Theory: The Key Writings That Formed the Movement*. Kimberle Crenshaw, Neil Gotanda, Gary Pellar, and Kendall Thomas, eds. New York: The New Press.

Persons, Stow. 1987. *Ethnic Studies at Chicago, 1905–1945*. Urbana: University of Illinois Press.

Platt, Jennifer. 1904. "The Chicago School and Firsthand Data." *History of the Human Sciences* 7: 57–80.

Popkin, Richard H. 1974. "The Philosophical Bases of Modern Racism." In *Philosophy and the Civilizing Arts*. Craig Walton and John P. Anton, eds. 126–165. Athens: Ohio University Press.

———. 1978. "Pre-Adamism in 19th-Century American Thought: Speculative Biology and Racism." *Philosophia* 8: 205–239.

Proctor, Robert N. 1988. *Racial Hygiene: Medicine under the Nazis*. Cambridge: Harvard University Press.

———. 1991. *Value Free Science? Purity and Power in Modern Knowledge*. Cambridge: Harvard University Press.

Provine, William B. 1973. "Geneticists and the Biology of Race Crossing." *Science* 182: 790–796.

———. 1986. "Geneticists and Race." *American Zoologist* 26: 857–887.

Puzzo, Dante A. 1964. "Racism and the Western Tradition." *Journal of the History of Ideas* 25: 579–586.

Quinlan, Sean. 1996. "Colonial Bodies, Hygiene and Abolitionist Politics in Eighteenth-Century France." *History Workshop Journal* 42: 107–125.

Reilly, Philip R. 1991. *The Surgical Solution: A History of Involuntary Sterilization in the United States*. Baltimore: Johns Hopkins University Press.

Richards, Evelleen. 1989. "The 'Moral Anatomy' of Robert Knox: the Interplay Between Biological and Social Thought in Victorian Scientific Naturalism." *Journal of the History of Biology* 22: 373–436.

Richards, Graham. 1997. *"Race," Racism, and Psychology*. London: Routledge Press.

———. 1998. "Reconceptualizing the History of Race Psychology: Thomas Russell Garth (1872–1939) and How He Changed His Mind." *Journal of the History of the Behavioral Sciences* 34: 15–32.

Richards, Robert. 1987. *Darwin and the Emergence of Evolutionary Theories of Mind and Behavior.* Chicago: University of Chicago Press.

Rigotti, Francesca. 1986. "Biology and Society in the Age of Enlightenment." *Journal of the History of Ideas* 47: 215–233.

Ruse, Michael. 1979. *The Darwinian Revolution: Science Red in Tooth and Claw.* Chicago: University of Chicago Press.

Russell-Wood, A. J. R. 1978. "Iberian Expansion and the Issue of Black Slavery: Changing Portuguese Attitudes, 1440–1770." *American Historical Review* 83: 16–42.

Samelson, Franz. 1978. "From 'Race Psychology' to 'Studies in Prejudice': Some Observations on the Thematic Reversal in Social Psychology." *Journal of the History of the Behavioral Sciences* 14: 265–278.

———. 1986. "Authoritarianism from Berlin to Berkeley: On Social Psychology and History." *Journal of Social Issues* 42: 191–208.

———. 1997. "On the Uses of History: The Case of *The Bell Curve.*" *Journal of the History of the Behavioral Sciences* 33: 129–133.

Schiebinger, Londa. 1990. "The Anatomy of Difference: Race and Sex in Eighteenth-Century Science." *Eighteenth-Century Studies* 18: 347–405.

Sloan, Phillip R. 1973. "The Idea of Racial Degeneracy in Buffon's *Histoire Naturelle.*" In *Racism in the Eighteenth Century.* Harold E. Pagliaro, ed. 293–322. Cleveland: Case Western Reserve University Press.

———. 1976. "The Buffon-Linnaeus Controversy." *Isis* 67: 356–375.

Smedley, Audrey. 1999. *Race in North America: Origin and Evolution of a Worldview.* 2d ed., Boulder, CO: Westview Press.

Spiro, Jonathan P. 2000. *Patrician Racist: The Evolution of Madison Grant.* Berkeley: University of California Press.

Stanfield, John H. 1982. "The 'Negro Problem' within and beyond the Institutional Nexus of Pre-World War I Sociology." *Phylon* 43: 187–201.

———. 1985. *Philanthropy and Jim Crow in American Social Science.* Westport, CT: Greenwood Press.

———. 1995. "The Myth of Race and the Human Sciences." *Journal of Negro Education* 64: 218–231.

Stanton, William. 1960. *Leopard's Spots: Scientific Attitudes toward Race in America: 1815–59.* Chicago: University of Chicago Press.

Staum, Martin S. 2000. "Paris Ethnology and the Perfectability of the Races." *Canadian Journal of History* 35: 453–472.

Steinberg, Stephen. 1995. *Turning Back: The Retreat from Racial Justice in American Thought and Policy.* Boston: Beacon Press.

Stepan, Nancy Leys. 1982. *The Idea of Race in Science: Great Britain, 1800–1960.* Hamden, CT: Archon.

———. 1986. "Race and Gender: The Role of Analogy in Science." *Isis* 77, no. 287: 261–277.

Stephens, Lester D. 2000. *Science, Race, and Religion in the American South: John Bachman and the Charleston Circle of Naturalists, 1815–1895.* Chapel Hill: University of North Carolina Press.

Stocking, George W. 1968. *Race, Culture, and Evolution: Essays in the History of Anthropology.* Chicago: University of Chicago Press.

———. 1987. *Victorian Anthropology.* New York: Free Press.

Stuurman, Siep. 2000. "Francois Bernier and the Invention of Racial Classification." *History Workshop Journal* 50: 1–21.

Sweet, James H. 1997. "The Iberian Roots of American Racist Thought." *William and Mary Quarterly* 54: 143–166.

Thomas, Hugh. 1997. *The Slave Trade: The Story of the Atlantic Slave Trade, 1440–1870.* New York: Simon and Schuster.

Thomas, William B. 1984. "Black Intellectuals, Intelligence Testing in the 1930s, and the Sociology of Knowledge." *Teachers College Record* 85: 475–501.

Thurtle, Phillip. 2002. "Harnessing Heredity in Gilded Age America: Middle Class Mores and Industrial Breeding in a Cultural Context." *Journal of the History of Biology* 35: 43–78.

Tucker, William H. 1994. *Science and Politics of Racial Research.* Urbana: University of Illinois Press.

Urban, Wayne J. 1989. "The Black Scholar and Intelligence Testing: the Case of Horace Mann Bond." *Journal of the History of the Behavioral Sciences* 25: 323–334.

Vaughn, Aldon T. 1982. *Roots of American Racism: Essays on the Colonial Experience.* New York: Oxford University Press.

Wacker, R. Fred. 1979. "Assimilation and Cultural Pluralism in American Social Thought." *Phylon* 40: 325–333.

Waller, John C. 2002. "Gentlemanly Men of Science: Sir Francis Galton and the Professionalization of the British Life Sciences." *Journal of the History of Biology* 34: 83–114.

———. 2001. "Ideas of Heredity, Reproduction, and Eugenics in Britain, 1800–1875." *Studies in the History and Philosophy of Biology and Biomedical Sciences* 32: 457–489.

Weidman, Nadine. 1997. "Heredity, Intelligence, and Neuropsychology: or Why *The Bell Curve* Is Good Science." *Journal of the History of the Behavioral Sciences* 33: 141–144.

Weikart, Richard. 1993. "The Origins of Social Darwinism in Germany." *Journal of the History of Ideas* 54: 469–488.

———. 2002. "Darwinism and Death: Devaluing Human Life in Germany 1859–1920." *Journal of the History of Ideas* 63: 323–344.

Weindling, Paul. 1985. "Weimar Eugenics: the Kaiser Wilhelm Institute for Anthropology, Human Heredity and Eugenics in Social Context." *Annals of Science* 77: 303–318.

———. 1998. "Dissecting German Social Darwinism: Historicizing the Biology of the Organic State." *Science in Context* 11: 619–637.

Weingart, Peter. 1989. "German Eugenics between Science and Politics." *Osiris* 5: 260–282.

———. 1995. "'Struggle for Existence': Selection and Retention of a Metaphor." in *Biology as Society, Society as Biology: Metaphors.* Sabine Maasen, Everett Mendelson, and Peter Weingart, eds. 127–151. Dordrecht, The Netherlands: Kluwer Academic Publishers.

Weiss, Sheila Faith. 1986. "Wilhelm Schallmayer and the Logic of German Eugenics." *Isis* 77, no. 286: 33–46.

———. 1987. "The Race Hygiene Movement in Germany." *Osiris* 3: 193–236.

Williamson, Joel. 1984. *The Crucible of Race: Black-White Relations in The American South Since Emancipation.* New York: Oxford University Press.

Wilson, Philip K. 2002. "Harry Laughlin's Eugenic Crusade to Control the 'Socially Inadequate' in Progressive Era America." *Patterns of Prejudice* 36: 49–67.

Young, Robert. 1985. "Darwinism *Is* Social." In *The Darwinian Heritage.* David Kohn, ed. 609–638. Princeton: Princeton University Press.

Zenderland, Leila. 1997. "*The Bell Curve* and the Shape of History." *Journal of the History of the Behavioral Sciences* 33: 135–139.

Index

About the Authors

John P. Jackson, Jr., received his Ph.D. in the History of Science and Technology from the University of Minnesota–Twin Cities in 1997. He writes on the history of the scientific study of race and how scientific arguments interact with political and legal ideas. He is the author of *Social Scientists for Social Justice: Making the Case against Segregation* (2001) and the editor of *Science, Race, and Ethnicity: Readings from Isis and Osiris* (2002). He is an assistant professor in the Department of Communication at the University of Colorado—Boulder.

Nadine M. Weidman received her Ph.D. in history and philosophy of science and technology from Cornell University in 1994. She writes on the history of the human sciences, especially psychology and anthropology, and the ongoing debates over nature and nurture, biology, and culture in those sciences. She is the author of *Constructing Scientific Psychology: Karl Lashley's Mind-Brain Debates* (1999). She is a lecturer in extension studies in the Division of Continuing Education and associate of the Department of History of Science at Harvard University.